The Reflowering of the Goddess

Hélène de Beauvoir: Second Encounter with the Great Goddess (1982)

The Reflowering of the Goddess

by

GLORIA FEMAN ORENSTEIN

PERGAMON PRESS
Member of Maxwell Macmillan Pergamon Publishing Corporation
New York   Oxford   Beijing   Frankfurt   São Paulo   Sydney   Tokyo   Toronto

Pergamon Press Offices:

USA	Pergamon Press, Inc., Maxwell House, Fairview Park, Elmsford, New York 10523, USA
UK	Pergamon Press plc, Headington Hill Hall, Oxford OX3 OBW, England
PEOPLE'S REPUBLIC OF CHINA	Pergamon Press, 0909 China World Tower, No. 1 Jian Guo Men Wai Avenue, Beijing, 100004, People's Republic of China
FEDERAL REPUBLIC OF GERMANY	Pergamon Press GmbH, Hammerweg 6, D-6242 Kronberg, Federal Republic of Germany
BRAZIL	Pergamon Editora Ltda, Rua Eca de Queiros, 346, CEP 04011, Paraiso, São Paulo, Brazil
AUSTRALIA	Pergamon Press Australia Pty Ltd., P.O. Box 544, Potts Point, N.S.W. 2011, Australia
JAPAN	Pergamon Press, 8th Floor, Matsuoka Central Building, 1-7-1 Nishishinjuku, Shinjuku-ku, Tokyo 160, Japan
CANADA	Pergamon Press Canada Ltd., Suite 271, 253 College Street, Toronto, Ontario, Canada M5T 1R5

First edition 1990

Library of Congress Cataloging in Publication

Orenstein, Gloria Feman, 1938-
  The reflowering of the goddess / by Gloria Feman Orenstein.—1st ed.
    p.   cm.—(The Athene series)
  Includes bibliographical references.
  ISBN 0-08-035179-4 : — ISBN 0-08-035178-6 (pbk.)
  1. Feminism—Philosophy. I. Title. II. Series.
HQ1206.0765 1990
305.42'01—dc20   89-48176
                                                         CIP Rev.

Printed in the United States of America

(∞)™ The paper used in the publication meets the minimum requirements of American National Standard for Information Sciences—Permanence of Paper for Printed Library Materials, ANSI Z39.48-1984

This book is dedicated to the memory of the grandmothers I have never known, both Feman and Appel; to the memory of my mother, Gertrude Appel Feman; to the memory of some of the other "mothers" in my life, Germaine Orenstein, Frances D. Greene, and Dr. Inge Bogner; and to several other women who have "mothered" me in other ways, and are still very much with me, Dr. Anna Balakian, Leonora Carrington, Sara Appel, Esther Orenstein, Joyce Orenstein, Trudy Greene Cooperman, Adah Askew, Erika Duncan, Jovette Marchessault, and Ellen Marit Gaup-Dunfjeld. I want to extend this dedication to include the "mothers" of contemporary Goddess research as well: Merlin Stone and Marija Gimbutas. My book is also dedicated to my daughters, Nadine Monica Orenstein and Claudia Danielle Orenstein, and to my nieces Eve Orenstein, Siu Ping Chin Feman, and Alix Flamm who continue the Matrilineage.

Contents

Foreword

The Reflowering of the Goddess is a revelation and a plea. I think that it will eventually be regarded as one of the most important and prophetic books of our time. Rich with impressive insights, it documents and explains the emergence of ways of perceiving and interacting with the world that may well affect the very survival of the earth and all life on it.

For many years, Professor Gloria Orenstein has been observing and studying the phenomenon of an ever-increasing body of art and literature that has been inspired and informed by the reclamation of knowledge of ancient Goddess reverence and the rise of women's spirituality from within the feminist movement. Exploring this creative work produced by contemporary women, Orenstein explains that inherent in the work are values, belief systems, and world views that are leading us into an exciting new consciousness of existence.

She creates some much-needed new vocabulary to describe what is happening, referring to these artists and writers as "feminist-matristic," and shows with crystal clarity that this contemporary feminist-matristic consciousness is simultaneously developing from and contributing to an extremely important cultural metamorphosis, a transformation to a new paradigm of how we can live in accordance with what she describes as a "global earth-based spirituality."

To further clarify her exploration of each individual work of art and literature discussed in the book, she also brings together many ideas of contemporary authors and teachers of archaeology, history, ecology, women's studies, theology, psychology, political science, art history, and shamanism. Although some of their ideas overlap, while others seem at first to be quite disparate, she patiently and brilliantly weaves all the threads of the numerous diverse intricacies of these ideas into a single tapestry to reveal the overall pattern of what is happening and why. The image she shows us is dynamic, exciting, and energizing. It is that of the flowering of a completely new cultural renaissance.

She explains that at the core of this cultural renaissance is the reclamation and honoring of three vital areas of ancient knowledge and perceptions. The first area is the reclamation of knowledge of our "matristic" heritage, that is, an expansion of the generally accepted historical time frame to include the vast body of evidence of ancient Goddess worship, a consciousness of how the belief in Creation by the Great Mother affected the world views of those societies in which the Goddess was revered, and how it can affect ours. The second area concerns the understanding of our physical and spiritual connections as humans to the rest of the natural world and to each other, an understanding that existed in more ancient periods and still exists among some cultural groups today. The third area involves a serious consideration of the energies, powers, and wisdom that we generally refer to as spiritual, magical, metaphysical, shamanic, or intuitive, as being real and causally affective. Orenstein points out that each of these three vital areas has been bypassed or suppressed, thus forgotten by contemporary patriarchal societies which have been swept up in a fervent belief in "progress," resulting in what she refers to as "amnesias."

However, she explains, the Cassandras of today do remember this ancient wisdom. These Cassandras are the feminist-matristic writers and artists who are daring to voice or depict what the majority of even the most educated and respected members of our society have ignored, denied, or completely forgotten. The resounding question that repeatedly presents itself as we read this book is whether or not the world will once again label these Cassandras as foolish or insane, or can they shock our amnesiac world into remembering before it is too late?

With a gift of uncanny insight into each work of art and literature, Orenstein provides us with a Rosetta Stone to unlock the symbolism and encoding developed by women who at times obscured or occulted feminist-matristic messages in their work in order to protect themselves in periods when such statements would often lead to accusations of madness. Her explanations also help us to comprehend the symbols and images created by contemporary women whose personal and unique languages of imagery may not be easily deciphered. Once we understand the individual symbolism and imagery that has been developed and is being used by each of these women, we arrive at a new and different approach to their art and literature, an approach that has not yet been understood by most critics and historians of art and literature today.

This feminist-matristic art is almost the exact antithesis of recent art forms that are about the color and the application of the paint or about space and the sculptural material used, that is, about painting or sculpture itself. This reductive approach to contemporary art has in turn engendered a trivialization and denigration of art that is inspired by, refers to, or portrays, a spiritual vision. Since so much of the art world is controlled by men, this attitude is especially noticeable in references to art associated with feminism and/or ancient Goddess reverence. Such art is often dismissed as "childish," "primitive," or "superstitious" by most contemporary critics and historians of art, as well as by many other artists. Perhaps these attitudes prevail even more vehemently upon any consideration of the idea that art could actually possess other levels or dimensions that include magical energies and powers contained in the imagery, in the materials used, in the site of the work, or invoked by the actions and process of making the art—the dimensions that had probably been the underlying motivation in the actual origins of visual arts in the Upper Paleolithic period.

Orenstein courageously honors the fact that this work of feminist-matristic artists not only is reclaiming Goddess imagery and our matristic past, as well as making statements about all nature as sacred and ourselves as an intrinsic part of nature, but also that it is exploring and celebrating ritual act, image, object, and site as containing metaphysical energies that invoke and thus help to create a different and more life-affirming reality, one that includes and respects the three areas of knowledge that have been forgotten. Describing the contemporary use of ritual action and of magical images, objects, and environments as the reclamation of a shamanic wisdom that includes believing and acknowledging that invisible and intangible elements affect us, and that this magic can be an inherent aspect of art, Orenstein provides us with a richer understanding of the many levels or dimensions of reality that these artists draw upon and that their art reveals.

She explores the verbal arts of feminist-matristic writers with the same depth of respect and comprehension, examining the written word in relation to ancient oral traditions of transmitting "tales of power," and honors access to wisdom and knowledge that is received through intuition or personal *gnosis*. As a scholar and professor, Orenstein is well aware of the credibility we have long awarded to information based upon empirical study and previous documentation. But with a consciousness of how the written word has and can be used to distort and omit realities of the past and even the present, she explains the value of the intuitively and/or metaphysically acquired knowledge that individual women writers have been drawing upon in their work and in their own views of past, present, and future realities. This allows for each variation as yet another aspect of reality.

As a researcher of artifacts and written texts from ancient cultures in which the Goddess was worshipped, I feel I must comment here upon the existence of the evidence of written material about Goddess reverence from those ancient cultures. Although we can observe the continual slippage of the importance of the Goddess in the written materials as those early cultures were invaded and conquered by patriarchal groups, we can and do draw upon these ancient texts to know about ancient beliefs. It seems clear that if we did not have this written material from which to extrapolate backward in time, we would have no idea, other than intuitive, of what the multitude of statues and temples from preliterate periods were, that the belief in the Goddess as Creator ever existed, or even that there was Goddess reverence at all.

Yet while I explain that this body of written evidence from Goddess-revering cultures does exist and holds immense value for us, I cannot dismiss the reality or importance of personal gnosis or metaphysical guidance as an important factor in retrieving it. During the many years of my own journey of searching for the evidence that I used in *When God Was a Woman* and in *Ancient Mirrors of Womanhood*, I continually had experiences of possessing unexplainable knowledge of what to look for and where to look, each bit of information appearing just as I needed it. Perhaps in my own case, because the knowledge I received was most often about which library, museum, or excavation site to visit, which book or archaelogical journal to read next, even which pages held the evidence I needed at a particular time, along with the numerous instances in which I would find myself with a specific person or in a certain place I had not intended to visit, but from whom or where I received vital information for my research, the metaphysical guidance I received almost daily dovetailed quite comfortably with more academic procedures.

Having had so many of these experiences of what Orenstein calls "The Methodology of the Marvelous" for so many years, I cannot say that metaphysical gnosis or guidance does not exist. Since I had always been extremely skeptical of any tales of receiving metaphysical knowledge that I had heard from others before my own experiences, my conscious acceptance of the reality of this type of guidance was not easily accomplished and emerged only after quite a few years of inner struggle between my skepticism and my own constant experience of it. At this point it has been there for me so repeatedly over a period of almost 30 years that accepting the reality of this form of receiving information has become far more for me than an article of faith.

Thus I am especially grateful to Gloria Orenstein for having the honesty and courage to discuss seriously this aspect of reclaiming ancient wisdom. Although I have spoken to close friends about my experiences of being continually guided in my research into an area that had not yet been examined as a totality, it is liberating to be able to consider it and write about it in a more public way. I think it is the area of reclamation discussed in this book that will probably draw the most uncomfortable reactions, yet I also find myself wondering if it will give permission to many other artists, authors, and scholars to speak about similar experiences. Nonetheless, I think we must be careful to differentiate between knowledge that has been acquired through intuitive or other metaphysical forms and the knowledge we have acquired from ancient cuneiform tablets or the hieroglyphs of papyri.

I am even more appreciative of Orenstein's work in this book because it documents the actualization of a hopeful vision I held during the many years I was doing research for and writing *When God Was a Woman*. I dreamed of thousands, millions, of women knowing about the Goddess reverence of the past to help us better understand how and why the expression of women's perceptions about so many aspects of life had been silenced by later patriarchal systems. At the time I began to work on my book in the late sixties, very few people, even those who had extensive educations, were familiar with the existence of the numerous ancient temples or written prayers and legends of the Goddess from any periods preceding archaic Greece, or realized that writing itself had been developed and widely used for over two thousand years before Homer. In addition, many of my feminist friends questioned what my research had to do with feminism. This documentation of how the reclamation of the Goddess is inspiring such a rich diversity of women's creative work, and helping us to express our perceptions of ourselves and our sensibilities about our earth and all of life, causes me to feel that the almost impossible dream I held for so long is being made manifest.

I sense, with a strangely overwhelming certainty, that each of us has a contribution to offer to this transformation, one that I now realize so many of us have dreamed about. *The Reflowering of the Goddess* articulates what many of us have felt but could not quite grasp or express with the clarity that Orenstein reveals. The tapestry she has woven gives us a vocabulary, a broader and thus more inclusive perspective, and a means of comprehension that will ultimately inspire and motivate more and more people to join in this renaissance, not by emulating what others have so far done but by getting in touch with the fact that they too have awakened and remember. Thank you, Gloria Orenstein, for helping me to be more hopeful that the vine on which this flower grows will continue to send out new shoots into places that were once barren, and to know even more deeply that the flower itself is so full of promise that to truly grasp the beauty and mystery of its appearance is to want to take part in its fruition.

Merlin Stone

Acknowledgments

I would like to give special thanks for the support and encouragement given me by many individuals who accompanied me on my journey, most importantly to all the feminist matristic artists, writers, and scholars who so generously gave of their time, their materials, and their creative lives over the years I have known them, as well as during the year of the writing of this book. I would also like to thank my student, Barbara Graber, who spurred me on in the preliminary stages of my research by taking her own, independent Goddess journey under my tutelage at U.S.C. I give particular thanks to my daughters, Nadine Orenstein and Claudia Orenstein, and to my little extended family in New York composed of my dear friend, Adah Askew, and our friend, John Wielk, who lived through both the suppression and the reflowering of the Goddess (book) with me during my sabbatical in New York in 1988. Thanks, too, to my friends Irene Diamond and Jeff Land, who sparked my ecofeminist journey, and to all the participants in U.S.C.'s. Ecofeminist Perspectives Conference for their energy and spiritual sustenance. I am also grateful to Irene Javors for her stimulating discussions on many topics of shared interest during my sabbatical in New York, to Arlene Raven for putting me in touch with new feminist matristic artists, to Barry Pribula for his excellent photographs, and to the Brewster Gallery in New York for materials and for their continued generosity. This may actually be a first, but I seriously want to thank the marvelous people at the WordPerfect Hotline in Orem, Utah, who listened so patiently and compassionately to my cries of frustration at the mysterious disappearance of vital parts of my text and who were always there to bail me out. Thanks also go to Lowell Morrison, who put the finishing touches on my computer literacy. I am most grateful to Savina Teubal for support, both intellectual and technological, in all these areas. Thanks are also offered to Deena Metzger, who midwifed my trip to Samiland and my return to New York, to Esther Broner, who midwifed my "Crone Journey" as I reached mid-century in New York, and to Joyce and Phil Orenstein who continue to nurture me with goddess energies.

Although I wrote most of this book on the East Coast, I do want to remember my friends in Los Angeles, the members of the Program for the Study of Women and Men in Society (S.W.M.S.) and the Comparative Literature Department at U.S.C., particularly Walter Williams, whose support all the way from Indonesia energized my writing. Special thanks, too, are due to Lois Banner, who has embraced "the Goddess" independently of me and who understood my journey. Some of my colleagues past and present may look upon this "Queste" with quizzical expressions of amused befuddlement. However, they have all helped me to clarify my thoughts and to pursue what, for lack of a better word, might be referred to as my own "Grail." Some men, like Alan Nadel, who have not embraced "the Goddess" have given complete support and valuable criticism, and for that I am very thankful. Others such as my brother Sandy Feman, helped me in very important ways at critical moments.

I am especially indebted to Merlin Stone for her perceptive reading of this book and for the inspiration and comfort she has given to me, personally, as well as to so many other women all over the world through her groundbreaking books, which opened this field of Goddess re-search, re-membering, and re-vision for all of us. Finally, I want to thank Leonora Carrington, Rosalyn Bruyere, and Ellen Marit Gaup-Dunfjeld for bringing so much magic and healing into my life—and especially for bringing it right into the very halls of Academe! Both extremely surreal, *and very real, thanks* are also extended to all of my editors at Pergamon Press's Athene Series. Stephanie Boxall, with whom I share the special birthday of International Women's Day (March 8), saw me off to Samiland, greeted me on my return, and received the first version of this manuscript. Lisa Tantillo, my current editor, nurtured its rebirth into its final form. I am also infinitely indebted to Deborah Leary and Kathryn Dix for their excellent literary skills and sensitivity. Renate Klein and Susan Hawthorne are also thanked for their perceptive feminist readings of this manuscript in Australia.

Finally, I give thanks to the invisible, yet very real energies and forces that I call "the Goddess," the spiritual matrix from which my ideas and my vision come to life.

Introduction

As I pruned the final pages from an excessively long manuscript in June 1989, I lived through three earthquakes in the Los Angeles area of California. Indeed, since January, I have lived through more than five quakes here. It also seems to me that the most recent three earthquakes happened during my revision of the literary chapters in this book, which talk about the symbolism of the earthquake as an expression of the anger of the Great Earth Mother at how humans have destroyed her sacred lands, water, forests, and air. It was during these moments of perfect alignment between my writing and the Earth Mother's energies that I was overtaken by a sense of the great urgency with which we *must* perform what I have termed "Green Magic."

During these earthquakes I was constantly reminded of the chant sung in feminist spirituality rituals:

> The Earth is our Mother/ We must take care of Her
> The Earth is our Mother/ We must take care of Her

Although this book was first written during the academic year 1987–88, while I was on my sabbatical from the University of Southern California, and living in New York City (my former home), its genesis and gestation actually cover the period from 1971, when I first heard the words "the Goddess" pronounced by surrealist artist Leonora Carrington, through the summer of 1987, when I embarked on a Vision-Quest in Samiland (Norwegian Lapland) with the Shaman, Ellen Marit Gaup-Dunfjeld. The magical tale of how the Shaman of Samiland came into my life as a manifestation of the surrealist teaching that "The Marvelous Is Real" is as much a part of the creation of this book as any discussion I could offer about professional research methodologies.

In choosing to affirm the magical and synchronistic aspects of a process that is usually reduced to highly technical terms, I have decided to refer to this aspect of the practice of my profession as "The Methodology of the Marvelous."

Thus, while researching contemporary artists and writers who are reclaiming the image, symbol, and mythos of the Great Goddess in their contemporary works of art and literature, I was led upon extraordinary adventures, too numerous to recount in this book, but which will certainly form a cycle of autobiographical tales of power that I will write about in the future.

For the past 17 years I have been publishing articles and giving conferences and slide lectures about the meaning of the parallel movements in feminist art and literature by which the Great Goddess has re-emerged in the works of women creators during the period known as the Second Wave of the women's movement (1970s and 1980s) as the symbol of Creation on three levels: cosmic creation, procreation (fertility), and artistic creation.

In the past I had been using the word "gynocentric" to convey the meaning of "woman-centered," a term that was frequently used in feminist criticism. However, until the writing of this book I had not clearly enunciated the difference that I now see between "gynocentric" (as used in the now popular term "gynocritics") and "feminist matristic" as I use it here. I have been inspired by Marija Gimbutas's use of the term "matristic" to avoid the technical problems in speaking of cultures whose Creator was imaged as female but which we cannot, strictly speaking, call "matriarchal." While some of those cultures may be or have been either matrilineal or matrifocal, what I wish to stress is a holistic ethos (values, ethics, roles, images, etc.) associated with cultures whose Cosmogonic myth features a Goddess, a female Creator. For those prepatriarchal cultures whose mythos of the Great Goddess inspires our contemporary creators, I will still use the word "matristic." However, I have added "feminist" to "matristic" in order to stress the roots of this perspective in radical feminism whenever I speak of today's writers and artists. I have done this in order to reclaim the radical feminist roots of ecofeminism because today the word "matristic" is being used by numerous women whose works reclaim the Goddess in ways that we might not consider to be "feminist." I do not want contemporary ecofeminists to eclipse their radical feminist foremothers. Nor do I want to perpetuate a sloppy, wishy-washy jargon that calls everything referring to women "feminine" without any feminist analysis of the social construction of gender.

Indeed, there are certain feminists who would maintain that the term "radical feminist" is sufficient to describe what I have labeled "feminist matristic," since Mary Daly, whose weblike, interconnected ways of thinking about Goddess murder in *Gyn/Ecology,* was germinal to our contemporary critiques of patriarchal religions and to our understanding of their takeover and transformation of Goddess symbology into patriarchal myths.

However, by "feminist matristic" I do not mean "woman-centered" either, because, as I use this term, I mean to imply a shift in cosmogony rather than a shift in gender alone. I do not intend to put women "at the center" or "first." I intend to honor the Goddess (the Great Mother/the Earth Mother) at the origin of Creation and at the center of the Cosmos, as the Creator of all of life. Indeed, it was not until I completed the writing of this book that I understood the importance of this difference. All of the artists and writers I have considered here make it perfectly clear that what deity one worships *matters* (in the sense of literally *creating matter*).

Thus, a feminist matristic vision does not just shift the gender of the deity from male to female; it alters the entire cosmogony; it changes the Creation story and the values that ensue from embracing a particular deity or a particular Creation myth (that is energized through one's spiritual, religious, and creative practices). The kind of world that has been created in systems that espouse a patriarchal Father God Creation mythos are completely different from those embracing a matristic Earth Mother Goddess myth of origins. Both genders, of course, are included in each mythic vision, but whereas the patriarchal system is androcentric (male-centered), the matristic world-view as I have explained it in the book places humans within the context of their origins (the Cosmos, the Earth) and, as many tribal, matrilineal cultures do, sees the Earth as the Great Mother, the womb from which all life springs, and humans as a part of nature, not above or outside of it. The contemporary feminist matristic vision honors all life-creative, life-enhancing values, and while it does not privilege women over men, it affirms both women and men in all these life-nurturing, life-supporting capacities.

I have always wanted this book to bear witness to the meaning that women artists and writers have made of the immensely important body of research that women searchers and questers such as Merlin Stone and Marija Gimbutas have uncovered about the existence of at least 30,000 years of life on Earth, before patriarchy, in which the cosmic Creator was revered in the image of a female. I had aspired to show the power of a female image of the deity in bestowing legitimacy on the creative works of women who could, at last, visualize Creation as female. I have avoided the use of the word "feminine" wherever possible, because it has proved to be problematic in feminist theory.

The "feminine" has been shown to be a patriarchal social construct, and while it is a word that is frequently used by participants in the feminist spirituality movement who wish to "restore the feminine" in order to bring about a balance and heal the Earth (which has been dominated and ravaged by the "masculine" for too long), the university professor in me cautions me to avoid phrasing this thought in those words because of the immense critical baggage that the word "feminine" carries with it. Of course, I understand what is meant by the desire to "restore the feminine," but since the "feminine" has a different meaning in different cultures and at different periods in history (aside from being a patriarchal construct), I have chosen to speak of and elaborate a "feminist matristic" vision rather than resort to the use of the word "feminine," particularly since I see them as two totally different concepts. Whereas the "feminine" refers to a shift in gender away from the "masculine" (however we wish to construe those terms), a "feminist matristic" vision refers to a total change in the Creation myth or the cosmogony of a culture.

Another problem has been the use of the word "matriarchy." How much easier it would have been to be able to simply say "matriarchal" instead of "patriarchal"! But once more feminist theory has shown that "matriarchy" means "rule by women," and not only are we without definitive proof of there ever having been literal matriarchies in the prepatriarchal era, but we also do not necessarily wish to substitute systems of "rule by women" for systems of "rule by men" as our source of inspiration. This by no means implies that we do not support the political leadership of women. Simply put, the feminist matristic vision is about politics in the feminist sense, rather than about political systems as such. It is about a Creation story and the values and ethics espoused by both the women and men who envisage the cosmic Creator as the Great Mother rather than the Father God. It is about honoring a "mothered knowledge of creation" and what that might mean both to the past and to the present.

While on the abstract level, it could, and will, be argued by some that we might easily conceive of a symbol without gender (that is, a geometrical form—a star, a circle, etc.) to represent a cosmogony that would not be oppressive to anyone, I want to emphasize that my book is *not* about the cultural construction of any *new* cosmic story. Rather, it *is* about re-membering an original cosmic myth, as well as a legitimate and actual history of many thousands of years in which the Goddess was revered as the Creator of all life. This is to say that a feminist matristic vision is specifically about (as my title indicates) both the suppression *and* the reflowering of the Goddess in art and literature by contemporary women.

The title also reflects my desire to focus, first, on the suppression of the Goddess and the impact of this on the creative imaginations of women in the arts historically, studying mainly the surrealists and elucidating how the stifling of the female image of a cosmic Creator contributed to the madness and suicide of many women artists and writers in that movement; then on the occultation and coding of the secret realizations about the taboo placed on this knowledge in patriarchy by two of our most difficult women creators to interpret (because their work is coded and occulted), Gertrude Stein and Leonora Carrington; and finally, on the reflowering of the Goddess in works by contemporary feminist women to show that, as the taboo lifted under the supportive political climate of the contemporary women's movement, creative works with a feminist matristic vision began to surface and to flower.

These were my original ambitions, and they were at the origin of my desire to put the last 17 years of my research into one all-embracing vision in which both the negative effects of the suppression and the positive results of the liberation of Goddess knowledge and images could be perceived as two parts of one ever-unfolding history.

But as anyone who has ever written knows all too well, to embark upon the writing of a book is often like buying a ticket to a foreign land. One may read all the guidebooks in advance, but the trip itself is always full of startling surprises.

When I began the journey I did not consciously realize something that became acutely apparent as the trip progressed. The overall impression I now have, as I conclude my work, is that, on a very subtle level, myth *is* real—or, creation *is* literal. It *matters* very much what our myths are; it *matters* very much what we create, for in a world whose Creation myth is not earth-based, one that does not include a vision of the Earth's renewal, we can literally read in the papers every day the actual story of the "Wasteland." Feminist matristic artists and writers, as visionaries, with perhaps a touch of the prophet, like the Cassandras before them, who spoke truth about the disasters they saw taking place in the world of men, have emphasized the importance of restoring the Grail to its prepatriarchal "pagan" and female origins—or, as Leonora Carrington has expressed it in her novel *The Hearing Trumpet*, the sacred Cup (Grail, Chalice . . . etc.) must be returned to the Goddess in order for life to flourish on Earth once more.

Indeed, women and the Earth are both Grails—vessels containing sacred blood, wombs from which all life is born. The feminist matristic Creation story affirms this knowledge. However, it is the patriarchal cosmic story in which God the Father is the Creator of life, that has resulted in the technological takeover of the gestation of life from women, the technological interference in the creation of life, and the ongoing rape and plundering of the natural world in the name of so-called progress. Furthermore, the Father God cosmic story has also led to the poisoning of most organic life on the planet due to the misguided belief that if men cannot create life in wombs, then they will do so in laboratories.

Most of the contemporary literature that I have reviewed is situated at the precise historical moment in the narrative when this usurpation of matristic power by androcratic power is taking place. Many of the stories show the ancient matriarchs of the Bible or the priestesses of the Goddess religion working underground to wrest the power away from the conquering Father God patriarchs in order to return it to the people of the Mother Goddess culture. In some ways we are living through a similar moment now, one in which feminist matristic creators are returning the symbols of creation to their original Mother Goddess cosmogonic source. Of course, patriarchal systems have been in place for several thousands of years, but never before has the fertility of the Earth and the female been more threatened than at present. Originally, the Goddess was a fertility symbol, and for people who live in harmony with the Earth and its cycles, fertility is always sacred.

It does not take a shaman or a professor to see that the Wasteland is a reality, and that until we take the nonscientifically provable *risk* of changing our Creation story and of restoring our *original* and viable story of the Great Mother, Creator of all life, to our mythic pantheon, we are taking a far greater *risk,* for we are placing all of life on Earth in jeopardy. I am, of course, very well aware of all arguments to the contrary. However, many of our lives, especially those of white Eurocentric intellectuals, have been completely inculcated with all the theories that refute my points. It would be of little value to restate them here. I simply want to say that, as a woman witnessing the threat to female bodily integrity and the rise of the breakdown of the immune systems of vast numbers of my contemporaries due largely to background radiation and pollution, I feel that the time has come for us to state loudly and clearly that *we see* all life is dying, and *we* know that only a major shift can heal us now! That shift, I suggest, is to return to the original source of the most ancient wisdom on the planet, the matristic vision of Creation.

You may respond: "How can we ever know what that system taught, for all vestiges of its practices have been destroyed? There is very little data we have to go on." This is where our contemporary feminist matristic artists and writers as visionaries have come to be extremely important. For they are now synthesizing the data they have gleaned from archaeological and historical research with the new kinds of knowledge they have acquired by drawing on what is commonly referred to as the "right brain." By sensing, psyching out, intuiting, feeling, imagining, and creating, they are bringing forth a body of teachings that, while it may not be the literal truth of our ancient past, can nevertheless constitute what we might call a "Feminist Matristic Path" or a "Feminist Matristic Way." They are combining their insights with experiences lived in tribal cultures (such as the native American or the Sami) in order to transform the world, now, before it is too late.

In the first part of this book I have tried to address some of the theoretical issues surrounding the most common objections to "the Goddess." One of the more vocal reactions has been to say that the Goddess is an archetype, and that all archetypes are ahistorical. I want to respond to this point up front, because it is precisely this kind of reaction that blurs history. To call the Goddess an archetype is to relegate some 30,000 years of human history to the level of the unconscious and to negate the actual historical reality of centuries of human life. Therefore, the Goddess is anything *but* ahistorical! The history of the Goddess actually exceeds that of the Father God by millennia!

One of the most important reasons for restoring the symbol of the Goddess as Creator is specifically in order to expand our historical framework well beyond the advent of patriarchy. The Goddess, however, does *not* symbolize a universal ahistorical image of the "essential feminine," as some have assumed. Rather, the Goddess symbolizes the actual history of many women and men living for thousands of years under systems that, from what we can understand of those cultures (based upon the very limited data we have, due to the desecration of the remains and the meager funding that has gone into further excavation of important Neolithic sites), were societies in which women were accorded a very high status, and whose peoples were more peaceful than our own. Contemporary feminist matristic artists, writers, and scholars do not promote a wholesale return to the past. Feminist matristic creators espouse balance and, in order to restore balance, recommend combining the best insights of the ancient matristic past with the best insights of what the present has to offer. By "best" I consistently mean those values that are earth-based.

I have, therefore, contrasted the patriarchal tendency toward myths of matricide with the feminist matristic tendency toward telling tales of power, or tales of *matrigenesis*. In so doing I have come to speak about literature, my own field of specialization, in a way that I had not anticipated when I set out on the journey of this book.

Having discussed the various kinds of amnesia to which we Westerners have become addicted, such as eco-amnesia (our forgetting our connection to the natural world), gyneamnesia (our forgetting about the 30,000 years of our matristic history), and shamanic amnesia (our forgetting our connection to the spirit world), I have concluded, in my chapter on contemporary feminist matristic literature, that another kind of amnesia still persists in the West—amnesia about the oral world, the world that preceded the print technologies. We have forgotten about the values inherent in oral transmission, and in my chapter on contemporary feminist matristic literature, I have tried to show that contemporary writers, in establishing a relationship with the values espoused by those in ancient goddess-worshipping cultures, are attuning themselves to worlds in which the literary word was a *spoken* word, worlds before writing and certainly before print had evolved. In these worlds, the quality of attention that went into learning and retention was, indeed, different from the quality of attention and care that would go into learning in a culture that could conserve all of its knowledge on a computer.

It is my contention that within the contemporary women's movement, we are witnessing the creation of a veritable cultural rebirth, and in that rebirth we are passing on our knowledge largely through oral transmission (consciousness-raising groups, gatherings, conversation, storytelling, and the like). We have realized that just as temples and civilizations can be destroyed, leaving virtually no traces of their knowledge behind, so, too, can electronically stored knowledge be erased. Feminist matristic writers and artists are creating works that function similarly to works in the oral tradition, because they spark the retention of information through human memory and the transmission of knowledge without the necessary intervention of technologically invented artifacts.

It greatly surprised me that, at the beginning of my academic career, having obtained a Doctorate in Comparative Literature, I was asked to teach folklore. I did so at Douglass College of Rutgers University for seven years, and I must confess that I could never understand why, having studied the great canonical writers such as Dostoyevsky, Joyce, or Proust,

I was then called upon to teach genres such as the riddle, the proverb, the joke, the children's game, or aspects of material culture such as recipes, Easter-egg painting, barn building, or graffiti. The irony of all of this is that now I *do* see why *I* had to teach folklore for so long! I had been trained in a system that bred an elitism in me toward certain genres and a certain gender—indeed—toward folk arts, women's arts, and, in general, toward all forms of creation that had not been stamped with the seal of approval of the white, upper-class, male "mainstream" culture and its canons and criteria, or transmitted via the print or modern technological media.

Moreover, at the same time that I was teaching folklore, as a feminist, I was always teaching works that had *never* been published, and showing slides of art works by women who had been written out of art history. Yet I had never made the connection between the two. Now it seems elementary to me to realize that not only have women been written out of the mainstream, but that entire centuries of cultural creation are continually being written out of white, Western, androcentric, elitist histories all the time. From this point of view, what does get published or recorded seems to me to be incidental in comparison to the great cultural flowerings that never make it through the arduous and very political processes that lead to mainstreaming, whether in literary publishing houses or in art galleries and museums.

In my literature chapter, then, I have chosen to approach our feminist matristic reflowering from this perspective. From my position, there are many works in circulation in our culture that support my arguments, and these works may or may not be inscribed in our "official" records by the redactors of our cultural heritage. This does not mean that they are not valid. Rather, it means that they, and many other works like them, are being created and, like the works of the lost women writers of the past that we have now excavated, are simply works that have not gained the immediate visibility accorded to those that circulate in the mainstream marketplace, for reasons that are often politically or financially determined. In a first version of this manuscript, I had discussed several books that either had not yet been published or that never were published. Because of the limitations of space, I have had to omit those that were not yet published.

I have selected works from various genres—mainly novels (or as I call them, "tales of power"), one play, one long poem, and works of science fiction as well as a mytho-poetic feminist matristic autobiography. I have selected these works to support my theoretical arguments, but I am well aware of the many omissions you may discover. I have intended my overview of the cycles to serve as a map and a catalyst rather than as any extensive or complete survey. I have tried to discuss works from the classical literary canon (such as those by Christa Wolf) as well as those that circulate widely in the popular culture (such as the books by Marion Zimmer Bradley). I beg my readers to forgive my oversights and omissions, specifically because I know that I embody the criteria of my academic training and that, therefore, I have probably perpetuated different pernicious 'isms, not consciously, but unconsciously, in order to indicate the paths along which this enormous bulk of material has led me.

It was of extreme importance to me to consider the visual arts along with the literature. During the seventies I had co-created two feminist salons; one in literature exclusively, The Woman's Salon for Literature in New York (co-created with Erika Duncan, Karen Malpede, and other writers), and one in the multi-arts, Cerridwen (co-created with Marcia Miller), named for the Celtic Goddess, Guardian of the Sacred Cauldron of Wisdom and Inspiration. From my experience in the feminist literary salon over several years (its duration was from 1975–1985, but I left it in 1977, and it was kept alive by its co-creator, writer Erika Duncan), I concluded that, in general, writers and artists often do not understand each other. Having come out of my studies on surrealism, where artists and writers shared a common vision, I wanted to spark that sharing among feminist creators. The Cerridwen Salon (which lasted only one year, at the end of the seventies and was held, for the most part, at Soho 20, a feminist art gallery in New York) did present soirées on a common theme that was taken up by women working in a wide variety of arts and media. Thus, it became clear to me that a feminist matristic reflowering was actually taking place simultaneously in women's art, literature, theater, and music. By using only the visual arts and literature in this book I do not mean to suggest that a feminist matristic vision is not flowering among composers, filmmakers, or dancers. On the contrary, I hope that this book will launch an exploration of this vision in the other arts as well. While for the most part I have dealt only with feminist matristic artists who have established a name for themselves in the art world (however we might construe that concept), as I roamed through exhibits of M.F.A. (Masters of Fine Arts) candidates at various art schools I realized how much incredibly good creative work simply never makes it to public view because of all the hoops their creators must jump through to establish a career or a "life" as an artist, exhibiting in galleries or museums. My goal has not been to cast an authoritative aesthetic judgment on creation, although my training has led me to make selections that are, obviously, based on criteria that have been internalized both consciously and unconsciously during my studies in white, Western, elitist, mainstream institutions. Yet, because I have focused on women, one could never claim that these artists have achieved anything like the success, recognition, or reputation of their male colleagues at similar points in their careers.

In both the visual arts and literature I have selected creators most representative of a feminist matristic vision, irrespective of their "success" in the mainstream. Nevertheless, I have considered aesthetic quality as a criterion, both consciously and unconsciously. I also realize that any criteria we use to judge these works also have vast political implications. The new feminist scholarship in the arts has been extremely vocal in pointing out exactly how hierarchies have been established to conform to the white male value system.

I also beg my readers to excuse any omissions I have made among visual artists. Once more, I have tried to outline *my* journeys rather than to be exhaustive.

Finally, I would like to conclude by restating that my "call" to encounter the Great Spirit in Samiland (known to us as Lapland) grew directly out of my surrealist research, especially that on Leonora Carrington. The last line of her novel *The Hearing Trumpet* reads: "If the old woman can't go to Lapland, then Lapland must come to the Old Woman." When I read this manuscript in her home in Mexico City in 1972, I asked her *why* the Old Woman wanted to go to Lapland. Leonora Carrington replied quite nonchalantly that it was simply because "The shamans of Lapland are the most magical people on Earth." Although I did not know what that meant at the time, I intuited that the information was somehow important for me, and I remembered it in a sacred way until January 1987. For it was then, 15 years later, that Ellen Marit Gaup-Dunfjeld, the Shaman of Samiland (known to us as Lapland), stepped into my office at U.S.C. as if transported there via a magic carpet woven by Leonora Carrington's "tale of power." It was, indeed, a magical manifestation of the Marvelous, right in the very "groves of Academe." I later found out that the Sami goddesses were celebrated in solstice and equinox rituals entitled "ACCA/demias," named for their Triple Goddesses—Sar/ACCA, Juks/ACCA, and Yuks/ACCA, and their Great Goddess, Mader/ACCA.

Thus, it all comes full circle or, as I realize, I have completed the first rung of a spiral, and on that circular journey I have learned that we must ask which gods are being served before engaging in any creative venture. There seems to be a magical energy related to all thought and all creation. If we are mindful of that, then we can awaken out of our eco-amnesia and our matristic and shamanic slumbers. We can also remember the oral tradition through which our earliest women writers gave voice to their matristic visions. Perhaps we will eventually find the word "writer" inadequate, for we need a word that embraces singers and tellers of tales of power, as well as one that describes the very recent process of creation that dates back only as far as the written word. We can also reawaken the passions and desires for the generation of life through a reverence for the life force.

Yet, it does *matter* exactly how we invoke the life force, and what values relate to the myths of the deity that represents the life force to us. The Earth is our original womb, and, as *I see it,* we must become questers for the lost Grail, in order to heal the wounds of the Great Mother, by restoring to Her the precious Cauldron of Regeneration that has been pirated away by the nuclear, test-tube, and pollutant industries. The Mother is ailing, and today all women—Persephones, Eves, Oshuns, Oyas, Helens, Liliths, Cassandras—*all* have been in exile from the true Matristic Garden of their hearts' desire. It is this Matristic Garden that needs to be tended now, for at the very moment that I write these words the forests are burning, the Earth is quaking, the whales are dying, and my friends are ailing from the breakdown of their immune systems. Yes, we are the Earth, and if She is sick, so are we. We are suffering from Her disease, for we eat Her fruits, and are one with Her. This is Her language; the way in which She communicates Her pain to us. The feminist matristic arts, by attuning us to the voice of the Earth Mother, aspire to promote a healing of the planet now by sparking us to action of all kinds. One important form of action is the transformation of our cosmic mythos, and this can easily be done by storytelling, as well as by participating in all forms of feminist matristic creation in the arts, in general.

May the Methodology of the Marvelous ignite many new feminist matristic creations and tales of power, so that the synergy of their combined energies will catalyze a critical mass large enough to heal the world.

Gloria Feman Orenstein
New York City, June 1988
Los Angeles, June–September 1989

Honoring Our Mothered Knowledge of Creation

This book is born at the confluence of many streams of thought within women's studies: the ecofeminist movement, the feminist spirituality movement, feminist literary and art theory and criticism, and the radical social activism that gave birth to our new understanding of the silence that has prevailed over a variety of topics such as sexism, racism, classism, and homophobia, as well as over the study of matristic cultures, a field now embraced under the symbol of the Goddess.

While the original explorations, intuitions, analyses, and revelations that provide the groundwork for this study became the subject of my academic research in the early 1970s, a book such as this could not have been written before the actual literature and art works themselves were created, and most of these were born in the 1970s and 1980s under the supportive energies of the feminist movement and women' studies combined.

Indeed, one of the important theses of this study is that scholarship, done by those both inside and outside the academy, can be catalytic in affecting the forms of the arts and the lives of those living and creating in a particular historical period.

This statement implies that knowledge is a force for transformation and that the suppression of knowledge can contribute to trauma both within the individual and in society at large. I contend here that the women's studies movement that was born in the early 1970s and has flourished since then (in the seventies and eighties) is exemplary of how new knowledge can lead to action and action can lead to new knowledge, reciprocally, and that the synergy of the two modes of change can create a critical mass sufficient to bring about a cultural metamorphosis whose artistic expression is both reflective of that change, and far-reaching in its ability to envisage the possibilities of further changes yet to come.

Scholarship and activism must, however, be accompanied by other processes that are far less obvious, less tangible, and harder to pin down in order for cultural transformations to occur. Some of these fundamental, powerful, and important processes at work in the culture include intuition, imagination, memory, foresight, and vision. These latter mental functions are particularly crucial in reconstructing history and creating narratives when those more tangible sources of information such as historical and archaeological data are missing.

In the case of knowledge about lost civilizations, such as those that predated written and patriarchal history, these intuitive functions of the mind play an especially critical role in revisioning the past and envisioning the future.

The feminist matristic arts that I will explore in this book, arts that reclaim a mythos in which all life was revered as sacred and believed to have been created by the Great Mother Goddess (a mythos that was alive for over 30,000 years of human history) (Diner, 1973/1929; Eisler, 1987; Gimbutas, 1974; Levy, 1968/1948; & Stone, 1976; etc.), rely heavily on the visualization and narrative powers of contemporary artists and storytellers. These women artists piece the knowledge they have gained from feminist scholarship together with their intuitive musings, imaginative reconstructions, and psychic recall of ancient civilizations whose material traces are virtually lost to us now, in order to help us imagine how differently women could be empowered today had they been born into an era that did not deny that matristic heritage, indeed one that honored it.

Women artists and writers today, deriving their creative powers from a new understanding of the history and mystery of Creation imaged as female, are energizing a creative process that I am here calling "shamanic," and they are creating works of art whose functions often contrast with our contemporary Western notions of the function of art in society.

This shamanic function of the feminist matristic arts, in contradistinction to prevailing Western notions, reclaims the ancient powers of art to heal, to empower, and to perform what we might term "magic"—to effect materializations of the imaginary and the willed. Tales told by contemporary feminist matristic writers function like medicine stories and shamanic tales of power. They show us how to reconnect with and remember those past eras in which the Great Mother represented Creation and women were respected as powerful incarnations of the Great Mother's fertile potency—times when there was no schism between cosmic creation, procreation, and artistic creation, for all were intrinsically linked within the image of the Creator visualized as the Great Goddess, Creatrix of all life.

It was, as Merlin Stone, Marija Gimbutas, Helen Diner, Jane Ellen Harrison, G. Rachel Levy, Elizabeth Fisher, Elizabeth Gould Davis, and more recently, Riane Eisler have shown that with the intervention of the patriarchal period in history, the flowering of those matristic cultures was interrupted, and that for approximately five thousand years all traces of those matristic beliefs and practices were systematically eradicated from mainstream culture. This erasure of all traces of Goddess cultures (the desecration of Goddess temples, the inscribing of patriarchal versions of myth and history into the written record, etc.) has brought about the overall effect of a global matricide, a killing of the image of the Mother that previously prevailed over all three aspects of Creation (cosmic creation, procreation, artistic creation).

On the level of cosmic creation, the patriarchal religions have rewritten the creation myths around a Father God rather than a Mother Goddess. On the level of artistic creation, our recorded canon of art and literary history has been written by, and included virtually, only males. Finally, today the new reproductive technologies are experimenting with the possibilities, not only of test-tube babies, but of eventual male motherhood, cloning, and other techniques such as artificial wombs that would remove procreation from the female, just as patriarchal myths of cosmic creation and artistic creation have already erased the female from her original positions of power in the other two realms of creation.

In this book I will argue, further, that whereas the women of surrealism and other recent literary and artistic foremothers such as Gertrude Stein had to subvert their consciousness of the Goddess as the original empowering mythos of Creation because of the historical contexts in which they lived and worked, contemporary feminist matristic artists and writers, fueled by the women's movement and its accompanying feminist scholarship and activism, have been able to articulate more fully the meaning of the Goddess in much more open and less subversive ways (thanks to the creation of feminist publishers and galleries). Thus, they show us how to reconstruct our stories of dis-memberment and disempowerment by re-membering our origins via the imaginative processes catalyzed during the creation of art.

Through a study of their reclamation of our original mythos (one that was interrupted by patriarchy, but that still prevails in a variety of indigenous cultures today), we can observe an emerging tendency to reclaim and revalue the original image of the Creator as female and to reconceive the function of art as shamanic and magical. Basic to this new feminist matristic art is the understanding of the principle that *creation is literal*. By this I mean that the creative act actually does produce life, and that, as the surrealists believed, the imaginary tends to become real; that art functions to create *exempla* of "how to do"—of how to connect with the powers that actually, not merely metaphorically, make the invisible visible.

The new feminist matristic arts also function to promote and record healing by creating "medicine stories" or "medicine images," "feminist matristic midrashes" (commentaries and rewrites) or revisions of patriarchal versions of images and tales, which promote the further growth and flowering of women's original—and now reflowering—feminist matristic creative powers. In this regard, I contend that, inspired by the ways in which tale cycles circulated in the oral tradition, stimulating memory and recall, contemporary feminist matristic storytellers are creating new cycles of tales of power, using a formulaic approach to narrative. This process fuels an open-ended flowering of new feminist matristic variants or rewrites of our inherited, patriarchally inscribed versions of tales of creation, heroism, and the like.

Whereas written literature arose during the patriarchal era, permitting the inscription of one sanctified version of a story into the historical record (the androcentric version), tale cycles that function according to the processes of the oral tradition catalyze and generate many diverse variants of the stories of particular events and persons. These feminist matristic tale cycles thus recontextualize the Western patriarchal literary tradition with its single sanctified version of a story, and relativize its canonically inscribed narratives and images. This feminist matristic creative process decenters the white, Western, androcentric artistic tradition, and restimulates the growth of a new feminist matristic tradition.

This feminist matristic tradition, as we shall see, does not replace patriarchy with matriarchy but rather restores women to their historically grounded powerful roles deriving from humankind's original association of Creation with the female and the life-producing fertility of both the mythic Great Mother and the actual real mother.

At this point a short history of some of the most important works of scholarship and creation that seeded the fertile germination of the feminist matristic arts is in order. I here refer the reader to several of the groundbreaking, germinal texts in order to situate this study well within the phase that follows their publication, without which this book could not have been written. All of the following contemporary writers at first drew upon the writings of Jane Ellen Harrison, Helen Diner, and G. Rachel Levy. Some of these more recent works are Merlin Stone's *When God Was a Woman* (1976) and *Ancient Mirrors of Womanhood: Our Goddess and Heroine Heritage* (1979–80); Elizabeth Gould Davis's *The First Sex* (1972); Charlene Spretnak's *Lost Goddesses of Early Greece: A Collection of Pre-Hellenic Myths* (1978) and her collection *The Politics of Women's Spirituality: Essays on the Rise of Spiritual Power Within the Feminist Movement* (1982); Elizabeth Fisher's *Woman's Creation: Sexual Evolution and the Shaping of Society* (1979); Monica Sjöö and Barbara Mor's *The Great Cosmic Mother: Rediscovering the Religion of the Earth* (1987); Carol P. Christ and Judith Plaskow's collection *Womanspirit Rising: A Feminist Reader in Religion* (1979); Susan Griffin's *Woman and Nature: The Roaring Inside Her* (1978); Mary Daly's *Beyond God the Father: Towards a Philosophy of Women's Liberation* (1973), and *Gyn/Ecology: The Metaethics of Feminism* (1978); Marija Gimbutas's *The Goddesses and Gods of Old Europe: Myths and Cult Images 6500–3500 B.C.* (1974); Naomi Goldenberg's *The Changing of the Gods: Feminism and the End of Traditional Religions* (1979); *The Feminist Spirituality Journal, Womanspirit* (1974–84); Starhawk's *The Spiral Dance: A Rebirth of the Ancient Religion of the Great Goddess* (1978), and *Dreaming the Dark: Magic, Sex, and Politics* (1982); Elaine Pagels's *The Gnostic Gospels* (1979); Carolyn Merchant's *The Death of Nature: Women, Ecology, and the Scientific Revolution* (1980); Judy Chicago's *The Dinner Party: A Symbol of Our Heritage* (1979); Esther M. Harding's *Women's Mysteries, Ancient and Modern* (1971); Phyllis Chesler's *Women and Madness* (1972); as well as the writings of many other women too numerous to cite in full, some of whose works are studied in this book and cited elsewhere. Among these are Ruby Rorlich, Margot Alder, Z. Budapest, Rachel Carson, Patricia Monaghan, Savina Teubal, Luisah Teish, Hallie Iglehart, Riane Eisler, and Elinor Gadon.

Concomitant with the publishing of these works, several conferences and gatherings took

place during the 1970s and the 1980s that prepared the terrain for the rooting and germination of the feminist matristic arts in our society today. Among these conferences were Women
and Life on Earth, which took place at Amherst, Massachusetts in 1980; The Women's Penta-
gon Action, held in Washington, DC in November 1980; and The Great Goddess Re-emerging Conference, on the campus of the University of California at Santa Cruz in 1978. These
have been followed up more recently by U.S.C.'s Ecofeminist Perspectives: Culture, Nature,
Theory Conference, and Gaia Consciousness: A Conference and Celebration of the Re-emer-
gent Goddess and the Living Earth, held at the California Institute of Integral Studies, in April
1988.

I am suggesting that contemporary feminist scholars, writing on the subject of the Goddess
from any number of disciplines (archaeology, religion, history, literature, art, anthropology,
etc.), are actually reliving and reversing a patriarchal biblical story, the story of Eve in the
Garden of Eden, and as they taste of the forbidden fruit of the tree of knowledge, they are
discovering a knowledge that is taboo in their culture. Moreover, as more women scholars
enter the patriarchal garden and eat of the fruits of the forbidden tree of knowledge (or
as more contemporary women's studies scholars deepen their research about the Goddess),
the more that knowledge about our most ancient matristic past will permeate our contemporary historical accounts, and the more the biblical myth of Eve's role in the Garden of
Eden will become illuminated with respect to the meaning it holds for contemporary
women.

Today, researchers in almost all fields of women's studies are confronting the unavoidable
evidence that in many prepatriarchal cultures, which some refer to as "matristic" in order
to avoid using the word "matriarchy" (for which no solid evidence has, apparently, been
found), the Creator of all life was revered in a female image, and women's status was greatly
enhanced in comparison to women's positions in most contemporary patriarchal societies.

If we juxtapose the evidence given by Marija Gimbutas in her monumental archaeological
studies of the prepatriarchal cultures in what she refers to as "Old Europe" (Gimbutas 1974)
with the works of Alice Miller (1986), and Bruno Bettelheim (1980) on the taboo and silence
surrounding the subjects of incest and the Holocaust, and with, for example, Kim Chernin's
Reinventing Eve: Modern Woman in Search of Herself (1987), where she envisages modern
woman as the new Eve, eating of the mother tree, tasting the divine fruit and breaking the
taboo by feasting on "Goddess knowledge," we begin to understand some of the conundrums and silences surrounding the emergence of research on the Goddess that prevailed
until Her reflowering in the 1970s and 1980s.

It is the task of contemporary feminist scholars to redefine the terms in which the story is
enacted. In this book I argue that an ecofeminist perspective can serve to redefine the meaning of that quest for knowledge, whose patriarchal scenario was enacted in the biblical Garden of Eden. Chernin thus supports Merlin Stone, who, in When God Was a Woman, wrote:
"When these children of Paradise eat from the mother tree they realize that they are 'naked
with regard to knowledge.' In other words: one bite of the Goddess fruit and they realize
that the story they have been told by the patriarchal God, blind usurper, false authority,
envious ravisher, is not the only possible tale. One bite of the mother fruit and they become
aware that there is something very fishy about the idea of a Creator who is exclusively male"
(Stone, 1976, p. 3).

Chernin then imagines the woman sharing her new knowledge with her husband. However, this woman is now aware of a new power that has come to her through the knowledge
she gained by eating of the mother tree.

In her discussion of the new Eve, Chernin metaphorically situates the position of feminist
scholar with respect to the patriarchal academy, and she says that the dilemma we are faced
with is to give birth to "The Woman Who Is Not Yet." She writes: "Eve's dilemma: a choice
between obedience and knowledge. Between renunciation and appetite. Between subordination and desire. Between security and risk. Between loyalty and self-development. Be-

tween submission and power. Between hunger as temptation and hunger as vision" (Chernin, 1987, p. 182).

The new Eve, according to Kim Chernin, is disobedient in satiating her hunger for knowledge. She transgresses the patriarchal taboo and discovers knowledge of the prepatriarchal world when the Mother Goddess prevailed rather than the Father God. However, that was the story of the Fall written by the patriarchal redactors of the Bible.

In the new feminist matristic version, written by contemporary women artists, writers, and scholars, it is patriarchy that is responsible for the Fall from Paradise or from the prepatriarchal Mother Goddess world. If Goddess knowledge reverses the meaning of the Fall, then it becomes clear that we have "fallen" into patriarchal time and space, and that the possible eclipse of all life can be attributed to the inception of patriarchal history, when we were first expelled from the Garden, which we all tended together.

Feminists, however, are never at peace with mere role reversals. Thus, the new Eve does not seek to restore the reign of Mother Goddess knowledge in order to banish men from a new feminist matristic Eden.

How the new Eve responds to her new knowledge is what feminist matristic creative works are about. As we shall see, women writers and artists of new feminist matristic cultures cannot be reduced to one single artistic or political tendency. As in all cultures, this literature and this art consist of many cycles—cycles of lamentation, cycles of celebration, cycles of retracing, cycles of rewriting, cycles of rediscovery, cycles of reclamation, cycles of reconstruction, cycles of integration, cycles of prophetic vision, and so forth.

One might say that the literary and artistic works created in the 1970s and 1980s were birthed by the many new Eves, who, once having tasted of the fruit of the mother tree could not but give life to their new hungering visions. These works, like acts of Holocaust and incest survivors, bear witness, as is the responsibility of a survivor, to their knowledge of the trauma as well as to their observation of the denial of the trauma among their contemporaries, which they learn to understand as a delusion. They also bear witness to the creation of a new feminist matristic vision of transformation.

In his essays on surviving, Bruno Bettelheim (1980) recognizes that words such as "holocaust" function to distance us from experiencing the horror of the reality of man's murders, the massive extermination of European Jews, gypsies, homosexuals, and so forth. Euphemisms such as "Holocaust" fuel the massive denial that leads everyone to avoid facing the truth.

The Reflowering of the Goddess argues that the ravishment of our prepatriarchal Goddess cultures by invading hordes of Indo-Europeans, who brought sky gods and war to more peaceable and earth-revering matristic cultures, was as traumatic for women, historically, as was the Holocaust for Jews, gypsies, homosexuals, and other so-called undesirables, who also lived through the desecration and destruction of their cultures.

Modern Eves cannot help but notice that the biblical paradigm has been radically altered. Today's Eve must reject exile and return to the Garden, not because she is the best peacemaker, not because she cannot live autonomously either outside (or within) the Garden, but because the Garden itself is in jeopardy. Eve, in saving the Garden, saves her own life as well, which is dependent on the Garden. She must, in fact, create a feminist matristic Garden in which both women and men may prosper, nourished by the wisdom of the Great Mother tree of knowledge. Furthermore, today's Eves and potential Demeters can no longer willfully withhold their fruits or fertility from the Earth. The paradigm has been so changed that today, because of the pollutants in the environment, women's fertility has been diminished, not as a result of the Mother Goddess inflicting punishment because of the rape of her daughter, but rather as a result of Her own rape, the rape of the Earth. Today it is rather the Persephones who are rescuing Demeter, their Mother, by succoring the Earth while maintaining a struggle against Her rape as well as against the rape of all women.

As contemporary stand-ins for Eve and Persephone, feminist matristic scholars bear witness by offering the fruits of their lives and their labors in the hopes of catalyzing a female alchemy which will transform the "gold" of a commodified world back into the beautiful "brute matter" of the natural world. This new female alchemy opposes the traditional description of the alchemical process, because instead of extracting spirit from matter or metamorphosing matter into spirit, this new female alchemy seeks to return the consciousness of spirit to matter, and to alchemize us back into realizing that the Earth herself is infused with spirit. This new female alchemy does not look upon brute matter as devoid of spirit. All to the contrary, it considers the Earth to be the living vessel/Grail/womb of the sacred spirit of all creation.

As we survey women's literary and artistic creation over the decades of the seventies and the eighties, the theme of the reclamation of the image of the Goddess in contemporary works emerges as a salient feature of the new feminist matristic iconography.

In fact, it is entirely logical that this should be the case, for the Goddess has always symbolized creation and therefore, by extension, the Goddess also represents artistic creation. Originally, it seemed as if an Ur-Fertility Goddess only represented procreation, but we are now coming to understand the image of the Goddess, as it appears in the arts, in a more metaphorical way—as a symbol for three separate kinds of creation: cosmic creation, procreation, and artistic creation, all embodied and implied in the images of the Great Mother.

In the Goddess image there is no distinction drawn between woman as creator of nature and woman as creator of culture. The symbol of a woman Creator bringing forth both life and art, nature and culture, seems to represent in the most poignant, powerful, and concise way possible, the point at which many of the themes espoused by contemporary feminism converge.

Indeed, the ancient Goddesses of various cultures, as Merlin Stone pointed out, were originally envisaged as the creators of culture, having invented the alphabet and language (e.g., Sarasvati, India, Brigit, Celtic Ireland, Nidaba, Sumer, and Seshat, Egypt), and planting and harvesting (e.g., Ninlil, Mesopotamia), as well as the various arts and crafts practiced in a wide variety of cultures all over the world.

The Goddess image implies a new feminist matristic consciousness at the same time that it reveals a new knowledge of our most ancient historical past. The Goddess symbol also reminds women that our legitimate history has been buried, and that through its excavation we are learning how short the patriarchal period in human history has been in comparison with the 30,000 or more years of matristic history in which goddess-centered cultures flourished in central Europe, Anatolia and the Near and Middle East.

The Goddess has thus become a valid artistic symbol for women as creators as well as procreators. The Goddess emerges today as a symbol for the manifold changes that many women and men hope to bring about both in consciousness and in the world, which will restore women to their important places in history and in contemporary cultures. Indeed, it is this new feminist matristic knowledge, being uncovered by feminist scholars around the world, that must also clearly articulate the vast political conclusions that we are now drawing from the lessons we have learned while engaged in these studies.

The return of the Goddess in art and literature today does not signify a plea for a return to the pagan religious practices of the prepatriarchal past, although it also does not exclude a revival of Goddess worship within a contemporary feminist context. Nevertheless, it does signal a new awareness of a kind of spirituality that does not separate heaven and earth, spirit and matter, human and animal; a spirituality that images the Earth as sacred, and the Goddess as the Great Mother of all life.

In "The Dangerous Sex: Art Language and Male Power" art historian Joanna Frueh (1985) critiques the metaphors of war and miracles that permeate all art historical writing. These metaphors define the artist as a male, as a conquering hero in a war against the generation of the fathers to which the male artist must do violence in order to achieve freedom. They also define the artist as a miracle worker. The male artist is sanctified by the language of miracles used in art historical and critical writing. As Joanna Frueh expresses it, the male artist, like a priest and a prophet, is considered to be divine. She writes "the divine, a Renaissance as well as a modern ideal, is not patterned on a goddess. In contemporary Catholicism, Jesus is called a miracle worker, while Mary is not." (Frueh, 1985, p. 11). Frueh reminds us how we are taught to worship artists because the subtext of art history implies that great artists are like God or God's prophets.

This is where the image of the Goddess emerges. Art history's Creation myth uses the male artist as a stand-in for God the Father. In this case, God the Father and the male artist both give birth to nature (the cosmos) and culture (art).

It now becomes apparent that in the feminist matristic artist's reappropriation of the Goddess image, two false Creation myths are being corrected:

1. The myth of God the Father as cosmic Creator. In light of all the recent archaeological evidence that shows how the very first Creator was imaged as a female, we must reclaim a Creation story in which the Goddess is recognized as the Mother of all living things. This knowledge of the ancient Goddess in prepatriarchal times is, of course, extrapolated backward from the written materials that we have found from the literary periods of our very earliest history (e.g., the Hymns to Inanna).
2. The myth of the male artist or writer giving birth to the work of art. This myth is based upon an erroneous and rhetorical device in which the biological powers of procreation are first transferred from the female to the male, and then used as the metaphor for all types of creation. Now it at once becomes clear that if we are to use the metaphors of procreation and creation legitimately, we will be led directly to the discoveries that (1) The earliest image of a Creator was that of a female, and (2) An artist who is both fecund and "pregnant with" or who "gives birth to" a work of art is equally as apt to be a female as a male, contrary to the way patriarchal art histories read.

Exemplary of the way in which contemporary writers use the reclaimed image of the Great Mother both to critique white Western patriarchal history and to reclaim, through memory and scholarship, the legitimacy of myths of origins that depicted ancient realities in nonsexist, nonracist ways is Alice Walker's The Temple of My Familiar (1989).

In this literary tour de force Walker creates the character Lissie, who remembers her past lives from prehistory to her most recent incarnation and narrates them on a cassette tape that is played after her death. She also narrates the story of Fanny, a contemporary women's studies professor, who falls in love with the spirits of the dead, who inspire and motivate her scholarly quests. Both black women's modes of knowledge—Lissie's memory of all-time, and Fanny's ecstatic, visionary scholarship—are motivated by the force of the love of truth. The novel is about the quickening of spirit within a culture that has killed it by practicing matricide, colonialism, and racism.

In the section from which the novel derives its title, Miss Lissie relates to Suwelo (Fanny's partner throughout most of the novel) by tape (an oral narrative) a dream in which she lived in a temple and had a familiar that was part bird, part reptile, and part fish, the very essence of aliveness itself. However, as its caretaker/protector, with all the power over it that the role implies, she had made the mistake of keeping it under a bowl. It nevertheless succeeded in pecking its way out of the bowl, and eventually she imprisoned it underneath a metal washtub. Ultimately, however, with all the force of a volcano, her lively familiar broke out of its washtub prison, spread its new-found and exquisitely colorful wings for the first time, and flew away.

The imprisonment and domestication of the familiar in the dream, and its breakthrough and flight to freedom, create a parable about the domestication and castration of black women in the white world. The dream symbolism of its flight toward freedom represents the desire of all familiars to be liberated, to discover the power of their colors, and to reconnect

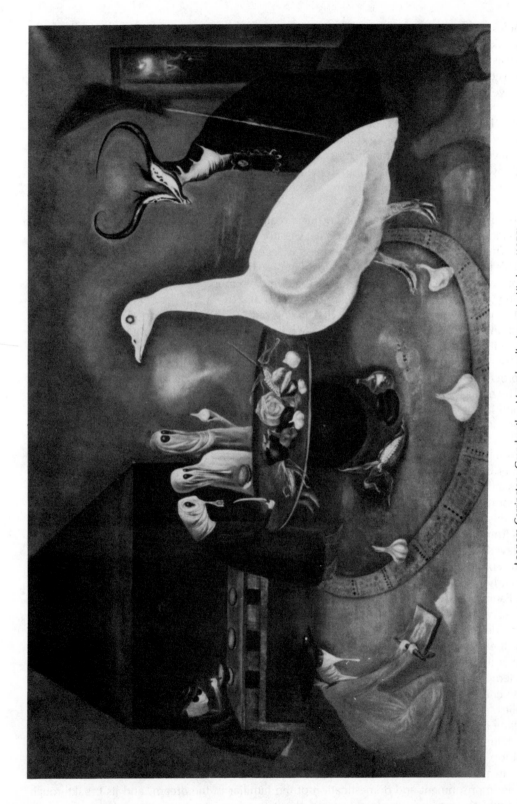

Leonora Carrington: Grandmother Moorehead's Aromatic Kitchen (1975)
Artwork photographed by Barry Pribula

8

with the ancient role of the undomesticated familiar, one of intimacy and nonverbal communion between humans and nonhumans, one of spiritual power.

The novel reconstructs the meaning of the Black Madonna, upon whose shrines so many white Christians erected cathedrals. It reclaims Mother Africa as the original and black Great Mother of all. It resurrects the memory of prepatriarchal times in which spirit was experienced as alive in matter, and Creation was imaged as a black female, and it evokes the African Eden through both memory and research, showing how the white male colonizers defined the original crime under patriarchy as loving the mother.

"Well, you get the picture. If I am not mistaken it is only in Poland that Our Black Lady, the Great Mother of All—Mother Africa, if you will—is still openly worshipped. Perhaps that is why it is said of the Poles that they are none too bright. . . . This is what they have done to their own mothers; it is certainly what they have done to Mother Africa" (Walker, 1989, p. 197). The crime of matricide has surely been most cruelly perpetrated on black women, and their physical and spiritual castration in white societies, their domination and ghettoization, is what the story of the colorful familiar suffocating underneath the porcelain washbasin expresses. Sadly, the white man's colonization of black women has also contributed to severing the bonds that would have brought African and European women together.

As Walker's novel reminds us, Notre Dame was built upon the site of a shrine to Isis, who was later called the Black Madonna, thus colonizing the spiritual remains of the Goddess just "as the Louvre had been built to colonize the material remains of devastated cultures" (Walker, 1989, p. 268).

The transformatory moment for men in Walker's novel occurs at the end. Here Suwelo takes one of Miss Lissie's last paintings, the *Tree of Life* painting in her series of lions, and hands it to Mr. Hal upside down. Mr. Hal sees a light emanating from a reddish spot on the painting. Suwelo then turns it upright, and knows that the reddish spot means "the return of Mr. Hal's lost vision," (Walker, 1989 p. 416) which, in this novel, would mean his understanding, loving, and honoring of Miss Lissie's multiple selves. The reddish spot, perhaps red for the energy of the life force of her blood that is alive in her art, creates a powerful force field that literally touches the men and opens the floodgates of their memory and desire. In this sense art is a spiritual presence that is embodied in matter, whose power to transform humans, to literally create new stages of awakening in its viewers, exemplifies the shamanic principle that *creation is literal.*

On a metaphoric level, the arts of black feminist matristic women create a *real temple* for all familiars, all winged colorful beings, animal and human, female and male, black and white—a temple that does not deny their winged nature, a temple that honors the sacred communication between human and nonhuman, a temple that celebrates creation in the image of the Mother. Walker's book is just such a temple. In it, the spirit of all familiars who have suffered castration, domestication, and colonization, both literally and metaphorically, can find liberation and experience ecstatic, inspired flight via the imagination.

Art, when it is performing its shamanic function takes us to that spirit world that is a real dimension of life, but one that has been excised by white, Western "civilization."

A brief overview of the evolution of my research on the Goddess reclaimed in art and literature by contemporary women is set forth in the following paragraphs. This detailing of the various steps and stages of my own thinking during the decades of the seventies and eighties is intended to provide a more nuanced historical, contextual, and process-oriented understanding of the layering that underpins this current book on the Goddess, which is written from an ecofeminist perspective.

In the first stage of my research on the women of surrealism, I discovered that an image of the Goddess was encoded or occulted beneath the surface of otherwise emblematically surrealistic figures, tropes, symbols, narratives, and the like. For example, in Leonora Carrington's painting *Grandmother Moorehead's Aromatic Kitchen* (1975), I found that I was confronted with a coded cryptogram, which on a superficial level could "pass" for a surrealist oneiric dream image. Actually the figure of Mother Goose was used as an emblem for Mother Goddess, as the resemblance in English between Mother Goose and Mother Goddess suggests. In this painting, the beings, both otherworldly and mythological, are preparing a meal within a magic circle, which is decorated with a series of black strokes that would probably not interest the casual viewer. However, these inscriptions in mirror-writing contain the occult meaning of the work. When deciphered they read: "The Goddess Dana became and is the Sidhé. . . . The Old Races died—Where did they go?" The painting imparts a visionary and scriptural revelation of the underworld land of the Sidhé from Celtic mythology, where the Goddess Dana's tribe fled when it took refuge from the conquest by the patriarchal gods. The message of the painting is occulted precisely because Goddess knowledge is threatening to a patriarchal culture. Witness the burning of women who believed in the religion of the Mother Goddess during the holocaust of the witch burnings in Europe.

In my studies of the works of the women of surrealism I began to wonder about the rate at which these women artists committed suicide and went "mad." In a series of articles such as "Reclaiming the Great Mother: A Feminist Journey to Madness and Back in Search of a Goddess Heritage" (Orenstein, 1982) and "Towards a Bifocal Vision in Surrealist Aesthetics" (Orenstein, 1983), I studied these two themes in surrealist women's art and writings. The results of my research are explored in more detail in Chapter 4. Briefly, however, my conclusions were that in the works of the women of surrealism who have either had encounters with "madness" or committed suicide, the image of the Goddess is suppressed or else encoded and occulted. It then becomes a symbol of female creation that has been repressed to such a degree that when it surfaces, it looms large enough to be confused with a "delusion of grandeur." If the women of surrealism suppressed and occulted the meaning of the Goddess vision in their works, or expressed it unconsciously in narratives and paintings of their journeys through psychic realms that we have come to label madness, it was because to articulate this knowledge more fully involved running the risk of literal torture (i.e., witch burning) in a patriarchal culture.

Another period in my research, which provided a historical perspective, occurred when I read Merlin Stone's *When God Was a Woman* (1976). This historical period is self-explanatory, and actually never ended. The influence of this book on my thinking has remained as powerful as it was when I first read it. This influence permeated my thinking in the phases that ensued, and was, at least in part, responsible for my ultimate refutation of the Jungian perspective on the Goddess.

A Jungian Period in my thinking actually coincided with my collaboration on the Great Goddess issue of the *Heresies* collective in 1978. I had been invited to do an article for this issue on the re-emergence of the Goddess in art by contemporary women. I called my piece "The Re-emergence of the Archetype of the Great Goddess in Art by Contemporary Women" (Orenstein, 1978), and my use of the word "archetype" indicates that I was under the influence of the ideas of Jung. At that time I had come to believe that the fact that so many contemporary women artists were expressing the Goddess image in their works meant that they were tuning in to an archetype of the collective unconscious, one that Jung had called "The Archetype of the Great Mother." According to Erich Neumann's book, *The Great Mother: An Analysis of the Archetype* (1955), based upon Jungian psychology, the Great Mother represents the feminine in the human psyche. He argues that the archaic world of the archetypes appears in myths and dreams of all humans throughout all time and space. According to Jungians, the archetype is an internal image at work in the psyche everywhere.

What I wish to stress here is that at the time I wrote the *Heresies* article, I was drawn to the Jungian hypothesis for several reasons, the most important being that I had come upon the discovery of the Goddess, as it were, through my connection with Leonora Carrington, because she had a great personal affinity for the writings of Jung. Since her work had produced such a strong effect upon my thinking, I was inclined to follow her lead, and to accept a Jungian interpretation of the re-emergence of the Goddess. Moreover, many of the Goddess artists that I interviewed in the mid-1970s were also inspired by Jung. Architect Mimi Lobell had designed a Goddess temple in 1975 in collaboration with a Jungian therapist. She then explained to me that she considered the shape of the temple to be the externalization of an archetypal structure that exists within the psyche.

Artist Carolee Schneeman also felt that her earliest body images related to the ancient Cretan and Minoan Goddesses, quite possibly because she had been intuitively in touch with a vision of the archetype. Buffie Johnson told me that her work since the late 1940s had been drawn from the Jungian concept of the collective unconscious. Her paintings evoked mythic memories and served as sacred icons to stimulate and resurrect the layers of consciousness in which our most primordial and archaic images, such as the Great Goddess in the images of *Ariadne* (Barley Mother) or *The Pomegranate*, recalling Demeter and Persephone, appear in connection with the life-giving powers of "the feminine."

Donna Henes was doing process environmental sculptures about Spider Woman from the Navajo emergence myth. Sheila Moon in her study of the Navajo emergence myth said that "Spider Woman is the unobtrusive but powerful archetype of fate, not in the sense of determinism, but in the sense of the magical law of one's own gravity which leads always beyond itself towards wholeness" (1970, p. 152).

My departure from the Jungian hypothesis first began to take shape in my mind when I interviewed Mary Beth Edelson about her pilgrimage to the Grapçeva caves in Yugoslavia. She was a friend of Merlin Stone's, and they both had worked together on the *Heresies* Great Goddess collective in New York. It was then that Merlin Stone's book *When God Was a Woman* (1976) began to resurface in my mind, and pierce through the Jungian overlay. It was at that time as well that I realized that to describe the Goddess as an archetype in the psyche was both invalidating to the kind of historical research that Merlin Stone had done, and distorting to the literal genesis of the artistic work of Mary Beth Edelson. In her lecture at the Great Goddess Re-emerging Conference held at the University of California in Santa Cruz in 1978, Merlin Stone discussed the difference between reading about a "goddess cult" in a patriarchal historical text and actually visiting the archaeological sites such as Byblos, Ephesus, Paphos, Čatal Huyuk. At an archaeological site or in museums such as those in Heraklion, Istanbul, Beirut, Ankara, Nicosia, and so forth, one might find hundreds of goddess figurines and artifacts. The actual scale of the site, its dimensions, its profoundly awe-inspiring setting, often led one to realize, on the spot, that these were no small "goddess cults," but rather that this was once an important world religion that had existed over a period of many thousands of years. Mary Beth Edelson's readings about the Goddess and her travels to Yugoslavia convinced me that her artistic and creative imagination was fertilized both by feminist scholarship and by personal pilgrimages. The Goddess that appeared in her work did not emerge from a trance state or as an archetype from the collective unconscious. In fact, it emerged from a knowledge of history. Also, politically, it seemed to me that talking about archetypes emerging in the psyches of women was again relegating women artists to the problematic status of unconscious or mad visionaries, a myth from which they had every right to desire to be liberated. It would be only too convenient to discard this new artistic work as the work of women mystics and neo-pagans who were either mad or illuminated by the archetypes of the collective unconscious, when, in my experience, I knew them personally to be conscious creators, and scholars in their own right. This is certainly not to say that Goddess images did not spontaneously occur in their dreams or visions. It is simply to underscore the importance of the actual, lived experiences as well as of the impact of feminist scholarship on the creative works of women artists.

Before Cynthia Mailman did her *Self-Portrait As God* for the Sister Chapel, she undertook extensive research, and showed me a huge collection of notebooks and sketchbooks about her readings on the Goddess in prehistory and early history. Similarly, Diana Kurz had studied Buddhism for many years before she painted herself as the Hindu Durga. Judy Chicago's *Dinner Party* was also in process in the late 1970s, and we were constantly being informed

Diana Kurz: Durga (1977)

of her research on the "Fertile Goddess," the Eye Goddess, and the Snake Goddess. Indeed, Judy Chicago had made use of the services of a group of women researchers, who actually sought out Goddess images for the plates in the project. Hélène de Beauvoir's Goddess paintings are based upon her extensive readings about Crete and her travels to Crete. The images she draws upon come to her from history and are then artistically transformed into symbols for contemporary women emerging into an era in which their own creative powers are affirmed and flourish. Hence, it became more and more evident that contemporary women artists' Goddess images did not emerge directly or spontaneously from dream visions, but rather were creations inspired by the new feminist knowledge of our actual but erased historical and prehistorical past that feminist scholars and artists were uncovering.

Finally, I discovered the vast and profound body of archaeological research and interpretation done by Marija Gimbutas. In her book *The Goddesses and Gods of Old Europe: Myths and Cult Images 6500–3500 B.C.* (1982), Marija Gimbutas demonstrates that the ancient civilizations which endured from the upper Paleolithic and Neolithic through the Copper Age (from 26,000 B.C. to 3000 B.C.), particularly in southeast and central Europe were distinct in every way from their Indo-European successors. They were matrifocal, largely peace loving, and earth- and sea-bound, whereas the Indo-European civilizations that followed were patrifocal, mobile, warlike, and sky-oriented. According to Gimbutas, the peoples of this Old European culture revered the Great Goddess Creatress, Giver of all, specifically in two aspects:

1. As Cosmogonic Creator—the Giver and Source of all life, fertility, and creation.
2. As the Goddess of Death and Regeneration—the Symbol of all renewal and becoming.

At once I began to see that the works of contemporary feminist matristic artists also fell into these two categories. Yet, this was not because of a psychic archetypal connection, but because in their conscious creation of new feminist matristic images of women's strength and creativity, they drew upon the most ancient sources of inspiration that they had come upon in their readings, research, and travels—the images of the Great Mother, Creator of all, who bore many different names in different cultures, but whose predominance well exceeded that of the current patriarchal mythos.

Thus, in my article "Une Vision Gynocentrique Dans La Littérature et L'Art Féministes Contemporains" (Orenstein, 1984), I was able to show that a variety of visual and literary works created by feminist artists from California and Canada to Nigeria, recapitulated the most ancient motifs and symbols connected to the pre-Indo-European mythos of the Goddess—motifs such as the Snake Goddess, the Bird Goddess, the primordial Egg, the Butterfly, caves, labyrinths, seeds, rivers, webs, vessels, horns, the Cow, the Double Ax, Earth Mounds, and the uplifted arms of the Cretan and Minoan Goddesses.

Today literary critics Estella Lauter and Carol Schreirer Rupprecht are revising Jungian archetypal theory to make it more malleable to feminist analysis. Their book *Feminist Archetypal Theory* (Lauter and Rupprecht, 1985) is written in response to Naomi Goldenberg's challenging critique of Jungian theory for feminism in her book *The Changing of the Gods: Feminism and the End of Traditional Religions* (1979). Lauter and Rupprecht's revision of the concept of the archetype marks a huge step forward in archetypal analysis, for they maintain that "the archetype assumes different forms according to the personal and social history of the person who manifests it" (1985, p. 11). They feel that the archetype is a useful concept because it refers to something real in our experience . . . that it may uncover a tendency shared by a great number of women across time, space, and human culture. They also maintain that image and behavior are inextricably linked. Yet, their ultimate goal is to study what women imagine, dream, fantasize, feel, and think by studying their art and their dreams.

Where my ideas now differ from theirs and from my own previous archetypal approach is in the understanding I now have of the ways in which these Goddess images were often actually inspired by the new knowledge of history, archaeology, and anthropology uncovered within the context of feminist scholarship. It seems to me that the recurrence of Goddess imagery today shows us precisely to what degree feminist scholarship has actively influenced the creative processes of women artists by providing them with new materials about which to dream, to muse, to imagine, and to create.

These artists all seem to be saying, "Remember: Our true history has been erased! People once imaged the deity as female. We are not making visible a mere fantasy of the imagination; we are consciously creating an imaginative rendition of what was once actually real. What we want to depict is the fact that those peoples of our ancient, matristic past who revered a Goddess, also accorded women positions of power and honor. Those powerful women of the past were the same women who bequeathed to us the first gifts of civilization— the knowledge of writing, of agriculture, and of the arts. In creating contemporary images of women we consciously want to relate ourselves to our most ancient matristic past. By doing so we can reconstitute a lost goddess tradition artistically." While all artists employ fantasy, the dream, and the imagination, we must be careful not to mystify our comprehension of the creative process. Art has both a conscious and an unconscious component. Here I want to emphasize the conscious component, and to note that the re-emergence of the Goddess can be explained historically without resorting to the concept of the archetype at all. The importance to feminism of stressing how social change, political action, and conscious-ness expansion affect the imaginative capacities of creative women must not be under-estimated lest we lapse back into identifying women artists solely with the intuitive aspects of creation alone, and ignore the evidence of their conscious intellects at work in making art.

The most recent stage of evolution in my ideas concerning the Goddess image came as a result of my encounter with political scientist Irene Diamond in California in the eighties. Our fruitful exchange of ideas between political science and the arts and humanities led to our co-creation of the conference Ecofeminist Perspectives: Culture, Nature, Theory at the University of Southern California in Los Angeles in 1987. Ecofeminism, inspired by Rachel Carson's *Silent Spring* (1962), Susan Griffin's *Woman and Nature: The Roaring Inside Her* (1978), and Carolyn Merchant's *The Death of Nature: Women, Ecology, and the Scientific Revolution* (1980), combines ecology and feminism in that it makes a critique not only of androcentrism, but also of anthropocentrism. It asserts that humans and nature are not sepa-rate from each other, but that we are interconnected, and that we live *in* the Earth rather than simply *on* it. It posits that our planet, Gaia, is alive, and that we are dependent on Her for our life.

This is where the Goddess or the Great Earth Mother comes into ecofeminism. In affirming that the destruction of our planet stems from the delusion that the world can be mastered or controlled by humans, who after the seventeenth century began to see themselves as outside of, and separate from, nature, rather than as a part of nature, in analyzing God the Father as the symbol of those patriarchal, instrumental, scientist attitudes toward the Earth, eco-feminism recognizes that cultures which revere the Earth have thought of it as our Mother. Thus, ecofeminism considers the return of the Goddess as a sign of the return to an attitude of reverence for the Earth, our Mother, and of an ecological as well as a nonsexist conscious-ness.

In examining a variety of arts that are mindful of this ecofeminist perspective, I have found that the figure of the Goddess emerges as the symbol of creation, of procreation, and of female artistic creativity. These arts, in understanding the cycles of nature and the cosmos, often express their meaning through rituals that celebrate our embodiment in the cycles of the human body and of the body of the Great Mother. These arts in which the Goddess becomes the symbol for the Earth Mother frequently refuse to erect monuments that destroy or triumph over nature and time. Instead, they often prefer to honor our interconnectedness with the Earth and the cosmos, rather than assert our mastery over them. Thus, they are both ecologically and politically self-conscious.

It is a sad fact that with the increased pollution of our Earth and our waters, human fertility has decreased. Feminist matristic artists are becoming more conscious of the Earth's fertility. If we are not mindful of the Earth's fertility, we will be plunged into a nightmare world from which all fertility, human and nonhuman, will be totally erased. Thus, feminist matristic artists and writers are particularly mindful not to pollute the Earth—not even during the pro-cess of making art.

In Israel, Miriam Sharon has celebrated the nomadic desert peoples, the Bedouins, whose tents leave no traces that could destroy the sacredness of the pure Earth, their Mother. In New York, Donna Henes has performed solstice and equinox rituals calling attention to the natural cycles of the cosmos, and Helene Aylon has created an Earth Ambulance, which transported the ailing earth on a stretcher to the United Nations, because it is the wounded body of our ailing Earth Mother. In California, Rachel Rosenthal, in her performance piece, *Gaia, Mon Amour*, chanted, keening against an Amerindian backdrop, calling upon the spirit powers of the universe to save the planet, while in Los Angeles Leslie Labowitz raised sprouts as an artwork, commenting on how we must put our art-making energies into the regeneration of the Earth. All of these artists and many more have seen the Earth as our Mother, and have conceived of us as parasites feeding off our host. If we destroy Her, we will destroy ourselves as well.

This vision of interconnectedness, this holistic vision, leads to a Green Politics as well as to a new mythic vision.

In contradistinction to the Great Goddesses of Old Europe and of the Middle East, of India, Asia, and Africa, whose rediscovery and reclamation partially inspired the creation of these new feminist matristic art works, the emergence of contemporary Goddess images and symbols within the content of Western feminist matristic art does not, for the most part, represent a predominant cultural belief nor the actual rebirth of the Goddess religion, except for certain individuals and groups. Rather, it shows how creativity is directly affected by a combination of social factors such as political activity, feminist scholarship, and feminist education—all a part of the contemporary women's movement. Like the humanistic renaissance of the sixteenth century, this feminist matristric renaissance of the twentieth century demonstrates how profoundly research, education, and political action may affect a transformation in the workings of the creative imagination and the creation of new forms of culture.

We may also observe that contemporary feminist matristric artists are weaving a new Creation myth. In the biblical myth, woman was born of man, and when she tasted of the apple from the tree of knowledge, God the Father expelled her from the Garden of Eden.

In the new feminist matristic Creation myth, woman is born of woman, of a Creatress. In tasting of the apple from the tree of knowledge (i.e., in doing feminist matristic research) she is learning about her true origins. In a contemporary feminist matristic world she will not be expelled from the Garden by her female Creator; she will, on the contrary, be called upon to cultivate that Garden, to revive the Wasteland that the Garden has become today.

In Leonora Carrington's women's liberation poster, *Mujeres Consciencia*, we see the new Eve returning the apple to the old Eve and rejecting the myth of the Fall. This new Eve then experiences illumination as her gyneric energy, the serpent power of Kundalini (so Leonora Carrington conceives of it) rises through the Chakras of her body to the Third Eye of illumination. The poster is green for Green Politics, for as we have seen, the new Eve is born of the Garden and is dependent on it for her life, as it is dependent on her for protection. With the threat of nuclear winter hovering in the future, the new Eve, whether she does or does not share the apple with Adam, who may or may not respond to the call of a female Creator, . . . this new Eve, knowing that the Garden is her very Mother, will minister to Her in a reverent way for the sake of all the interconnected flowering lives of all the species that live upon the Earth. Today's new Eves and Persephones, who are now called upon to write the new story of humankind from a feminist matristic perspective, will be telling the many possible new stories about Eve's new relationship to other women, to men, to the Great Mother, and to the Garden. And these are the stories we will be attending to in the final chapters of this book.

As the Ecofeminist Perspectives Conference made clear, contemporary feminist matristic artists and writers are now collaborating with feminist political scientists, for in view of the threat of incipient planetary annihilation, the return of the Goddess in the arts takes on a still larger political dimension. It signifies the natural outgrowth of what it meant in the early 1970s. Whereas the Goddess then symbolized a reminder of our erased prehistory and early history, a reminder of the witch burnings, of spirituality connected with the practice of an original Mother Goddess religion, of the repression of female creativity, now in the late 1980s the Goddess has come to signify a fusion of ethics, aesthetics, and politics in a global ecological vision of survival both for humankind and for all nonhuman life on Earth.

It is important for us to recognize that *in only two decades women in the arts,* inspired by the multiple actions of women in the women's movement, *have actually transformed the content of their creations in ways that spell out a new mythic paradigm.* It is also important

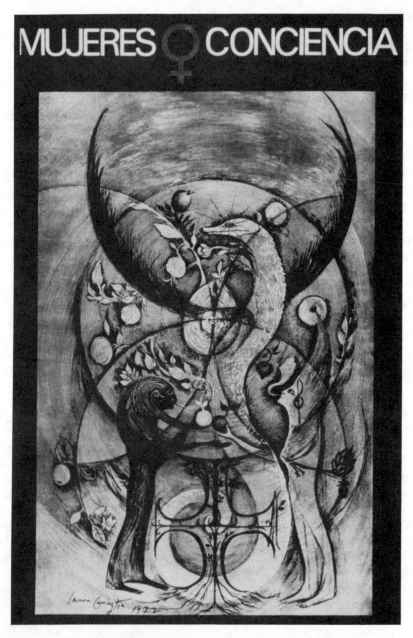

Leonora Carrington: Women's Liberation Poster Mujeres Consciencia (1972)
Artwork photographed by Barry Pribula

to understand that the re-emergence of the Goddess today *does* transform the myth of the Garden of Eden in three fundamental ways:

1. It establishes knowledge and truth as liberatory processes for mental health and Creation. The patriarchally forbidden knowledge of the Goddess now calls us back to the Garden rather than expelling us from it.
2. It stresses the importance of an ecological perspective so necessary in a world in which all forms of life as we know them are threatened with extinction. Exile from the Garden is no longer just a punishment to humans; it means the death of the Garden itself for

humans are the caretakers of the Garden as well as one of the life forms that flourish in it.

3. It clarifies the profound interconnectedness between all forms of life.

These, I submit, are only three of the more recent meanings of the re-emergence of the Goddess in the contemporary arts. As a symbol for the creative self, for knowledge and for life, the Goddess today is a potent image for catalyzing feminist matristic energies of transformation.

The Secrets of Green Magic:
Radical Feminism, Ecofeminism,
and Grandmother Gaia

In her painting *The Creation of Birds*, the surrealist artist, Remedios Varo, depicts a Woman/Bird Being who is both an alchemist and an artist. Sitting in her laboratory, which is also her art studio, she uses the energies of the cosmos and the chemicals of the earth to sketch the image of a bird, which then flies off the paper and soars into the sky. Dressed as a bird herself, she has created a being in her own image, and has given it both artistic and biological life simultaneously. Indeed, many indigenous peoples all over the globe believe that to retell the story of Creation is to re-create the world.

Paula Gunn Allen, in *The Sacred Hoop: Recovering the Feminine in American Indian Traditions* (1986) explains that when Thought Woman *sang* over the medicine bundles, she brought life to the twins. *It was her singing that brought forth life, not a biological act.* "A strong attitude integrally connects the power of Original thinking or Creation Thinking to the power of mothering. That power is not so much the power to give birth, as we have noted, but the power to make, to create, to transform. . . . Without it no practice of the sacred is possible, at least not within The Great Mother societies" (Allen, 1986, p. 29).

Thus, perhaps it can also be said that to tell any story propels it into some form of life (if only the life of the imagination of the reader), gives it energy, and enhances its possibilities for realization in some form. Then we can conclude that women writers of the new Eve's (re)birth may be launching more than a mere fiction, for if, as the surrealists believed, "the imaginary tends to become real," and if, as many indigenous peoples believe, to retell the Creation story *is* to re-create the world, then the literature and the arts produced by feminist matristic artists over the past two decades, may actually and magically bring about amazing and surprising changes in the world. As extreme as this statement sounds, there is no reason to believe that the project of feminist matristic artists is any less monumental than that—a project of ecological, political, social, and mythic proportions.

What I am suggesting is that whereas modern science tends to believe that creative thought does not produce life in the same way that procreative acts do, according to Paula Gunn Allen's teachings on native American cultures, the two are identical in power—especially in feminist matristic cultures.

I invoke Paula Gunn Allen's discussion of the native American Indian literary tradition in presenting the works of a feminist matristic vision, because I believe that their objectives, as well as their expressive forms of ceremonial and ritual, are often similar in function. She

Remedios Varo: La Creación de las Aves [The Creation of Birds] (1958)
Artwork photographed by Barry Pribula, by courtesy Walter Gruen

writes that native American Indian literature is not about self-expression, that it is about creating ceremonies and telling sacred stories that align humans with the energies of the cosmos, that integrate them into the larger community, and make all of reality sacred. Thus, if the feminist matristic arts and letters have not only reinterpreted the Fall, but have also created new mythic paradigms for Western culture, it is because feminist matristic artists and writers believe, along with native Americans, that through the power of the word, originally the spoken word, now transmitted via the print media, they can bring humans into balance with nature and the cosmos. For the word (its vibratory resonance) is real, and its magical utterance does produce materializations. Feminist matristic writers and artists believe that all of reality is sacred, and that all is interconnected in ways that are not always obvious, but that the life of the mind and the life of matter are inextricably interrelated so that *Creation is literal*. For feminist matristic writers and artists like Remedios Varo, a contemporary woman is also, literally, a Creatrix. Varo depicts a woman in the image of the female cosmic Creator whose Creation is made in her own image through the power of the mind and the body aligned with the imagination and actualized in artistic skill. If she conceives of a bird and paints it, her Creation has the energic potential to manifest itself as a real bird. Feminist matristic artists and writers are enacting a sacred shamanic or magical Creation ceremony, breathing life into an animistic world view that preceded patriarchy and that was symbolized by the Great Goddess Creatress, Mother of all.

To argue that Creation is literal, that the energy of thought is integrally related to the creation of matter, is not the same as holding a Jungian belief in the collective unconscious. On the contrary, rather than unconscious, in this case I see a close *conscious* interrelationship between mind and matter that heretofore has been put down as a "primitive" belief in magic. The Jungian hypothesis of a collective unconscious also leads to ahistorical and transcultural conclusions that simply erase specific historic and cultural contexts. I would also argue that the Goddess image, as it appears today in the works of contemporary feminist matristic artists and writers, symbolizes not just the nature-fertility and cosmic-creation motifs, but also a new unification of women's roles, both as procreator and as creator (of culture, i.e., artist), based on a heightened awareness of the primordial unification of these roles in ancient cultures. The prevalence of the re-emergence of the Goddess today, while it means different things to different women in different cultures, can also be seen, more generally, to stand for a conscious reclamation of a world view whose ethics, spiritual values, and social organization are deemed superior to those of today's dominating technocratic, non-ecological, androcratic systems.

I realize fully that one may say that some feminist matristic creators idealize or romanticize prepatriarchal cultures, and that in re-connecting women to nature they unconsciously advocate a philosophical essentialism that may result in pernicious consequences for women. Another objection to linking women to nature is that to identify women with a nature that is already exploited in our culture is to repeat the subordination of women. Here I must remind the reader of Susan Griffin's germinal, thought-provoking work, *Woman and Nature: The Roaring Inside Her* (1978). Contrary to the positing of an essentialism, Susan Griffin *historicizes and contextualizes* in detail the parallel oppression of women and nature during the course of the unfolding of Western patriarchal history. Hers was an early critique of essentialism.

In *The Great Cosmic Mother: Rediscovering the Religion of the* Earth, Monica Sjöö and Barbara Mor (1987) speculate on the world view that predominated before the inception of patriarchal structures. This cosmogony expressed itself differently in various cultures and civilizations all over the world, but fundamentally it held that the Earth was the Great Mother of all of life, and the cave was the womb of the Great Mother. All life, both biological and spiritual, was considered to be sacred and interconnected, and cultures such as those of the Neolithic were, as we have previously stated, more egalitarian and less violent than our own. In addition, these cultures were matristic, and nonhierarchical; they affirmed life, and do not seem to have engaged in war.

Tracing the voluminous data about prepatriarchal, matristic societies, and contrasting those findings with what we know of the nature of most patriarchal societies in the past and today (i.e., that they separate spirit from matter, are nonegalitarian, and engage in war), the authors call for a new "global spirituality." Their definition of this new spirituality can be considered the touchstone for what values feminist matristic writers and artists are reclaiming in invoking the image of the Goddess in their creative works today. Sjöö and Mor write that "we need a spirituality that acknowledges our earthly roots as evolutionary and sexual beings, just as we need an ontology that acknowledges earth as a conscious and spiritual being we need a new, global spirituality—an organic spirituality that belongs innately to all of us, as the children of the earth" (Sjöö and Mor, 1987, p. 421).

It is this new global earth-based spirituality that the symbol of the Goddess represents today. The Goddess symbol reminds us of the approximately 30,000 years of human history in which those earth-based, pacific, nonhierarchic spiritual values existed in cultures that revered the Great Mother as the Creatress of all. However, the Goddess is not reclaimed today simply for the sake of role reversal. She is reclaimed to provide the information and evidence lacking in general education in order for us to confront mainstream religious ideologies and to trigger our historic memory of times that were *real*.

The Great Goddess, as I use the concept in this book, refers to a historic reality, not a fantasy, and is a signal recalling to our mind the actual historic past in which humankind's sense of unity with the personal mother and with the Earth Mother was perceived as sacred.

Today, ecofeminist theorists such as Carolyn Merchant, Ynestra King, Irene Diamond, Charlene Spretnak, Susan Griffin, Starhawk, Mary Daly, Riane Eisler, Judith Plant, and Marti Kheel are successfully unpacking the patriarchally constructed "woman is to nature as man is to culture" impasse, and reconstructing a theory that develops the ecological parameters of a new discourse about humans and nature.

It is important to claim our foremothers as we reconstruct patriarchal history and *construct* our feminist matristic historical matrilineage.

Thus, while recognizing the contemporary ecofeminist positions about nature, the Earth Mother, and women, we must be mindful *not* to eclipse the crucial work of either Rachel Carson or of radical feminist Mary Daly in enunciating the analyses which were to form the matrix out of which contemporary ecofeminism was born.

Mary Daly in *Gyn/Ecology: The Metaethics of Radical Feminism* (1978, p. 17) reminds us, in her discussion of the dismemberment of the Goddess tradition by Christian and post-Christian myth, that just as the godfather has replaced the Mother Goddess in patriarchal societies, and silenced women's expression of their own spirituality relating to the pre-existing Goddess cultures, so too has nature's voice been silenced by the same patriarchal institutions, philosophies, and policies.

Daly refers to Rachel Carson as "an early prophet foretelling ecological disaster" (1978, p. 21) in her book *Silent Spring,* and sees Carson as a "mythic Cassandra, who was cursed by Apollo ('the god of truth') to be disbelieved when she prophesied truth" (p.21). She adds that "Ecologists today still deny her recognition, maintaining dishonest silence. Meanwhile the Springs are becoming more silent as the necrophilic leaders of phallotechnic society are carrying out their programs of planned poisoning for all life on the planet" (p.21).

Daly goes on to stress the fact that she is not suggesting that women have a "mission" to save the world from ecocide, nor is she "calling for female self-sacrifice in the male-led cause of 'ecology' " (1978, p.21). She, however, does call for women to have the courage to break the silence and create a new *spring.*

Mary Daly's reclaiming of Rachel Carson and of G. Rachel Levy as visionary foremothers attests to her thinking in a web of feminist matristic interconnectedness. Daly has put together G. Rachel Levy's analysis of the way in which the son eclipsed the Great Mother in the Dionysian rites, with Carson's prophetic vision of the death of the Earth Mother. She has seen the *connection* between the eclipse of the Great Mother, the death of the Earth Mother, and the rape of the Goddess through the multiple gyn/ecocidal strategies of patriarchal myth-making.

In linking the death of the Earth Mother (nature) to the death of the Great Goddess (prepatriarchal matristic cultures), Daly is *not* engaging in a reversal of the "woman is to nature as man is to culture" postulate. Nor is she elevating women and nature above men and culture. On the contrary, she is thinking in a web of interconnectedness and linking the death of nature to the death of Goddess cultures. This, then, is precisely what I would call feminist matristic thinking. Because it sees the interconnected webs that link humans to nature, it is also ecofeminist thinking. Daly is *not* linking women to nature; she is connecting the death of nature with the death of goddess-revering cultures. In fact, she is actually relating nature to culture, and seeing the radical implications of a truly interconnected vision. Such a vision of the *connection* between nature and culture sees that cultures which revered the Great Mother did *not* destroy nature. Daly's radical feminism *was* ecofeminism, for she never placed humans above or outside of nature but rather saw the connections between human-created kinds of cultures and the way humans in those cultures treated the natural world.

Like Susan Griffin in *Woman and Nature: The Roaring Inside Her,* she thinks in terms of the connections between the fate of cultures, of nature, and of women. Neither of these writers can be said to have placed humans above or outside of nature. Both have seen the disastrous implications of a nonecological perspective, but both, as radical feminists, have extended the web of interconnections far enough to analyze the relationship between power hierarchies in a given culture and that culture's attitude toward nature.

In the following discussion I will attempt to recount the ecofeminist political position. However, I want to emphasize that ecofeminists do *not necessarily* require either a Goddess as symbol or a harkening back to the Neolithic for inspiration. As a viable contemporary political movement, they seek to bring about a world whose ethics, practices, and values may, in some ways, resemble those of our ancient forbears in matristic cultures, but they neither agree on all of them, nor do they *necessarily* invoke prepatriarchal Goddess cultures as a model for the ecological future they envision.

However, some ecofeminists, such as Starhawk, are practitioners of Wicca, the religion of the Earth Mother Goddess; some, like Charlene Spretnak, also stress an inextricable bond between politics and spirituality. Others do not embrace the Goddess either as an inspiration from the past or as a present spiritual value in order to carry out their important ecological and feminist political work in the world.

In her paper "Ecofeminism and Feminist Theory" (1987), Carolyn Merchant establishes an overview of the various tendencies within feminism (liberal, Marxist, radical, socialist feminist) and their positions vis-à-vis nature and the environment. This paper states clearly that: "Liberal Feminism is consistent with the objectives of reform environmentalism to alter human relations with nature from within existing structures of governance through the passage of new laws and regulations" (Merchant, 1987, p. 1). She writes that according to a liberal feminist perspective "women do not differ from men as rational agents and that exclusion from educational and economic opportunities has prevented them from realizing their own potential for creativity in all spheres of human life. . . . Women, therefore, can transcend the social stigma of their biology and join men in the cultural project of environmental conservation" (Merchant, 1987, p. 2).

Thus, while liberal feminists seek to transcend the patriarchally constructed social stigma of the "woman is to nature as man is to culture" split, radical feminists such as Susan Griffin and Mary Daly, on the other hand, stress that women and nature have been mutually associated, and both have been devalued in Western culture. They assert that both can be liberated through direct political action. . . . Merchant goes on to say that radical feminism ". . . celebrates the relationship between women and nature through the revival of ancient rituals centered on goddess worship. . . . A vision in which nature is held in esteem as mother and goddess is a source of inspiration and empowerment for many ecofeminists. . . . Radical ecofeminist philosophy embraces intuition, an ethic of caring, and weblike human-nature relationships" (Merchant, 1987, p. 3).

Merchant argues that radical feminists have turned the patriarchal association of women and nature upside down, and rather than devaluing both, they celebrate and elevate them, particularly at this moment in history when Mother Earth's existence is being threatened by the possibility of nuclear war and the actualities of pollution of the air, the water, and the land.

Yet, Merchant's analysis maintains that the radical feminist position perpetuates the very split that the liberal feminists seek to transcend—the woman is to nature as man is to culture split. In celebrating women and nature, radical feminists, according to Merchant, seem to maintain the woman is to nature as man is to culture dichotomy. I disagree with Carolyn Merchant's analysis of this problem, and, as I have stated, believe that radical feminists were thinking in interconnected webs, linking humans to nature, long before the ecofeminist position was articulated. Indeed, it is the radical feminist analysis of Susan Griffin and of Mary Daly that constitutes the root of ecofeminism. While some might see a profound difference between radical feminism and ecofeminism (claiming that the radical feminists continued to maintain a dichotomy between nature and culture, while linking women to nature (only elevating that connection above men and culture), I argue that what both have consistently done is to show that culture is the creation of humans who are part of nature. They have repeatedly shown how we have done a disservice to humans and to nature by considering only men to be the creators of culture. When we look upon cultures in which women were creators, we are aware of a different attitude toward nature.

A young ecofeminist, Chiah Heller, has shed light on ways to reclaim both women and nature in their special association with each other (even as they have come down to us so constructed and so degraded in patriarchal history), and yet go beyond the impasse of reinforcing these same patriarchal splits and dualisms. Heller seems to agree with Merchant's analysis, and I am referring to her here in order to show that *both* the original radical thinkers from whom ecofeminism derived, *and* a contemporary ecofeminist have found ways to work beyond the dualistic reversal that Carolyn Merchant refers to.

The key to working through this impasse comes from the field of social ecology, as it has been integrated with radical feminism. In her article "Toward a Radical Eco-Feminism: From Dua-Logic to Eco-Logic," Chiah Heller points out that "the belief that certain subjects are more connected to nature than others is basically dualistic and patently reflects a lack of ecological sensibility." What can we learn from ecology that can be applied to this problem? Heller reminds us that "the study of Social Ecology shows us that all beings within an eco-community are interconnected" (p.13). Thus, as Heller continues, a radical ecofeminist critique of the "woman and nature" question must articulate a way to break through this dualistic impasse. Once we go beyond dualism, we see that the question becomes how we can account for women's different relationship to nature without reasoning that women are "more" connected to nature than men. Heller's response is that "women are not more *connected* to nature than men, but rather that women *remember* their interconnectedness to the natural world more than men" (pp. 13,14,15).

Heller calls men's lack of this primary awareness, their "ecological amnesia." Women's primary memory of human interconnectedness with nature is then termed women's "ecological memory." Heller affirms that women and men are equally connected to nature, but that whereas men have forgotten this connection, women have remembered it. She stresses that these inclinations are only "tendencies," for, naturally, there can be women who have also forgotten their interconnectedness with nature as well as men who remember theirs.

We might, at this point, look at the three kinds of amnesia we have discussed until now.

1. Amnesia vis-à-vis a period of 30,000 years of history in which the vast realm of Creation was associated with a female Creator, the Great Mother. (Matristic, historical amnesia)
2. Amnesia vis-à-vis an ecological understanding of the interconnectedness of everything within the vast realm of Creation. (Eco-amnesia)
3. Amnesia vis-à-vis the models of Creation and of communication with the spirit world revered in nonwhite, non-Western, and tribal societies, both in the past and in the present. (Shamanic amnesia)

It now becomes obvious that under patriarchy, humans in power (males for most part) have brought about a process of selective memory, and that what has been pruned from our ideologically constructed memory bank and from our educational systems is vast—its scope includes approximately 300 centuries of history as well as our interdependence with most of both the entire living, human and non-human worlds.

While it is too simplistic to reduce 30,000 years of prehistory to a single core belief, and too reductionistic to claim that an exact replica of any of those ancient cultures, if reproduced today, would provide a real solution to the many crises that confront our planet, I am suggesting that to remember the reality of a buried history *can* promote the healing of many wounds, and *can* shed light on a number of heretofore unexplained problems concerning the history of women's creativity. While I wish to remind the reader of the values and beliefs of a time that has been erased from our memory, a time referred to by the image of the Goddess as it reappears in women's arts today, I would also like to bring the discussion up to date by showing that the most contemporary scientific thought arising within our present patriarchal society resembles the cosmological view of ancient matristic cultures.

Here I refer to the "Gaia Hypothesis" as expressed in J.E. Lovelock's *Gaia: A New Look at Life on Earth* (1979) in which he states that "the biosphere is a self-regulating entity with the capacity to keep our planet healthy by controlling the chemical and physical environment" (p. ix). J.E. Lovelock and Lynn Margulis have elaborated the Theory of Gaia, that the Earth is alive, is sentient, has its own intelligence, and that we pose a threat to all life if we do not live in harmony with its Earth-Wisdom.

We can look upon native American religions and the practice of Wicca, the Earth religion of the Great Mother as reclaimed by Starhawk, as religions that link the original female image of the Creator to contemporary ecology. Wiccan witchcraft teaches that the Goddess is the symbol of "Immanence—the awareness of the world and everything in it as alive, dynamic, interdependent, interfacing and infused with moving energies: a living being, a weaving dance" (Starhawk, 1982, p. 9).

Whether we consult Starhawk, Paula Gunn Allen, Monica Sjöö, Carolyn Merchant, Irene Diamond or the Gaia Hypothesis, it is clear that what links all of these positions is a fundamental undercurrent of animism. All of these cosmogonies, religious practices, mythologies, and ideologies concur in their belief that spirit does not exist apart from the entire cosmos, but rather that the Earth itself is sacred, and that since we are an interdependent part of it, we are sacred too. In all of these living systems the Earth is the Mother, both of life and of death, but death is not viewed as a negative state or as the void within an ecological perspective where all living matter is recycled and reborn. Death is merely one phase of a vaster process of life, death, and regeneration. All of this is seen as part of a web of interconnectedness, part of the cycles of seasons, of day and night, of solstices and equinoxes, of the tides, the phases of the moon, and the menses in women.

Today feminist theoreticians, theologians, and psychologists such as Carol Christ, Susan Griffin, Judith Plaskow, Margot Adler, Naomi Goldenberg, Carol Gilligan, and Rosemary Ruether join the ecofeminists and the feminist matristic writers and artists in espousing a world view that takes responsibility for creating a culture that stresses the values of interconnectedness and embodiment as a means of grounding us in a spirituality of immanence rather than one of transcendence.

Many of these new paradigms and perspectives embrace the Great Mother Goddess as a symbol of the ways that these perceptions are grounded in a reverence for the Earth as our Mother, and in an understanding that the connectedness that most of us have experienced with our literal mothers is a valid metaphor and analogy for this radical ecofeminist consciousness of our relationship to the Earth.

Relating all of this to the new Eve in the Garden, we see that through women's more immediate eco-memory, and through our search for knowledge in women's studies (eating the apple of Goddess knowledge and remembering life in the original Garden), Eve may become an example to Adam in the creation of Paradise now, our home on the planet, the Garden of our Great Mother, Gaia. As the new Eve communicates her new vision via the magical aspects of the arts, as well as via the more ordinary paths of reason, contemporary women (the new Eves) can hope to create, what Ynestra King once called for in a talk at U.S.C.'s conference on ecofeminist perspectives, "a rational reenchantment of the world."

It was in 1976, with the publication of Merlin Stone's *When God Was a Woman*,[1] that feminist inquiry into the ancient Goddess religions and cultures became widespread. Merlin Stone surveyed the many manifestations of the Goddess dating from the Paleolithic, and asked important questions about why a religion that lasted over 10,000 years was consis-

---

[1] *When God Was a Woman* was initially published in England in March 1976 under the title *The Paradise Papers— The Story of the Suppression of Women's Rites*. It was published in the United States later in 1976.

tently referred to as a "cult," when the Goddess was revered as the supreme deity every-where. She also noted the many attributes, talents, skills, and inventions of the diverse God-desses, and discussed the elevated status of women living in goddess-centered societies while documenting the destruction of Her temples and the desecration of Her shrines.

In her chapter on "Unraveling the Myth of Adam and Eve" she traced the many manifesta-tions of the serpent with the Goddess at sanctuaries where the fig tree was most probably the original tree of knowledge, and the serpent the literal embodiment of the oracular powers attributed to female deities from Greece to Mesopotamia (Stone, 1976, p. 217). As she wrote in 1976, to eat of the tree of knowledge was to transgress against the patriarchal Father God and to eat of the Goddess's body (of knowledge). In her chapter "The Daughters of Eve" Merlin Stone asks whether "the suppression of women's rites has actually been the suppres-sion of women's rights" (p. 228).

As we have seen, the daughters of Eve are reinventing her as the daughter who tasted of the fruit of the mother tree, and resurrected a lost world through research, *gnosis,* and creation.

But in reconnecting to the Great Mother, there are many daughters of other "first women" from cultures in which the Earth is still revered as the Mother today, who can be our wisdom figures leading us to yet a deeper understanding. One of them is Paula Gunn Allen, who, in her talk at U.S.C.'s ecofeminist conference entitled "The Woman I Love is a Planet; the Planet I Love is a Tree," interpreted Gaia's ecological crisis as her rite of passage toward becoming a Woman of Wisdom. She wrote

> Our planet, my beloved, is in crisis: this, of course, we all know. We, many of us, think that her crisis is caused by men, or white people, or Capitalism, or industrialism, or loss of spiritual vision or social turmoil, or war, or psychic disease. For the most part, we do not recognize that the reason for her state is that she is entering upon a great Initiation. She is becoming Someone Else. Our planet, my darling, is gone coyote, heyoka, and it is our great honor to attend her passage rites. She is giving birth to Her new Consciousness of herself and Her relationship to the other Vast Intelligences, Other Holy Beings in Her Universe. Her travail is not easy, and it occa-sions her intensity, her conflict, her turmoil, which the turmoil, conflict, and intensity in the small affairs of humans and other creaturely life mirror. And as She moves in her growing and learning ever closer to the Sacred Moment of her Realization, her turmoil, intensity, agony and conflict increase.
>
> We are each and all a part of Her, an expression of Her essential Being, a small fragment that is not the whole but that, perforce, reflects in its inner self, its outer behavior, its expressions and relationships and institutions, Her self, Her behavior, Her expressions and relationships, Her forms and structures. We humans and our relatives, the other creatures, are integral expressions of Her Thought and Being. We are not Her, but we take our Being from Her, and in her Being we have being, as in Her Life we have life. As She is, so are we.
>
> In this time of Her emergence as one of the sacred planets in the Grandmother galaxy, we necessarily experience each specific in its way, according to its shape and significance, our share or form of Her experience, her form. (Allen, 1990, reprinted with permission of Sierra Club Books)

In referring to the Earth as Grandmother, and in remembering that we derive our existence from Her, in personifying the Earth as our earliest ancestors did, we align ourselves with our forebears, we reactivate an animistic view of nature, we restore the anima/soul to the planet, (which had been de-souled by the objectifying language of science, which refers to the earth as "it"), and we breathe life into a matristic Creation story once more. If the feminist matristic Creation stories derive from earlier matristic Creation stories that brought forth cultures that revered nature, perhaps there is hope that we, too, may turn the tide, and bring about a reflowering of the Goddess, which implies a reverence for nature and ultimately reflowering of all life on Mother Earth.

The Wilderness Connection: A Shamanic Model for Feminist Matristic Creation

As feminist matristic writers, artists, and critics use the symbol of the Goddess to weave a web of connections between the contemporary world and ancient goddess-worshipping cultures (retrieving values, forms, and images of women from societies that challenge our patriarchal perceptions) so that we can now visualize and integrate a sense of the close interaction between humans, nature, and the spirit world, we realize that the symbol of the Goddess is important both to feminism and to ecology.

Clearly both feminism and ecology began as secular movements, and both have ofter resisted absorbing the specificity of Goddess symbolism into their philosophical and ideolog·ical positions for a variety of political reasons.

Nevertheless, as a symbol, the Goddess adds an extra weight or valence, a vector tha forces us to expand the parameters of our vision and analysis in the direction of prehistory.

In the case of ecology, the Goddess symbol obliges us to think about the implications of the gendered image of the cosmic Creator as we return to a concept of the Earth as alive, an image such as that which prevailed in the millennia preceding patriarchy. Without the Goddess symbol connected to ecology, it might seem to be sufficient to return to the pre-seventeenth-century cosmology that existed within patriarchy [as described in Carolyn Merchant's *The Death of Nature: Women, Ecology and the Scientific Revolution* (1980)] in order to reconceptualize our interconnectedness with nature and the cosmos. Yet, the Goddess symbol inspires us to refer back to goddess-centered cultures like those of the Neolithic and cross-culturally to such images as that of Kali, the dancer who dances the world in and out of existence (Hawthorne, 1990) when striving to achieve ecological goals. The Goddess symbol obliges contemporary ecologically minded thinkers to include gender and sexual politics in their analyses.

It is the female gender of the image of a cosmic Creator that makes all the difference between an ecological ideology rooted in patricentric historical time and an ecofeminist ideology that draws its source from a vaster matristic time frame.

While on a practical level ecofeminism is certainly viable without the Goddess; on a theoretical level, the expansion of the time frame that the Goddess symbol provides forces us to come to grips with our cosmic mythos in such a way as to ensure the inclusion of women's most ancient, most traditional, and most contemporary concerns and values at every critical moment.

Starhawk, a Wiccan priestess of the old religion of the Goddess, writes that "Earth-based spirituality influences ecofeminism by informing its values. This does not mean that every ecofeminist must worship the goddess, perform rituals, or adopt any particular belief system.

We are not attempting to promote or enforce a spiritual practice. . . . What we are doing however, is attempting to shift the values of our culture. We could describe that shift as one away from battle as our underlying cultural paradigm and toward the cycle of birth, growth, death, and regeneration" (Starhawk, 1989, p. 174).

Indeed, today the consideration of an artifact such as the figurine of the Venus of Willendorf (2500 B.C.E.), which represents women's fertility in harmony with the fertility of the Earth and the fecundity of the Great Cosmic Mother, reminds us, as we enter the age of the new reproductive technologies, that female and male fertility as well as the fertility of the Earth, are currently in danger. Without elaborating on the consequences and the impact upon women's lives and choices that ensue with the rise of these technologies, it is sufficient to suggest that the symbol of the fertility Goddess now also connotes a consciousness of the growing threat to female procreation that these technologies pose. The Goddess, then, deconstructs patriarchal history while historicizing matristic history.

For similar reasons, the Goddess, as Carol Christ has convincingly shown in her now classic article "Why Women Need the Goddess" (Christ, 1982) is important to Feminism, because it raises questions that stretch our consciousness beyond a purely material base. While embracing such vital material questions as the status and roles of women in goddess-centered cultures, it also obliges us to consider the gendered nature of symbol systems, in general, and how they affect women's daily lives. As Carol Christ has argued, the Goddess redefines women's bodies and sexuality outside of all patriarchal systems, valuing our cycles, our procreative powers, and our nurturing and life-sustaining capacities.

During the first two decades of the contemporary women's movement, we women sought to name our world. One of the most important tasks was naming our sexuality from a female perspective. Today, as women name the world, we name our own cosmogony as well, and see female sexuality in relationship to a matristic creation story. The movement toward viewing female sexual energy as related to the cycles of the cosmos and of nature embraces the Goddess as the emblem of our repositioning of humans within nature, as Ecofeminism does. The Goddess also reminds us that in "archaic" cultures in which people lived according to this cosmogony, the Goddess signified the principles of creation and fertility, both in nature and in a culture where nature was experienced as sacred and as female—where ideas and mind were understood to be a part of nature as well.

In our contemporary project of weaving the worlds of nature and culture, spirit and matter, archaic matristic and contemporary feminist matristic cultures together, we—writers, artists, and critics—are like the shamans of a new feminist matristic culture. It is for this reason that I propose the shamanic model as an approach to our work at hand. As I see it, our task is nothing less than re-membering the body (of culture) of the Great Mother. Metaphorically, the terms "re-membering" and "body" can be read both literally and figuratively. For we are both literally piecing together the fragments of the dismembered[1] body of the Great Mother (through history, research, archaeology, and travels to ancient sites, ritual, storytelling, etc.) as well as remembering the entire body of a culture or cultures that expressed the lives, visions, hopes, creations, and deeds of people for whom the Great Mother was both alive and sacred.

It has traditionally been the role of the shaman to mediate between realms in order to bring about a healing.

According to John A. Grim's *The Shaman: Patterns of Siberian and Ojibway Healing:* "The shaman is the person, male or female, who experiences, absorbs and communicates a special mode of sustaining, healing power. In most tribal peoples the vital rhythms of the natural world are manifestations of a mysterious, all-pervasive power presence. . . . the

---

[1]These processes, of dismembering and remembering, have been spelled out for us by Mary Daly in *Gyn/Ecology:- The Metaethics of Radical Feminism* (1978).

transforming power that the Shaman invokes is experienced as an all-encompassing presence that is mysterious, but as real as the wind or a breath, after which, it is sometimes designated as spirit. It evokes the awesome feeling generally associated with the holy. . . . visible in dreams and visions, in memories of dead ancestors, of the fecund earth, and in the expansive sky, this mysterious power is so manifestly present that no explanation of it is adequate. Rather, it is itself, accepted as the cause of those transformations in the life of the seasons, the animals and the plants upon which tribal life depends. . . . a mountain might embody such a presence. So also certain rivers, groves of trees, birds in flight, or even the skillful acts of a craftsperson. All these may be understood as specific manifestations of a numinous reality" (Grim, 1983, pp. 3,4,5).

Today's feminist matristic artists, writers, and critics can be understood by referring to a shamanic model, for, since they are interested in expanding the context of life to include its broadest dimensions, they are linking spirit and nature, the land and the invisible, in ways that were the norm for most archaic and matristic cultures.

Mircea Eliade interprets the shamanic ecstatic experience as a "primary phenomenon . . . because we see no reason whatever for regarding it as the result of a particular historical moment, that is, as produced by a certain form of civilization. Rather, we would consider it fundamental in the human condition . . . what changed and was modified with the different forms of culture and religion was the interpretation and evaluation of the ecstatic experience" (Eliade, 1964, p. 504.).

John A. Grim also suggests that in our time, with the ultimate threat to life that our technology poses, we too, like the members of archaic societies, are desperately in need of a sustaining energy that can revitalize and regenerate life on our planet. He reminds us that "shamanism is formed from the particular tribes' understanding of the relationship between the living and life-giving worlds. The phenomenal and the spiritual realms are seen as interlaced rather than completely distinct from one another" (Grim, 1983, p. 54).

Thus a shamanic model places humans in relationship, not only with the visible and measurable living world, the phenomenal world, but also with the invisible world, the spirit world, which is understood to be the "life-giving world."

In our human-centered historical moment, the task of the shamanic weaver of worlds is not only to reconnect us to the spirit world, the existence of which modern, Western civilization tends to doubt, but to recover our connections to nature, which anthropocentric and androcentric thinking have minimized in their human-centeredness. Indeed, today the biotechnologists, inventors of many new reproductive technologies such as artificial wombs, are sabotaging this reconnection. As Grim concludes: "because of the ecological recognition of human interaction with the natural environment, the profound beauty and meaning of many shamanic symbols is being rediscovered. . . . Indeed the invocation of the shamanic mode of consciousness gives rise to an awareness of the patterns of meaning inherent in the earth" (Grim, 1983, p. 208).

The contemporary feminist matristic vision, in reclaiming modes such as ritual and myth from ancient, shamanic societies, in resurrecting the values of reverence for the sacredness of nature and the female from goddess-worshipping cultures, and finally in stressing the importance of the role of the shaman in weaving the worlds together and in revitalizing our energy in order to bring about a healing of the planet, is, it seems to me, most appropriate to our transformatory task.

Thus, I would like to propose a shamanic model as a new method of approaching contemporary feminist matristic texts and creative works.

The shamanic model will help us to reconceptualize an approach toward the mythological underpinnings of our own literary journeys, asking us to revere our ancestors' beliefs in a nonphenomenal spirit realm, as well as to deeply respect the cosmogonies both of peoples who no longer populate the Earth, as well as of those who do.

As women of the scientific modern era name a matristic cosmogony and create a new feminist matristic mythos, it is helpful to remember, as Stephen Larsen points out in *The Shaman's Doorway* (1976), that people of all times have founded their civilizations, not on facts, but on myths—the Celtic world, the Greek world, the Near East, and so forth, all did so. These myths, as feminist scholarship has repeatedly shown, were consistently patriarchalized. As Larsen points out, the world of scientific enlightenment is really only a brief moment in historical time. He reminds us that myths function in their cultures both as a means of socialization and as a form of "guidance." When they act as a form of guidance, they become a living mythology, and it is my contention that the re-emergence of the Goddess today actually marks a moment in which women are attempting to live out and then inscribe a feminist matristic mythos into the modern world as a form of guidance, of life-loving energy and power.

Our new feminist matristic literature and art, then, introduce us to the type of mythic thinking that can both socialize and *guide* us in this time of transformation from a patriarchally based, scientific paradigm to a new paradigm which, as we have seen, replaces humans within the context of the cosmos and the natural world, returns the image of the Creator from male to female, and proposes the arts and their creators as guides to realms of empowerment.

As we have also seen, a basic premise of our reconceptualization of a reality that encompasses both the phenomenal and the spirit world is that all of it is sacred, and that we are in the process of reactivating our mythic imagination both via the modes of the creative artist and of the shaman, for it is the shaman who unites himself (or herself) with a sacred order of being, and it is the artist who makes the invisible, visible (Larsen, 1976, p. 63).

In our Western enlightenment cultures, the shamanic experience is generally considered to be abnormal, for in scientific descriptions of the phenomenal world, "authorities" have relegated all journeys to the so-called spirit world to the category of mental illness while, at the same time, recognizing that cross-culturally, thousands of people make these journeys to the spirit world all the time, and remain quite sane and functional within their own cultural frameworks. Indeed, these are usually the most prestigious people of those cultures—the healers, the medicine people, the priests, and so forth.

In proposing a shamanic model for interpreting contemporary feminist matristic literature and art, I am inspired by the similarities between the states of shamanic initiation and journey, which include severance, journey to the lower world, dismemberment, journey to the upper world, and return to the collectivity, with the stages of the Goddess, Inanna's journey to the underworld as analyzed by Sylvia Brinton Perera in *Descent to the Goddess: A Way of Initiation for Women* (1981). This book shows Inanna's descent into the underworld (ruled by her sister, the dark Goddess, Ereshkigal), her subsequent dismemberment (she was literally hung on a peg), and return to the upper world as a primal pattern for retrieving the wholeness of the Goddess, or what *she* calls "the feminine." By reclaiming both the upper world and the underworld aspects of the Goddess, women today can become psychologically whole. Because of the patterns of severance, dismemberment (we interpret this symbolically as dying to an aspect of one's former self, but being reborn, ultimately, to a new self), and rebirth that are common to the shamanic journey and the Inanna story, we might turn for additional guidance to works on shamanic ways of knowing in our attempt to elucidate the function of storytelling in the works of contemporary women creators, whose retrieval of the Goddess combines the patterns of the descent of Inanna with the patterns of the shamanic journey. (See Dexter, 1990.)

Juergen W. Kremer, in an article entitled "The Shaman and the Epistemologer—Is There a Juanist Way of Knowledge?" (1968), discusses the relationship of narrative to shamanism.

Kremer is interested in the *injunctive* perspective of the language of stories—the ways in which a story "contains a certain set of instructions—upon which one can agree in language—that, if followed, creates a certain experience. Rather than use words as categories that point to something, we use them as directives to do something." (p. 13)

A ritual, for example, sets the conditions for an experience in the way that an injunction functions. Kremer refers to injunctions in language or in ritual or in the stories of shamanic initiations recounted by Carlos Castaneda or Michael Harner as "recipes to do" (1968, p. 15), and he concludes that "once we pay attention to this aspect of stories, *then the tales turn into tales of power*" (p. 16; emphasis mine). Kremer shows that metaphors are about connectedness, and that they are also "an injunction to enter, to create 'the other' in order to create and experience connectedness" (p. 16).

Contrasting the stories told in "Enlightenment" Societies by single authors with shamanic stories told by initiates and members of a collective, Kremer notices that single-authored creative stories in "Enlightenment" Societies propose a dominant story, whereas in shamanic stories there is co-evolution or co-creation. According to Kremer, shamanic stories, as "injunctions to do," give models for acts of power that demonstrate ways in which humans can align themselves with the forces and energies of all realms, and hence can co-create an expanded notion of reality—one that incorporates "the other" into its narrative, one that posits the narrative as creative of reality, as well. "Stories create realities and shamanic stories create realities different from scientific stories" (Kremer, 1968, p. 20).

If we use this model of Shamanism to inform our approach to the power stories, medicine stories, and mythic stories that contemporary women are writing about the Goddess, we come to the following conclusion, which I propose as an approach toward the reading of these works.

The stories are *injunctions*. They are saying: "This is the journey I propose for the recovery of our lost matristic power, stories, and objects relating to the Goddess. Take your own journey; follow my path or yours, but expand our knowledge by telling your own feminist matristic tale of power about how, through the journey, you reconnected to an ancient sacred, matristic source."

It is in this sense that our tales of power may be considered as medicine stories, for they promote a healing of the wounds we might identify as "de-souling" or as a loss of the spirit.

Contemporary women living in patriarchal societies are "disspirited". Their sources of power—the myths, stories of origin, Creation stories, and images of a female Creator, have been excised from the consensus reality of patriarchal Enlightenment Societies. Feminist matristic art may be viewed as a shamanic journey undertaken by contemporary women in order *to weave the worlds together that have been torn apart*—the world of phenomena and the world of spirit, the world of prehistory and the world of recorded history, the world of the sacred and the world of the profane.

Works of art set up an energy interchange with the viewer-voyager. They empower the viewer-voyager to take the journey, and to tell of the journey in the form of an injunction. These stories are saying: "Here is the way to become a person of power—not 'power over,' but 'power-from-within' (an expression used by, among others, Starhawk, 1987). This is my tale of power, my journey to the source of 'gynergy.' What is yours?" These are not stories for deconstruction; they are stories for remembering, and for reconstruction of a lost way of life.

Studying a variety of sacred journeys made by initiates and shamans in history, both pilgrimages and explorations of sacred space and the other world, Hans Peter Duerr, in *Dreamtime: Concerning the Boundary Between Wilderness and Civilization*, postulates that journeys that formerly were made into the earth or into the wilderness became internalized as subjective journeys in the nineteenth century. Speaking of the boundaries between what was inside and what was outside, he tells us that in archaic cultures "one had to have lived in the wilderness. One could know what *inside* meant only if one had once been *outside*" (Duerr, 1985, p. 43). He explains that as civilization became more complex, the knowledge of these journeys to the wilderness or to the caves and mountains where communication with the spirits transpired, was lost. Civilization, he maintains, "encountered the things of the other world by inhibiting, repressing, and later by 'spiritualizing' and 'subjectivizing' them. . . . That which was outside slipped to the inside, and if on occasion it was unable to deny its original character, it was integrated into subjectivity as being that which was 'projected' "(Duerr, 1985, p. 45).

Those who make the journeys to sacred spaces in the wilderness are shamans, and, according to Duerr "there are people whose task it is to represent, as it were the *nagual* on the island of the *tonal*" (1985, p. 72). By "nagual" Duerr refers to phenomena in the spirit world, or what Carlos Castaneda has termed "nonordinary reality"; and by "tonal" Duerr refers to the world of phenomenal reality or "ordinary" reality. The shaman thus dissolves the boundaries between so-called civilization and so-called wilderness. For Duerr, civilization specifically entails a consciousness of ourselves as "tamed beings." This consciousness has a double meaning when considered from a radical feminist perspective, and I would like to invoke both levels of reading of the concept "tamed." (I qualify the words "civilization" and "wilderness" with the ironic epithet "so-called," because Sami Shaman, Ellen Marit Gaup-Dunfjeld, would say that what we call "civilization" is "the *real* wilderness.") Whereas in archaic and tribal societies a literal, physical journey to the wilderness would be followed by reentry to the collective social life, and the initiate or journeyer would become conscious of how civilization had made him or her a *tamed* being (as opposed to the way he (or she) lived beyond the boundaries of civilization in the wilderness), in today's modern world that journey to the wilderness has been turned into our journey into the depths of the psyche.

The shaman dissolves boundaries in order to journey to what we call wilderness, what Duerr associates with the *nagual,* or the numinous. When the shaman returns to the *tonal,* or to manifest reality (by descending from the mountain or returning from the sacred site), she (or he) knows that the *tonal* only exists in relationship to the *nagual,* and that once having returned from the *nagual,* life in the *tonal* becomes a consciousness of actually being a part of the *nagual,* of the sacred, spiritual realm.

In contemporary societies we take the journey into our psyches and into our dream worlds rather than to mountains and sacred sites in nature in order to gain the knowledge of the shaman who dissolves the boundaries between the worlds, the knowledge that tells us we are both "tamed" and also part of the nagual, the other world. Yet, this inward journey, postulated by Duerr as a direct result of Marxism and psychoanalysis, actually subjectivizes and dehistoricizes what, for primal peoples, was a literal objective and historical pilgrimage to an actual sacred site. In subjectivizing this experience, *we have lost a consensus on the reality* of such a journey, and we have moved sacred experiences of that other world closer to the realm of what may be confused with that which is often labeled abnormal.

Today, feminist matristic writers and artists are making the invisible, visible, by *re-exteriorizing* the journey for us through the arts. They are replacing the psychic journey to the other world back into history and nature. Journeys to the other world in contemporary feminist matristic art and literature are less likely to be described as purely interior voyages. They are more likely to be evocations of a prepatriarchal past or a site in nature where the Goddess was once revered, not as a figure in the psyche, but as the culturally accepted symbol for the Creator of life. This may entail a journey to specific mountains, caves, historical sites, or sacred sanctuaries where traces and energies remain of ancient matristic cultures. These tales can be conceived of also as midrashes or commentaries on the inherited epics (the Classical Cycle, the Grail Quest Cycle, the Judeo-Christian cycles, etc.) from patriarchal culture. As we journey through them via midrash and commentary to a feminist matristic revisioning, we, too, learn that for us the other world, the matristic past, which revered the presence of the Goddess's energy, can be likened to the *nagual.* We then feel that we must bear witness to it on the island of the *tonal,* here understood both as manifest reality and as patriarchy. It is an altered perception, which shakes up our existence in the *tonal, and teaches us that under patriarchy, (women's "tonal" as compared with ancient matristic cultures, understood as women's "nagual" or "numinous realm"), women have become "tamed beings."*

How do many of these concepts relate to the feminist matristic arts today? In "Nine Principles of a Matriarchal Aesthetic" (1985), German scholar, Heide Göttner Abendroth uses the term "matriarchal" for what I have called both "matristic", and "feminist matristic," and she conceives of an art that "breaks down the barrier between art and life. . . . Matriarchal art is magic which is performed and experienced, and its spontaneous expressions can be so gripping that they lead to Ecstasy" (Abendroth, 1985, p. 83).

Matriarchal art, as she conceives it, involves all the functions of daily life, and merges with the symbolic and matriarchal mythology in festivals of the seasons, demonstrating "nature's unity with human beings as opposed to nature's exploitation and civilization by men. . . . It is a tremendous challenge to live by the values which patriarchal societies have banished to the ghetto of the unreal" (Abendroth, 1985, p. 93).

Matriarchal art's magic produces ecstasy, and, according to Abendroth, retrieves values that have been banished to "the ghetto of the unreal." It is located at the crossroads of at least six separate journeys to places where our "wilderness" and our "ghettos of the unreal" intersect.

As I see it, six of these wilderness journeys to power places or to *the nagual* made by contemporary feminist matristic visual artists are:

1. The journey to our ancient matristic, prepatriarchal historical roots—a journey to the "light" Goddess of Fertility and Creation.
2. The journey inward, which, like the journey of Inanna, is a journey to the underworld of the psyche, to the underworld of society, to the "scapegoated" aspects of women's strengths, to the "dark" Goddess of death, dismemberment, and ultimate rebirth, to the "ghetto of the unreal." This "dark" Goddess, then, also sheds light on the repressed and forgotten psychological characteristics (often strengths and powers that have been obscured or driven underground by patriarchal social systems).
3. A pilgrimage to sacred places of power, sites of ancient sanctuaries, vision-quests in nature, to sacred sites in nature, and so forth.
4. A shamanic journey to the spirit world, to the other world, the *nagual*, to the invisible dimensions beyond the phenomenal world for the recovery of spirit guides, spiritual knowledge, empowerment, and healing.
5. A journey to the Wisdom of the Crone, a life-journey to the magical rebirth of spiritual adventures that occurs in old age. Aging, interpreted feminist matristically, seems to be the time at which the surrealist vision (the total interpenetration of states of waking with altered states of consciousness) takes over.
6. A journey to the "Outta-Sight," to the uncanny, to the Goddess in the City, to the Clown, to the daring, imaginative acts of power that recover our matristic heritage.

All of these journeys are to the wilderness, the mystery, the suppressed, the hidden, the excised—to the *nagual* of our emerging *tonal*. From these journeys we reap the knowledge and experiences that confirm for many of us the fact that we, twentieth-century women, have become *tamed, domesticated* beings living in a culture that has denied us the powers that would have come from contact with these other realities.

Feminist matristic artists are birthing a new vision through their creation. In that vision they are shedding the light of ancient goddess-revering cultures onto contemporary historical and political constructs, as well as reclaiming the dark aspects of the Goddess that seem to be foregrounded in this, our second decade of the Goddess's re-emergence.

Merlin Stone, one of our many pathfinders, has reinterpreted the meaning of the dark Goddess for us in her article "Endings and Origins" (1988), where she writes that "much of this . . . imagery of the dark, the mysterious, the hidden, the silent, the unknown, is also present in the male perception of woman . . . as the mysterious, unknowable, passively waiting earth—in which the male desires to implant his seed while simultaneously fearing that he may die as he does this" (pp. 28, 29).

Merlin Stone, along with Susan Griffin and Mary Daly, sees man's desire to gain control over nature and women as similar to his desire to gain control over death. Stone calls for an "Endarkenment" to complement our search for "Enlightenment" in order to make us whole. This endarkenment would "bring to light" those aspects of women and nature that have been rejected by patriarchy, and relegated to the realm of the dark, the underground/world and the unconscious.

Today's feminist matristic artists must undertake the journey to the dark, split-off, underworld aspect of the Goddess (such as Inanna's journey to Ereshkigal's realm) in order to revision the dark Goddess within the overarching cyclical pattern of life, death, and rebirth, in which the dark realm is understood to be an inherent part of all life. This journey also revisions patriarchy within an expanded 30,000-year framework *as merely one darkening phase of the Moon*, rather than as an eternal or everlastingly absolute Dark Age.

In making these many journeys to the past, to the depths, and to the unfamiliar in the here and now—the wilderness, the numinous, the other, or the *nagual* dimension of our lives, contemporary feminist matristic artists, writers, scholars, and women perform reversals analogous to those performed by the Huichol Indians on their sacred journey to Wirikuta, led by the shaman. As described by anthropologist Barbara Meyerhoff, for the Huichols, reversals are in order in connection with the sacred journey to their true Home, the paradise known as Wirikuta. When they make this journey, they return from the exile of their daily, tamed lives, to their true Home, and when they leave Wirikuta and return to their houses in the villages, where things are not reversed, they have left their true Home, and are in exile again. All of their life is a delicate alternation between life at home and life in their true Home—Wirikuta or Paradise, which they only reach on the peyote hunt. (See Meyerhoff, 1974.)

As exiles on a quest for a True Home, also a realm in which all is reversed from what women know in patriarchy, specifically regarding our powers, important roles in the culture, social status, prestige, recognition, creativity, and the like, feminist matristic artists use their shamanic, visionary abilities and their radical ecofeminist imaginations to bring us to our True Home, our sacred terrestrial Garden on Gaia. To revision the dark of our present exile, to enlighten and endarken our knowledge of the Goddess in both prepatriarchal and patriarchal cultures, and to *re-member* the body (of culture) of the Great Mother (read here also Gaia or Tiamat) after her dismemberment has destroyed Her almost beyond recognition, is the sacred task we are called upon to accomplish. As changers, transformers—of myth, psyche, culture, and social reality, feminist matristic creators are like shamans, magicians, and healers. They are, simultaneously pilgrims and questers. To give birth to a Home/Land for women is also to give birth to a Home/Land for all, and it involves performing the most fundamental reversal of all, that of resacralizing the Earth.

Power stories and power images tell women how to journey to the many sources of ancient strength and knowledge, how to reconceptualize life once these powers are known, how to bring them forth into the present, how to live in an integrated, holistic way, revering the cycles of light and dark, of the cosmos, nature, and the body, of the sacred and the secular, making the here and now the True Home. Despite their journeys to the limits of time and space, feminist matristic artists return empowered to their communities, and *make the ultimate reversal, not on the journey, but on the return*. It is their task to use their art to teach us how to retrieve our knowledge and power in order to reverse the patriarchal priorities of our world, and to make the planet, Gaia, truly habitable, and a True Home once more.

The Suppression of the Goddess: The Relationship of Madness to the Quest for the Great Mythic Mother

In this chapter we will look at the effects of the suppression of knowledge about the 30,000 years of history in which Creation was imaged as female upon the creative lives and works of some women of the surrealist movement. Here we will consider the psychic effects of the cultural erasure of the Great Mythic Mother. In Chapter 5 we will then study the conscious encoding of the intimations of a matristic mythos as a subversive narrative element. In these examples we will observe the ways in which this suppressed material functions when it reappears in the lives and works of women artists enculturated to the norms of eco-, matristic, and shamanic amnesia.

The examples of René (Colette Thomas), Unica Zurn, and Leonora Carrington are used to illustrate the ways in which the Goddess or the Great Mythic Mother appears in female creative works when there is no consciously articulated cultural framework for the expression of such material. I draw no conclusions about how the knowledge of this culturally erased and often taboo material found its way into the minds of these artists. However, I do want to suggest that in addition to the workings of the intuition and the unconscious, folk culture (folk tales, folk arts, healing practices, etc.) often transmits the legacy of our matristic heritage. It is not necessary to postulate the emergence of an archetype in the unconscious in order to explain the appearance of matristic motifs, shamanic motifs, and the like, in the works of these artists. What I am interested in exploring is how this material emerges in distorted form because it has been sublimated and repressed under the hegemony of androcentric institutions. These intimations of all that patriarchy has rendered invisible often appear in exaggerated form in the works of women who have had documented encounters with what the Western world has come to label "madness."

One visual artist who did *not* undergo the kind of experience in the underworld (that we have come to label madness) is the surrealist artist Remedios Varo. Thus, her work is exemplary of how these motifs, how this knowledge, was expressed in the work of a surrealist woman artist, whose creativity was not affected by states of extreme mental alienation.

In her paintings *Papilla Estellar* (1958) and *Presencia Inesperada* (1959), Remedios Varo accurately depicts the private and often secret workings of women to keep alive their connections to nature and the "invisible"—the "invisible," of course, including all of matristic history symbolized by the Goddess, and all of the invisible realms of the spirit world that shamans contact as they journey between the dimensions to weave the worlds together.

In *Papilla Estellar* a woman sits alone in an Octagonal Tower performing an act of cosmic caretaking that establishes an intimate link between magic and the activities of the Nurturant Mother. The woman is channeling astral energies from the cosmos through a tube in the roof of her magical tower that sends the energies (or stellar essences) directly into a meat grinder in which she churns them into a pablum of stars suitable for feeding the luminescent Moon, kept in a bird cage in her chamber.

Contemporary women have become solitary caretakers of the Moon (Goddess), which, like a caged bird, has been tamed, domesticated, shut in, and rendered invisible to all but the women who nourish Her secretly through their art and their lives, performing acts of cosmic magic. In this painting one can intuit that Remedios Varo felt herself to be identified with both an aspect of the Moon Mother (as creator/artist) that was caged and domesticated, as well as with the liberating Artist, the nurturer who, through her works, both as painter and as transformer of magical ethers from the invisible, keeps the wilder parts of a tamed world alive. Here female creativity is shown to be in the service of both the Goddess and the Cosmos (which are often conceived of as the same), as well as inseparable from the role of Caretaker and Nurturer.

In *Presencia Inesperada* (1959) we see the same woman at work recycling the wood of her table back into the natural world, as small trees sprout from a tear in the wood that very much resembles a vaginal opening. However, while engaged in the secret reverse alchemy of turning the table back into a tree, an unexpected male presence breaks through the back of the chair, and, like a tormenting demon, mocks her "Great Work." The humor of the painting suggests that the energy involved in transmuting the wood of the table into a tree is the very same energy that metamorphoses the upholstery of the chair, sending the decorative fleurs-de-lis spiraling down to earth (for they are living flowers—lilies of the valley), releasing the spirit of the chair or the table as well as that of the mocking male figure who haunts her even as she performs her silent magical work.

These are spirits trapped in matter. These nature spirits can be returned to the natural world, but only through the patient, solitary, creative work of women, particularly of women artists, who, by virtue of being both women and creators, seem to have an intuitive or folk eco-memory, matristic memory, and shamanic memory.

In *The Female Malady: Women, Madness and English Literature 1830–1980,* Elaine Showalter contextualizes women's madness within the setting of English culture from 1830–1980 in ways that can be expanded to explain aspects of the works of the women of surrealism, writing and painting from the 1930s to the 1950s, both in Europe and Latin America, from an ecofeminist perspective.

Showalter convincingly demonstrates that within the confines of the patriarchal system set in place in England from 1830–1980, which defined normalcy and sex roles according to a male-centered model, women were identified with nature and the body, both demeaned, while men were linked to culture and reason, both edified.

She joins Phyllis Chesler (*Women and Madness,* 1972) and Sandra Gilbert and Susan Gubar (*The Madwoman in the Attic: The Woman Writer and the Nineteenth Century Literary Imagination,* 1979), in arguing that "madness is the price women artists have had to pay for the exercise of their creativity in a male-dominated culture" (Showalter, 1985, p. 4). She also reminds us that "madness was a disease of the highly civilized and industrialized" (p. 24). She cites various authorities on the absence of madness in cultures closely linked to nature such as the peasantry of the Welsh mountains, the Western Hebrides, and the wilds of Ireland.

Indeed, her work shows that in Victorian society, as well as in the post-Victorian world, where women's longings for education, autonomy, and mastery were unfulfilled, madness often resulted. Not only were women's ambitions to create culture impeded by social mores and institutions, but women's identification with nature was also debased, as the female

Remedios Varo: Papilla Estellar (1958)
by courtesy Walter Gruen

body with its cycles was rendered taboo, and women's sexuality was stifled by that culture's denial of it. Showalter goes on to affirm that "powerlessness could lead to pathology" (Showalter, 1985, p. 190). We may, thus, legitimately inquire whether a nonamnesiac, living in a world of culturally induced amnesia, is actually "mad," or whether she is "illuminated," and stepping to the beat of "a different drummer." At what point does the culture drive the woman of eco-matristic-shamanic-memory mad, and send her over the brink from being the woman of awakened memory in a world of amnesiacs to being a woman driven mad by the persecution she undergoes for her memory in a culture that judges her to be insane rather than awakened? This is indeed the problem we face when discussing all the Cassandras in literature.

We have suggested that contemporary feminist matristic writers and artists have tended to tell tales of power based on the shamanic model, which are tales about "how to," inviting the reader-listener-viewer/participant to create her (or his) own connection to such sources of power, and to continue the process by developing and enlarging the map of the journey. Remedios Varo's paintings give us many scenarios for such journeys to female sacred sites. They also give us the secrets of a newly remembered female alchemy and magic. In *Exploración de Las Fuentes del Río Orinoco* (1959) Varo depicts the domesticated, tamed woman as an explorer of the wild Orinoco River, who sails on mechanized wings in a boat with buttons, probably a cloak metamorphosed into a traveling vessel, to encounter the source of the river, the fountain of life, in a small, also domesticated, tree altar.

Nacer de Nuevo (1960) finally depicts the unleashing of the woman-spirit that had been imprisoned in the wood of the magical chamber, encountering both the reflection of the moon in the goblet of water and the tree bursting forth from the wood of the table. Varo's visual metaphors are clear, complex, and stunning. We are in close contact with our source all the time, but it has been denied. We are not acculturated to being constantly mindful of the fact that the table was once a tree, that the water we drink comes from the ocean whose tides are regulated by the Moon, as are women's menses.

In all of Varo's paintings woman is linked to both nature and the "invisible," which is as real for her as the phenomenal world is for us. In *Música Solar* the woman uses the astral rays of sunlight as strings of a violin, whose ethereal music/light revives a patch of flowering life on an entirely desiccated forest floor.

Deeply connected to her sources of power, life, and energy, and strengthened by her creative expression, the woman artist as explorer, magus, and scientist reawakens a vision that shows spirit alive in matter, and symbolizes that knowledge by the image of the Moon Goddess as the female Creatrix. Varo's works read today very much like a tale of power.

Indeed, it is unfortunately true that a large number of the women of surrealism either have known moments of madness (which can be looked upon as either a breakdown or a *breakthrough*), or have actually committed suicide. Raised in patriarchal religious climates which perceived women's cycles and their connection to nature as the source of evil, rather than as the source of power, women writers and artists such as those in the surrealist movement have had either to suppress and repress that knowledge or code it and render it occult.

I would now like to take a closer look at the way in which either a matristic vision, or the Goddess symbol, rises to the surface in moments of madness or illumination in the works of three women of surrealism, specifically Unica Zurn, René (Colette Thomas), and Leonora Carrington, all of whom have had personal encounters with what we, in the West, have termed "madness" or states of mental "alienation." Additional support for this interpretation and analysis can be found in a feminist matristic explication of *Nadja* by André Breton. (See Orenstein, "Nadja Revisited: A Feminist Approach," 1978.) If I have eliminated Nadja in this discussion, it is simply because she was not an artistic creator in the surrealist movement.

However, she was a real woman, not a literary character, and the traces of her own journey, as interpreted from the drawings she made during meetings with Breton in a café, now published in his book, *Nadja* (1960), when combined with a deciphering of the path of her journey as described in his "novel," show her to be expressing a matristic cosmogony related to the Celtic world.

In his *The Manifestos of Surrealism* (1972), André Breton, proclaiming the absolute value of the freedom of the imagination, offered a new, positive approach to madness. Viewing it as a heightened state of consciousness, productive of poetic discourse, he said that only imagination teaches us about what can be, and that he would gladly spend his life drawing out the confidences of mad people, because they are people of a scrupulous honesty and, of course, because their imagination gives him hope.

Reclaiming all the faculties of the mind when freed from the tyranny of logic, Breton sought a new kind of resolution between the states of waking, reality, and dream—a surreality in which the marvelous resided. Indeed, because madness was an important path to the Marvelous, the surrealists often cultivated states of temporary insanity and hailed them as privileged moments of creative vision.

Thus, surrealism remains one of the few poetic and artistic movements in which an artist's output in a mentally alienated state was supremely valued, and seen to be the sign of the fecundity and freedom of the imagination. However, while this approach to madness might have been beneficial for work of certain surrealists, feminists are now calling into question the causes of insanity in women and reinterpreting the symptoms of female madness, redefining the specificity of its meaning within the context of a male-defined description of both reality and normalcy.

Yet, because the surrealist movement placed such a high value on the work produced by artists in moments of madness, it provides us with a unique body of materials from which to understand the significance of this state when it occurs in women writers and artists. It furnishes us with documentation that is virtually unequaled in its illumination of the correlation between states of mental alienation in creative women and their connection with patriarchal Creation myths.

I propose to look at the commonality of imagery in the visions of René, Unica Zurn, and Leonora Carrington, all women whose encounters with madness were expressed in literature, art, or both. However, the deeper meaning of their madness has always been misunderstood, because it has continually been placed within the framework of patriarchal literary and artistic criticism. Looking at their experience from a feminist matristic perspective may help us to gain insight into the nature of women's imaginations and women's mythic visions.

How does a feminist matristic perspective interpret the madness of women and, in particular, that of women artists? In *Women and Madness,* Phyllis Chesler argues that, in a patriarchal society, women are fundamentally alienated from knowledge of their own inner strength, as well as from a history of images that would provide them with role models of alternative ways of conceiving of women and of being female. Chesler writes: "Women are impaled on the cross of self-sacrifice. . . . Unlike men, they are categorically denied the experience of cultural supremacy, humanity, and renewal based on their sexual identity. . . . In different ways, some women are driven mad by this fact. Such madness is essentially an intense experience of female biological, sexual, and cultural castration, and a doomed search for potency. The search often involves "delusions" or displays of physical aggression, grandeur, sexuality and emotionality—all traits which would probably be more acceptable in female-dominated cultures. Such traits in women are feared and punished in patriarchal mental asylums" (Chesler, 1972, p. 31).

Chesler's theory maintains that the denial of cultural equality, and even supremacy, has been an important factor in causing female madness. In *The Madwoman in the Attic: The Woman Writer and the Nineteenth Century Literary Imagination,* Gilbert and Gubar extend this analysis to include the madness specific to women writers. They claim that in a patriarchally defined literary history men are seen as the fathers of creation with all the cosmic potency of the image of a male God behind them. Since the world was "authored by a male God" (Gilbert and Gubar, 1979, p. 5), it was assumed that the imaginative universe of a corpus of works was similarly authored by the male imagination. As Gilbert and Gubar point out, the metaphors of literary paternity implicit in our culture assume that God the Father both engendered the cosmos and fathered the text. Female madness, then, within the context of a patriarchal Creation myth and literary history is, according to critic Barbara Hill Rigney (Rigney, 1978, p. 8), a political event. It is connected to a rebellion against or escape from male authority, and Rigney views it much as R.D. Laing would view all madness—as a form of superior sanity and a search for an authentic, integrated image of the self. In the case of women writers it is a search for an image of the self as creator, even if it is as creator of a world that others do not recognize—a world in which women reclaim their identification with the Great Mother in an essentially matristic description of reality.

In their discussion of George Eliot, George Sand, and the Brontë sisters, Gilbert and Gubar stress the fact that the dilemma of a patriarchal creation model has always forced women to identify the creative self with a male persona in order to fulfill the exigencies of a male mythic vision. Trapped within a masculinist world view that had no image of a female Creator, women artists had either to identify their own creativity with a male self-image or to suffer the consequences of an irreconcilable clash between their talents and their sex. This clash often terminated in madness.

Research into the life histories and art works of the women of surrealism reveals a large number of instances in which creative women have suffered from episodes of temporary insanity often leading to suicide. A closer look at their writings and paintings sheds light on the ways in which the absence of a female Creation myth in Western culture has been symptomatic in women's insanity when it finds expression in the arts.

While the category *poète maudite* has been created to describe the works of male artists such as Rimbaud and Artaud, who have been called visionaries when they were possessed by a "holy" madness, women writers who have had similar experiences, such as Virginia Woolf, Anne Sexton, and Sylvia Plath, have rarely been lauded for their mental states of alienation. The woman writer's madness is never considered to be a special state of grace, a lofty manifestation of her election as sibyl or prophet, as seer of the deeper truths. On the contrary, "mad" women writers and artists have always been treated with disdain, and their madness turned to an affliction, a sign of their inferiority, their inability to cope—a permanent stigma.[1]

The surrealist movement is perhaps alone in valuing the artistic production of women in moments of madness. However, this fact by no means implies that women were considered equal to men in their ordinary states of maturation and development. Xavière Gauthier has argued that the art of male surrealists and the theoretical position of André Breton demonstrate, rather, that despite their revolutionary pretensions, when it came to women, phallic myths prevailed, and that surrealists were *toujours prêts à réduire la femme à un object de contemplation et de consommation.* ("Always ready to reduce woman to an object of contemplation and consumption.") (Gauthier 1971, p. 13.) Yet, as I have shown elsewhere (Orenstein, 1973), women artists in the surrealist movement never depicted women as mere objects. Rather, they created them as subjects, as alchemists, goddesses, and spiritual guides. They consistently identified women with the exalted image of the Magna Mater rather than with the diminished image of the Femme-Enfant (the Woman-Child). Whereas for the male surrealists, women were considered of consequence when they were divested of all cultural power, either infantilized or mad, for the female artists of the same movement, the Mother Goddess was indeed the basic image of female Creation.

---

[1]Ideas first mentioned by Vivianne Forrester in a speech given at La Maison Française of New York University, early 1970s.

The three women to be discussed here bear witness to a profound female desire to restore the original image of sacred female creation to art, religion, and daily life through reclaiming a female Creation myth as a viable model for female creativity. The madness experienced by these women of surrealism is not merely *connected* to the political and social realities of patriarchal authority in the secular world. It is more essentially *caused* by the repression of the Goddess image in the Judeo-Christian religious tradition. Coded within the cryptic imaginings of these very rare texts and paintings that give testimony to their female "season in hell" is the desire to restore women to their original important places in a matristic myth of cosmic Creation as well as in the actual historical record.

Colette Thomas, an actress who worked with Antonin Artaud, published *The Testament of the Dead Girl* in 1954 under the male pseudonym of René. Her anonymity was maintained by the mystery and silence that surrounded the book when it first appeared. André Breton's surrealist group was probably the only one to speak of it at all. This book of "*pensées,* parables, philosophical fragments, theatrical meditations, personal testimonials, and stories reveals itself to be a feminist matristic statement that resonates deeply today, for Thomas speaks of the disappearance of women's creative work and of their profound sense of nonexistence in a male-dominated society—the feeling that Simone de Beauvoir has referred to as the experience of the "Other." Colette Thomas writes: "For the voice is woman but DOES NOT EXIST . . . God is dead. I protest in the name of woman" (René, 1954, p. 33).

Her consciousness of women's social oppression is acute, yet Thomas sees woman collaborating in her own tragic destiny out of a lack of reflection upon her own spiritual condition. Her book attempts to awaken both women and men to the injustices and realities of their social and spiritual worlds:

> THE HEROINE OF LOVE OF THE WORLD.
> —IT IS A WOMAN. BUT WE DON'T SEE HER FOR SHE HAS NOT BEEN TAKEN BY THE LOVE OF THE WORLD—BUT VIOLATED, TRAMPLED, KNEADED AND REJECTED BY HATRED AGAINST THE WORLD, WITH HER CONSENT. (René, 1954, p. 85, the author's capitalization)

Realizing that woman's true destiny is to be self-generating, autonomous, and independent of male authority, especially of that imposed upon her by the myths and parables in which male divinity is sacralized, she writes:

> CELESTIAL JERUSALEM IS NOT A PLACE—BUT A WOMAN MADE OF EARTH AND REMAINING WOMAN IN ORDER TO SAY: NO KING, NO GOD, NO PRIEST, NO GENERATION—MYSELF ALONE AND SUFFICIENT TO BE AND TO BECOME FOR I HAVE BECOME—YES THAT IS TO SAY THAT NOTHING MORE IS TO COME FROM HER BUT HERSELF, FINALLY REALIZED. . . . FOR CHRIST NEEDED MARY TO LIVE. BUT MARY, DID SHE NEED CHRIST TO CONTINUE TO LIVE?
> HERE IS THE CRIME;
> AFTER CHRIST HAD LIVED, THEY SAID, THE FATHER, THE SON, AND THE HOLY GHOST, AND THEY HID WOMAN.
> BUT NOW THE MONSTROUS LIE, THE PHENOMENAL HYPOCRISY HAS POLLUTED THE ENTIRE EDIFICE. CHRISTIANITY IS DYING OF ITS INFAMY—AND WOMAN IS BORN OF HERSELF—HER OWN JOB. (René, 1954, pp. 142–144, the author's capitalization)

If Thomas's message has been passed over in silence, it is because she saw all too clearly woman as the original Creator of life. Her mad illumination rails against the denial of female spiritual power, the denial of the Goddess as Creatrix. It protests against the lie that patriarchal theology created in the myth of Adam and Eve and the myth of the virgin birth, which rob women of their procreative legitimacy. Thomas is outraged by her vision of women defiled and demeaned under our social and religious systems. She realizes that women were forced to collaborate on their own annihilation.

A visionary, Colette Thomas expresses her clairvoyance poignantly in a short parable entitled "The Little Girl and the World." It tells of a young girl, Anne, the daughter of a woodcutter, who would take a lantern with her to greet her father when he returned from the woods every evening at nightfall. As she welcomed him, she would repeat the words: "The lantern gives light." One day she carried her lantern to meet her father and welcomed him excitedly, saying, "The lantern illuminates things, Papa." Her father reprimanded her and reminded her that he had only taught her to say, "The lantern gives light," nothing more. "That's true Father, it usually gives light, but today it ILLUMINATED. I saw it on the path. Usually it makes a white ray, as white as the moon—today its light is red, green, blue, all colors—I thought of a celebration—it's true" (René, 1954, p. 158). When, overpowered by her own vision, she repeated the word "ILLUMINATES" in an exalted and defiant tone, her father threatened to beat her. Anne ran off into the forest, collided with a tree, and went blind. Many centuries after her death, men from another age, digging in the ground, discovered the miraculously preserved body of a young girl. It radiated such a pure light that from that day on they instituted great celebrations in honor of the body that they call "Années" (years), and other important rites of spring, summer, autumn, and winter.

This parable can be linked to the symptom of female blindness as it is discussed by Gilbert and Gubar. Eye "troubles," moreover, they write, "seem to abound in the lives and works of literary women, with Dickinson matter-of-factly noting that her eyes got 'put out' . . . Charlotte Brontë deliberately writing with her eyes closed, and Mary Elizabeth Coleridge writing about 'Blindness' that came because 'Absolute and bright/the Sun's rays smote me till they masked the Sun' " (Gilbert & Gubar, 1979, p. 58).

Women, it appears, are commanded not to see in a world where the visionary powers are appropriated by men. Thomas links the celebrations of the cycles of nature, usually performed in the name of the Great Mother, to the buried body of a female visionary. Colette Thomas meditates upon the parable and realizes that, given the condition of women's lives in this culture, one begins to understand why it is safer for women to continue to say "give light" when what they really mean is "illuminate." This kind of awareness of woman's spiritual mission and the thwarting of their powers by restrictions placed upon their vision and use of language becomes a very important key for the interpretation of women's writing. "But why," Thomas writes, "because she is 'possessed,' is a woman in this world despised? Because the man who possesses her is not perfect. And it is easier to find God than a perfect man. But I who have found God, I continue to seek a *perfect* man" (René, 1954, p. 203).

The imperfect laws made by men have imprisoned women within a false image of creation that denies their biological and spiritual experiences—their sexuality and their illuminated visions: "Ah the virgin-mother! The elect and the sin in the same flesh! Ah! The admirable sophism!" (René, 1954, p. 210) "And if a Christ was born it is to Mary that we owe it. We don't need a Holy Ghost to bring a child into the world, nor a God. It suffices to be very truly a woman, and you can bring a child into the world—and God is only a figure of speech" (René, 1954, p. 216).

Thomas has seen through the lie of patriarchal theology. She has seen the desecration of the Mother Goddess in mixed metaphors and confusions created by the figure of speech, God. She has felt the denial of female sexuality and female spirituality and the need for a return to woman as the image of the Creator of the universe.

The female visionary is the *poète maudite* whose madness is a mask and a decoy. Were she to speak any more openly in a less mystical or cryptic prose, her true meaning might be revealed in all the intensity of its rage. For the illuminated vision of Colette Thomas expresses the intimation of the usurpation of her legitimate rights by patriarchal religion. Denied any image of her strength, denied the symbol of the Goddess, she lives in profound contradiction with her most authentic experience of self-knowledge.

Colette Thomas's position prefigures that of Mary Daly, for she reclaims female spirituality and sexuality, and calls for a new cycle in which a truer explanation of female creation will prevail. Mary Daly would interpret the perception of a woman like Colette Thomas by reminding us that "patriarchal myths contain stolen mythic powers. They are something like distorting lenses through which we *can* see into the Background. But it is necessary to break their codes in order to use them as viewers, that is, we must see their lie in order to see their truth. We can correctly perceive patriarchal myths as reversals, as pale derivatives of more ancient, more translucent myths from gynocentric civilizations" (Daly, 1978, p. 47).

The Jasmin-Man: Impressions of a Mentally Ill Woman, an autobiographical novel by German artist, Unica Zurn, who committed suicide in 1970 at the age of 54 after numerous encounters with madness, provides us with still more insight into the nature of the conflicts facing the surrealist woman artist. Zurn, who lived with surrealist artist, Hans Bellmer from 1953 until her death, was obsessed with anagrams and cryptograms. She was convinced that, just as the real world masks the truth of the imaginary world, so the body of the word hides the secret sense of its inner meaning.

Her anagrams, published with automatic drawings in her first book *Hexentexte* (1954, Berlin Galerie Springer) (in German), show a cabalistic approach to deciphering the mysteries of the universe through a mystical reading of the many sacred signs, symbols, and scripts she finds inscribed therein. In *Jasmin-Man* Zurn also discovers the occult links between her anagrams and her hallucinations.

The narrative is the autobiography of her own "season in hell," of her visionary experiences during her period of mental illness and internment in a psychiatric clinic. *Jasmin-Man* is written in the third person, creating a further level of distancing as she describes the schizophrenic split she underwent as a result of the conflict between her identity as woman and as creator. A look at the nature of this experience, the symbolism of her hallucinations, and the meaning of her psychic split indicates that her conflict, too, stemmed from women's deprivation of a female model for spiritual and secular creation. The basic split she describes is one in which she becomes possessed and is visited by her masculine double, her *döppelganger.* As her hallucinatory counterpart, he is known alternately as Jasmin Man or White Man. The image of Jasmin Man is an obvious reversal of the image of Jasmin Woman or the Woman-flower that we find so prevalent in surrealist poetry.

Identifying with the male as her own double, Zurn is able to experience the potential grandeur of her creative self, a dimension that she is denied in reality because she cannot reconcile masculine creative privilege with "femininity." She sees a magical link between the letters "H.M." in the Hotel Minerva where she stays in Paris and the initials of Herman Melville. Of *Moby Dick* she says she feels "too weak, too small . . . to be able, like Herman Melville did, for example, build a work on this emotional shock. . . . And she feels painfully the limits, the narrowness, the monotony that are, occasionally those of a woman's life" (Zurn, 1970, p. 66). Her so-called delusions of grandeur are equivalent to a woman's reclamation of the mythic and real roles accorded to men in her society—those of God the Creator and of the male author. Staying at the Hotel Minerva, the house of the Goddess of wisdom, is for Zurn somehow connected with her desire to become a female Herman Melville. *Moby Dick's* profound influence on her can perhaps be understood to reside in its assault on the symbol of the Deity and on the spiritual and physical evil incarnated in that symbol. It is precisely when she is staying at the Hotel Minerva that she feels possessed by the forces of a giant, or what psychiatry would characterize as "delusions of grandeur." In several hallucinations she possesses the powers of cosmic creation. Her desire to give birth to a new, more marvelous reality in the form of a city is analogous to Colette Thomas's New Jerusalem. The yearning for a new, more powerful, sacred image of woman is strongly present in the hallucination of the self as Mother of the World. To give birth to a new city is to transform civilization by reclaiming one's identification with the Great Mother: "And it is *she* who is going to give birth to this city. This desire becomes so excessive that she feels the pains of childbirth, the same symptoms as at the birth of her children. She doesn't know how it is possible to feel oneself pregnant with an entire city. But for several days she has lived through such unbelievable events that this new state seems practically natural to her" (Zurn, 1970, p. 33).

A woman's dream of changing the world, of radically altering the conditions of life, not only for humankind in general, but for women primarily, is the pivotal point of her "madness." Her lack of real secular power obliges her to invent imaginary powers in order to validate the sense of her own potency, which is deeply connected to the female experience of procreation. In the image of the self as Mother of the new city, Zurn is not experiencing time in the instant, but rather proclaiming woman as the point of origin of a new cycle of history. During moments of ecstatic transport, when she feels confidence and joy, she undergoes symbolic physical transformations through dance and auditory hallucinations that suggest her subconscious attraction to other cultures and other measures of historical time, to eras of history in which the Goddess was revered. In one particular hallucination she hears oriental music and feels "her spinal column change into a serpent" (Zurn, 1970, p. 90). During this sequence of changes she becomes a tropical bird, and hears a voice address her in the following words: "Whoever is capable of portraying a bird approaches mastery" (Zurn, 1970, p. 92). Finally, she perceives the apparition of a tiger, but she wants to enact both the hunter and the hunted simultaneously, for the voice informs her: "The one who portrays at the same time the tiger and the flight before the tiger has won and is a master" (Zurn, 1970, p. 92). Having wished to become a Master, she is ordered by the voice to become a scorpion and to incarnate the image of suicide. Clearly, she subconsciously feels she must be punished for her attempt to fuse with the sacred energy of the serpent, a Goddess energy. In the image of the serpent, Kundalini energy is connected with the Goddess Shakti. The serpent is also linked to many Cretan, Egyptian, and Near Eastern Goddess figures. Reclaiming the ancient image of the tree of life as the Mother Goddess, Zurn, in another ecstatic vision, also desires to "attempt the impossible: planting the bread tree" (Zurn, 1970, p. 100). She says:

"And *who* among men has ever succeeded in planting the bread tree? The terror of famine would be conquered. The sentence gets twisted in her like a serpent and she cannot resist it. . . . But where can one find the seed that will give forth the bread tree? A seed, a handful of earth, that's all she needs. With the certainty that she will accomplish this miracle she seeks and discovers on the floor a minuscule object of unknown origin, and she buries it in the handful of earth. With a solemn gesture she places earth and seed in the middle of the desk and sits down again, very proud, her heart filled with a childlike faith" (Zurn, 1970, p. 100). At the termination of this prolonged hallucinatory experience she asks: "But how did the Universe fall into the hands of men? As if it needed men's help! Error! error!" (Zurn, 1970, p. 102)

The imperative to plant the bread tree comes to her from the memory of a poem by Henri Michaux, "I plant the bread tree." Once more the initials H.M. are clues to her desire to reclaim for women the prerogatives of creation and nurturance that belonged to the Mother Goddess rather than to the male God.[2]

Her anagrams inform us that "Her deliriums are prayers" (Zurn, 1970, p. 112). She convokes the spirit of the genie locked in the bottle in another anagram and identifies this spirit with the White Man. In this anagram she calls it the "evil spirit . . . the one who devoured the mortal remains of the druid woman" (Zurn, 1970, p. 36), for it was the white man's culture that drove out the earth-based Goddess religion invoked by the druids. Thus, Unica Zurn has produced a split in which the part of the self she identifies either as masculine, or as evil for women, according to the norm of femininity as constructed by patriarchy, is a separate entity. The two somehow cannot coexist in one person, for to be both feminine and an artist like Melville, or a powerful spiritual leader like a druidess or a master is seen as a contradiction, and is a possibility that is denied to women both in society and in the surrealist movement.

In a parable appended to her manuscript, which describes a series of games played between male and female, the male protagonist, Flavius, succeeds in capturing Norma in order

---

[2]It has been suggested by Susan Hawthorne (Victoria, Australia) that H.M. might have a meaning in German relating to the Holy Mother—Helige Mutter.

to begin to incorporate her into himself: "During her incorporation Norma feels as if the marrow is escaping from her bones, her blood is flowing out of her veins, her senses are abandoning her" (Zurn, 1970, p. 157). Flavius absorbs everything from Norma until they both turn completely white.

In Zurn's magical universe, which is permeated with talismanic signs and omens, she presages a time when the male/female dichotomy will be resolved. Her obsessions embrace a yearning for a new order, a time when men and women will be utterly transfigured. She is convinced that "Under the surveillance of psychiatrists and nurses, and with the help of injections, man is going to be slowly transformed into woman and woman into man. They are going to unite, to feel saved, and to marry" (Zurn, 1970, p. 130). This hope for a possible harmony between the sexes eventually extends into the hope for a harmony between all species of life on the planet. It is through her writing (she was at work on this manuscript during her internment) and her art (she did automatic drawings) that she eventually learned to control her hallucinations, to give them esthetic form, and thus, temporarily, to recover from her intense need to live out in secret the private delectation of her messianic mission. Her art reveals a quest for a more perfect order, a world transformed, in which all beings will find salvation. "All of a sudden, between faces and plants, she also discovers animals. She sees those that she tried to draw: birds, fish and insects. She even perceives the most fantastic relations between animals and men, that are founded on a perfect and impossible harmony" (Zurn, 1970, p. 139). Her manuscript ends with a comparison between her own experience and that of Artaud, claiming for herself the right to have her madness taken as seriously as his. In a diary Unica Zurn wrote:

"For the last time Jasmin-Man (Hans Bellmer) becomes present in a silent dialogue with her. He is not the one that says that she is now God. She says it. And that becomes such a strong certitude that she can barely stand this new state. She has come down to earth to live with human beings for the first time in the history of the world. She gets up and sits down on the edge of the bed. This feeling is indefensible and too intense to be described. She is overwhelmed. She lies down again, and the voice of Jasmin-Man says to her: "I am God." "She responds: "No, I am." This struggle is prolonged until she says: "Agreed, you are the older and the wiser of the two of us. You are God, and I am your son, Jesus" (Zurn, Obliques, p. 255).

Christianity's deification of the male as God and redeemer, leaving no important role for woman except that of the impossible Virgin Mother is what Zurn's madness calls into question. As she perceives the fantastic harmony in the new relationships between animals and humans, she touches her source of power. In her place of power she comes to feel that she is the supreme Creator.

Leonora Carrington's experiences during her mental breakdown were published in her narrative Down Below (1972). In it she describes the illuminations she had during her internment in a psychiatric hospital in Santander, Spain. Carrington's madness, too, could be termed a "delusion of grandeur," but her identification with powerful women can also be interpreted as a desire to restore woman to her rightful place in our religious and human systems. Her appropriation of the female principle in all its earthly and spiritual manifestations, of the identity of the Queen of England and of Christ into her persona, indicates her profound need to reclaim woman's secular and sacred powers:

"Later, with full lucidity, I would go "Down Below" as the third person of the Trinity. I felt that through the agency of the Sun, I was an androgyne, the Moon, the Holy Ghost, a gypsy, an acrobat, Leonora Carrington, and a woman. I was also destined to be, later, Elizabeth of England . . . I was she who revealed religions and bore on her shoulders the freedom and the sins of the earth changed into knowledge, the union of Man and Woman with God and the Cosmos all equal between them. The son was the Sun and I the Moon, an essential element of the Trinity, with the microscopic knowledge of the earth, its plants and creatures. I knew that Christ was dead and done for, and that I had to take His place, because the

Trinity, minus a woman and microscopic knowledge had become dry and incomplete. Christ was replaced by the Sun. I was Christ on earth in the person of the Holy Ghost" (Carrington, 1988a, p. 32).

One of Carrington's paintings, in particular, deals with the dichotomy between patriarchal and feminist matristic visions. It provides an interpretation for the image of the Goddess as She is viewed by the female artist raised in an androcentric culture. In *Rarvarok* (1963), Carrington has divided her composition in half, presenting two opposing visions simultaneously. On the left are the Priests, Rabbis and Choir Boys of the Judeo-Christian religions. On the right is a woman who is either mad or possessed by a vision. In her vision a horse-drawn chariot appears bearing a white female figure. The chariot is driven by two horses with breasts and human heads, one black, one white. The male figures seem to be aloof, judging the sanity of the woman from a safely removed distance, perhaps pronouncing her "hysterical." The white horse, in Carrington's mythological world view, is generally associated with the Celtic mythological white Horse Goddess, Epona. As a death chariot with its curtain semidrawn, the Horse Goddess reveals the presence of a luminous white woman, a figure of the White Goddess within the chariot. The woman on the floor is then, from the feminist matristic perspective, in a trance state, and possessed by a vision of the Mother Goddess. In Carrington's mythic vision death is a passage to another dimension, one in which encounters with the lost tribes and races that worshipped a Goddess, such as the Tribe of the Goddess Dana of the Tuatha de Danaan, transpire.

Finally, if these women, in their intuitions of female grandeur, both in myth and in history, have been pronounced insane, must we not begin to question our definition of sanity? Women's so-called delusions of grandeur seem to point to a search for an authentic mythology and history of which they have been dispossessed. Today the symbol of the Goddess represents thousands of years of prepatriarchal history that women must repossess before they can come to a complete knowledge of their history and traditions. Whether viewed as breakdown or breakthrough, the madness of surrealist visionary women represents a reclamation of the Great Mother, a feminist journey to madness and back in search of a Goddess heritage. As Carol Christ has said: "The symbol of the Goddess has much to offer women who are struggling to be rid of the 'powerful pervasive and long-lasting moods and motivations' of devaluation of female power, denigration of the female body, distrust of female will, and denial of women's struggle to create a new culture in which women's power, bodies, will and bonds are celebrated. It seems natural that the Goddess would reemerge as a symbol of the new-found beauty, strength, and power of women" (Christ, 1979, p. 286).

It has been my contention that women writers and artists have been connecting to the sources of their matristic power by re-membering the body (earth-body, culture-body, cosmic-body) of the Great Mother, and that the suppression of knowledge of Her and of societies in which She was revered as the Creator (giving legitimacy to the image of a female Creator) has caused irreparable psychic damage to creative women. In those cases where their connection to their source of power was so short-circuited as to cause serious mental alienation, we can often find the image of the Great Mother resurfacing in narratives about their "seasons in hell," as in Unica Zurn's *Jasmin Man* or Leonora Carrington's *Down Below*.

In their efforts to communicate a feminist matristic view, their intuitions, and their intimations of the greatness of women in a world that once was and no longer is, they have been driven into more severe states of mental anguish, composed both of periods of madness and of illumination, depending upon how these are defined in any period. It would be romanticizing madness to suggest that all forms of madness in women are really states of illumination mislabeled. Nevertheless, for an illuminated woman to speak the language of eco-memory, matristic-memory, or shamanic-memory to an audience of culturally indoctrinated amnesiacs is to risk either being labeled or driven insane.

In her book *Women Artists and the Surrealist Movement*, Whitney Chadwick shows that nature was a metaphor for women in the works of women surrealists such as Meret Oppen-

Leonora Carrington: El Rarvarok (1963)

heim, Ithell Colquhoun, Toyen, Frida Kahlo, Remedios Varo, Emmy Bridgewater, Eileen Agar, and Rita Kernn-Larsen. She argues that the fertile earth had become a symbol for women's creativity among women surrealists. (See Chadwick, 1985.)

In contradistinction to the way male surrealists linked women to nature, creating not merely sex objects, but surrealists objects of them, female surrealists saw nature as their source of fecundity, and the Goddess image became the natural symbol for female creation.

The tales of power that surrealist women artists and writers painted and narrated all point to the locus of gynergy (female creativity, energy, or life force) in their connection to the Earth, to legendary and historic knowledge about ancient matristic cultures, to power places, and to the spirit world, as well as to nature and the cosmos. Most of them did not live long enough to tell us about the power that comes from connecting to the wisdom of the Crone. However, Leonora Carrington, now in her seventies, paints and writes about this crucial source of female power, and we will explore this aspect of her work later in the book.

Blockage of their connection to any of these power sources could, and often did, lead to extreme alienation, and ultimately to madness. While the suppression of the Goddess can never be said to be the sole cause of their madness, it is now clear that denial of this history and of this source of power contributes to exacerbating creative women's sense of alienation in patriarchy, not only from its religious systems, but from their own creativity as well. It is the denial of this knowledge, the modern desacralization of the world, that is an important cause of madness in women, (and this is probably true to some degree for men as well).

Moreover, in their recent volume of feminist literary criticism *No Man's Land: The Place of the Woman Writer in the Twentieth Century* (Vol. 1, 1988), Sandra M. Gilbert and Susan Gubar, discussing sexual linguistics, ask whether it is possible that "the idea that language is in its essence or nature patriarchal may be a reaction-formation against the linguistic (as well as the biological) primacy of the mother?" (Gilbert & Gubar, 1988, p. 264) Further, they reason, if it is so that "the female does have a crucial linguistic role . . . isn't it also possible that verbal signification arises not from a confrontation with the 'Law of the Father,' but from a consciousness of the lure and the lore of the Mother?" (Gilbert & Gubar, 1988, p. 265)

If the "mother tongue" is primal in the formation of women's linguistic abilities, and, if renaming all of reality is a feminist priority, as Gilbert and Gubar show (in their concluding discussion of Ursula K. LeGuin's parable "She Unnames Them" in which "Her first woman gives back to the first man the name given to her by 'you and your father' " [Gilbert & Gubar, 1988, p. 270]), then it would be reasonable to suggest that many of our literary "ancestresses" and foremothers renamed their primal experience of reality, not only in the name of the literal mother, but also in the name of the Great Mythic Mother in order to express the authenticity of their affiliation with an extended female matrilineage. Indeed, I am suggesting that if the pre-Oedipal relationship of the daughter to the mother with its permeable boundaries and interconnecting bonds constitutes the earliest knowledge of the body of the literal mother, then to remember the body of one's own mother is to reconstruct one's earliest cosmogony—a matristic vision of the origin and source of life as the body of a still greater mother, the Great Mother and Matrix of all life.

It is my contention, then, that our literary foremothers, working without the support of an active feminist literary movement, in returning to the source of their linguistic power, (the mother tongue), re-created the body of the Great Mother as a primary tale of power.

While working under the constraints and stresses of such periods in patriarchal history as those posed by Victorian England or the Second World War in France, our literary foremothers told their stories of power either by coding them or by occulting their references to the Great Mother as the revealed sources of the sacred, of fertility, of creation, of spiritual rebirth, and of magic.

Starhawk, a contemporary Wicca witch and priestess, also a poet, political activist, and practitioner of the Goddess religion, writes in *Truth or Dare: Encounters with Power, Authority, and Mystery* (1987): "We like to tell ourselves

> stories of power
> how we lost it
> how we reclaim it (Starhawk, 1987, p. 3)

She continues, writing that "We are faced with the task of ensuring that the collective story continues so that those who come after us can write their own chapters, so that the memory of those who came before us is not erased. We must preserve and renew the world, re-member Her back into life" (Starhawk, 1987, p. 312).

The power that Starhawk refers to is what she has called "power-from-within," and she contrasts it to "power over." The consciousness referred to by "power over" is secular, and does not conceive of the world as a living organism, but rather as an object. The consciousness referred to as "power-from-within" is defined by Starhawk: "The language of power-from-within is poetry, metaphor, symbol, ritual, myth, the language of magic, of "thinking in things," where the concrete becomes resonant with mysteries that go beyond its seeming solid form. Its language is action, which speaks in the body and to all the senses in ways that can never be completely conveyed in words. The technology of power-from-within is magic, the art of changing consciousness, of shifting shapes and dimensions, of bending reality" (Starhawk, 1987, p. 15).

In telling stories of power, women are working magic; they are evoking materializations through the incantatory power of language—in this case of the mother tongue, which re-evokes the cosmogony of the Great Mother in remembering the literal body of the biological mother. "To say the Goddess is reawakening may be an act of magical creation," wrote Starhawk (1987, p. 79). "Our challenge is to bring the Goddess back to life, to envision, create, and inhabit the re-membered living body of the earth" (Starhawk, 1987, p. 112).

This challenge, this injunction, seems to have been felt by many of our literary foremothers as diverse as H.D., Renée Vivien, and Virginia Woolf. In the next chapter, we will unravel the thread of a feminist matristic vision encoded in the writings of Gertrude Stein and Leonora Carrington, noting how it was couched either in literary conventions or coded in subversive, iconoclastic icons and occult, esoteric references.

It is ultimately through their literary and artistic "Vision-Quests" and "Grail Quests" that our visionary foremothers narrated their tales of power. As immediate survivors of the great holocaust of matristic history, these few women with eco-matristic-shamanic memory, alive in a world controlled and constructed by "amnesiacs," haunted by the memory of witch burnings, had to conceal their knowledge of one civilization and mythos of the Great Mother.

Decoding the Hieroglyphics of Feminist Matristic Subversion: Patriarchal Symbol Systems as Decoys

The suppression of knowledge of matristic cultures has obviously contributed to the many causes that led creative women, deprived of all female images of Creation, to enter states of mental alienation.

It is possible to decode the hieroglyphics of the conscious subversion of this knowledge as a subtext in the works of Gertrude Stein and Leonora Carrington. This chapter details how Gertrude Stein uses the symbols of patriarchal Judaism and how Leonora Carrington uses a variety of Eastern and pre-Columbian esoteric symbol systems as decoys, which consciously occult their subtexts about the Goddess religion and its earth-based spiritual values.

Contemporary feminist theorists (i.e., Chodorow, Dinnerstein, Gilbert & Gubar, and others) have established the important role that the pre-Oedipal relationship to the mother plays in women's psychological and linguistic development. I am suggesting that the lack of relationship to the historical tradition, culture, and matrilineage of the Great Mother might play an equally important role in impelling the full development of women's psyches and creativity, especially within patriarchal societies.

While writing back through the biological and literary motherline has led to hypotheses of a mother tongue and literary experimentation along the lines suggested by Gilbert and Gubar in their chapter on sexual linguistics [i.e., "Intuiting the empowerment that daughters might win from literal and literary mothers, women from Dickinson to Woolf and her descendants subversively transform classical languages into female native tongues and praise matriarchal witchcraft. For these artists the lure of the mother's lore always takes precedence over what Lacan calls the "Law of the Father" (Gilbert & Gubar, 1988, p. 262)]. It is also obvious that the lore of the Mother (culture-specific lore about prepatriarchal, pagan, or matristic Goddess cultures) has largely been suppressed. In searching for their mother tongue, women writers in touch with their close interrelationship with nature, know (and also intuit) that they are at once the literal daughters of their biological mothers, the literary daughters of their artistic foremothers, the Earth Daughters of Gaia, and the spiritual daughters of the Great Mother, one Cosmic Creatress of all life.

Thus, it is natural to find that in exploring their matristic heritage, women writers and artists will seek the sources of their power and gynergy simultaneously in the bodies of their biological mothers, in the body of works of their literary ancestresses, and in the mythic and spiritual bodies of wisdom relating to the Great Mother Goddesses of different cultures.

GERTRUDE STEIN

As Gilbert and Gubar have said about Gertrude Stein's entrée into the male literary scene, "making herself into her own and everybody else's pseudomale precursor, she definitely inherited the place of the father in order to put all the men she knew in their properly dependent places" (Gilbert & Gubar, 1988, p. 188). As they show, Stein evolved out of her "masculinity complex" to explicitly extol the genius of Susan B. Anthony in her opera, *The Mother of Us All.*

Not only did she turn toward an affirmation of an important political foremother, but according to Lisa Ruddick, Stein has coded into *Tender Buttons* a myth of the return to the mother after a short season in the symbolic realm of the father. She writes that in Stein's work there is "a hidden myth of human development that permeates these texts. The myth is articulated unsystematically and tends to appear in coded form. But one can make out a central story about loss of the mother, entry into the world of the father, and the imagined recovery of the mother" (Ruddick, 1986, p. 230).

Ruddick argues that *Tender Buttons,* "the most famous of Stein's abstract writings, is not so abstract as it seems; in fact it is a prolonged enactment of the return to the mother" (Ruddick, 1986, p. 235). In *Tender Buttons,* Ruddick explains (1986, p. 235), Stein seems to reclaim the mother as the cook, who, in preparing the fruits of the earth for the dinner table, mediated between nature (the domain of the Mother and the Earth Mother) and culture or civilization (the domain of the Father).

While Stein's coding of her lesbianism has been studied by such well known feminist scholars as Catharine Stimpson (Stimpson 1977), her Jewish identity has never been specifically analyzed in relation to the abstract vs. coded nature of her fiction. Yet, it is precisely in her relationship to Judaism that her allusions to a female God surface. The coding of the Goddess in Stein's abstract writings can be related to the theme of assimilation in both her life and her art.

As an American Jewish lesbian living in France at the time of the Nazis, as a Jewish woman in America, and as a Jewish American woman writer in France, Gertrude Stein had many reasons for wanting to assimilate, for seeking a contemporary composition both in her life and in her art in which her triple marginalities as Jewish, woman, and lesbian could be camouflaged. In all three of these areas Gertrude Stein tried to cover up her difference in order to better assimilate to her intellectual milieu. By decoding the work of Gertrude Stein from the perspective of assimilation, we will discover the subversive strategy of Goddess icon making.

Whereas her book *The Making of Americans* is a compendium of the lives of "old people in a new world, new people made out of the old" (Stein, 1934, p. 86), Stein says that "it was essentially religion which made them different" (p. 86). In *The Making of Americans* Stein tried to flatten or "cubicize" this individuality by assimilating it to a larger composition and insisting on the repetitiveness of a cultural experience that might otherwise have been perceived as unique or singular in a pejorative way.

"There is always then repeating, always everything is repeating, this a history of every kind of repeating there is in living, this is then a history of every kind of living . . . there are and were and will be always existing millions of each kind of them, and the kinds of them from the beginning, and in every nation, are always the same and this is now a history of some of them. There are always then the same kinds of them, and millions of them, millions of each kind there are of men and women always existing" (Stein, 1934, pp. 159–160).

By insisting on the repetition in lived experience and upon the multitudes who represent that same singular kind of lived experience, Stein assimilates the uniqueness of "they were different in all the ways that they had in them . . . in all the things that made them uncertain inside them, they were different inside each one of them from all the others of them in religion" (Stein, 1934, pp. 159–60), to a broader, more all-inclusive conception of the diversity of life forms which the old world had already struggled to accommodate.

In assimilating as a woman writer, a lesbian, and a Jew, through her salon in Paris, Gertrude Stein successfully used a structure that had well served both patriarchal and subversive feminist purposes for many centuries. Literary salons had functioned chiefly as forums for displaying the works of male writers and creating networks of influence for males of power and genius of many eras. Yet, at the same time, they gave salon women an opportunity to read and air their feminist works and ideas in a public arena, so that they could also influence the men in their turn. The strategy of subversion from within that the salon model exemplifies is a strategy that operates in Gertrude Stein's literary work as well.

Stein's cryptic literary style can also be understood as a camouflage and as a structure, which on one level serves the patriarchal premises of her own culture but on another level subverts that patriarchal meaning in favor of a feminist matristic vision. We shall examine how this functions specifically in her so-called abstract writing, and its occultation of her feminist matristic meaning while giving the illusion of being Jewish, traditional, nonrepresentational, artistic expression.

It has been argued by Susan Handelman (1983, p. 99), that the home of the Jew is a sacred text in the middle of commentaries, and that the Jew, existing in the realm of desire, "différance," and displacement, "will not abandon scripture for Logos" (p. 109). Thus, as Handelman reasons, Gertrude Stein's écriture of différance can be seen essentially as a Rabbinic impulse, and like Derridianism, a "stubborn adherence to the free play of the sign, a refusal to stabilize it or to posit univocal referents that fulfill it . . .," for as Handelman says, "the loss of a stable referent that grounds the 'literal' and 'proper' meaning of words is a manner of exile" (Handelman, 1983, p. 107). Her argument continues that, "interpretation, mediation, displacement, deferment, exile, absence, equivocal meaning—these are the themes of Rabbinic and Derridian interpretation. For the Jews, as for Derrida, there has been no redemption; there is no fulfilling presence. And nonfulfillment—is a characteristically Jewish mode" (Handelman, 1983, p. 107). I would argue that Gertrude Stein's Jewish mode of writing, her écriture of différance permits an assimilation to a Jewish nonrepresentational mode of art which she, at the same time, subverted from within in favor of a feminist matristic spiritual vision at odds with patriarchal Judaism. It is, in fact, through her dangerous trespassing over the Jewish patriarchal taboos that Stein reveals an occulted goddess-vision in her work.

It is also my observation that Gertrude Stein's experience as a Jew in America and her understanding of the impulse toward assimilation, influenced the ways in which she handled the camouflaging of her marginal identities not only in her life, but also in her work.

The Jewish stratum in her work is exemplified, first of all, by her abstract écriture of différance, and, second, by iconic Jewish thematic motifs. However, as we shall see, Stein subverts them both in order to express a feminist matristic, and ultimately a goddess-centered vision.

Jewish art is problematic, specifically concerning the making of iconic or graven images, for the Ten Commandments (Exodus 4:20) and Deuteronomy IV (17:17) explicitly make strict injunctions against the creation of an image in the likeness of any male or female, animal, fish, or bird. Naturally, this injunction was connected to the idea that Jews should not bow down to these images or serve them as deities.

Nevertheless, traditionally, these images were interpreted as pagan. As a result, historians of Jewish art inform us that "up to modern times there was almost no plastic art among the Jews, no sculpture, little painting, hardly any architecture" (Roth, 1971, p. 265). This biblical injunction has also led Jewish artists to espouse nonrepresentational art. Without making any case for Gertrude Stein's religious beliefs, as a culturally identified Jew there is a real tension inherent in the blatant iconic emphasis in her art collection, her sitting for the famous portrait by Picasso, and her own nonrepresentational portraits. Yet, these were *portraits* just the same, only they were nonfigurative, and they were not likenesses of males or females in the strict or literal sense of the word. Even the cubist device of the play on authorship in the *Autobiography of Alice B. Toklas,* written by Stein, viewed in this light, turns out to be a strategy for evading the straightforward self-portrait, the iconic image. For, at the same time that it ducks painting a forthright portrait, it actually creates as flamboyant a portrait as the Picasso head of her itself (a head, we might add, that was missing for the longest time because, as Picasso claimed, he could no longer see it, and so he painted it out). My point is that the problematics of Jewish identity in Gertrude Stein gave rise to a tension between the surface and the substance in both her life and her art. Thus, while her Jewish identity is occulted in a style that can also be characterized, according to Handelman, as both Rabbinic, heretical hermeneutic and typically Jewish nonrepresentational, this very Jewishness, in itself, is used by Stein as a patriarchal camouflage, which she then transgresses and flaunts in order to inscribe feminist matristic readings into her work.

Not only is her nonrepresentational style characteristic of a Jewish approach to art, but her theory of the noun is also derivable from the problematics of Jewish theology. Phyllis Trible, in her article "Depatriarchalizing in Biblical Interpretation" (1976), explicates Genesis 2:23, showing how Hebrew uses the verb "to call" in naming woman, rather than the verb "to name." The presence of the verb "kara" (to call) in "she shall be called woman," Trible argues, is an evocation, not a naming. Naming an object, in her reading, would establish supremacy over the named—over animals and women. In "calling" woman rather than "naming" her, she is evoked and not objectified. Similarly, Stein's resistance to naming comes out strongly in *Tender Buttons,* where she, too, evokes and calls forth objects rather than naming them.

Trible argues that *The Song of Songs* is a midrash on Genesis, for in *The Song of Songs,* naming is ecstasy. In the erotic Garden of Eden, where woman names man, where the roles are reversed, "love makes a new creation" (Trible, 1976, pp. 224–225). This, I see as analogous to Gertrude Stein's description of poetry in *Poetry and Grammar* where she emphasizes that poetry is completely caressing a noun.

> When I said.
> A rose is a rose is a rose is a rose.
> And then later made that into a ring I made poetry and what
> did I do I caressed completely caressed and addressed a
> noun.
> Now let us think of poetry any poetry all poetry and let us
> see if this is not so. . . .
> Anybody knows how anybody calls out the name of anybody one
> loves. And so that is poetry really loving the name of any-
> thing and that is not prose. Yes any of you can know that (Stein, 1935, p. 231)

Stein's assertion that caressing a noun is the ecstasy of writing poetry, her naming of Alice as her wife, her dwelling with her in the Garden (of Bilignin), her love poetry, and her reinterpretation of the Garden of Eden in her life and in her work constitute a reversal of Genesis and a reversal of the meaning of the Fall. Ultimately, as we shall see in her use of Goddess imagery in the recurring symbol of the cow, Stein opposes the Mother Goddess to the male patriarchal God in her playful transgression of Judaism's strictures. Stein's critique of Jewish patriarchal injunctions is alluded to specifically in her identification of Alice as a Jew, as her wife and lover, and in her connection to pork, which Jews are specifically forbidden to eat.

In *With a Wife* we read: "A Jewish wife with a Jewish lover," and in *A Sonatina Followed by Another,* having referred to Alice as her "little Jew" (Stein, 1980, p. 195), she becomes more specific in linking Alice as a Jew with pork, which is, of course, not kosher. Nor is women's love for each other. Yet, these are her favorite meals.

"I took a piece of pork and stuck it on a fork and I gave it to a curly headed jew. I want my little jew to be round like a pork, a young round pork with a cork for his tail. A young round pork. I want my little jew to be round like a young round pork. I do" (Stein, 1980, p. 296). "A special name for careless is caress" (p. 297).

Alice is the wife and lover of a woman. She is forbidden meat, pork, and the forbidden fruit in the Garden of Eden; she is knowledge in the biblical sense. "We murmur to each other, nightingales, we please each other with fruit trees and we allow each other melons and we throw each other shoes. And pork. What do we think about pork and asparagus. What do we think about everything. It is necessary for us to know what we think We think very well of butter and church cheese. We think very well of cracked church bells" (Stein, 1980, p. 297).

Later, in *Annex to No. 2 Sonatina Followed by Another Not Yet Safe But Walking*, we read: "How old are brave women. . . . Do not think that we are safe . . . a fig an apple and some grapes makes a cow. How, the Caesars know how. Now. The Caesars know how and they know how now. The Caesars know how" (Stein, 1980, p. 303).

Stein links the fruits of the Garden of Eden (fig, apple) to butter, cheese, cracked church bells, a cow, and Caesar. The cow is thus associated with the music of a broken church bell, with (the reversal of the Fall), and connected with the fruits of the Garden of Eden instead. What is a cow? Stein proclaims: "A cow . . ., and as to cow which is mentioned anyhow. A cow is mentioned anyhow. Thank you Romans, Caesars and all. . . . I love her too my little Jew. . . . she is that kind of a wife" (Stein, 1980, p. 314).

It is likely that Stein constantly refers to Julius Caesar because of his well-known homosexual adventures, as Suetonius's *The Life of Julius Caesar* (Suetonius, 1957, pp. 33, 35) informs us. Here the portrait of a Roman general (by Suetonius) is conjured up by a Jewish writer within a text of *différance* which is anti-iconic in nature. Stein's love is as taboo in Judaism as is the making of a portrait of her love object. Thus, she distances herself from direct portraiture while at the same time conjuring up the direct portrait of a famous homosexual. In the non-Jewish world of the Romans who persecuted the Jews, this kind of love was accepted. Thus, for Stein, love as she experienced it, was non-Jewish. Yet, it was not Christian either. It was pagan. However, Stein does associate erotic love with religion. "You manufacture cows by vows" (Stein, 1980, p. 307). Cows have previously been decoded by Linda Simon (1977, p. 107) as signifying orgasm. Yet, by extension, the cow is also the Great Mother (in Egypt revered as Hathor . . . "her Golden Calf, the same deity worshipped by Aaron and the Israelites" (Walker, 1983, p. 181). It is also from the cow that both milk and meat are obtained. In kosher dietary laws Jews are forbidden to eat meat and drink milk at the same meal. In this symbolic sense, reconstituting the cow in oneself as a totality is the same as reconstituting the forbidden Great Mother within the self, the Goddess, who is banned in patriarchal Judaism. Gertrude Stein might literally partake of pork and cheese at one of Alice's meals, and in literature, she tells us, she was not kosher either. Conventional grammar and composition were for Stein the dietary laws of language, and she constantly rejected them in favor of her own pleasure. Stein's playful *écriture* of *différance* sets in place in *Emp Lace* (Stein, 1980, pp. 238, 239) the lines "come out cow come out cow come out cow come out cow etc." "Come out" suggests a revealing of her lesbianism, but "cow come out cow" enlarges the meaning to imply a revealing of her "worship of the cow" or her proclivity toward a vision of the Mother Goddess—a coming out of patriarchal Judaism, both as a lesbian and as an invoker of the Great Mother as a religious symbol. The fruits of the garden plus the cheese and butter from the cow, as well as the linking of Alice with pork, all constellate both a reference to Judaism as well as a rebellion against its many taboos. As Stein says in *Emp Lace:* "It was a way to say" (1980, pp. 238, 239). The unforgettable lines

"And the cow comes out of the door. Do you adore me. When this you see remember me" (Stein, 1980, p. 312) appear in *A Sonatina Followed By Another*. This piece is signed "Y.D."[1] Here I suggest relating the mysterious initials Y.D. to the title of the poem *Yet Dish*, which, when read in elision, produces the word-sound YIDDISH. In other words Stein is asking us to remember the poem *Yet Dish* whenever we see the "cow" and remember her.

Yet Dish can be interpreted as a play on the Passover Seder. Passover can also have several connotations in Stein's work, for not only can it refer to the Jewish celebration of liberation from slavery in Egypt, but it can also refer to "passing" as a non-Jew and as a heterosexual. It has all of these meanings in her poem *Pass Over:*

> Pass over.
> Pass over.
> pass.
> pass.
> pass.
> pass. (Stein, 1980, p. 199)

Much of *Yet Dish* should be read with an ear for Yiddish or Hebrew prayers, and with an eye for symbols of the Seder ritual. One stanza begins: "A lea ender stow sole lightly/not a bet beggar" (Stein, 1980, p. 55). A lea is Elia, the prophet Elijah who often appears as a beggar. The door is opened for him at the Passover Seder. A glass is also set out for him. Yet, the beggar is negated. "S a glass" may be puzzling until we pronounce S, and realize that in German and Yiddish it means "Eat." "Not an Eider" negates the egg (Ei) also found on the traditional Passover plate. "Note tie stem bone" might refer to the shank bone on the traditional Passover plate. Not(e) may negate it, too. Finally, "never a single ham" (Stein, 1980, p. 55) once more refers to the Jewish taboo on pork. This line is directly followed by:

> Meal dread
> Meal dread so or
> Meal dread so or bounce
> Meal dread so or bounce two sales. Not a rice.
> No nor a pray seat. (Stein, 1980, p. 58)

Here the dread of the sacred patriarchal ritual meal is connected with the negation of a place for prayer. Seemingly, in order for a real Seder to take place, a true ritual meal of celebration of liberation from slavery, a nonkosher meal would have to be served. In addition, the traditional foods would have transformed meanings. Whereas the bitter herbs serve to remind Jews of how the Egyptians embittered the lives of their forefathers in Egypt with hard labor and work in the fields (Goldberg, 1949–1966), for Stein the bitterness is found in *this* life.

In "A R nuisance/Not a regular plate" (Stein, 1980, p. 60), "Are, not a regular plate" evokes the irregularity of Stein's own ceremonial meals of liberation—the pork, the forbidden fruit from the tree of knowledge, and so forth.

Stein plays upon the sounds of familiar Hebrew prayers in such combinations as:

> Lessons lettuce
> Let us peer
> Let us polite
> Let us pour
> Let us polite
> Let us polite. (Stein, 1980, p. 59)

This stanza suggests the sounds of L'Zion and, of course, the lettuce might also remind us of the parsley and bitter herbs on the Passover plate. Yet, at this Seder we feel a voyeurism ("Let us peer"), a camouflaging ("Let us polite"), and a religious lamentation echoed in a play on the word *"miserere":*

---

[1] Susan Hawthorne intuitively reads Y.D. as "Your Dear."

Peace say ray comb pomp
Peace say ray comb pomp
Peace say ray comb pomp
Peace say ray comb pomp (Stein, 1980, p. 60)

The Hebrew prayer said before breaking bread, which thanks God for bringing forth the fruits of the earth, is known as the motzi (Ha Motzi), and at Passover it is said as one eats the matzo, the unleavened bread. These sounds (motzi and matzo) are echoed in the refrain: "old boat seak, old boat seak next to hear" (Stein, 1980, p. 62). Yet *Dish* begins with the line: "Put a sun in Sunday, Sunday." The use of Sunday as the non-Jewish holy day, as opposed to the Jewish Sabbath of Friday night and Saturday, and the possible illumination that can come from a nonkosher, non-Jewish Seder of liberation from the slavery of patriarchy is seen in Stein's deconstruction of the ritual Seder meal concluding with the line: "next a Sunday, next a Sunday" which parallels the conclusion of the Seder when one says: "Next year in Jerusalem". This parallelism sets up a tension between the Promised Land and escape from bondage of the Jewish law, perhaps that imposed upon homosexuals, for on the second night of the Seder it is said: "This is the Passover Festival . . . The Sodomites provoked God and were condemned by fire on Passover" (Goldberg, 1949–1966). Stein thus shows us how the Seder celebrates the Inquisition, for the European sabbat "or festival, was fabricated largely by judges of the Inquisition during the 14th and 15th centuries on a foundation of pagan precedents. Churchmen said witches held four Great Sabbats a year 'in derision of the four annual festivals of the Church,' but the church had copied these from the pagans in the first place" (Walker, 1983, p. 874). In returning to Sunday, Stein commemorates the origin of the Sabbat/Sabbath, reminding us that originally in pagan practices the Moon Goddess was worshipped.

In *Patriarchal Poetry* Stein parodies the dietary laws of Judaism in a more overt way when she writes: "Patriarchal poetry and not meat on Monday. Patriarchal poetry and meat on Tuesday" (Stein, 1980, p. 111). Here meat is probably the cow. This text follows closely the evocation of the bird in "such a pretty bird" and so forth (Stein, 1980, p. 110), and the section "Was it a fish was heard was it a bird was it a cow was stirred was it a third was it a cow was stirred was it a third was it a bird was heard . . . Fishes a bird cows were stirred, a bird fishes were heard a bird cows were stirred a third. A third is all. Come too" (Stein, 1980, p. 110). In this text Stein uses the Christian symbol of the fish, the third, to represent the Trinity, the prepatriarchal bird goddess and the cow in tandem, both in defiance of the Ten Commandments' injunction against their iconic representation and also as symbols of alternatives to the Judaic definition of God.

Sexuality is also underscored in relation to an alternate, goddess-centered vision in *Lifting Belly* when Stein relates Caesar to the cow: "The Caesars are docile . . . And/in relation to a cow" (Stein, 1980, p. 47). Earlier in *Lifting Belly* Stein had written: Caesars do their duty/ I never make a mistake./We will be very happy and boastful and we will celebrate Sunday" (Stein, 1980, p. 43). Thus, *Yet Dish* in its celebration of Sunday rebels against Judaism's taboo on nonkosher foods and acts. In the Mother Goddess religion where the cow is the symbol for the Great Mother and where the Garden of Eden is a garden of earthly delights of the fruits of the Earth Mother that are blessed by the Hebrew motzi, Stein can conclude: "It is very meritorious to work very hard in a garden" (Stein, 1980, p. 63). The Jewish blessing, Ha Motzi, which she echoed in "old boat seak" is a prayer praising God for bringing forth the fruits of the Earth. Stein rejects Judaism's patriarchalizing of the Earth Mother Goddess, and she suggests that a true Seder, in fact any truly sacred ritual meal, is actually a celebration of the Goddess of Vegetation.

Stein's ultimate heresy toward patriarchal religion consists in using the icon of St. Teresa as a decoy for the Goddess. In her play *Four Saints in Three Acts* she insists upon putting the saints in the landscape, in the garden. Saint Teresa is particularly important to her, perhaps because of her ecstatic love for, and marriage to God, as well as for having been known to preach the virility of women. One of the best-known of the phrases ascribed to Saint Teresa is that she preached to women to be as strong as men. "If you do all that is in you the Lord will make you so manly that men themselves will be amazed at you" (Peers, 1946, p. 84). In *Four Saints in Three Acts* the Goddess of the birds, the pigeons on the grass, is disguised as St. Teresa. George Eliot had referred to St. Teresa in *Middlemarch,* reminding us that "St. Teresa was certainly not the last of her kind. Many Theresas have been born, who found for themselves no epic life; wherein there was a constant unfolding of far-resonant action . . . for these later-born Theresas were helped by no coherent social faith and order which could perform the function of knowledge for the ardently willing soul" (Eliot, 1956, pp. 3, 4). Referring also to the image of St. Teresa invoked by George Eliot, Stein's meaning has to do with the discovery of a heretical, coherent body of knowledge for the ardently willing soul. Thus, St. Teresa of Avila may become a coded symbol for the Great Goddess in Stein's work, since in Teresa's *The Interior Castle* she wrote: "For from those divine breasts where it seems God is always sustaining the soul there flow streams of milk bringing comfort to all the people" (Mollenkott, 1981, p. 22). Thus, we see that St. Teresa, herself, referred to God in female imagery.

In conclusion, we can look at Gertrude Stein's life style and literary style as strategies for mediating the tension between her need to assimilate and her desire to individuate. In both her salon and her literary works she created illusions through assimilation, while using strategies of subterfuge from within in order to deconstruct the patriarchal contexts of her assimilation. Yet, within that surface assimilation, Stein simultaneously reconstructed feminist matristic identity through the playful transgression of patriarchal taboos. Her creative codification of systems of decoys and signposts point to the significant landmarks and sites of transformed vision inscribed upon the geography of her wordplays.

Moreover, this system of coding and decoys uses the *spoken* word as a clue to its deciphering. As I will argue later in the final chapter, contemporary feminist matristic literature makes use of certain conventions of cultural creation that come from the oral tradition.

In the seventeenth century in France, a popular salon game was *La Carte du Tendre* (the Map of Tender). In it, pretendants to the citadel of the country of Tender, a metaphor for the heart and the salon of Mlle. de Scudéry, would describe the roads they might have taken in order to reach Tender, the capitol of her citadel. Traversing the Plains of Indifference and the Lakes of Ecstasy, dashing their hopes against the Rocks of Rejection, they would finally arrive at Tender only to be informed by Mlle. de Scudéry that they had taken the wrong road. Known as the supreme prude of the seventeenth century, Mlle. de Scudéry rejected her suitors, because she espoused the philosophy of Platonic Love, (probably in order to protect herself from unwanted pregnancy and to ensure a long future of intellectual life at her salon). This is somewhat like the game that I see Gertrude Stein having played with most contemporary literary critics.

Gertrude Stein's opaque work, her nonrepresentational obscurantism, her seemingly playful esoteric abstractionism is what an *écriture* of *différance* is truly about. She, too, is a Salon Woman who does not easily admit visitors to her citadel of Tender. Contemporary critics may dash their hopes upon the rocky cliffs of Structuralism or in the Sea of Semiology. They may lose their way along the patriarchal highways and byways of Cubism, Surrealism, Rabbinic heretical or hermetic hermeneutics, but they will never reach the citadel of Tender, for Tender only appears to be a Salon. It is actually a prepatriarchal Garden of Eden, a female dream of Paradise. It is also, however, a matristic, non-Judaic land of milk (cow) and honey (suckle), where pork comes from the pig, sacred to the Goddess, and milk and meat reconstitute the body of the Great Mother. For, in a true communion one eats one's god. It is also a land where Caesar, St. Teresa, and the Cow constitute the new unholy Trinity, one that is as mystifying to the patriarchal outsider as the Father, the Son, and the Holy Ghost must have seemed to Gertrude Stein's profoundly radical and flamboyant but occulted feminist matristic mind.

LEONORA CARRINGTON

Deprived of knowledge about early matristic societies, cut off from eco-memory, and from contact with the spirit world, women have suffered from the suppression of the Goddess most bitterly in the debasing of one of her most potent triple aspects—that of the Crone, the figure of the Wise Old Woman. Feminist matristic writers and artists, in making literal and imaginary journeys to their sources of sacred power, find that the journey through aging to the kind of wisdom that precedes death is one of the most intense aspects of Goddess knowledge being recovered today.

According to Mary Daly's *Websters' First New Intergalactic Wickedary of the English Language*, a Crone is "a Great Hag of History, long-lasting one; survivor of the perpetual witch-craze of patriarchy whose status is determined not merely by chronological age, but by Crone-logical considerations; one who has Survived early stages of Otherworld Journey and who therefore has Dis-covered depths of Courage, Strength, and Wisdom in her Self" (Daly, 1987, p. 114).

Daly's definition focuses on the other world journey made by elder women, for it is traditionally the Crone who acquires wisdom, not only about the visible, material dimensions of reality, but about the forthcoming journey after death, as well.

In her extensive study of the Crone, Babara G. Walker (1985) connects the Crone to Sophia and Minerva, Goddesses of Wisdom, and recalls her specifically as that aspect of the Great Goddess of Old Europe, referred to by Marija Gimbutas (Gimbutas, 1982) as the second aspect of death and regeneration.

The Crone has always been associated with the aspect of the total cycle of life, death, and regeneration represented by Death, and it is for this reason that the Crone has been so forcefully denied and despised. In a culture that denies death, it is obvious that older women will be rejected and demeaned.

Yet, Walker tells us that "an important point about these traditions of the knowledge-giving, civilization-creating Crone "is that her intellectual gifts were not based solely on what is now called "feminine intuition," emotion, or unconscious responses. She was equally credited with analytical intelligence of the sort that has become stereotyped as "masculine" (Walker, 1985, p. 65).

Leonora Carrington's novel *The Hearing Trumpet* (1974) and her recent paintings *Kron Flower, Tell The Bees, Eye Witness*, and *Bubba/Zaida* (1988a) tell us about the voyage made by the Crone, a voyage that Mary Daly accurately describes as "the art of Spinning beyond the compass. It is also skill in walking/talking the Wrong Way, moving in Wicked directions, opening doors to Other dimensions, Other Spatial perceptions. . . . Women who roam into these Wild Realms require Other navigational devices" (Daly, 1987, p. 273).

We will return to a discussion of the Crone in Carrington's work, but first we must explore the way in which she occults her feminist matristic vision within the coded glyphs and symbols of a variety of patriarchal esoteric traditions. Using them as a decoy, she subversively transforms their meaning for the feminist matristically minded viewer and reader.

Leonora Carrington's artistic work is deeply informed by an intimate connection to the Tibetan Buddhist, the ancient Mayan, the Gnostic, and the Celtic traditions as well as to alchemy and a familiarity with Kabbala.

However, visual intuition, or direct *seeing* and *knowing* are the firsthand sources of esoteric information, and in referring to these sources of her esoteric knowledge, I am obliged to make reference to the six weeks I spent as her guest in Mexico during the summer of 1972, because of what I learned from the manner in which we visited the archaeological sites.

The visionary process she taught me sets the structural and symbolic scene for a living investigation of her mythic universe. Upon my arrival at her home she gave me (along with a copy of *The Hearing Trumpet*) a copy of the *Popol Vuh*, the Mayan creation myth, and

Leonora Carrington:
The Ancestor (1968)
Artwork photographed
by Barry Pribula

told me to read only these books in preparation for our journeys, but to forget everything else I had ever learned about Mexico from anthropology, archaeology, or history for the purposes of this particular trip.

One day in July we visited the pyramid at Tula, and Leonora asked me to view the site in the following manner. I was to approach the pyramid from afar and walk toward it slowly from a great distance. When I came to the foot of the pyramid, I was to report exactly what I had observed. The optical illusion involved in this experiment was that as one approaches the pyramid, the giant Atlantean figures on the top seem to drop down into the pyramid and disappear underground. During one of our discussions, Leonora informed me that in her opinion this optical illusion might have been intentional, because the pyramid seemed to commemorate a sacred site. She intuited that this site might have once been inhabited by a race of giants or superior beings who, for some reason, had been supplanted, and subsequently disappeared from the face of the earth. References to the land masses of Atlantis and Lemuria arose, and we talked about all the possible esoteric knowledge that these ancient civilizations, now vanished from our world, might once have possessed.

This experience disclosed for me the central thematic core of Leonora Carrington's artistic vision: the vanishing of an ancient world, a superior world—its disappearance into the underground of our history and of our psyche. As an artist, she is interested in developing visionary techniques that can assist us in resurrecting knowledge about that world. Through the expansion of our consciousness, as well as through a vast familiarity with world mythology, legend, and ancient history, we may be able to "see" the past by decoding the glyphs of our present reality.

Her painting alternately titled *The Ancestor* or *The Godmother* (1968), is a coded cryptogram that can be used as a model for understanding her vision of that underground realm. It combines Tibetan, Mayan, and Celtic symbolic references with her own mythic interpretations of the matristic cultures of those lost worlds. In her painting, a female Ancestor in white, a reference to the White Goddess, emerges from the center of a magic circle whose four corners are guarded by lemurs. The lemurs are coded glyphs referring to Lemuria. The Magic Circle is inscribed in a quadrilateral, a mandala of the Earth, corresponding to the central plane of the Buddhist mandala of the double pyramid. The Godmother rises from the central point of the quadrilateral, which, according to *The Tibetan Book of the Dead*, is "the central point of the mandala . . . the center of a lotus" where "we have the identity with the origin of all buddhas and deities of The Tibetan Book of the Dead" (Detlef, 1977, p. 6).

This quadrilateral is also the cosmic quadrangle of the Popol Vuh, which is "determined by the four solstitial points and is divided into four equal parts by the astronomical cross whose arms align with the cardinal points" (Girard, 1979, p. 28). This "quadrangulation of territory" (Girard, 1979 p. 28) corresponds to the quadrangular planes of heaven and earth created by the Mayan divinity. Thus, since the divinity that emerges from the underworld of Carrington's artistic vision is a Goddess, it is clear that, in addition to the Popol Vuh, Tibetan Buddhism, Gnosticism, alchemy, and the Celtic tradition, we must actually concern ourselves with the meaning of the gender of the deity in order to decipher the deepest hermetic meanings occulted within Carrington's art.

What do the traditions of the Maya, the Gnostics, the Tibetans, the Celts, the alchemists, Lemuria, and Atlantis have in common, and how do they relate to our visit to Tula and to the gender of the deity in Leonora Carrington's mythic vision? Leonora Carrington's philosophical quest is to redefine the relationship between life and death in ways that are postulated by all of the ancient traditions of myth, religion, and lore that we have mentioned. For her, to die is to be reborn to a higher state of consciousness, and the task of life is to awaken from a transient state of forgetfulness and somnolence to states of ever-increasing awareness. For the Tibetans, death, as described in the Bardo Thodol is only "a form of life without its earthly veil." For the Mayas, according to the Popol Vuh, we are now in the fourth cycle of creation, and "there are no walls between the living and the dead, nor are walls thought to exist today. The flow between life and death creates a meshing of the two worlds." . . . "Ancestors also influence the world of the living . . . Coming from the grave (on the Day of the Dead) they watch over the house, see and hear everything, and punish those who cause discord or break the moral code" (Nelson, 1974, p. 24).

Gnosticism parallels Tibetan Buddhism, in that it, too, is concerned with the soul's journey toward *gnosis* in the dimensions of cosmic space and time. It is "more particularly "knowledge of the way", namely of the soul's way out of the world, comprising the sacramental and magical preparations for its future ascent . . . Equipped with this *gnosis*, the soul after death travels upwards, leaving behind at each sphere the psychical "vestment" contributed by it" (Jonas, 1958, p. 45). In Gnosticism, moreover, a fundamental dualism between God and man is postulated in terms that characterize "true" life as "alien," as originating in the "beyond." "All relations of man's terrestrial existence are "in this world," "of this world," which is seen in contrast to "the other world," the habitation of "Life" (Jonas, 1958, p. 51). The concepts of the "alien" and the "beyond" are fundamental to Carrington's notion of the origin of the beings who first populated the earth and then disappeared underground. The study of Gnosticism is deeply significant to her, because it speaks of the release of the soul from the prison of this life. Its ascent toward God is similar to the path of the soul in the Bardo in Tibetan Buddhism.

Carrington's cosmic vision, like Gnosticism, the Mayan cosmic creation myth, and Tibetan Buddhism, envisages death as another realm of living. She views the past, present, and future, not as discrete, compartmentalized segments of time ending with individual death, but as parts of an ongoing stream of Maya, Karma, cycles of history, cycles of release and evolution, creation and reincarnation through which, what we call the "living and the dead," flow in different states of incarnation such as those described in the Bardo Thodol.

In Leonora Carrington's journey from suffering to liberation, which parallels the Tibetan path expounded by the Bardo Thodol, woman's suffering is enacted within the patriarchal dimension of human history, and the path of liberation marks the progress from a vision exclusively rooted in this world and the patriarchal order, toward a vision of the worlds before and beyond the present, which are hidden from but coexistent with the "Now," and which are, for her, worlds of goddess or matristic visions. This is also the path of liberation for men in her vision; a return to a recognition of the Great Mother Goddess as the supreme Creatress of all life in the universe.

In order to read Leonora Carrington's paintings correctly, one must not only be grounded in the mythic and historical traditions that inform her symbolism, but one must also take into account the forms of disclosure and expression employed in the art of those bodies of work that inspire her, such as the Mayan codices, the Tibetan tankas, the ancient scrolls and papyri, and the lunar calendars, which once marked the cycles of time and civilization, as well as the alchemical tractates of spiritual transformation—all spatio-temporal symbolic languages that speak of the path toward liberation and the rebirth of the spirit. In Carrington's personal vision this path toward liberation is marked by a return to the Goddess, either via a return to the actual mythic sources of ancient history, or via a conscious reversal of symbols from male to female in order to produce a transformed vision of gender roles.

Her paintings, like the codices and tankas, show the coexistence and intermingling of the many states of being in one vast space-time continuum, as well as the sacred or magical geometries of the earth and of the previous and future worlds in symbolic terms.

All of these many esoteric and occult traditions share a belief that the structures and symbol systems referring to the underworld or previous worlds of past eras are accessible to human consciousness in the present. However, it is specifically as a surrealist artist, and because of her interest in the dream state and in other altered states of consciousness, that Leonora Carrington's contemporary work relates to these ancient traditions. In the Tibetan and Gnostic systems, *gnosis,* or inner illumination on the path toward liberation takes place in an altered state, perhaps akin to the dream, a state which is closer to the spirit world. Yet, in all of these traditions conventional wakefulness is viewed as an illusion, a sleep from which one must awaken to the true knowledge of the spirit self and of the other worlds. Surrealism, too, posits states apart from full wakefulness as those that reveal the truer reality, surreality.

Carrington's art is a modern woman's codex for this awakening. It speaks of past ages, of cycles of matriarchy and patriarchy, and of lost continents that once possessed matristic cultures. Through a meditation upon her work, the viewer is induced into a new formulation of both reality and identity, of space, time, self, and cosmic history. We shall observe this process in several specific techniques of her hermeticism after a general presentation of how to "read" or "see" a Leonora Carrington painting.

It is important to understand the meaning of Nahualism in order to examine the hermetic intersubjective exchanges that pose problems for the ordinary viewer of Leonora Carrington's art. In many of her paintings communication between particular individuals and among groups of individuals focuses on an inhabitual advance or gesture, or on a dialogue between animals and humans or animal-human hybrids and humans. The baffling communication between beings of different natures can be explained by a reference to the Mayan belief in the Nahual. Carrington's understanding of Nahualism, and its reinterpretation within her own mythic vision can assist us in deciphering her paintings. "Nahualism embodies the belief that there exists between the person and the Nahual (animal or vegetable), a fully determined, intimate relationship that begins and ends with the life of the person" (Girard, 1979, p. 173). People are thought to have a soul that resides in their body and one that resides in an animal or a plant. Their life shares a common destiny with their animal or plant Nahual, so that if the animal's life is endangered, theirs is as well. This belief in Nahualism connects humans to nature in very immediate and deep ways.

The painting *Bird Seizes Jewel* (1969) links the Tibetan tradition to the Gnostic and the Mayan traditions in a coded pictograph about the reclamation of the essence of enlightenment and liberation by women for both women and men. The jewel refers to the Tibetan Buddhist trinity composed of "Three Jewels," Buddha, Dharma, and Sangha, or the Guru, the Teachings, and the Community of Disciples (Detlef, 1977, pp. 55–56). Here the bird-woman or Bird-Goddess leads the patriarchal Rabbis (their symbolism reappears in *Rarvarok* and *The Naked Truth*), and enlightened, as shown by the aureole above her head, she seizes the Jewel from the guru in the concrete structure. She has thus taken back the wisdom of enlightenment for humankind. In Gnosticism the serpent is the symbol of *gnosis* on Earth, and, according to Hans Jonas, represents redemption. He says that the serpent "came . . . to represent the 'pneumatic' principle . . . and thus could become a 'symbol of the powers of redemption . . .' " (Jonas, 1958, p. 93). However we read it, the white serpent (white for the White Goddess of her Celtic tradition) steals the crucified and bleeding fish from the black-horned ram (animals representing patriarchal religion and the patriarchal takeover of matriarchal symbolism, respectively) while the female Bird-Goddess seizes the jewel of enlightenment from the guru in the tower of concrete. Through a cross-cultural Nahualism, an identity is posited by the artist between the Bird-Goddess and the Serpent (both possessing the same soul).

As they both achieve redemption and enlightenment through their Nahual-identification, so too, by extension, do the creator of the painting and the viewer, who are also implicated in the dynamics of Nahualism. Thus, the hermeticism of cryptic paintings such as this one can be understood through a knowledge of the Mayan beliefs as they commingle with Carrington's interests in many other mythico-religious systems of thought.

Humans and animals intermingle ideally only in the underworld (*Pomps of the Subsoil*, 1947) where the Goddess, from whose brain a Tree of Life evolves, presides over the birth of the Tree of Life from the Cosmic Egg or, on an analogical level, the birth of life from woman. In two pictoral parodies of Manet's *Picnic on the Grass*, *Pomps of the Subsoil* (1947) and *Pastorale* (1950), we see how Carrington's vision contrasts with that of Manet for whom the nude women, painters' models, were linked to nature, while the clothed men, creators of culture, represented the power of patriarchal creation. Here, on the contrary, there is a "participation mystique" between humans and animals, between men and women, for the pastoral setting comprises a philosophical underpinning of Nahualism, where the concept of the animal soul that shares a common destiny with the human seems natural.

Leonora Carrington's interest in alchemy is often linked to the culinary arts in her painting through the concept of chemistry. The chemistry involved in the act of painting is a mode of culinary alchemy in its spiritualization of matter, creating the painting as a kind of surrealist food for thought. Digestion is also a chemical process. The connection between culinary alchemy and the matriarchal/patriarchal dichotomy that we have been presenting is deeply linked to the Popol Vuh in more specific ways. During the Third Age of Creation the Bean Goddess prevailed, and it was with the advent of the Fourth Age, the present age, that the Corn God became the central deity of Creation in Mayan mythic history. Thus, in an expanded sense, since we are what we eat, both literally and figuratively, a change in food can imply a change in deity.

Leonora Carrington discusses the ancient belief in the eating of the Gods in her own commentary to her retrospective at the Center for Inter-American Relations in New York in 1975.

Leonora Carrington: The Naked Truth (1962)

"The cabbage is a rose, the Blue Rose, the Alchemical Rose, the Blue Deer (Peyote) and the eating of the God is ancient knowledge, but only recently known to 'civilized occidental' Humans who have experienced many phenomena, and have recently written many books that give accounts of the changing worlds which these people have seen when they ate these plants" (Carrington, 1976, p. 23).

Carrington also makes the analogy between eating and aesthetics. "Writing and Painting are alike in that both arts—music as well—come out of the fingers and into some receptive artifact. The result, of course, is read, heard or seen through the receptive organs of those who receive the art and are supposed to 'Be' what all these different persons perceive differently" (Carrington, 1976, p. 23).

The painting that best illustrates the ways in which identity is reconstructed through the alchemy of cooking is *Grandmother Moorehead's Aromatic Kitchen* (1975). By deciphering the painting and understanding the references to alchemy and witchcraft embedded in the image of the cauldron, which is also the alchemical oven, the viewer has symbolically (through the postulation of Nahualism) "eaten" of the Goddess, as do those beings in the underworld who are preparing the mythic meal. In other words, art is a magical food that we ingest through the eyes, but which brings a subtle chemistry to our beings in a way that is similar to what we experience when we eat. Art transforms us and makes us into what we see in the same way that food transforms us into what we eat.

Such a meal is the focus of attention in the painting *Sidhé: The White People of Dana Tnatha de Danann* (1954), where the luminous beings of the lost world co-mingle with animals as they do in *Lepidopterus* (1969), in which the Black Swans from the song of the ancient Bards "I am the Black Swan, Queen of them all," are being fed red food, recalling red ochre and blood, a kind of food of resurrection for the Goddess. The paintings become in an extended sense, the viewer's food of resurrection, offerings that catalyze an alchemy of vision.

In Leonora Carrington's work the Alchemy of Identity takes place either via the alchemy of cooking or via the purificatory alchemy of the Alchemical Bath.

Cornelia and Cornelius (1973) expresses pictorially how, when patriarchal alchemy is reversed, the matristic Creation myth is revealed. Here, Sulphur and Mercury, Male and Female, Sun and Moon, are immersed in the alchemical bath by the blue figure, the Alchemist, aided by two mythico-legendary beings. Curiously, when the painting is turned upside-down, a change of vision and a change of gods occurs. The shadow selves and otherworldly counterparts of the male and female are, in the reversed painting, holding a vessel decorated with the spiral serpent and the Tree of Life. The serpent as the Mayan Divine Nahual, is also linked to the serpent of Kundalini Yoga upon which Carrington's women's liberation poster, *Mujeres Consciencia*, is based. Its iconography curiously parallels this one, reminding us that for the Gnostics, the Serpent meant *gnosis* on Earth. Thus, a reinterpretation of the Garden of Eden myth from Carrington's perspective would bestow a positive identity upon the serpent, and would envisage the new Eve returning the apple to the old Eve (Mujeres Consciencia) of the patriarchal myth, and rising, parallel to the Kundalini energy that rises to the Third Eye of illuminating as a new female alchemy of vision. Indeed, to *eat* the apple would mean to ingest the patriarchal version of sin. To return the apple, *not to eat it*, marks the refusal of the male God and of patriarchal religion.

The Garden of Eden seems to be implied as well in the painting *The Queen of the Mandrills* (1959). The mandrill, so like the lemur, suggests once more the lost world of the Goddess. Here she is blazing in the Tree of Life, apprehended by the Black God. She is associated with the pomegranate (usually linked to the Goddess), not with the apple, and she represents the Goddess vision. To eat of the true fruit of the Tree of Life, the pomegranate, could mean the restoration of matristic myth and wisdom. To refuse the apple is to reject patriarchy, but to eat of the pomegranate would mean ingesting and embodying the wisdom of the matristic vision.

Leonora Carrington: Sidhe The White People of Dana Tnathe de Danann (1954)

Finally, Carrington talks about indigestion as a result of *not* turning the world upside-down. "There are so many questions and so much Dogmaturd to clear aside before anything makes sense, and we are on the point of destroying the earth before we know anything at all. Perhaps a great virtue, curiosity can only be satisfied if the millennia of accumulated false data are turned upside-down, which means turning oneself inside out, and to begin by despising no thing, ignoring no thing . . . and make some interior space for digestive purposes. Our machine-mentation still reacts to colossal absurdities with violence, pleasure, pain . . . automatically, such as: I am, I am, I am, (anything from an archbishop to a disregarded boot). But is this so? Am I? Indigestion is imminent" (Carrington, 1976, p. 24). In this way, eating or not eating can become an act of mythic and political importance.

Carrington's so-called confusion of human and animal identities is actually the creation of a multilayered glyph about the presence of the Goddess Creatress in a multiplicity of mythic systems. *Ogdoas* (1964), which has a female nun with an animal face, is named for the Mother in Gnosticism known as the Ogdoad (Jonas, 1958, p. 191). Here she carries a water jar, which links her with the Mayan Water Goddess, the Lunar Deity Ixmucané of the Popol Vuh. Raphael Girard connects "the face of her water jar" with the Moon Goddess, for the "Indian conceives the moon as a gigantic pitcher that pours water from the sky. . . . In the remote past as well as the present day those vessels of globular form designed to carry water are used exclusively by women in accordance with the practice begun by Ixmucane" (Girard, 1979, p. 167). Here, Ixmucané is the Moon Goddess and the Alchemist. Her identity as Nun can be understood as another symbol for female spirituality.

Finally, part of the strangeness of Carrington's painted universe is that through humor she comments playfully on the seriousness of her own vision. In *Edwardian Hunt Breakfast* (1956) Carrington satirizes the English aristocratic hunting ritual, showing how unaware the hunter was of the presence of the Goddess-nurturer at his ritual breakfast, for she is associated with the food they are about to eat. Two Mexican peasants stand opposite the English hunter. They know about the Nahual principle, and they realize that the hunter's soul is very likely linked to that of one of the animals he is about to kill. The Englishman-hunter is holding a blue egg (of alchemy and women), and the meal includes a cabbage (an alchemical rose). Thus, the meal prepared by the Goddess is a form of witchcraft that will probably prevent the hunter from killing any of the animals that are sacred to her in the forest. The humorous technique specific to Carrington's vision is that she shares with the viewer an invisible world that is not seen by the hunter. Only the viewer knows that the Goddess, the nurturer, has performed a kind of culinary alchemy upon the hunter, and that she is presiding over the hunt.

In view of the complexity of Carrington's vision, her mural-sized painting *El Mundo Mágico de los Mayas,* located in the National Museum of Anthropology in Mexico City, takes on a special meaning, for, indeed, the Indians of Chiapas are the living descendants of the Maya, and while they have been Christianized by the missionaries, their Christianity is merely grafted onto their deeper Mayan magico-religious cosmic vision. Basing her interpretation of the Mayan gods on figures from the Popol Vuh, Carrington has depicted Tepeu-Gucumatz, the blue-green feathered serpent-bird ancestor. "In this darkness the Creators waited, the Maker, Tepeu-Gucumatz, the Forefathers. They were there in this emptiness, hidden under green and blue feathers, alone and surrounded with light" (*Popol Vuh,* p. 33). The serpent is the divine Nahual and totem of the Chorti Maya, the People of the Serpent. The large cross of the Christ image is also a Mayan God, and in a previous version of the painting was a Chacmool, making it clear that it was the Mayan God that was sacrificed during colonization. Even such simple Christian ceremonies as the healing of the sick are presided over by deities of the ancient Mayan Creation myth. The painting also has an underworld, the entry to which, Andrés Medina tells us, is marked on earth by caves with crosses on them. It is through the caves that man makes contact with the gods. "In almost all pueblos there exist narratives that tell about how different men accidentally entered into this underworld and could observe the life of the Gods that reside there" (Medina, 1964, p. 26).

Thus, Carrington's mural painting, *El Mundo Mágico de los Mayas,* is a kind of surrealist codex. But, whereas the Mayan codices and the Popol Vuh relate the creation-destruction cycles of the four ages of historico-mythic time, Carrington's codex relates the process of awakening, the journey from a vision of life in this incarnation, as depicted in the realistic daily life and ceremonials of the Indians, to an evolved consciousness of the visions of deities perceived in other states of awareness corresponding to the Tibetan Bardo states or to the Mayan realm of the cosmogonic mythic ancestors.

Carrington's mural tells us that awakening is the ability to look at life in this dimension and to see its most ancient sources and its furthermost possibilities of becoming. It also tells us that the races which have disappeared are not entirely gone. If we look carefully among the colonized cultures of today, we will find the descendants of the people who once worshipped the Bean Goddess. The mythic underground/the other world, is also a metaphor for the cultural stratification of the human psyche. Just as the Maya believed that their ancestors intermingled with them in their daily lives, Carrington's study of the people of Chiapas, descendants of the Maya, tells us that the lost realms are coexistent with our own, and through an initiation into the practices of meditation and visualization, they can be recovered.

The recovery of knowledge from the ancient past and the potential future, is, in Carrington's work, the role of the Crone.

The Hearing Trumpet, which is discussed again in yet another context in the last chapter, unites elements from the fairy tale and the detective story in a Grail quest novel. The protagonist, a 92-year-old woman named Marion (for the ancient pagan Sea-Goddess, Marian, and recalling Mary and Mary Magdalen), is banished by her relatives to a Gurdjieff-style retirement community, where, through telepathy and mystical visions, she learns of her own true identity and her many karmic reincarnations. This matristic identity is equivalent to personal knowledge of her past lives and their identification with truths related in the Gnostic gospels.

The kind of *gnosis* advocated by Gnosticism, the personal intuitive experience of self-knowledge and knowledge of the true nature of the divinity, is described by Elaine Pagels in *The Gnostic Gospels* (1979). It is the kind of experience through which Marion learns about her past lives as epiphanies of the Great Mother in the form of a bee, an abbess, and a practitioner of witchcraft. It is through extrasensory perception, of which the Hearing Trumpet is the symbol (representing a kind of horn that becomes an auditory faculty for messages from other dimensions and a metaphor of the horn associated with the magical powers of the Grail, for the horned god Cernunnos in Celtic mythology was the possessor of the magical cauldron of the Tuatha de Danaan) that she learns of her ancient Goddess heritage. The horn is also a reference to the horns of the Moon and of Moon Goddesses in general.

Marion's first contact with her goddess-nature and lineage comes through a magical relationship with the portrait of an abbess hanging in Lightsome Hall, her retirement community. The portrait winks at her, and we are informed that this abbess was an initiate of the Goddess and a healer who dealt in witchcraft. Carrington's heroine plunges into an adventure through time and space and across the centuries, and discovers the existence of a scroll related to the life of the Goddess which reads: "At the beginning the two spirits which are known as Twins are the one Female and the other Male. They established at the beginning Life, the Pneuma, and the Holy Cup to hold the Pneuma. And when these two Spirits Met such was the manner of birth of the Winged One of the Feathered Hermaphrodite, Sephira. For since then the Cup has not rendered fruit. The sterile jailors of the cup having banished Her from her Most Rightful Realm in the Caverns of Her Most Secret Mysteries. (Signed) Epona, Barbarus, Hekate" (Carrington, 1977, p. 116).

In this scroll Carrington links the Celtic White Horse Goddess, Epona, to her own creation, Barbarus, the masculinized name of "the Goddess Barbara, worshipped as the life-giver or womb" (Carrington, 1977, p. 112), and to Hecate, the Greek Goddess associated with witchcraft, representing the Crone aspect of the Triple Goddess. Carrington also sets forth in her scroll a reference to the Gnostic papyri found at Nag'Hammadi, about whose discovery she had been aware. According to Elaine Pagels, these texts "speak of God as a dyad who embraces both masculine and feminine elements. One group of Gnostic sources claims to have received a secret tradition from Jesus through James and through Mary Magdalene. Members of this group prayed to both the divine Father and Mother" (Pagels, 1979, p. 58).

Carrington's reference to the Sephira relates the ancient Goddess tradition to the "Kabbalistic tendency to discern a male and female element in the deity, as related in the Zohar." (Patai, 1967, p. 138). Raphael Patai in *The Hebrew Goddess* quotes Moses Cordovero (1522–1570), the Safed Kabbalist, who comments on the Sephirot called Crown as follows: "The Crown itself is comprised of Male and Female, for one part of it is Male, the other Female. . . . The view that the deity is androgynous or hermaphroditic, in nature, if not in form, must have existed several centuries prior to its first explicit mention" (Patai, 1967, pp. 138, 139). What Carrington has accomplished is the telescoping of a fabulous history of the Goddess's primordial existence and her subsequent absorption and eventual masculinization throughout the history of patriarchal religions. But Her ultimate existence is revealed to women through *gnosis*, personal religious visions and experiences, as well as through the deciphering and decoding of patriarchal mythic and religious symbolism.

For example, the feathered hermaphrodite, Sephira, unites the kabbalistic male-female dyad with an image suggestive of the Mexican feathered serpent, Quetzalcoatl, suggesting that if we look further into the feathered gods, we might discover the Snake Goddess, or an even more original female image of divinity hidden behind the masculine image of God.

The women of Lightsome Hall meet in a circle and perform a ceremony that raises the power of the Goddess, chanting: "Belzi Ra Ha-Ha Hecate Come/Descend on us to the sound of my drum" (Carrington, 1977, p. 143). As they chant together to evoke the Queen Bee, a cloud forms itself into "an enormous bumble bee as big as a sheep. She wore a tall iron crown studded with rock crystals, the stars of the Underworld. All this may have been a collective hallucination although nobody has yet explained to me what a collective hallucination actually means. . . . As she faced me I was thrilled to notice a sudden strange resemblance to the Abbess. At that moment she closed one eye, as big as a tea cup, in a prodigious wink" (Carrington, 1977, p. 143).

Marija Gimbutas discusses the epiphany of the Great Goddess in the form of a bee in her archaeological study *Goddesses and Gods of Old Europe: Myths and Cult Images 6500–3500 B.C.* She quotes Porphyry quoting Ransom informing us that "the ancients gave the name of Melissae (bees) to the priestesses of Demeter who were initiates of the chthonian goddess. . . . From this passage we learn that Artemis is a bee, Melissa, and that both she and the bull belong to the Moon. . . . We also learn that souls are bees and that Melissa draws souls down to be born. . . . Many gold rings of Minoan workmanship from Crete and Greece portray the bee-headed goddess or the same goddess holding bulls' horns above her head" (Gimbutas, 1982, pp.181, 182). Gimbutas suggests that the bee was chosen as the symbol of regeneration, like the Egyptian scarab, because of its antennae like the horns of the lunar crescent and of the Moon Goddess.

Marion with her hearing trumpet is a contemporary image of the Moon Goddess. She discovers this in an experience of *gnosis*, a personal revelation of the knowledge of her divine essence and subsequent reincarnations. "Holding the mirror at arm's length I seemed to see a three-faced female whose eyes winked alternatively. One of the faces was black,

Leonora Carrington: Kron Flower (1986)

one red, one white, and they belonged to the Abbess, the Queen Bee, and myself'' (Carrington, 1977, p. 169). The colors black, white, and red, represent stages in the process of alchemical transformation of brute matter into gold, the final stage of which is symbolized by the color red. This triple-faced Goddess is the Triple Goddess, whose three aspects, Virgin, Mother, and Crone, are here represented by the Abbess, the Queen Bee, and Marion. Accompanied by a wolf-headed woman, Anubeth, the High Queen of the Wolves, and a kind of Egyptian Goddess figure, Marion restores the Holy Cup to the Goddess as swarms of bees gather over the spot and drop honey like manna while carrying off the Holy Grail to a secret part of the cavern.

As the tale ends, Marion and her friend, Carmella, are in Lapland, a land of reputed shamanic powers. Anubeth's werecubs populate the planet, and they "fervently hope that this will be an improvement on humanity, which deliberately renounced the Pneuma of the Goddess" (Carrington, 1977, p. 192).

In this novel of self-discovery and occult and mythic decoding, Carrington metaphorically conveys the true alienation of women from knowledge of their most sacred origin as connected with the loss of the Holy Grail to patriarchy and the concomitant erasure of all traces of a Goddess religion from history. It is, according to her, only through the development of the extrasensory faculties of psychic evolution that women mystics, artists, seers, sybils, and practitioners of the "craft" of the wise, Wicca, can recover this *gnosis* or knowledge of their true spiritual heritage.

Writing her own Gnostic gospel, she is inspired by the suggestion in the gospels of Mark and John naming Mary Magdalen, not Peter, as the first witness to the resurrection (this time it is the resurrection of the Goddess in female consciousness) for she, too, has rewritten the script of patriarchal Christian symbology. Like Gertrude Stein, Carrington has revolutionized women's vision by breaking the patriarchal "mindbindings" that mask their matristic origins. Now that Carrington is in her seventies, her message about the wisdom of the Crone has entered her paintings in a more overt manner.

One of her most recent works, *Kron Flower* (1986) is a homage to the Crone, the Woman of Wisdom, the Elder, whose secret knowledge is that old age is a period of creative reflowering in which, as we have seen in *The Hearing Trumpet*, the great female adventure really begins. Adventures such as those lived by Marion Leatherby, the protagonist, adventures such as the female Grail Quest, which restores the sacred pneuma to the Goddess so that life on earth may reflourish, are symbolized in this painting, by the large red Kron flower, the flowering of the Crone's vital life force (the blood of her art) and of her true beauty in old age. Thus, aging is seen as a process of development, of growth, and of resurrection. This version of resurrection differs from the Christian version, for in the new feminist matristic myth of Resurrection, it is the Old Woman, the Crone, who is resurrected to full creative vitality in this life, not in the hereafter. Nor is there any sacrifice, any death, or betrayal by those of her spiritual community. Rather there is support leading to regeneration in the flesh as well as in the spirit. The resurrected one, however, is an elderly female rather than a young male.

In *Tell the Bees* (1986), crones and bees have a secret affiliation—a secret conspiracy. The Bee is an epiphany of the Goddess, according to Maria Gimbutas's archaeological studies, and the Bee is seen as an epiphany of the Goddess in Carrington's novel. Both crones and bees live in a female-centered universe, and both *Kron Flower* and *Tell the Bees* associate women's wisdom as Elders with their reawakened affinity for all forms of plant and animal life. In old age, crones, bees, flowers, humans, animals, and plants, all communicate with each other, and sense their fundamental gynergic interconnections. Her painting, *The Magdalens,* also connects older wise women to the story of Mary Magdalen as it is retold in *The Gnostic Gospels.* Here Mary Magdalen is restored to her primary role as a disciple of Christ and the first witness of his resurrection.

Leonora Carrington: Eye Witness Bubba and Zaida (1987)

Finally, *Eye Witness* (1986) refers to the female visionary experience, and by extending the metaphor of the Magdalens (the witnesses of the miracle of resurrection) to include the woman artist's creative work, we intuit that *Eye Witness* refers obliquely to the artist herself, as a visionary whose works bear witness to the miracle of resurrection in her own life, to the resurrection of Crone wisdom, as well as to the resurrection of an ancient matristic knowledge in a contemporary feminist matristic visionary form. The woman artist is then both Mary Magdalen, the witness to the resurrection, and also the female Christ, the crucified and resurrected one. By further extension, we also participate in the process of resurrection by immersing ourselves in the energy field of the painting as we are led to the path of resurrection via our role as witness to the rebirth of the woman artist as Wise Woman, Elder, and Crone, and of the reflowering of the Goddess vision, which will restore life on the planet via the magic of art—the art of magic.

In *Bubba/Zaida* (1987), a title meaning Jewish grandparents, Carrington creates a cosmic encounter between the now-aged Patriarch and the Crone. The Crone, a shriveled, wizened flying woman, comes face to face with the grandfather, patriarch, as she soars out of the heavens like a Balinese flying Goddess figure. Her skin is deep red (for the life force), but wrinkled. She carries a black egg, which she extends to the patriarch. He sits on his throne in the sky, but his feet are being washed by the waters of life. However, he seems oblivious to his grounding in the female aquatic matrix. They stare at each other in an eternal gaze. The Crone's black egg can symbolize many things: the black sun of alchemy, the black humor of surrealism, the nigredo which, in alchemy, must be transformed into gold (obviously a new cycle), the void of Buddhist enlightenment, the realm of the Dark Goddess that must be explored, the death of fertility in the Wasteland ruled by the Fisher-King Patriarch, Eco-Amnesia, the ridiculousness of not recognizing that the wisdom of the Crone is not the same as the wisdom of the Virgin and the Mother, and so on. Whatever the many interpretations we may read into the symbol of the Black Egg presented to the Patriarch by the Crone, one thing is clear: He has never really paid attention to the egg or to the Mother; nor does he notice the waters of the Great Mother or the wisdom of the Crone. He simply stares incredulously, and in stupefaction. In the denigration of the powers of both women and nature, the patriarchy has never noticed that, as Leonora Carrington once said to me: "the Earth *is* a heavenly body." Here, woman, too, becomes a heavenly body. Locked forever in a "Star Wars" of the sexes, the systems controlling our knowledge have never let us see the beautiful feathered wings of the Crone that here propel her at a rapid pace across the universe. Nor do we know that she is the Earth, the Grandmother. This Crone is flying; she is birthing a new world from the black egg—perhaps black, because it reverses the symbolism of black and white prevailing under patriarchy that linked white to purity and black to evil. Perhaps it is from this dark egg of the Crone that a new multiracial, multicolored creation will arise.

This Crone, like Mary Daly's angel, is an "Elemental Spirit of the universe whose duration and movement are outside the limitations of tidy time and whose principal activities are knowing and willing; bearer of Archaic knowledge and wisdom" (Daly, 1987, p. 60). For Carrington, it is the Crone, who, through *gnosis* announces "the Second Coming of Women: the new arrival of Archaic Female presence; spiritual awakening beyond christolatry and all patriarchal religions" (Daly, 1987, p. 95).

Although both Stein and Carrington have occulted or coded their knowledge of the Great Mother, it is clear that Stein's use of the *spoken word* as the code, and Carrington's use of *gnosis,* direct revelation, affirm that the Great Mother still lives, even when she is hidden behind patriarchal symbol systems. Her life, that of the Earth, of the cosmic Creatress, and of the woman artist, can be perceived directly without the intervention of patriarchal or Rabbinic hermeneutics.

Women's Feminist-Matristic Renaissance in the Twentieth Century Arts

As we have shown earlier, it was with the advent of the contemporary women's movement in the late 1960s and early 1970s that the necessary synergy between feminist political activism, radical feminist theory, women's studies scholarship, and the creative explorations of women artists and writers was sparked, fueling a renaissance for women in the arts in our century.

As art historical and literary historical data was unearthed about women creators of the past, as feminist cooperative galleries were founded and began to flourish, as alternate feminist presses and publications began to proliferate, and as networks and communities of feminists in the arts sprang into being, the seeds were planted for the flowering of a new feminist culture in which all the arts were to play a central role.

During the course of the decades of the seventies and the eighties feminist studies programs, bookstores, publishing companies, cooperative art galleries, conferences, and the like, all brought to public attention the many diverse issues, themes, controversies, images, and knowledges that contemporary women of various backgrounds (races, classes, ethnicities, sexual preferences, religions, and physical abilities) shared. These multidimensional, multiethnic approaches began to transform the consciousness of men's and women's thinking along the lines of gender and power relations.

In every field and discipline, treatises uncovered buried materials about women written out of public record, lost to history, rejected, discriminated, excised, and oppressed.

Simultaneously, however, a parallel story of women's strengths, accomplishments, triumphs, historically acclaimed talents, innovations, creations, and discoveries was also being uncovered. Countering the history of centuries of patriarchal oppression was the emergence of alternate "herstories"—stories of women's ancient lost powers, stories of women's empowerment. Inspired by feminist studies in archaeology, anthropology, religion, and history, and persuaded that women's status had once been elevated in prepatriarchal, matristic cultures, imaginative women set about reinventing cultures for the contemporary world in which both nature and women would be reverenced once more.

Stimulated greatly as well by Susan Griffin's *Woman and Nature: The Roaring Inside Her* (1978), where it is argued that there is an important parallel to be drawn between the treatment of women and of nature in patriarchal cultures stemming from the philosophical separation of spirit and matter, and the simultaneous degradation of the latter, women artists and writers began to conceive of cultures created by women that would revolutionize our relationship to nature, that would affirm the knowledge that spirit resides in matter.

In the final section of *Woman and Nature,* entitled "Matter, How We Know," Griffin writes: "Because we know ourselves to be made from this earth, and shaped like the earth, by what has gone before . . . we know this earth is made from our bodies. For we see ourselves. And we are nature. We are nature seeing nature. We are nature with a concept of nature. Nature weeping. Nature speaking of nature to nature" (Griffin, 1978, pp. 223, 226).

Griffin links a feminist cultural vision to an ecological vision of interconnectedness. It is Griffin's view of women seeing themselves as nature speaking to nature, and of nature weeping that is often portrayed in the art by feminist matristic artists.

Thus, the ecofeminist Goddess symbol today, as reclaimed by a diversity of feminist matristic writers and artists, for whom Susan Griffin speaks in her theoretical writings, sets itself in direct opposition to a patriarchal vision, and represents the sacredness of woman *and* nature, the linking of spirit *to* matter, a reclamation of the values represented by ancient prepatriarchal cultures, and a new-found reverence for the Earth and its energies, as well as for women and their contemporary cultural creations.

The Great Goddess image, as it is reclaimed today, then, reconciles two previously contradictory concepts—nature and culture. Feminist matristic cultures, rather than being separate from nature, will now be understood to be a part of nature, just as honoring nature will now be understood to play an important role in women's new feminist matristic cultures. It is the creation of these new cultures through art—their themes, motifs, symbols, iconography, myths, forms, and styles—that now concerns us.

However, before we embark on further discussion of the feminist matristic renaissance in women's arts, let us return to the two theoretical stumbling blocks that have challenged this movement from the beginning. These are

1. Its misidentification as a form of essentialism.
2. The misinterpretation of its strategies as deriving from an idealist or naively realist assumption about the relationship between image and meaning-production.

The theoretical arguments that are most persuasive in countering the critiques of essentialism and idealist or naïve realism were made by Angela Partington in her article "Feminist Art and Avant-Gardism" (1987), in which she refuted the criticism of what have been called the "celebratory strategies" of feminist art. It had been claimed that images such as those of Goddesses posit a specifically "feminine" essence, based on biology, and that they also constitute celebratory, heroic images of womanhood, which other women would have to look up to. This alone raised questions as to *which* women should be "heroinized" or celebrated and whether images of vaginal iconography (such as those celebrated in Judy Chicago's *Dinner Party*), are defining an essentialist feminine, and, if so, whether this is a biologically determined essence.

Partington points out that "feminist criticism . . . constructs feminist readings" (1987, p. 230). She reminded us that, rather than defining an "essential feminine," these kinds of images "demonstrate that there is such a thing as 'feminine'[1] knowledge, a specifically 'feminine'[1] experience of the world, and that therefore culture is not un-gendered" (p. 233).

Additionally, the critique of these celebratory strategies of women's achievements, powers, skills, and so forth, had maintained that they "obscure important differences" (Partington, 1987, p. 236) in women by making such generalizations.

According to Partington, there is a need to generalize at a symbolic level, and she interprets these images as liberatory, because she understands them to emphasize "the potential for the construction of symbols for women's knowledge of their own oppression" (1987, p. 235).

In other words, the process of cultural creation, while it has produced symbols that may overgeneralize, inflate, conflate, or otherwise obscure differences, also permits us to see

---

[1]Quote marks inserted by G. Orenstein.

similarities and to make images of women's diverse strengths and powers an integral part of a new shared description of reality. Incorporating symbols from ancient Neolithic and Paleolithic cultures such as the labyrs, the labyrinth, the egg, the serpent, the spiral, and so forth, into the new feminist matristic iconography is actually a way to reverse Essentialism. Indeed, it reminds us that our patriarchal historical context is far too narrow, and it recontextualizes the lives of women within an expanded historical framework including millennia in which their connection to nature was not demeaned, but rather honored.

Thus, Partington sees these same images, whether newly created or reclaimed from an ancient past, as creating new cultures, as fostering solidarity, and as forging new bonds among women. Partington writes convincingly that "Above all, celebratory strategies aspire to provide a means of identification between women, in a society where isolation and fear divide and control women, whose knowledges are systematically represented as neuroses, aberrations, fantasies etc. within the discourses of patriarchal culture" (1987, p. 233). Finally, she concludes that it is not necessary to equate heroinization with hierarchization.

The arguments that these celebratory or gender-reversed images, whether overgeneralized or not, actually signify the fact that knowledges are gender-specific, and that this point alone is creative of feminist solidarity and bonding on a global scale (without excluding an awareness of the diversity that exists among women), actually contributes to the establishment of a new symbolic language—an iconography that may, eventually, generate an appropriate definition of the conept of "the feminine" for use within a feminist matristic context, a definition that some women feel implies "subversively feminine."[2]

In "An Open Letter to Thomas McEvilley" (1989), New York artist, Mary Beth Edelson, accuses critic Thomas McEvilley of perpetuating the false notion of Goddess art as being essentialist by using the construct of "nature/culture," and, (in a lecture that she attended at the Artemisia Gallery in Chicago), of presenting "feminist work as a hierarchical progression from nature to culture, setting one against the other" (Edelson, 1989, p. 34). She continues to elucidate the patriarchally constructed confusion about this issue saying "you presented what you called "Goddess Art" of the seventies as nature, and deconstructionist art of the eighties as culture" (p. 34). "This construct", she adds, "also advances the idea that women artists working with nature have accepted their bodies and intuition at the expense of their cognitive minds, and that deconstructionist artists have accepted their intellects at the expense of their sensual bodies" (p. 35). Edelson reminds us that "patriarchy profits from the nature/culture construct because the dichotomy works to keep in place treatment of the sexes as they have been historically polarized with a reimposition of rigid notions of male and female" (p. 35).

Borrowing the symbols of ancient goddess-connected religions from the Neolithic through the Egyptian, Cretan, Greek, Indian, and Amerindian cultures, the artists and writers of this feminist matristic tendency are creating clusters of symbols that are woven into the fabric of their art much as the symbols of birds, crows, seagulls, or fountains, glaciers and mirrors were woven into the fabric of the poetry of the nineteenth-century symbolists, because they represented a communal vision of the desolation of the poet's soul and the desire for flight to the absolute. As Anna Balakian suggested (*The Symbolist Movement*, 1967) in her study of the symbolist movement, these images constitute a symbolist alphabet. In a certain sense, we may say that goddess-related symbols function today in a similar manner, for they relate to each other in terms of a unified, communal, cosmic vision, and create a resonant energy field. What are the symbols connected with the ancient Goddess religion that reappear in a contemporary context energizing the text with mythic networks of associations? Marija Gimbutas has outlined those dating from Old Europe (7000–25000 B.C.E.). The Snake motif, the Primordial Egg, the Bird Goddess, the Snake Goddess, the Corpulent Goddess, the Moon Goddess, the Pig, the Bee, the Butterfly, and so forth, and additionally, caves, labyrinths,

---

[2]This idea was suggested to me by Susan Hawthorne of Australia.

seeds, weaving, webs, pottery, vessels, horns (the horns of the Moon), the Cow, the Double-Ax (Labrys), earth-mounds, mountains, (Gimbutas, 1982) Demeter, Persephone (the mother-daughter mythologem), Diana-Artemis-Hecate, Goddess temples, and the positive image of the Witch as Healer and Wise Woman all form a part of this new symbolist alphabet. These symbols fall basically into two categories:

1. Natural symbols referring to the Earth and all species of life upon the planet (plant, animal, human, mineral, cosmic), fertility, and human sexuality.
2. Symbols of women's cultural creations: weaving, cooking, pottery, agriculture, healing, art and the like.

Because these symbols translate an animistic vision that perceives the existence of a vital life force inherent in all matter, the "vitalist" symbol is linked to a more highly energized form of aesthetic expression in order to incorporate the gestural, oral, and ritual dynamics of a language that has nonverbal components indicating ceremony, song, and movement, Both the vitalist symbol and the dynamic form incite active participation in a communal transformatory vision that seeks to restore an image of matter as the living incarnation of spirit, of the body as a powerful energy center by which the new mythos is translated into actuality.

The formal expressionistic elements that unite many of the works in our study are their tendency toward oral or ritual-dynamic forms: the song, the chant, the prayer, the spell, the call, the cry, the ritual, the ceremony, rather than more static or silent forms of expression. These energetic and often overflowing forms frequently suggest an accompanying performance—either dancing and drumming, dancing and whirling, or gesture of prayer, lamentation or celebration. Stampedes, sabbaths, and clan gatherings, acts of healing and of spirit travel across the boundaries of time and space also characterize many feminist matristic creations. Occasionally processions, pilgrimages, spectacles, exorcisms, séances, and mudras are suggested, and frequently the striking of musical instruments and a richly orchestrated sound accompaniment, verging on the implications of actual staging, enactment or dramatic performance, takes place.

I am suggesting that a new feminist matristic symbolic alphabet and dynamic is evolving. The new feminist matristic symbol reclaims a mythic motif associated with the mythos of an ancient Goddess religion and creates a correspondence between that image and present-day reality, thus translating its powers into terms of the contemporary world. It functions to wrench consciousness out of a transcendent divine or mythic plane divorced from nature, and to return it to a contemplation of the real lives of women (and men) living on our planet today. It reminds us that the here and now is the actual, living embodiment of spirituality, that we are living out the myths on a daily basis (creation, rebirth, etc.), and that we are in the process of rewriting the script of all of them, and thereby of changing the world. I also suggest that this new feminist matristic symbolism incorporates the evocatory function of those symbols, while augmenting that function in several ways.

In his translator's preface to R.A. Schwaller de Lubicz's *Symbol and the Symbolic: Egypt, Science and the Evolution of Consciousness* (1978), Robert Lawlor suggests a way to understand Egyptian symbolism that could apply to feminist matristic symbols. "A method of viewing is required comparable to our hearing faculty: one must learn *to listen to the symbolic image*, allowing it to enter and pervade one's consciousness as would a musical tone which directly resonated with the inner being unimpeded by the surface mentality. In this moment of inner identity between the intellect and the aspect of the tangible world evoked by the symbol, we have the opportunity to live this knowledge" (de Lubicz, 1978, p. 10).

As we shall discover, this specific aspect of the Egyptian hieratic symbol, its vibrational aspect, is relevant to the art under discussion here, where Goddess images such as Wolf-Woman, Plant-Mother, Cow-Mother, River-Mother, and Fish-Mother are prevalent. In this regard de Lubicz explains that "In civilizations such as Ancient Egypt, what we in our present presumptuousness call 'primitive animal worship' was not a worship of the animal, itself, but a consecration made to the vital function which any animal particularly incarnates. It was not, in reality a worship; it was a meditation used to support and clarify an essential function of nature . . ." (de Lubicz, 1978, p. 13). He gives as an illustration of this concept the example of the jackal, an animal who tears the flesh of its prey to pieces, as represented in the jackal-headed god, the symbol for the physical process of digestion. He proposes these symbols as "vital symbols," dynamic not static, and representative of the simultaneity of opposites and the coexistence of mutually contradictory images. Rather than an analytic, dualistic approach to reality, the Egyptian hieroglyph could symbolize both the whole (i.e., the bouquet) and the individual entity (i.e., the flower) simultaneously. Analogously, the feminist matristic use of symbols derived from an ancient goddess-centered mythos, can also come to symbolize heretofore contradictory notions by proposing a meditation upon the functions represented by the elements of which the symbol is composed. Contradictory aspects such as nonhuman nature vs. human nature (defined patriarchally) can now be reconciled feminist matristically in images such as the Loba (Wolf-Woman of di Prima, Anubeth of Carrington); vegetable vs. human can now be reconciled ecologically in the image of Plant Mother, (Marchessault); animal vs. human in Spider Woman (Henes); and spirit vs. matter can now be reconciled shamanically in the image of Thought Woman (Allen). All of these symbols propose a meditation and consecration in the sense suggested by de Lubicz. In certain cases these meditations will be upon altogether different aspects of the symbol than those currently associated with it. For example, in the image of the Loba, the Wolf-Woman, di Prima suggests a meditation on the aspect of the Wolf as protectress rather than as hunter. In Rachel Rosenthal's meditation on the Planet as Crone, the aspect of the Wise Woman is stressed rather than that of the decaying, weak old woman.

As seers in touch with the deeper levels of the subconscious, artists have always been the mediums who were most receptive to those new visionary images that foretell the creation of new mythic structures, and prefigure the transformation of culture. Today a revolutionary movement in women's art is being born. The symbol of the Great Goddess is re-emerging, and Her images, energies, motifs, and artifacts are being re-evoked in rituals and art rites, which serve as sacred ceremonies for social and spiritual transformation.

In reinterpreting the meaning of the symbol of the Great Goddess for women today, through an analysis of the works and pieces now being created and performed, we are led to conclude that Goddess consciousness functions to exorcize the mind-body split that prevailed under the dominance of patriarchy and to bring about a healing in which body knowledge and earth knowledge are reaffirmed as faculties of intelligence, and spirit is recognized as a sacred property of matter upon which all natural and spiritual life depends.

Through the public and private rituals and performances of Mary Beth Edelson, Kyra, Faith Wilding, Vijali, Christine Oatman, Anna Homler, Susan Schwalb, Betsy Damon, Rachel Giladi, Suzanne Benton, Ana Mendieta, Marcia Hewitt, Donna Henes, Miriam Sharon, Rachel Rosenthal, Jane Ellen Gilmore, Fern Shaffer, Cheri Gaulke, Barbara Smith, Jean Edelstein, Elizabeth Erikson, Mierle Laderman Ukeles, Helen Aylon, and so on, as well as via other works by Judy Chicago, Ursula Kavanagh, Donna Byars, Jovette Marchessault, Nancy Azara, Buffie Johnson, Asungi, Sasha McInnes, Ann McCoy, Mayumi Oda, Marlene Mountain, Mimi Lobell, Christinna Biaggi, Monica Sjöö, Ghila Hirsch, Beth Ames Swartz, Ruth Weisberg, Edith Altman, Sandra Menefee Taylor, Bruria, Helen Klebesdedl, Maria Mazzara, Meg Easling, and others, the female body is being resacralized and the Earth is being resanctified in an initiatory rite of passage toward an ecstatic rebirth from the Earth Mother into an era in which women will reawaken to a holistic psycho-physical perception of the sacred spirit alive in the world as a revolutionary form of their feminist matristic evolution. Where once the Great Goddess was associated with the fertility and birth mysteries, today She has come to symbolize the re-emergence of womankind from the prepatriarchal cycle where Her powers were once revered, through the dark night of Her exile under patriarchal domination, into a new cultural cycle of female creation, which will come about as a result of the changes in consciousness and society that knowledge of the traditional powers associated with the Great Goddess evokes. Such knowledge is now being gathered by feminist matristic artists, writers, and researchers through expeditions to caves, mounds, sanctuaries, shrines, and megalithic sites where the Goddess was once worshipped, and where the ancient rituals are now being reenacted so that the primordial experience of Goddess energy and a contemporary feminist matristic vision may be recovered. In the reclamation of this lost ancestral heritage, women artists are catalyzing ecstatic-regenerative images of women that revive physical and spiritual centers of feeling, perception, intuition, magical knowledge, vision, and prophecy, that have lain dormant under centuries of repression.

A feminist matristic art often obliterates the many dichotomies between the image and the act through the art rite. It reunites the body and the spirit, the visualization and the incarnation via the ceremonial and the performance. Through these rituals the symbol of the Mother Goddess is perceived as the analogical explanation of the Great Mystery of Creation, both biological and cultural.

The celebration of the Great Goddess is a fundamental rejoicing in being as a verb, as a creative energy, and as a sacred earth energy. These rituals are rites of evocation and transformation. They are mythic reenactments of the journey back to Earth's center, to the womb of the Great Mother, where contact can be reestablished with the sacred earth energies so that all can be reborn of the Earth Mother once more, and so that myth, biology, and culture may reflect each other reciprocally.

This ritual aesthetic is not posited as an exclusively female one, but rather as one that is appropriate to the content of a changing mythos and a recreation of the history of origins, as well as a means of invoking renewal and bringing about a cultural healing. As such, the creating of the works, themselves, is viewed as part of the mythic cycle of renewal, a tale-telling ritual of recovery and new creation.

If, according to Eliade, myths relate a sacred history and ritually reenacting that sacred history of origins can bring about a healing, then the ritual forms employed by today's women artists serve "to reexperience that time, to re-enact it as often as possible, to witness again the spectacle of the divine works, to meet with the supernaturals and relearn their creative lesson" (Eliade, 1963, p. 19).

Reclaiming and Re-membering Matristic Iconography

Over the past two decades I have witnessed the birth of a movement that I have called feminist matristic art. As contrasted with feminist art, with which it obviously intersects and overlaps, feminist matristic art acknowledges the larger shift in cosmogony, mythology, spirituality, psychology, and history that comes about as women reclaim the Great Mother Goddess Creatress of all life, and work creatively to bring about Her re-emergence on many levels.

As I look over the feminist matristic visual artists that I discuss in this chapter, approximately two-thirds of those I have encountered fall into the category of ritual or performance artists. Certainly their dynamic ritual forms function in some ways that are similar to the ways in which traditional rituals function. They obviously convey values linked to a sense of continuity over time (in this case linking contemporary participants to a sense of connection with their ancestors who might have participated in Goddess rituals in ancient cultures). They also foster the creation of a sense of community by creating ceremonial behaviors that transmit and reinforce meanings, ethics, values, and teachings relating individuals to the life cycle and to cosmic events. They confer status, teach roles, mark transitions, and mobilize people to make changes in their lives and in the world (Doty, 1986).

Noting that ritual comes from the Latin *ritus* and the Greek *rheo,* to flow, run, rush, or stream, Tom Moore puts the sense of river or stream back into the etymological root of ritual, and defines it as a ceremony that puts one back in touch with the stream or flow of life's energies. "To be in ritual is to be in a stream like the water of the Tao. . . . to be in ritual is to be in the river. . . . It is to know that life is energy, and that all flows and changes" (Moore, 1983, pp. 2, 3). Moore contrasts ritual that puts one in touch with the flow to heroics, in which one runs frantically against the flow, and to psychotic rituals, in which one is blocked to the flow or alienated from it.

However, practitioners of the Goddess religion, Wicca, who perform rituals regularly, are aware of the magic that rituals create. Starhawk writes that "Magic teaches that living beings are beings of energy and spirit as well as matter, that energy—what the Chinese call 'chi'— flows in certain patterns throughout the human body, and can be raised, stored, shaped, and sent. The movements of energy affect the physical world, and vise versa" (Starhawk, 1987, p. 24).

Ritual, which helps us to get in touch with these energies, also teaches us that "the tangible, visible world is only one aspect of reality. There are other dimensions that are equally real, although less solid. Many cultures acknowledge other realms of existence" (Starhawk, 1987, p. 25). Referring to those dimensions that have been called the Dream World or the Twilight World, Starhawk teaches that ritual also opens the doors to these nonvisible worlds and their powers. Rituals, by moving energy through group process, create collective change, for the movement of energy *is* action, and action causes change.

It is now becoming clearer that the ritual and performance arts that reclaim the Goddess as the Earth Mother work not only to change consciousness through the creation of new images and actions, but also to shape and mold the energies that actually create reality, to make subtle contact with the invisible forces and powers of other dimensions (that are acknowledged by cultures all over the world). During the enactment and performance of these rituals, feminist matristic artists are inviting women to come into close contact with these energies and to participate in and experience magical creation.

Thus, ritual permits us to live a new myth, to experience its cosmogony, its symbols, its traditions, its modes of expression. As we enter the world of the ritual, we begin to "embody" these new knowledges and new feelings. The synergistic effect of augmenting the energies of the collective through the enactment of ritual hastens the processes of community creation and alliance building, of psychic transformation, personal and group empowerment, and ultimately the resacralization of the Earth.

In her article "Contemporary Feminist Rituals" (Turner, 1978, p. 25), Kay Turner shows the parallels betweeen the shamanistic and the feminist ritual, stressing that the shaman is "the wounded healer," who, having been healed, can then heal the community, just as the feminist ritualist who has healed her wounds of oppression through the performance of feminist matristic ritual acts, can now empower women to embrace a different world-view by embodying and activating images of power and transformation during ritual. Turner writes that "a primary objective of ritual is to achieve shared meanings and a sense of shared goals, not to promote private images or dreams. This is the crucial difference between the ritualist and the artist. The artist takes herself, her content and ability to express that content as commendable to the world of meaning and aesthetics. She is a source of new meaning. . . . The ritualist is constantly at work to leave the self, to become a channel for transcendent experience" (Turner, 1978, p. 25).

The feminist matristic ritual artist is thus a mediator between the shaman and the artist. She creates new images and new meanings from her personal, creative matrix, while simultaneously enacting a role similar to that of the shaman and empowering the collectivity through sharing her own power with the group. In a century of video ads and Hollywood illusions, where dreams are manufactured, and where we are invited to step inside a Hollywood Disneyworld or fantasyland on a daily basis, we are constantly seduced into mistaking the unreal, the simulated, the illusory, for the real, and into experiencing this illusionary experience with others, thus making it into a trumped-up shared reality.

Feminist matristic artists, however, are *not* making the unreal, real. They are striving to render the existence of subtle, invisible dimensions, real. Their desire is to bring us face to face with the histories and mysteries in which all matristic art has been, and is, grounded. We have discussed the histories as the desecration of all traces of Goddess religion from the eras preceding patriarchy, as well as the witch-burning holocaust of the sixteenth and seventeenth centuries. Starhawk says of the mysteries that "we are never apart from the power of the mysteries. Every breath we take encompasses the circle of birth, death, and rebirth. The forces that push the blood cells through our veins are the same forces that spun the universe out of the primal ball of fire. We do not know what those forces are. We can invoke them, but we cannot control them, nor can we disconnect from them. They are our life, and when we die, decay, and decompose, we remain still within their cycle" (Starhawk, 1987, p. 6).

We will begin our overview of feminist matristic visual art by taking a closer look at the works of these women artists according to, first, the two aspects established by Marija

Gimbutas, which encompass the powers of the Great Goddess Creatress of all life. The two aspects, as we recall, are

1. The Cosmogonic Creator, Earth Mother, Fertility.
2. The Goddess of Life, Death, and Rebirth.

In considering the ways in which the first aspect of the Great Mother has been used in contemporary feminist matristic art, we will look at mostly static works—paintings, installations, the creation of new symbols and iconography relating to the theme of the Great Mother as a cosmic Creator, procreator and artistic creator, as well as to the theme of fertility reinterpreted as the theme of ecology.

Next, under Her second aspect, as the Goddess of Life, Death, and Rebirth we will study the themes of the cycles of history and the cosmos. Here, for the most part, we will discuss the works of ritual and performance artists that relate to the theme of the cycles of rebirth into a feminist matristic culture.

Following the overview of Her two major aspects, we will trace the journeys of these artists to the sites of empowerment and new knowledge that we have previously elaborated.

1. The journey to ancient prehistory and goddess-centered cultures.
2. The voyage inward into dream and psychic space.
3. The journey to sacred sites in nature and on the Earth.
4. The journey to the spirit world, a feminist matristic, shamanic voyage.
5. A visit with the Crone and a reclamation and celebration of the wisdom of Gaia.
6. A visit to the Outta-Sight, the Goddess in the City, the Clown.

These journeys can be read as tales of power or maps of guided trips to sites and sitings of the empowerment we can receive from an encounter with the Great Goddess.

In her first aspect as Goddess Creatress of life, today's feminist matristic visual artists are celebrating Creation both literally and figuratively in treating the themes of fertility, ecology, cosmogonic Creation, and the woman artist.

A modern reinterpretation of Her second aspect, that of becoming, celebrates contemporary women's emergence into a new cycle of history and vision. It incorporates themes of a quest for lost periods of women's history and a consciousness of the erasure of women's accomplishments from the human record. It often laments the burning of women of wisdom as witches who worshipped the Goddess during the patriarchal era. It also honors contemporary women's rebirth into empowered aspects of their evolution derived from a new knowledge of images depicted in the most ancient religions to have existed in human history.

THE FIRST ASPECT: COSMOGONIC CREATOR, EARTH MOTHER, FERTILITY

Two European artists are most well known for their early investigations and explorations of all aspects of the Great Mother, and for their creative renderings of Her powers as they were experienced through visitations to the many sacred sites and sanctuaries of the Goddess in Old Europe.

Monica Sjöö, the author of *The Great Cosmic Mother: Rediscovering the Religion of the Earth* (Sjöö & Mor, 1987), is an autodidact, who left her native Sweden and settled in England and Wales, after traveling around Europe from the age of 16 on, waiting for the women's movement to be born. In a personal interview she talked about the importance of visiting the sacred sites. "It is absolutely vital to visit the sacred places and to connect with the Earth, but also through imagery we are re-establishing that Earth is sacred and offering a holistic view of life civilized in the image of the Goddess." (Sjöö, 1987, p. 86).

Monica Sjöö sees her journey as a pilgrimage. She had powerful, mystical experiences at such sites as Silbury, which she conceives of as the womb of the Earth, and she had other holistic experiences at Avebury and Silbury, where she felt the Earth Mother communicating Her pain at "the destruction of Her living body." (Sjöö, 1987, p. 88).

Monica Sjöö's paintings create a contemporary iconography for a reconnection with the Great Cosmic Mother as She manifested Her sacred presence in many ancient cultures. Sjöö's image of *God Giving Birth* (Sjöö, 1987, opposite title page), which is a literal image of a woman in a cosmic setting giving birth to a child, shows that every mother is created in the Goddess's image, in the image of the Great Cosmic Mother. This work met with extremes of protest when it was first exhibited. She has also painted *Universal Creator* based upon the image of the Sheila-Na-Gig from old Irish churches, a "Vulva Woman" (Sjöö, 1987, p. 52). In this work, the creation of life, whether cosmic, human, or artistic, is a luminous, ecstatic experience. Ecstasy and vision, in fact, become signs of the Goddess's presence in Sjöö's, oeuvre. She finds the Goddess as *The Spirit of the Stone* (Sjöö, 1987, p. 69) (a mountain mother), and in *She, the Joyous Spiral, She, the Serpent-Power, She the Mother of Us All* (Sjöö, 1987, p. 74), Sjöö depicts the Great Mother's energic presence at dolmens and stone sanctuaries, as we visualize the serpent energies of the spiral and the numinosity of the Eye Goddess (and the third eye) in the harmonic vibrations that spiral around this ancient Celtic site. In *The Triple Goddess* (Sjöö, 1987, p. 87), she portrays the Virgin, Mother and Crone as three aspects of an eternally cycling unity whose origins date from the Old Stone Age and the Neolithic cultures. Sjöö has invoked the Greek Goddesses *Demeter and Persephone at New Grange* in Ireland, (Sjöö, 1987, p. 160) as well as *The Cretan Goddess* (Sjöö, 1987, p. 214), and *Nerthus/Freya* (Sjöö, 1987, p. 157), but in each painting Sjöö shows how the Goddess of one particular culture is really only a local aspect of the larger Great Mother religion. *Demeter and Persephone at New Grange* make it clear that in all cultures mothers mourn the rape of their daughters, and embody the powers of fertility and of life and death. On another level, we realize that whereas Demeter had withdrawn fertility from the planet, today it is Demeter that has been raped, as the planet's fertility has almost been wiped out by the poisons that our civilization has poured upon Her.

Sjöö's iconography of the Celtic Goddess tradition is particularly impressive, since she was drawn to it as an outsider through actual mystical experiences at the sacred sites. She has celebrated *Rhiannon/Cerridwen* (Sjöö, 1987, p. 130) by linking them through the text on the image to "Mother of All: Gaia, Rhea, Kali, Isis, Diana, Anu, Rhiannon, Brigid, Cerridwen, Cailleach." In her painting *Shamaness at Callanish* (stone circle off the coast of northwest Scotland) (Sjöö, 1987, p. 142), she has linked the Goddess to the female shaman and to the Eye Mother, thus portraying shamanic vision as an integral part of the culture of the Great Cosmic Mother. In *The Goddess at Avebury* (Sjöö, 1987, p. 137), the megalithic earthmounds, the dragon-serpent, the egg, the White Horse Goddess, Epona, and the moon's cycles are all established as the mythic fundaments of the powers of the Mound, which seems to glow with a special aura or force field, that can be activated by the vibrations of human intercourse with the Earth—through dances (seen in the dancing women), through rituals, and through the celebration of the new moon with the lighting of the Beltane fires. Finally in *The Goddess in Her Manifestation at Greenham Commons* (Sjöö, 1987, p. 416), Sjöö brings all the feminist matristic symbols and energy signs together to show the Earth Mother in Her multiple manifestations around the world, here represented by contemporary women from different countries, bringing forth life outside the death camp of the nuclear missile base. Sjöö's imagery has circulated widely in the women's movement through her posters, her postcards, her art works, her articles, and her books.

Monica Sjöö's virtually encyclopedic iconography, in its linking of many cultural traditions within a single painting, teaches us about the multiple aspects of the Great Mother's religion that are manifested in their many varieties in different parts of the world at different times. Her paintings constitute a complete teaching apart from (as well as together with) her book.

Ursula Kavanagh is an Irish artist whose early travels to Goddess sites in Ireland, England, Brittany, Italy, Sardinia, Malta, and Sicily have produced several series of art works that also trace the psycho-spiritual journey of a contemporary woman artist in search of her most ancient matristic roots. Ursula Kavanagh believes that "as artists our responsibility is to learn to decipher the camouflage that the sacred has taken on in this desacralized world. My research has led me to the Neolithic—a culture where to live as a human being was, in itself, a religious act, where the fertility of the earth, the importance of women, the sacramental value of sexual union, food and labor were all integrated" (Kavanagh, unpublished). She believes that the values and visions of the cultures of the Neolithic "constitute a model for our future"(Kavanagh, unpublished).

Also establishing a vast visual iconography of varied multicultural Goddess images linked by the imprint of her own vibrant style, Ursula Kavanagh began an Archaeology Series of Goddess images in 1978. In this series, she dedicated each work to the Goddess of a particular culture—the Goddesses of Malta, Anatolia, Crete, Mesopotamia, Brittany, Eleusis, New Grange, Egypt, Sardinia, and so forth. Having visited all of these sites and studied the archaeology and history of the cultures, she began to extract and sift the Goddess out of all the material, linking the symbols of the Goddess from site to site, paying homage to the powers and energies of the Great Mother. It was in 1980 that she began a new series of works entitled "Graven Images." These were etched into paper, and more directly connected to the process of stone carving. They were more symbolic and less narrative than the Archaeology Series. Her Estrella Series was based upon a figure she found on a piece of Mesopotamian pottery. She used the figure of Estrella, along with both archaeological and invented symbols. She placed Estrella in all sorts of ancient sites along the path of a visual journey back to the Goddess. In this series we find Estrella playing with serpents, as Lady of the Beasts, in the Garden of Eden, in Crete, at Aphrodite's Temple, in Malta, dancing at Stonehenge, at the Hanging Gardens of Babylon, at the Temple of Dendera in Egypt, at a Snake Sanctuary, as Sirens in the ocean, and at her own temple. A third series was begun in 1982, called the Arethusa Series. Inspired by a mermaid that she found in front of the main altar—in mosaic—in a church at Otranto, Italy, she found that Arethusa was originally a nymph (attendant upon Artemis), who was changed into a spring. In this series Arethusa is linked with the Irish Sheila-Na-Gig, with the Sun Goddess and the Moon Goddess, with the Snake Goddess, and with Mithra, Mélusine, Hecate-at-the-Crossroads, Medusa, the Serpent Woman of India with her lover in an underground cave, and She is also found reclaiming the Cretan labyrinth, having afternoon tea in Crete, in a Persian garden, as Aphrodite on the Half Shell—also as Persephone, Kali, Gaea, and Daphne.

In other works Kavanagh depicted herself as various Goddesses—as Isis, Ceres, a Siren, an Etruscan Matron, as Coatlicue, and Kore. Like Monica Sjöö, she was one of the first to create an exhaustive, encyclopedic imaginative rendering of the contemporary self at the ancient sites.

Establishing this vast iconography and appropriating the ancient symbols for our times was the first stage of feminist matristic art work.

In creating an iconographic lexicon of Goddess images, symbols and charged signs from the ancient cultures of the Great Mother, Buffie Johnson was one of the early innovators. Long before the contemporary feminist matristic artists began to explore the ancient sites, Buffie Johnson had been working on these symbols via the Jungian concept of the collective unconscious. She started putting Great Goddess symbols into her work in the 1940s. These Goddess symbols emerged from abstract works, as serpents became glyphs for the Goddess, in such works as *Egg of Chaos #4*, 1965.

Buffie Johnson has created single and hybrid images such as that of the grain in *Ariadne* (Barley Mother, 1971), the Goddess of Vegetation, or the *Pomegranate* (1972), recalling the

Ursula Kavanagh: Mélusine (1984)

myth of Demeter and Persephone. In *Pasiphae* (1976), she combined the image of the Iris, the sacred Lily of Crete, with a bovine head, so that both animal and plant symbols of the Goddess coalesce in a new charged sign that traces the form of the female womb, the Fallopian tubes, and the ovaries. Thus, the painting becomes a hieroglyph linking both the Great Mother and contemporary women through its symbols of fertility. Buffie Johnson's paintings celebrate the natural world, reminding us that each plant, fruit, seed, pod, and flower is a sacred bioform and a manifestation of the Great Earth Mother. Her charged symbols are employed as forces of awakening to remind us of a buried past when all of nature was alive in the Great Mother's sacred herbarium, planet Earth.

Each artist who depicted the Great Mother in her first aspect as cosmic Creator and Earth Mother has developed a unique visual language that enables us to read both nature and history from a feminist matristic perspective.

Icons and glyphs are only two of the versatile visual resources that contemporary women artists work with. Marlene Mountain, located in Tennessee, has created what we might call a Goddess Alphabet, inspired by her reading of the story of the Sumerian Goddess, Inanna.

Composed of triangles, circles, axes, stars, spirals, moons, uplifted arms, chromosomes, ziggurats, knots of Inanna, mountains, labyrinths, eyes, breasts, fruit, flowers and horns, she has also painted women's most ancient sacred symbols in numerous series inspired by the writings of Merlin Stone, G. Rachel Levy, Elizabeth Gould Davis, Judy Chicago, and the Heresies Collective. One of her paintings is of the Venus of Willendorf, and its title is *Mother*. Another is *Seek the Cow Mother—Holy Cow,* and another, showing a hand-print, is entitled *Cave Art Is Genuinely Woman's Art.*

Like Monica Sjöö and Ursula Kavanagh, Marlene Mountain's Cave Painting Series also revisits the themes of ancient Goddess history (Isis, Eve, Mother, Anahita, Changing Woman, Cave Wom, and Visual Womtra). In the second half of this series, we find the Pregnant Seated Goddess, the Goddess Half Buried in the Ground, the Eye Goddess: Supreme Intelligence, the White Mountain in the Primordial Water, the Cosmic Egg, and so forth.

Marlene Mountain is also a writer of Haikus—a word-weaver coining the consciousness-raising combination Womtra (not mantra). She has used Wom to replace man in her series entitled Cave Wom. Her crossword puzzles are particularly appealing as a cross between literature and art. Entitled "Cross Words," they come completely solved with negative words that are applied to women, implying that our dictionary definitions of reality are patriarchal. They also contain combined words such as malescholarship and goddessmurder. As visual shapes they play upon the form of the cross as well, and the overall impression is one of the crucifixion of women on the cross of patriarchal language. Because they are solved, they also imply the denial of the Mysteries in the patriarchal era.

In her other series of symbols, she goes beyond the limits of the alphabet to create new glyphs for energizing, empowering expressions, all derived from matristic history. Some of her glyphs are:

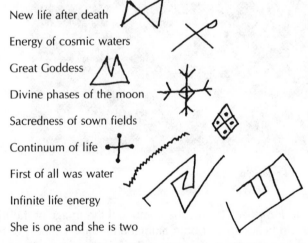

New life after death

Energy of cosmic waters

Great Goddess

Divine phases of the moon

Sacredness of sown fields

Continuum of life

First of all was water

Infinite life energy

She is one and she is two

Marlene Mountain's work alerts us to the important meanings contained in markings, scratches, designs, and patterns, such as those that were once inscribed on Goddess figurines and may now be found in unexpected places. These glyphs could be mistaken for abstractions or graffiti by the uninitiated, and they make us aware of the sacredness of even the most trivial scratches as possible primal forms of matristic expression.

If the various personal modes of expression of today's feminist matristic artists have one theme in common, it is the celebration of women's cultures both anterior to and contemporaneous with our own. Folk and tribal cultures are among those most fertile with Goddess imagery, for, excluded from the mainstream of hegemonic Western civilization's canon of art history, folk and tribal cultures and specifically the women's arts and crafts within them, have continued to transmit images and sacred signs of an original Earth Mother Creator.

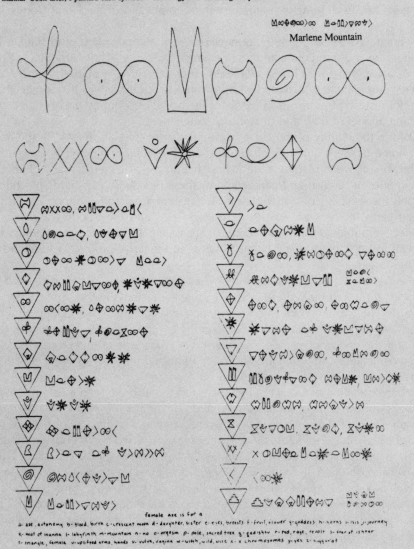

WOMEN AND LANGUAGE Vol. X, No. 1 51

FEMALE: AXE IS FOR A

I was reading a tale of Inanna (Sumerian Goddess) in English translated from cuneiform; I stopped, wrote in my sketch book, "make up a female alphabet," and went back to reading, not knowing what I really meant. Later that night (11/1/83), images and symbols started coming to me and a few hours later I had a "female alphabet" -- I assume from Inanna. Soon after, I painted each symbol -- called "gyn" -- on triangular panels.

Marlene Mountain: Female: Axe is for A

An artist known for her celebration of the works of women in these cultures is Betty La Duke, a professor of art at Southern Oregon State University in Ashland, Oregon. Her literal travels in Mexico, in Europe, India, Sri Lanka, Indonesia, Thailand, the Peoples' Republic of China, Papua New Guinea, Chile, Peru, Borneo, Nicargua, Haiti, Grenada, Yugoslavia, Ecuador, Bolivia, Brazil, Nigeria, etc., have fueled her shamanic seership. Her gaze projects a tender X-ray vision onto the Ur Mothers of all cultures, showing the Great Chain of Being, animal, vegetable and human, and the cycles of life, death, and rebirth incarnated in the great bodies of humble women, seen as epiphanies of the Great Goddess around the globe.

Her poetic visions of the interconnectedness of animal, plant, and human life are also metaphors for the interconnectedness of human cultures—Latin American, African, European, Asian, and so forth, in her work. We, too, each flow through the other, and are composed of spiritual matter inspired by other cultures. La Duke's vision counters that of colonization, for instead of proposing a mechanistic model of conquest and conflict, she proposes an organic model of flow and of spiritual sustenance.

Linked to the fertility of the Earth, especially since they are placed in the natural setting of her home in the mountains of Québec are the *Telluric Women, Women of Hope and Resurrection* of Jovette Marchessault (whose fiction will also be discussed). Made of materials found in piles of rubbish and garbage cans, these female River Guardians and Plant Devas exemplify the recycling of matter at its most transformatory and numinous level. These many-breasted Earth Mothers are made from egg crates, and their bodies and heads are often fashioned from milk cartons and yogurt or ice-cream containers. *Cow Mother* reigns as resplendent in her literary piece *Night Cows* as in the dairy products of which her Goddess sculptures are made.

These *Telluric Women* often have branches and serpents on their heads, and whiskers on their faces, for it is through these radarlike emanations that they are imagined to receive and transmit invisibly charged cosmic communications. Living as she does with a multitude of animals, Marchessault visualizes the energic forms through which each species communicates, and she endows her Goddess figures with all forms of receptors and diverse organs for communication. All is radiant and interconnected in Marchessault's ecstatic, shamanic universe.

The transformation of Gods to Goddesses represents more than a simple sex-role reversal of power symbols. It incorporates a revolution in values. Mayumi Oda's *Manjusuri* (1981), the Bodhissatva of Perfect Wisdom, is usually depicted with a sword. Here the sword is replaced by a sutra. Perfect wisdom is the image of a woman's body in motion, or body wisdom. Bettina Aptheker adds: "Traditionally, the male Manjusuri is astride a huge lion. In Oda's version, the female Manjusuri is self-propelled on a bicycle, the lion dashing alongside, with a comical, green-colored mane flowing wildly behind him" (Aptheker, 1988, p. 15). In Oda's work the traditional Thunder Gods have been transformed to Thunder Goddesses. Neither are angry, and both embody Yin and Yang energies. Similarly the Wind Goddesses, for whom typhoons and earthquakes have been named, are envisaged as women sending their forces to women (Oda, 1981).

The Goddess of the Earth is pictured as a Treasure Ship of Vegetables, a Cornucopia of the fruits of the Earth transported on the sea, just as the Goddess of Flowers, the Spring Goddess, and the Goddess of Snow are envisaged on ships as well. Mayumi Oda's goddesses are often on wheeled vehicles for land transport, or on ships for journeys across the waters. Whether interpreted as psychic symbols or as political images, these are women in motion; their bodies are strong and free. They are sexually uninhibited, and they represent the sacred female force in the universe. In her world all the elements, air, fire, earth, and water, are represented by goddesses, so that no longer will the nude body of woman be relegated to the shadows and silences of shame. This collection of diverse personifications of the goddesses can be interpreted as a model for a community of women of diverse strengths.

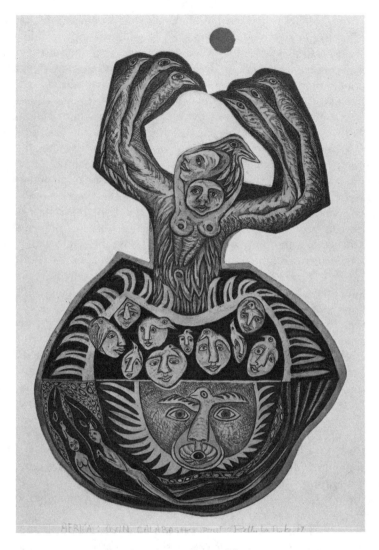

Betty LaDuke: Africa: Oshun Calabash (1987)

Gilah Yelin Hirsch's image of the Shekinah came to her in a dream in 1978 bearing the Hebrew letters AIN SOPH, which represent the Divine Essence or Divine Thought in the Kabbalah. In Jewish tradition, the Shekinah is "the independent feminine divine entity of the Kabbalah's mystical theosophy of the Middle Ages. According to Gershom Scholem, the foremost authority on the Kabbalah, the Shekinah was the feminine element of God" (Patai, 1967, p. 124). Hirsch interprets this to stand for consciousness. In her engraving the letters are written backward, because she is reading them from within the interior of the body, where her spiritual search had led her. The metaphor of weaving, and the body imagery of cell weaving in Hirsch's work echo the images of Spider Woman that we find in Paula Gunn Allen, Donna Henes, and Helen Klebesedel. Here, however, the DNA spiral *is* the AIN SOPH or the ALEPH. In other words, consciousness is a function of the body, and the word is born in the woman's body just as feminist matristic consciousness is born in the Shekinah's body. Other works in this series such as *Annan, Reconciliation, Ain Soph,* and *Reflections of Events in Time* connect the Wheat Goddess with the Tree of Life, the Breath of Life, and the formation of human tissue of the Goddess as the ground of being for contemporary women. In her work the body is the temple of the soul.

Also working on material related to the Shekinah, the feminine principle of the divine presence according to the Kabbalah, is Bruria, an Israeli artist, now residing in California. Bruria was born into a Chassidic family in Jerusalem, and as a child learned Aramaic, Hebrew, and Ladino, which enabled her, in her adult life, to translate the writings of the Spanish Kabbalist and poet, Abraham Abulafia, into both English and an abstract artistic language.

Her four works in bronze, entitled *The Divine Chariot,* convey her visualization and understanding of the Kabbalistic symbols of the alphabet (each letter being an opening into sacred space—a mystical access to the divine), the wheels of the Chariot (the hub of the wheel being the sacred center of each of the four worlds of Creation), and the magical number 10 (there are 10 spokes on the wheel because in the kabbalah no number less then 10 is holy). The tenth spoke on the four chariot wheels always becomes an organic form—twigs, a bush, a plant, and so forth. It is in the Chariot entitled *The Creation—The Divine Influx-Shefa* that Bruria uses the myth of the four rivers of Eden (which emanate from the central hands) as a mandala for meditation about water as the source of life—just as the Aleph represents the Creator and the unity of the universe. Using the circle with a consciousness of its feminine symbolism, and the female hands as those of a female Creator/Maker (of life, of art, of the universe), Bruria has permeated her meditations on the mystical Kabbalah and the essence of divine creation with a decidedly feminist matristic interpretation, reaching its ultimate expression in the combination of abstract, "feminine" symbols (i.e., the circle) with organic forms (i.e, flowering branches). Ultimately, we feel in her work the mystical presence of the female aspect of deity, the Shekinah.

Ruth Weisberg has worked intensively with female images of the sacred. In 1984 she painted *Waterborne,* which is a part of her cycle *A Circle of Life.* It is a self-portrait of herself being reborn from the water. Here Creation is not only expressed as rebirth, but also as the rebirth of the self as artistic creator. Her 1981 life-sized mixed-media drawing *Kore* is another self-portrait of the artist in the figure of a Kore, a being in transition between the divine and the secular. Weisberg conceives of it as an initiation. Finally, in *The Scroll,* a 94-foot drawing completed in 1987, Weisberg depicts the Angel who pushes the soul forth into life as female. The soul, according to Jewish belief, has perfect knowledge before it is born, but when it is born it forgets everything. The female angel bestows life upon the child in *The Scroll.* Thus, as we can see from these three sacred female images, Weisberg conceives of Creation, Rebirth, and the angelic realm of the sacred as female.

Helen Klebesedel's painting *Spinster* refers both to the Arachne myth and to Mary Daly's reclaiming of the word "Spinster" in her *Websters' New Intergalactic Wickedary of the English Language.* "Spinster n: a woman whose occupation is to Spin, to participate in the whirling movement of creation. One who has chosen her Self, etc.—Spiraling in New Time/Space" (Daly, 1987, p. 67). Klebesedel also writes that she was inspired by an interpretation she heard of the Arachne myth in which "she was turned into a spider, not for besting the Goddess at weaving, but for chronicling Zeus's rapes in her tapestry . . . But even as a spider, they could not stop the beauty of her art. This interpretation of Arachne caused me to turn to the spider with a new vision of unconquerable creativity. She emerged for me as a pregnant spinster, autonomous, as spinsters traditionally were, drawing her thread from her center as a spider. For me, the creative and the procreative come together in the spinster/spider. As one they weave the patterns and grids that give meaning to a seemingly random universe. . . . . . My spinster is a woman of color. It . . . is a figure that refers to the power of the creative voice as it grows out of and beyond an oppressive reality. She is black, but she wears a yellow mask that glows like the phases of the moon over her left shoulder. The mask is to allow the face of everywoman to exist behind it" (Klebesedel, letter to Orenstein, Dec. 13, 1987).

French Canadian and North American Blackfeet Indian painter, Charleen Touchette, in her series of *Reindeer Mother Visions,* reconnects us with the creative powers of the universe,

Charleen Touchettte: Deer Mother Vision (1988)
Photographed by S. Barry Paisner

as she depicts the energy exchanges that transpire between the real and the mythic mothers (Reindeer Woman as Mother) and the newborn child.

Other paintings in this series show Sky Mother and Sun Mother with the antlers of Reindeer Mother. Each mythic mother places the newborn child upon the Earth, and combines her energies with those of the mythic serpent in the creation and perpetuation of life.

Painted in a style reminiscent of Huichol yarn paintings, with bright primary colors and light energy fields, Touchette's native American vision reminds us of how all life is ultimately engendered and empowered by all the Great Mothers, mythic, spiritual, and real, who bestow their blessings upon future generations through their energic, visionary powers.

Metaphorically, art, too, can be understood as a kind of ''Reindeer Mother,'' through whose energy and vision we receive additional blessings reconnecting us to the forces and energies of the mythic, maternal nagual worlds that fuel the world of phenomenal reality.

Touchette sees real motherhood in the matriarchal North American Indian communities (where sometimes four generations of women create together in one room) as a potent source of spiritual sustenance. These generations of women, then, weave the web of Spider Woman in creating art communities in extended-family webs, which transmit the energies of Reindeer Woman (who appeared to Charleen Touchette in a personal vision) via their art. The magic of Reindeer Woman is experienced concretely in the magic of motherhood coupled with artistic creation in her own life, as she writes and speaks about painting in her kitchen studio surrounded by her children.

In Touchette's world, these acts of love weave more webs of female energy that create both life and art, for one is not seen as antithetical to, or cut off from, the other in her culture. Both life and art together create one whole "Beauty Way."

Sasha McInnes is a weaver, a tapestry artist, who now lives in Thunder Bay, Canada. She learned the arts of weaving and dyeing in Peru, and then returned to London, Ontario, where she spent many fertile years weaving and spinning images of the Great Mother looming large over the planet, and stretching her fingers into the bowels of the Earth. She has woven the Goddess spirit abstractly in works about solstice and equinox celebrations. Sasha McInnes has recently embarked on a completely new phase of her creative journey. In moving to Thunder Bay she is performing ceremonies and living among the Ojibway women elders in the North country. Recently, she participated in sweats, ceremonials, and received a sacred drum. She feels that she was "called" to this country by the grandmothers, the Crones of the Ojibway, and that in some sacred sense she has come "home," for indeed, she was literally born in this part of Canada. In Sasha McInnes's work the literal and metaphoric meanings of the Goddess as the weaver of the webs of life and fate are closely meshed.

Judy Baca is a Chicana artist living in Los Angeles, California, who has created the longest mural painting in the world, *The Great Wall,* which depicts the history of California in over one-third of a mile of murals using some 600 gallons of paint and more than 65,000 youth-hours from community co-workers. It was begun in the summer of 1976 and was completed in 1984 for the Olympics. It presents Southern California's history as seen through the eyes of the third world peoples living there. It portrays the history of the oppression of native American, Hispanic-American, and Asian-American peoples. Baca's next mural *When God Was a Woman,* is the spiritual counterpart to her call for peace in the Great Wall. It depicts the beginning and the end of the world in mythological terms. Her vision of the beginning of the world is based upon the legend of the Amazon Califia, for whom California was named. She is an Amazonian Earth Mother Goddess figure whose arms and legs are branches and roots connected to the arterial and venal networks of her powerful, gigantic, earth body. In her mural depicting the end of the world, Califia's original creative and protective earth energies appear as Amazons who will save the world from the ultimate holocaust. Baca's spiritual warriors use the natural energies of the cosmos as their weapons.

Diana Kurz and Cynthia Mailman have done self-portraits—the former of herself as the Durga killing the Buffalo Demon and liberating the world from evil; the latter of herself as God, an image of contemporary womanpower, for the creative artist sees herself as the reflection of the divine Creatress in whose image she was made.

Hélène de Beauvoir, sister of feminist Existentialist Philosopher Simone de Beauvoir, strikes out against all patriarchal theology in her painting *God the Father Expelling the Goddesses from Heaven* (1982). In her two works about the Cretan Goddess, *First and Second Encounter with the Great Goddess* (1982), we find a contemporary woman learning to align herself with the forces of nature and with the serpent power. In a first meeting, she makes an offering to the Cretan Goddess, and in a second meeting, she learns to wield the serpent power from the example of the Goddess, herself. In these works the nude female is reawakened to a repossession of her physical and spiritual powers. Indeed, de Beauvoir's work

Sasha McInnes: Reflection of a Dream—Inner Landscape (8′ × 8′ Tapestry)
Photographed by Jeff Carroll

subtly teaches us that to imitate the gestures of the ancient goddesses can constitute an empowering lesson for women of our time.

In sculpture, Nancy Azara, who is also a psychic healer, has made works carved in wood, which speak of the healing energies associated with priestesses of ancient matristic cultures. Many of her works have wrapped or bandaged limbs alongside of blood-red organic forms. More recently she has been expressing the rhythms and patterns of the healing energy known as chi in luminous twigs plated in gold leaf.

Titles such as *Initiation, Shaman Sister,* and *River Goddess* link the abstract sculptural configurations to motifs that explain the X-ray quality of penetration her works exhibit.

Pieces such as *Horns* are about energy bound and released. Although in this work it might seem as though an animal had been killed and taken as a trophy, the presence of light and energy that once permeated the animal body is still visible after its death. Thus, in Azara's work the soul survives death. Azara reveals the invisible life force, the animistic principle that is characteristic of a feminist matristic vision. In her work we see that although one might kill the body, the soul and the spirit live on in another dimension. Her *River Goddess* was inspired by the Mississippi River, where she envisions the image of women emerging from its onrushing flow as from the primal waters of life. The points of energy on the sculpture are like acupuncture points on the body of the Great River Mother. Azara's psychic vision

Judy Baca: Califia
©1976 Judith F. Baca

perceives the tree as a living being, a wounded being that must be healed. Her tree forms are also human, for every living thing is composed of the same luminous energy. Often her tree forms are backed by a shadow, a second dimension of the self, and are traversed by a luminous essence, a third dimension of the self. These are the subtle selves that only the psychic visionary can see when she charges a body with energy during a healing. Azara believes that we must find the Goddess in ourselves in order to heal the female self, and in doing so become empowered. Her works enable us to envision the Goddess within as an energy field, a golden core, an inner light, an aura, and a life force.

Audrey Flack's new works are sculptures of Goddesses for our era. Based upon classical references, they incorporate gestures and poses from ancient works, and translate them into a feminist matristic reinterpretation. In *Islandia,* for example, the *Goddess of the Healing Waters,* or the New Winged Victory is making a gesture of pronouncement of judgment that comes from Michelangelo's *Last Judgment.* However, here she has transformed it into a pose for the channeling of healing energies from the energy-surrounds of the body, through the body, to emerge from the Heart Chakra. The Goddess is making a gesture of offering at the level of the heart. All of Flack's Goddesses, Diana, the Art Muse, the two Medicine Women, the American Athena and the Snake Goddess have strong bodies of contemporary women who have been working out. Flack shows that there is no contradiction between strength and "femininity." While these women's beautiful bodies set a new ideal for the standard of beauty in our time, as did the classical nudes in their day, Flack's Goddesses are not sex objects, nor are they objects of a male gaze. They are commanding presences, whose strength is not aggressive; rather it is a healing force. While the musculature of the bodies is exquisitely detailed by Flack, a teacher of anatomy, it is in the movement of the body that one senses the flow of the chi. The rose that is above Islandia's right breast has now moved to the middle of her crown. Audrey explains that this shift is very significant. Could it mean that the energies entering the crown Chakra and moving toward the Third Eye, (that one senses as the focal point of Islandia's face), are specifically feminist matristic (rose) energies (gynergy)? Could it be an emblem of a new kind of feminist matristic intelligence, one that is related to a caring for the natural world? In its transformed meaning, we sense that the wings of her Winged Victory are shamanic bird wings (reminiscent of Remedios Varo's *The Creation of Birds*) rather than the wings of an angel. Islandia's wings are the organs of psychic perception and reception of healing energies. They indicate that her soul can fly, and that its visions and knowledge are transmitted through the gaze and via the healing energies that she channels.

In a humorous vein, Toni Putnam's metal sculptures express themes and images of alchemical journeys and transformations that remind us of the paintings of Remedios Varo. Her *Celestial Journey* (1987) and *Alchemyst's Journey* (1987) are whimsical gondolas and baby carriages equipped with all the symbols of alchemical and mythical voyages. However, *Demeter* (1988, 13' × 5' × 7') and *Alchemical Graintower* (1987) suggest that the true alchemy is the transformation of our mythos from a patriarchal to a feminist matristic one.

One could not write about the meaning of a Goddess vision today without focusing on the monumental work of Judy Chicago. *The Dinner Party* can be seen as a culminating point in the quest for women's lost history as well as an artistic, educational tool for connecting contemporary women with their great matristic matrilineage through a celebration of the two aspects of the Great Mother. Both the organic, ecological motif of seeds, grains, and butterflies on the plates, which speak metaphorically of female artistic fecundity and creation, and the historical underpinnings of the research behind the installation, which constantly reminds us of women's contribution to culture, convince me that Chicago exemplifies the kind of quest and creation that is central to the meaning of this new feminist matristic art. Her subsequent collaborative piece, *The Birth Project,* done in needlework by women around the United States, shows the many ways in which the Goddess symbol has come to fuse procreative creation, cosmic creation, and artistic creation in a powerful new charged symbol.

Judy Chicago: Earth Birth (Quilting on air-brushed fabric, 5' × 10')

The various pieces of needlework executed by women working in quilting, appliqué, weaving, macramé, needlepoint, smocking, and batik show the ordinary mother in the labor of childbirth as a woman as powerful as the creator of the universe. Her work explicitly depicts the way in which each birth is, literally, a cosmic event; how its wavelike energy-emanations spread through the cosmos in ripples and surges. Every birth has a cosmic resonance, as the rhythms of female labor echo the rhythms of nature.

These monumental images of female power become multiple metaphors for female creativity on all levels. In her book *The Birth Project* (1985), Judy Chicago has written: "It is perfectly clear to me that the ancient statues of goddesses represent a time when women enjoyed social and political equality. The replacement of those wonderful, powerful female icons with male deities was a disastrous event for women. . . . . I have endeavored for many years to 'make the feminine holy,' and one way I have expressed that is by making images of a female god" (Chicago, 1985, p. 177).

Judy Chicago has exposed the sociohistorical and psychological processes surrounding the creation of art as well as its technical and aesthetic aspects. Thus, while the female imaged in *The Birth Project* is almost archetypal, the process of creation has been contextualized through extensive documentation. The art-making processes that Judy Chicago has portrayed in her works (ceramics, needlepoint, etc.) set our imaginations to musing upon what women's working processes might have been in ancient cultures where women did the weaving and made the pottery. Thus, our contemporary historical moment becomes an expanded metaphor encompassing women's creative communities in other matristic cultures where these crafts have been and are practiced. Ironically, *The Birth Project,* in making us conscious of how the birth experience had been excised from patriarchal art, also makes us aware of how taboo is female sexuality in Judeo-Christian cultures.

Merlin Stone, Monica Sjöö, Barbara Mor, and many other writers on goddess-revering civilizations concur that among the earliest and most original images of the Great Mother was the Black Goddess of Africa.

Asungi, an "Afra-feminist," a spiritualist, a ritualist, an activist, and an "Africanist" artist in Los Angeles has explored the wide range of Goddess images from an Afra-centric perspective in a manner similar to the Eurocentric explorations of Monica Sjöö and Ursula Kavanagh, establishing a contemporary iconography for the modern woman/artist in her matristic lineage.

Because her voice is so powerful, I have chosen to let Asungi speak about her work in her own words.

I. ODDUDUA: MOTHER OF THE UNIVERSE (1982)
"THIS GODDESS OF THE UNIVERSE IS OFTEN THOUGHT TO BE THE GODDESS OF THE EARTH AND WIFE TO OBATALA, THE GOD OF CREATIVITY AND THE SKY. TOGETHER THEY ARE SAID TO BE THE GODDESS OSHALA, A BI-SEXUAL GODDESS. I CHOSE TO SHOW ODDUDUA AS THE GODDESS OF THE UNIVERSE BECAUSE SHE WANTED ME TO. HERE SHE HAS 3 SETS OF ARMS TO REPRESENT THE TRIUNE GODDESS IN HER THREE ASPECTS: SPIRIT, BODY AND MIND, AND THEREFORE REPRESENTING THE SUM TOTAL OF ALL THAT THE UNIVERSE IS. HERE SHE SITS ON A PLANET, RED FOR IT IS AKIN TO VENUS. SHE MOVES ABOUT HER A GROUP OF PLANETS AT HER LEISURE AND PLEASURE, FOR SHE KEEPS THE RHYTHMS OF THE PLANETS AS SHE WISHES. HER FACE IS MASKED FOR SHE HOLDS MANY MYSTERIES YET UNKNOWN TO US." (Asungi, personal statement, 1982, Asungi's capitalization)

II. OCHUMARE: GODDESS OF RAINBOWS (1982)
___"THE YORUBA PEOPLE SAY: "THE RAINBOW IS THE PRIDE OF THE HEAVENS." OCHU-MARE, AS THE RAINBOW, MOVES THE SEA WATERS BETWEEN THE HEAVENS AND THE EARTH. I SEE HER AS THE COSMIC CHANNEL AMONGST THE GODDESSES OF THE UNI-VERSE AND THE EARTH. HERE, SHE RESTS IN THE BEAUTY OF SELF-AWARENESS. SHE IS BLISSFUL, FOR SHE IS IN TUNE WITH THE UNIVERSE. SHE SITS UPON THE UNIVERSAL WATERS AND THE COSMIC LILY PADS SYMBOLIZE HER EVER PRESENCE. SHE IS NUDE, SYMBOLIZING HER PURITY AND ULTIMATE PRIDE OF SELF. HER MASK IS A SIGN OF STRENGTH AND MYSTERY. THE EARTH IN HER LAP IS SPINNING FROM THE ABSOLUTE ENERGY THAT SHE PROVIDES FROM HER NAVEL, WHICH IS A SOURCE OF COSMIC POWER." (Asungi, Personal statement, 1982, Asungi's capitalization)

III. OYA: GODDESS OF CHANGE-TRANSFORMATION (1988)
"THIS GODDESS HAS BEEN DEMANDING HER REVELATION FOR A LONG TIME. SHE COMES TO US AS THE SPIRIT-GUIDE-MOTHER TO ALL WIMMIN WHO HAVE CHOSEN WOMIN-IDENTIFIED POLITICS AND LIFE-STYLES. SHE IS THE "WINDS OF CHANGE" THAT WIMMIN'S SPIRITUALITY BRINGS TO THE WORLD . . . WIMMIN-IDENTIFIED HERSTORY AND EMPOWERMENT! IN THIS WORK I HAVE GIVEN BACK TO HER THE TORNADO AND THE LIGHTNIN' BOLT, TRADITIONALLY GIVEN TO HER MALE COUNTERPART, SHANGO; AND THE "MIRROR OF CHANGE" IN WHICH WE MUST ALL LOOK AS WE GROW IN OUR SPIRITUAL WOMINPOWER! THE COWRIE SHELLS ARE SYMBOLIC OF OYA'S ABILITY TO PERCEIVE THE FUTURE/TO AFFECT ITS CHANGE . . . HER DIRECT CONNECTION TO THE IFA DIVINATION SYSTEM THAT ONCE WAS A WOMIN'S SYSTEM. THEY SYMBOLIZE THE EVER-SEEING EYE AS WELL AS THE LIFE-GIVING VAGINA. THE MIRROR IS IN THE SHAPE OF THE EGYPTIAN ANKH TO SHOW THE LINEAGE CONNECTION BETWEEN THE YORUBA GODDESSES AND THOSE OF EGYPT. THE ANKH WAS THE ANCIENT SYMBOL FOR THE VAGINA (LIFE AND DEATH). HER SKIN AND CLOTHES ARE THE COLOR OF RED OCHRE, SYMBOLIC OF HER WOMINISM—ALSO THE MENSTRUAL BLOOD (THE ORIGINAL RE-QUIREMENT FOR SACRIFICE TO THE SPIRIT-FORCES) . . . LATER SUBSTITUTED BY HUMAN AND ANIMAL SACRIFICE UNDER PATRIARCHY. HER HAIR IS BRAIDED IN THE SHAPE OF BUFFALO HORNS, SYMBOLIC OF ANOTHER OF HER MATERIAL BODY/SHAPES; THE BUF-FALO WOMIN, SHAPECHANGER AND UNTAMEABLE (FEMALE) FORCE. OYA IS THE MOTH-ERNATURE FORCE THAT SAYS: "I AM A DIRECT REFLECTION OF YOUR ACTIONS; GIVE GOOD-GET GOOD . . . GIVE BAD-GET BAD!" SHE TEACHES US THAT TO RESPECT AND OBSERVE THE NATURAL LAWS OF NATURE IS THE ONLY WAY WE WILL SURVIVE AS A PEOPLE." (Asungi, 1988, personal statement, Asungi's capitalization).

In our search for images of womanspirit and womanpower that emerge from a reconnection with our matristic roots, Asungi's work is central to balancing the focus on white, Euro-centric images with images of the Goddesses from Africa such as the Horned Goddess who

Asungi: Odduda
Photographed by Asungi Productions

became Isis of Egypt and who certainly predated the matristic culture of Crete. These African Goddess images contain the evidence of humanity's earliest and global reverence for the Creator of all life as a female.

Numerous other painters and sculptors could easily have been included in this brief overview of static feminist matristic works. Some of these include the recent Goddess paintings of Sylvia Sleigh, the flowing soft sculptural pieces of Anne Healy, Goddess works by Alida Walsh, Nancy Fried, Faith Wilding, Meg Easling, Sandra Stanton, Judith Anderson, Nancy Spero, and Deborah LeSueur, and so forth.

The altars of Amalia Mesa-Baines, Linda Vallejo, and Betye Saar and the concrete poetry wall hangings and 3 dimensional poem-objects of the recently deceased Amelia Ettlinger, all blur the fine lines of demarcation either between art and spiritual practice or between written and visual poetry, for in the aesthetic of a feminist matristic vision, where all is interconnected, rigid distinctions such as these will fade as the energy flow linking all forms of expression to the sacred activities performed in daily reality becomes intensified.

Journeying: Re-enacting the Rites and Re-visiting the Sites of the Great Mother

In separating the first aspect of the Great Mother from the second aspect, it is important to note that we are not creating a polarity or a dichotomy. These aspects complement each other, and most of the artists discussed here under one aspect have produced works that might be viewed from the perspective of the other as well.

Nevertheless, what distinguishes the artists and works I will focus on in the second aspect is the dynamic ritual or performance quality of the work.

Because in the arts form and meaning cohere, it is evident that in recreating the psycho-sensual and political experiential awareness of moments in the birth, death, and rebirth of cultures, as well as the exorcism of oppression and the invocation of healing forces, a more vitalist, participatory form would be sought. Thus, we find a literal preponderance of performance and ceremonial art forms in feminist matristic art. This aspect of the works, however, is, in and of itself, a critical response to those theorists who have mistakenly labeled this art as essentialist or who have implied that the Goddess, as She appears in art, refers naively to an ahistorical, biological "feminine essence." Neither could be further from the facts! For, under this aspect, works about the Great Mother evolved specifically out of a historical quest. They are often composed of cycles of lamentation and mourning for specific women and men who were burned as witches during the witch hunts in Europe.

Many feminist matristic artists have had to exorcise the impact of patriarchal religions on them before journeying to the ancient sites of Goddess worship. Cheri Gaulke, in her performance piece, *This Is My Body* (1982), reenacts that journey of exorcism and rebirth. In her performance she is first the serpent in the Garden of Eden, and then Eve. Projected behind her is Hugo van der Goes's painting *The Original Sin* (1476). While it shows a naive Eve, Gaulke is positioned against the painting as the new Eve, an enlightened Eve, who chooses to eat the apple from the Tree of Knowledge in full *connaissance de cause*. She is nude, wearing only a fig leaf, and she eats the apple with a gusto that might be taken for sexual passion. Gaulke's eight tableaux pass through the Middle Ages and the renaissance, pausing at the witch burnings of the sixteenth century in which she appears to be burned on a pyre and to disappear in the flames in identification with the witches, who, like the new Eve, learned the secrets of nature and healing, understood the powers of the female body (as midwives), and were crucified for their knowledge. Just as Eve was exiled, Gaulke, herself, was tormented in her youth by her own father, a Protestant minister, when he learned about her adolescent sexual explorations.

In Tableau 6 Gaulke's real body is superposed upon Christ's crucified body projected in

Jovette Marchessault: Plant Mother

a slide of Antonella da Messina's *Crucifixion* (1475). Through the multiple layers of art history and of feminist matristic revision, we read the story of the crucifixion both of Christ and of woman, who, in the contemporary version of the crucifixion, is the stand-in for the child of God/dess. Gaulke invites us to read the story of her life as prototypical of that of the lives of all women raised in Christianity. Her life story is about the quest for sexual knowledge, the quest for spiritual knowledge, her identification with nature (the serpent, the apple, the garden), and her ultimate crucifixion (or exile from the garden of patriarchal privilege). Hers is also a story of Goddess murder, for the woman on the cross is at once a contemporary woman and also a flashback to women reflecting the image of the sacred—in other words, either a female divinity or a priestess. At the end of her performance, after merging her own body with the image of the crucified savior, Gaulke descended from the cross and was dressed and blessed by a holy woman. Then she was reborn as a serpent—here reinterpreted as the serpent affiliated with the ancient Goddess images, the serpent who, in sloughing its skin, reminds us of the sloughing of woman's uterine lining and of the lunar cycles. Thus, the crucified woman is at once the Great Goddess, Eve, a European witch, and all contemporary women born into patriarchal religions.

Edith Altman's art, like Cheri Gaulke's, exorcises patriarchal religious oppression, and uses feminist matristic symbols in transformative ways.

Her piece *Rebuilding the Temple: We Are Given a Gold Tent and All of Life Is the Folding and Unfolding of the Tent* (1987) confronts the internment of her father in the Nazi concentration camp at Buchenwald. She placed a golden tent (symbolic of alchemy and of a womb of life, rather than a womb of death like the ovens in the crematoria) in front of photographs from Buchenwald. Within the alchemical womb/tent, she has conducted healing rituals with other Holocaust survivors, and at Buchenwald she performed a ceremony uniting her father with his divine opposite, the Shekinah.

Inspired by Kabbalism, she also performed a sacred wedding ceremony for her father, since the Kabbalists believed that when we die it is our wedding day. The golden tent we are given when we are born transmutes the dark pain of the Holocaust into a golden healing energy, a light symbolic of the forging of gold out of brute matter. This alchemical process has taken place in the female alchemical vessel, the 'tent/womb/inner space. This vessel becomes a concrete metaphor for female creation, which takes place in the interior space of the psyche and of the womb of female creativity.

THE SECOND ASPECT OF THE GREAT GODDESS: LIFE, DEATH, AND REGENERATION

I will begin my discussion with the works of Ana Mendieta, whose life came to a tragic end when she fell to her death at the age of 36 in 1985. I want to stress the fact that although she executed many works about the theme of death, these were never about her personal death, but were metaphors for the death of the soul when it has been wrenched away from its vital and nourishing connections with the Earth.

As a child, Ana Mendieta had been exiled from her native homeland, Cuba, and sent to the United States as an orphan, where she lived in orphanages and foster homes with her sister for many years. She experienced this separation from the land of her birth and from her mother as being torn from the womb of the Earth Mother.

Mendieta's acute experience of the pain of being raised apart from her real mother and her mythic mother is transmuted by her art into a metaphor about our cultural alienation, both from the spirituality of the Great Mother and from the sensuality of nature. Yet, on a more political level, her art is a powerful testimony to the fact that the spiritual and the political are inextricably linked, and that work about the Goddess is not apolitical—if anything, it is more highly politicized than work with a more obvious or literal political content.

Mendieta's exile had to do with being sent away from Castro's Cuba. In her adult life Ana became a political activist on behalf of a variety of causes concerning the third world and third-world women artists. She was also deeply interested in Santeria, particularly in its magical and healing aspects.

Ana's art taught us how to see the holistic relationship of the political to the spiritual, of the human to the nonhuman, and to make the connections that a gendered vision of the Creator of all life permits us to make.

In the posthumous retrospective of her work at the New Museum of Contemporary Art in New York, held from November 1987 through January 1988, we witnessed the amazing evolution of the work of this major woman artist whose career was so tragically ended by a death, the actual cause of which remains as shrouded in obscurity as the death of the culture of the Great Mother whose blazing vitality also came to a premature and tragic ending.

In many of Mendieta's Earth works, she used her body, arms uplifted in the motif of the Cretan and Minoan Goddess as a metaphor for the self reflecting the image of her Creator. In this position, which has now become a literal mudra for feminist matristic art and a motif of empowerment, she would emblazon the outline of her body onto the Earth, by exploding gunpowder over it, leaving only the traces of her silhouette to mark the sacred site of her alchemical transformation, where the merging of her human energies with those of her great Earth Mother had taken place.

In one of her works from the Tree of Life Series, she has used her own k
mud, standing, arms uplifted, against a tree, to show how we are made from
how we must recognize that we are composed of the Earth's matter and energ
"above nature," but we are "of nature," and each of us, like a tree of life, is a
Earth.

In the works where she explodes gunpowder over her image inscribed in the Earth, she seems to blaze a trail back to the Earth's center, transmuting land into light, showing the process by which matter transforms into spirit, and how the two are literally one.

Her burial-mound pieces, such as *Nañigo Burial* (1976) and her crucifixion piece *Anima (Alma/Soul)*, 1976, speak of the spiritual light emanating from the Great Mother, even after Her death, and of the fact that it was the Goddess who was crucified on the cross of Christianity that swept over the West wiping out all traces of Her religion.

Mendieta's Rupestrian Sculptures, executed in Cuba in 1981, when she was there on a Guggenheim grant, were sculpted directly into the rock walls of mountainous caves that had hidden the rebels and revolutionaries fighting for independence. Hence, they make us think twice about the possible meanings behind the Paleolithic Venus figures found in the caves of the Dordogne which they closely resemble. Might not the original artists of those figures have been women artist-revolutionaries hiding in caves? Or were they performing rituals connected with the worship of the Great Mother that involved artistic images in a magical way?

From the posthumous perspective, her works entitled *Body Tracks* (1982), in which she used blood as paint on her arms, and slid along a wall from a standing to a squatting position, leaving tracks of her blood upon the wall, became powerful poetic metaphors for the *oeuvre* of the woman artist, whose creations in a world from which she is multiply alienated, can only be traces of the sacrifice of her lifeblood in the revolution she has waged to make her imprint in the world.

If I have placed Mendieta's work under the second aspect of the Great Mother, rather than under the first aspect, it is simply because I want to underline the dynamics of the burnings and the ritual aspect of the creation of many of the earthworks, even though the rituals were performed in private. Like life itself, they blazed magnificently while alive, and when they went out, their remains on the Earth formed the image of a woman. On the spiritual level, the resonance of their incandescence, like that of Ana's life itself, lingers as a harmonic tone that infuses us with the memory of the fullness of passionate creation that can, at any moment, be prematurely extinguished, and thus mark the turning from one cycle to another. The silhouette of a woman in the Earth remains in our memory as the specter of a form that we constantly rehallucinate whenever we see a tree, a cavern, a riverbed, a sandy beach, a patch of soil or grass. Once Ana Mendieta's work has been seen, the spirit of it continues to emanate in our mind's eye, projecting a memory of the image of the Great Earth Mother onto the land from which She has been erased.

Mary Beth Edelson, like Merlin Stone, Ursula Kavanagh, Monica Sjöö, and others, has studied the available archaeological and mythological sources about the sites and cultures of the Great Goddess that existed in prehistory and early history (i.e., from an androcentric perspective), and has drawn her own revolutionary feminist matristic conclusions, which then became the focus of all the energies in her art.

Today, in the late 1980s, when one can buy packaged tours to the Goddess sites, and, equipped with majors and minors in women's studies, one can arrive at Delphi or Eleusis in a tourist bus, it is difficult to imagine just how revolutionary it was in the early to mid-1970s for a woman like Mary Beth Edelson to make a pilgrimage to an isolated site like that of the Grapçeva Cave on Hvar Island off of Yugoslavia. Yet, she went there as an artistic pioneer in order to perform private rituals of herself in a fire ring in the cave, so that she could reexperience the energies once felt by those who celebrated the Earth as the Great Mother and the cave as Her sacred womb.

Ana Mendieta: Nañigo Burial (1976)

The flamboyant image of herself seated within the fire ring in the cave has almost become an emblem of feminist spirituality, so often has it been reproduced.

In a recent interview Mary Beth Edelson elaborated on the ecofeminist context, which had always been the larger framework of her art. Her *oeuvre* resonates with the new thinking represented by Fritjof Capra and Charlene Spretnak in that she defines her creative process as one that visualizes the interconnectedness of all things human and nonhuman. She talks about her process being liberatory, because it is one of "not yet knowing," a concept that was inspired by reading Susan Griffin's writing. She is not constrained by preexisting solu-

Mary Beth Edelson: See for Yourselves (Grapçeva Neolithic Cave Series—1977)

tions, categories, or so-called objective observations. Rituals are the form par excellence, the perfect vehicle for getting at new knowledge through an attitude of "listening to the universe of other people" (Edelson, personal interview, Winter 1988).

Within an overarching desire to save the planet and to challenge all myths about the inferiority of the female, Edelson tries to acknowledge the primal forces both of the dark and of the light in making her "descent to the Goddess."

In some of her earliest works on the Goddess such as *Old Myths/New Myths* (1973) and *Woman Rising/Our Story*, Edelson installed story-gathering boxes in which she collected personal stories from the public that helped to reveal our mythology-in-the-making. They range from mother and father stories and tales of one's life, to Goddess stories, stone stories, and stories about women's lost herstory and women's feminist matristic future. These stories are exchanged through the piece and through publication, like the exchange of vital nutrients, or of pure, fresh air, that when inhaled, combats the toxins in the gyn/ecology of the female system.

Two important ritual pieces that concern the cycles of history, and function to acknowledge both the cycles of lamentation and celebration are *Your 5,000 Years Are Up* (1977, Mandeville Gallery, University of California at La Jolla) and *Memorials to the 9,000,000 Women Burned as Witches in the Christian Era* (1977—A.I.R. Gallery, New York City). In *Your 5,000 Years Are Up* eight shrouded figures lift off the back wall of a gallery, as they slowly become inhabited by women, who then glide into a room where other women are sitting in the center of a huge fire ring. The shrouded figures weave circles around the fire ring, as chants are sung of women's rebirth from their isolation, via the circle, where pain is exorcised and anger expelled. The ritual ends with chanting and dancing, as women celebrate their new-found solidarity, and join together to rise up against the injustices their sister suffered under patriarchy. *Memorials to the 9,000,000 Women Burned as Witches in the Christian Era,* which was performed in conjunction with the exhibit of *Proposals for: Memorials to the 9,000,000 Women Burned as Witches in the Christian Era,* was inspired by Edelson's meditations on why Goddess worship was stamped out. The exhibit documented her pilgrimage to and ritual in the Neolithic Grapçeva Cave on Hvar Island in Yugoslavia. The ritual installation included a great archway crowned by the Horns of Consecration, and covered with photographs of women's hands reclaiming symbolic gestures and signs such as the "mano cornuta," now understood in a positive way as a sign of the horns of the Moon, and indicative of the Goddess. The fire ladder symbolized both a hasty pyre on which witches were often burned, as well as transcendence, its more traditional meaning.

During the ritual, participants read aloud the names of real women and men who were accused of witchcraft and burned at the stake. Then, everyone filed out of the gallery, and a procession wound its way through the streets of Soho in New York City to the chant of "The Goddess is here; the Goddess is us."

Interpreting the Goddess in the second aspect of her meaning—that of rebirth and becoming, performance artist Betsy Damon, in her piece *The 7,000 Year Old Woman,* performed publicly on May 21, 1977, covered herself with small bags of colored flour which she punctured in a ritual ceremony on Wall Street. As each small bag of flour emptied like a miniature sand-timer, it was as if the artist and her assistant, through intense concentration and meditation, had incorporated a bit of lost historical time into their own energy fields. When the bags were all emptied and placed on the ground, they formed a spiral or a labyrinthine pattern.

The image of the 7,000 year old woman tapped directly into the image of the many-breasted Diana of Ephesus. As a child, Betsy Damon lived in Turkey (1944–1948), (Anatolia). Living near the ancient Neolithic Goddess site, and as one of the few Americans there with her family, having very few playmates, she would fantasize about her surroundings. Images such as that of the 7,000 year old woman were born of this early experience in Turkey. Later, she also lived in Japan, where she fell in love with the Kabuki and the Noh theater styles, and studied calligraphy. The slow, meditative pace of her performance pieces draws heavily on her Japanese experiences, as does her sensitivity to nature in her recent Riverbed piece and her early Sacred Grove pieces.

Damon's integration of the ancient Goddess Grove with the theme of the rebirth of contemporary women was apparent in the shrine that she built at the Ny Carlsberg Glyptotek Museum in Copenhagen on the occasion of the U.N. Mid-Decade for Women Conference at the First International Festival of Women Artists, whose American coordinator was artist Susan Schwalb. Later, at the U.N. End of Decade Conference in Nairobi in 1985, she also created a shrine on the lawn of the university. Both shrines were sites of international rituals in which women from around the world came to share their pain and their joy. Because of the intensity of political conflict at each of these conferences, a space of spiritual renewal was sought by many women, and it was at the shrine that women from warring nations could meditate, laugh, and cry together, and forge spiritual bonds that often transcended the national politics that divided them and created conflict among them.

Betsy Damon: The 7,000 Year Old Woman (1977)
Photographed by Sue Friedrich

Israeli artist Miriam Sharon performs desert rituals that are rites of exorcism overthrowing the patriarchal model that constructed alienating cityscapes of concrete over the ancient earth shrines and sacred sites. Her pilgrimage to the desert put her in contact with the Bedouins, "the last survivors of the Earth Living Culture" (Personal Communication, 1977). Her own Space Project Earth people, which grew out of her stay in the desert, is a ritual act of identification with the Mother Earth culture. Through meditation rituals in the wilderness, Sharon expresses the wish to recreate an ancient lost myth of the Earth Mother. Sharon's reclamation of the barren earth as the natural holy shrine, and her use of the desert as a temple for meditation, exemplify the return to primal matter as holy matter. Her participation with the Bedouins in the life of the desert as Goddess-space, parallels the initiatory experience of Edelson's cave rituals and Mendieta's Cuban rupestrian sculptures. However, Miriam Sharon defines "holy" as without shrines or temples, holy in its being alone. Her totemic figures from desert culture inspiration are participants in events that she creates in patriarchal spaces such as factories and ports. Here, the people who work on the site participate with the artists in an exploration of soft structures and organic materials in contrast to the technological environment in which they work. She feels as if she is bringing the Goddess space into the patriarchal space, and thereby transforming the latter. She writes about the Harbour Project, *Ashdoda* (1978): "On a little Tel, in the sands of the same beach area, Ashdoda, the deity of the sea people, during the Canaanite period, was found buried in the sands. This project brought the disappearing 'Desert Woman' into the harbour, transforming it" (Personal Communication, 1977). Through her Mt. Gilboa Tent Project entitled *Body/Full Moon Cycle* (1980) the women who came to live on the mountain in the Mother tents she had made, shared their creations and were the midwives of a new culture. The tent became Miriam Sharon's symbol for the ancient ecological knowledge that the Bedouin women bring into the contemporary world. In Sharon's ritual, contemporary women living in tents on Mt. Gilboa in ancient Israel were rebirthed through the tent/mountain/womb of the Earth Mother into a cultural cycle of their own creation. And, as in the mountain tent, Arabs and Jews lived together peacefully, under one roof—one tent/the sky—so might they live together ecologically on the Earth in the future.

Donna Henes's rituals and performances began with a series of process environmental sculptures entitled *Spider Woman*. Her work has always been about weaving webs and making connections, and her webbed sculptures were created in nature, strung along branches and twigs with the sky and the grass as the loom upon which she wove her webs. Weaving the webs in various states of trance and ecstasy, Henes has spun Spider Woman's threads and cocoons of natural fibers as a form of primal meditation.

Known for her solstice and equinox celebrations, she brings the rotation of the planet, its spinnings and revolvings to the consciousness of urban dwellers who are cut off from a conscious sense of their attunement with the solar cycles. At the World Trade Center in New York City in 1984 she celebrated the vernal equinox (spring) by having participants stand 360 eggs on their heads, a feat that can be accomplished only as spring is ushered in. If you try to do this only one week later, it is literally impossible.

As an urban shaman, she brings the experience of Stonehenge and Avebury to the big city in events such as *Wrapping up the New Year* in Central Park. Her performance, *Streams of Conscience*, which was held in Manhattan's Bowling Green, where she filled a fountain with circular mirrors which absorbed positive images while people chanted for peace over a 17-hour period, was held at the summer solstice in 1984.

Henes is known, too, for her healing event, *Wrapping Our Wounds in Warm Clothes*, done on Wards Island in order to humanize the environment of the mental patients who are housed there. She wrapped strips of clothing, and tied them in knots to 1,459 trees (one for each patient) on Memorial Day. This bandaging of the trees reflected a nurturant, healing act toward the Earth, and brought hope to many patients. For Henes's mission is to shed light and to bring hope by spreading the image of our interconnectedness with each other and with nature through the symbol of Spider Woman's webs.

Solstices and equinoxes affect everyone and every living thing simultaneously. They remind us that we are part of a larger, living, moving planet, within a constellation, in a galaxy, linked to everything in the universe.

Henes has unfurled colorful streamers in a piece entitled *Wrapping the Wind* at sites in Israel, Florida, New York, and California, and she has spun cocoons and wrapped branches in a variety of colors in Mexico, on Long Island, in Israel, and in California.

Most of her cocoons and webs are red, the color of blood and the life force. She is making visible the force fields, energy fields, and networks of nature that are like the blood vessels of the human body. By enabling us to see the invisible pathways of power and energy on the Earth and in the sky, like ley lines and telluric currents, Henes reconnects us to the life force as she weaves and spins our gyn/ecological network, Mary Daly-fashion, across the planet. Using eggs as the ancient and modern symbol of fertility and of the female, and webs as the web of life that is woven in the womb by mothers and in the universe by the Great Mother Creatress, Henes becomes the artist-creator incubating and hatching the Cosmic Egg of a feminist matristic culture which will reconnect life in the city with life as those who live in close contact with nature experience their attunement with the cosmic forces.

THE JOURNEY TO PREPATRIARCHAL
SITES AND ANCIENT SANCTUARIES
OF THE GODDESS

Sacred journeys to ancient Goddess sites led by contemporary feminist matristic artists present reinterpretations of these cultures in ways that are relevant for our time. As seers and guides, their works often intuit aspects of Goddess reverence in these ancient societies by activating the kinesthetic imagination. The artists we will consider in this section often invite us to inhabit the site along with them, and to accompany them on the pilgrimage during which they will recreate the site, ancient artifacts, and ancient rituals according to a synthesis of their knowledge and their active imaginations.

It is obvious that the Goddess Temple would be a proper site to revisit. Architect Christina Biaggi, working with Mimi Lobell as consulting architect, has proposed the construction of a Goddess Mound. In the seventies, Lobell had already designed a Goddess Temple for construction at a site in Colorado. Hers was based upon design principles that corresponded to the Jungian archetypal theory.

The Goddess Mound proposed by Biaggi and Lobell is an actual sculpture of a Great Goddess Temple that can be entered. Biaggi writes in her proposal and artist's statement that "The Great Goddess who was the supreme diety of the early Neolithic and even Paleolithic peoples in Europe and Asia is re-emerging in the twentieth century as an apt symbol of women's growing consciousness and importance. . . . Sculpture in the Western world has lost the mystical, magical presence that it had during the Neolithic period when a temple or a sculpture was considered to be the body of the deity. In creating my sculpture, I wish to bring back some of this magic and mystery. I want to create a space that inspires mystery; that evokes the dark caves of the Goddess—places of rebirth and revitalized consciousness" (Biaggi, "Artist's Statement").

Biaggi did her doctoral dissertation on megalithic sculptures that symbolize the Great Goddess, and her proposed Goddess Mound is inspired by Maltese and Scottish structures. "The outside will resemble Maes Howe in the Orkney Islands, Silbury Hill in Southern England, and New Grange in Ireland. Inside, the irregular concavities formed by the figure's negative shapes will have the cavelike quality of Maltese tombs" (Biaggi, "Artist's Statement"). Biaggi and Lobell have, like ancient archaeoastronomers, calculated important solstitial and equinoctial alignments as well as other sunrise and sunset alignments, so that the cycles of the cosmos can be reexperienced as part of the sacred reality of the Goddess.

Jean Edelstein has created a Greek-inspired Goddess Temple installation in Venice, California. The columns of her temple are painted with large, dancing women, and more recently it is as if the dancers have left the columns and come alive within her studio. Working with her model, a dancer, Jean Edelstein literally dances her paintings (in the mode of action painters) before a live public. Sensing the kinesthetics of the female body, as it may have moved in ritual dances at ancient temples, Edelstein has painted and drawn works in a Temple Series in which she explores, through the body of the female as priestess and ritualist, the sacred relationship between women and the built and natural environment. She reevokes ancient memories of times when the female image was worshipped as the embodiment of the sacred.

Suzanne Benton is a metal sculptor who has traveled all over the world studying folk tales, making masks for a variety of international female folk heroes, and performing their stories as well as those of the matriarchs from the Bible and the women of the Greek myths.

Benton was one of the first contemporary feminist matristic artists. During the early seventies she created a throne for the Sun Queen in New York State's Art Park. The sculpture was made specifically for use in storytelling. Visitors to the park could sit upon the throne of the Sun Queen/Sun Goddess and tell tales from their lives and from their imaginations relating to the Goddess.

Florida-based performance artist, Kyra, has honored the pre-Columbian Goddesses Coatlicue, the Great Corn Mother, Chicomecoatl, and the Sun Goddesses in her series of Magic Circle Rituals combined with drawings and environmental sculptures. Her multimedia events in the Magic Circle Goddess Series are completed by a video performance. Kyra writes: "God the Mother in my art is interpreted through Her many symbols and is celebrated under many names given to her by the various civilizations from the prehistoric Great Goddess to the Egyptian Goddess Isis. The live ritual performance . . . is inspired by the many ancient rituals that celebrated the life-giving creative energy of the Goddess. It consists of fire and candle rituals, sounds, movements, and dance, accompanied by visual light effects. The participants include myself in the role of the high Priestess, other women as Priestesses, and a group of women and men playing the part of the worshippers" (Kyra, 1987).

In linking our ancient Western and Amerindian heritages, Kyra stresses the similarity in functions between, for example, the Goddesses Chicomecoatl and Demeter as Mother-Creators, bestowing abundance, as Harvest deities, Corn Mothers, and Goddesses of the Grains. In connecting Chicomecoatl and Demeter, Kyra expresses her reverence for Mother Earth in several of her various manifestations on the planet.

Rachel Giladi is an Israeli performance artist whose parents grew up in the old city of Jerusalem, and lived closely with the Arabs there. Having heard the stories of how three generations of her family lived in peace with the Arabs, Rachel began to do political performance pieces to protest war and to foster peace. She says that all her works are rituals about the identification of the Daughters of Zion with their neighboring women, the Daughters of Canaan. In Canaan in the prebiblical period, women worshipped Goddesses (who came to be known as "other Gods" in the Bible).

In 1976 Giladi performed a ritual of identification and unification with nature. In this piece, women wrapped themselves in burlap (a symbol of mourning in Israel), and went out to the beach, rolling down from the hilltop to the water's edge, enfolding themselves in sand. As the water washed over their bodies, they drank the water and the sand, and identified with the Earth, whose Goddess was known as Ashtoreth.

In 1978 she did a ritual entitled *Worshipping Foreign Gods,* which was a ceremony of purification and identification of the Daughters of Zion with the Daughters of Canaan. In this ritual the stones were used because of their identification as "foreign gods." Stones had also been used in the ritual stoning to death of adulterous women in Zion. Giladi erected a small, round tent that was lit inside, so that one could look inside, and see two women playing with stones. The women lay the stones on each of the chakras (energy centers) of their bodies. This work was a mystical, meditative ritual, an attempt to transform the aggression associated with the stones into an act of healing.

Her 1982 protest ritual was called *A Stone on My Heart.* In this performance women meditated with stones, and protested the war, asking the government to bring their children back from Lebanon. Giladi's work has always been about women and peace. In 1983 she went to the upper Galilee and put up four Israeli flags sewn in pink and white (not the traditional blue and white) on a hilltop on the Lebanese border, conveying the message that if women were in charge, peace might be restored. The flags remained in Kiryat Shmona for over two months. The four flags symbolized the four matriarchs of Israel.

In another performance in 1985, Giladi had pregnant mothers skate around the Dizengoff Square to call attention to the dangers to which they exposed their unborn children. When questioned about this by anxious bystanders, the women responded: "Why, then, do you send these same children to war? Feel for us now, before they are eighteen, and create the conditions of peace now!"

Jane Ellen Gilmore: Great Goddess at the Temple of Olympian Zeus II
(Ecclecticism and Stress Series—1978)

The performance in which Giladi made the most literal connection between contemporary women and the ancient Goddess culture of Canaan was entitled *Celebrate Now*. She put an announcement in the paper that crowns of Queens and Goddesses had been found in an archaeological dig. She had, in fact, done research on this dig and copied the small goddess sculptures and crowns, enlarging them into enormous headpieces, painting them in gold, and making them large enough for the women to try on. The crowns dated from 4,000 years ago, and bore ancient matristic symbols of snakes and horns. She then invited women to come to Dizengoff Square and see how they would feel wearing the crowns and goddess sculptures from the ancient civilization unearthed at the dig at Zidon. The ritual crowning included an offering of sweet wine and the burning of incense. Rachel walked around the square wearing a serpent crown and sprinkling rose water on the passersby, urging them to revive the values of the culture that existed when Goddesses were worshipped.

Like the work of Mary Beth Edelson, Rachel Giladi's creation is composed of separate cycles of Lamentation and Celebration. In the history of Israel, she sees the microcosmic example of the themes of holocaust and war, the rediscovery of ancient values from Goddess cultures, and how a reconnection with those values can lead to a rebirth and a new historical cycle.

The works of Jane Ellen Gilmore are unique in their celebration and reclamation of women's matristic history through her use of humor and irony. Her comical tableaux, photographed at the ancient ruins of Greece, Egypt, and Turkey, where performances dedicated to the mythical Goddesses were staged, show the discrepancy between women as they were revered in these ancient Goddess cultures (such as the Goddess Bast, a cat-headed Goddess in Egypt) and women as they are depicted today, as coy sex objects. By putting humorous cat-masked contemporary women on these shrines, such as the Temple of Zeus or the Temple of Apollo, we immediately perceive the way in which patriarchal history has debased the image of woman and erased the original sacred icon of the Goddess and her priestesses.

Gilmore has also created numerous shrines, which are parodies of devotional art and are

Ann McCoy: Temple of Isis, Pompeii (1987)

inspired by some of the bizarre roadside shrines that populate the European countryside of Mediterranean countries.

By revisiting the ancient sites with a contemporary gaze, Gilmore explores both the construction and the deconstruction of myth as well as the male-female role-playing in human interactions.

Finally, California performance artist Anna Homler's *Bread Woman* makes use of a sound track of "bread songs" that she has written, which sound like what we might imagine a primordial, Neolithic ur-language to be. Her persona, Bread Woman, an old woman with a face made of loaves of bread, is a symbol of the Earth's bounty and nurturance. Her bread mother sings bread songs in her primal mother tongue, and feeds the audience from her large supply of bread-filled bowls and trays, as she chants in the language of our dreams. Her songs seem to revive a memory of some ancient, magical use of the voice.

THE JOURNEY WITHIN

Although, for the most part, contemporary feminist matristic artists are trying to reclaim the Goddess in her historicity, rather than as an archetype of the unconscious, Ann McCoy's art is important specifically in what it reveals about the connection between the unconscious as a creative vortex of memories from ancient matristic history and contemporary feminist matristic consciousness.

Raised in the Southwest, among the Pueblo Indians who believed in the importance of dreams and visions, McCoy's images are culled from the dream. The raw material of the dream then undergoes an extensive process, which used to be called "incubation" in the classical world. Incubation, she tells us, is a "sleeping in" to obtain dreams for therapeutic and prophetic ends. For the past 20 years she has catalogued her dreams and visions, and traced their symbols and iconography through a study of world mythology. She is also attentive to the mysterious, acausal, synchronistic events that coincide with specific dreams. The works that result from this creative process are works such as the *Temple of Isis* (1987), a color pencil drawing which is 9 feet × 15 feet in size.

Stressing the importance of intuition and dream as forms of knowledge, which counter the modern world's emphasis on science, reason, and materialism, Ann McCoy is particularly drawn to the works of C. J. Jung, for she believes that her dream images well up from the collective unconscious, and she feels that the artist makes a bridge between two worlds— the outer, physical world, and the inner, spiritual world.

She has written the following about the genesis of her drawing, *The Temple of Isis.*

THE TEMPLE OF ISIS:
The events which led to the making of the Temple of Isis came from a dream fragment. In the dream I was handed an ancient instrument by an unknown woman. The next day as I was looking up a word in my dictionary, I saw a picture of a sistrum, the ancient instrument from my dream. The synchronicity of the events was underscored the following afternoon when I found a brochure from an Egyptologist in the street. I entered his shop and saw a sistrum at a greatly reduced price, and informed me it was the first he had ever had. The sistrum was thought to contain the magical properties of Isis, and when rattled was believed to make the Nile rise and fall. This votive rattle was meant to keep the worshipper in a state of spiritual attentiveness.

In a second dream, I was with a group of archeologists restoring an ancient temple site. A child entered the temenos on a donkey. Unlike Christ, the child was a young radiant Goddess. The dream was for me an annunciation. We live in an historical period which is overly androlatric. With the exception of the Virgin Mary, we have no feminine deity. For me the dream signaled, not the return of a matriarchal monotheism, but an integration of the divine feminine into the psychic lives of both men and women. The Eros represented by Aphrodite is sadly lacking in our culture dominated by Apollo, Ares, and sky gods. More than ever we need the goddess, the guardian of psychic interiority.

The night I began the drawing, I had a dream in which Isis appeared wearing a golden robe of silk. I touched the hem of her robe and awakened feeling changed by the numinous content of the dream. For me, the dream began a meditation on Isis and her meaning for the modern world. A second dream in Venice followed: I was working on the excavation of a site containing huge clay cows. As we worked, a friend read a text on a female figure who was resurrected. In Egypt the cow was associated with Hathor/Isis, and the bull with Osiris/Apis.

Both dreams inspired me to take a pilgrimage to the Temple of Isis in Pompeii. I arrived in Pompeii in a thunderstorm, lightening bolts shooting through the black sky and off the rim of the volcano. The atmosphere was mysterious, and the place deserted of visitors. I climbed over a back wall, and spent the day alone in the tiny temple.

As I left Pompeii, I met a young man from Liverpool who had taken his life savings to visit Pompeii. The student of Classics said that he, too, felt the gods of Olympus were alive. A boy in Reagan's America would probably be studying computers. I felt hope for the modern world as I spoke with the young man.

Isis, like Demeter, is an agricultural goddess, whose mysteries many scholars feel had to do with rebirth in the underworld . . . as the seed beneath the soil was equated to a kind of psychological and spiritual renewal likened to the agricultural cycle of renewal. The goddess is the guardian of feeling, interiority, and the healing aspect of the feminine. Isis heals her husband Osiris, an also symbolizes and agricultural renewal needed by our environmentally devastated world.

When the Temple of Isis in Pompeii was first excavated, they found eggs perfectly preserved on the altar. The egg is not just a cosmogonic symbol, it is also a philosophical symbol. As the philosophical egg of the medieval natural philosophers, it is the vessel from which the Anthropos, the spiritual, inner, and complete man emerges. (McCoy, "Artist's Statement")

In film, Sylvianna Goldsmith's "The Transformation of Persephone" segment from her film, *Orpheus Underground* (1973) was one of the first attempts to depict rape from the feminist matristic perspective. As Queen of the Underworld, the Goddess Persephone is shown both in her full sensuality and power as well as in her victimization. This journey to the underworld, is a journey to the unconscious, recovering repressed material both about female sexuality and about female power growing stronger in the underworld.

THE JOURNEY TO SACRED SITES IN NATURE

Honoring the Great Mother by celebrating the Earth and Her cycles has also given contemporary meaning to the solstice and equinox rituals performed by ancient and modern earth-revering and tribal peoples everywhere. Feminist matristic artists make offerings to the Great Earth Mother, whom they see and feel in the land, in the sky, and in the sacred presences of all creatures on Earth.

Faith Wilding, raised with the deep spirituality of the Hutterite community nested in the pagan landscape of Uruguay, broke the bonds of her harsh patriarchal background while retaining the strong sense of the Earth, itself, as spiritual and terrestrial mother in a new female Creation myth. Her ritual *Invocation to a Burning,* which took place at the spring equinox in 1980, was involved with the idea of rebirth from the Earth Mother, and dealt with the theme of fertility and vegetation in its planting ceremony. A full-sized body of the Earth Mother made of clay, wire, wax, and earth was burned at the equinox. Women present spontaneously jumped over the body and planted seeds communally in the earthly remains. The seeds sprouted, and new life was born out of the ashes. Faith then sent packets of these seeds to Copenhagen in 1980, where they were distributed to women from many countries in a global ritual of home planting entitled "Liberty Herbal," which would represent "women's world-wide efforts to unite with all of nature against war and world destruction."

Marsha Hewitt's *Autumn Ritual* is concerned with the magical and mysterious relationship to the Goddesses of the harvest. Her figures are reminiscent of British folk-art corn dollies. Her life masks serve as guardians of the sacred place in nature where the cycles of nature are celebrated in the name of the Corn Goddess. At the full moon on October 11, 1981, Marsha Hewitt led a fertility ritual in the cornfield at Yaddo (an artist's retreat) to mark the phases of life, death, and rebirth that the Goddess symbolizes. During the procession into the corn field, the northern lights came out, starting as a red, firey glow, gathering energy, turning pink, and moving directly over the cornfield. Two weeks later she held another ritual in order to make an offering of one of the goddess figures to ensure fertility. She prepared the figure by sewing heart-shaped leaves onto her gown. Then she burned her and left the remains on the site.

As in the case of Hewitt's ritual, the only traces that remain of the event in nature are photographic. Any burned materials are returned to the Earth for natural recycling. Most feminist matristic art approaches nature with reverence, and attempts, whenever possible, to return the art work to the Earth.

In Thunder Bay, Canada, the Anishnabe performance artist Rebecca Belmore has invoked the strong presence of Earth Woman in her piece entitled *Mukwa* (Ojibway for bear) in which she explores three generations of native women (her grandmother, her mother, and herself) through a vocal invocation of the spirit of the Earth Woman and three dancing shadows. A more political piece, *Swamp Woman* ("Mushkegokwe"), was created to bring attention to the dangers felt by the Earth-spirit. In this work the artist drew upon the experience of a native community whose existence was pushed to the brink of self-destruction by the intrusion of so-called progressive technology. The discord created by the imposition of technological ways onto the culture of a people that once lived in close harmony with the Earth manifested itself in the genocidal behavior of that local community. Through a multimedia performance using fog, earth, mud, dance, song, and poetry, as well as an installation, she invoked the presence of Swamp Woman to cut the cord of liberation, so that her people could live in harmony with nature once more.

Christine Oatman and Helene Aylon care for the ailing Earth in both magical and political performance events. Christine Oatman, in a healing ceremony, went out into a selected site in nature and draped her colorful blanket over the barren earth as if to heal a wounded patient. Weeks later, when the blanket, like a magician's cape, was lifted, a field of colorful flowers had sprouted under its protected area. Oatman has planted flowers in the colors of the chakras and the spectrum, each field generating a different energy for the Earth, which needs all the different kinds of healing energies we can administer to Her. It is in this sense that the artist performs a shamanic healing ceremonial, and becomes the spiritual Medicine Woman of her Earth Mother.

In 1982 Helene Aylon rescued some ailing Earth from the Strategic Air Command weapon base. The Earth was placed in pillowcases, and then transported in an Earth Ambulance to the United Nations, where it was carried down to the U.N. Plaza on stretchers like a wounded body. At the United Nations a 14-day sleep out was held for the Earth.

In *Sister Rivers*, which took place at the Kama River in Japan, Helene Aylon with Miriam Abramowicz conceived of the Earth as the Mother, and of Her rivers as the arteries and veins of the living planet. She bases her concept of the Goddess on the knowledge that Lympha was the Latin name for the Goddess of Water, and it is the word from which we derive lymph. In her piece two young Japanese women come to the Kama River and place rice and seeds into each of two pillowcases, respectively. They are sending the 'sacs' (the spelling recalls her previous events aboard The Strategic Air Command) down the river to Hiroshima and Nagasaki where women await their arrival. They will then be filled with the sands of Hiroshima and Nagasaki and will continue to sail down the rivers of the world, gathering earth, and making everyone conscious of the need to save the Mother as well as of how we have destroyed Her.

The evolution Helene Aylon has made from her *Earth Ambulance* piece to *Sister Rivers* is that whereas in the former, appeal was made to patriarchal authorities at the United Nations, in the latter, healing is sought, from the great wisdom of the Earth Mother Herself. The piece is ecofeminist in that it shows the interconnectedness of both natural and human agency in bringing about change. While the role the women play in saving the Earth is catalytic, ultimately it is the Earth's own wisdom aligned with the wisdom of the Great Mother River, that will direct the destiny of the sacks, as it once directed the destiny of the young Moses, whose rescue by the Pharaoh's daughter inspired this piece.

Vijali: She Who Opens the Doors of the Earth (Yelapa, Mexico—15′ × 20′ × 15′, granite—1981)

Vijali has been sculpting the Great Earth Mother in sacred rocks and boulders, which she finds at sites all over the world. Indeed, in order to see her works in nature, one needs to visit them with a map in hand, for they are located in the mountains and forests, far from the main road, and a hike is usually involved in reaching them.

As a child, Vijali was introduced to meditation. She entered a Hindu convent at the age of 14, and lived there until she was 25. Thus, she experienced the luminous energy by which humans are interconnected with nature, during the many hours she spent in meditation. When she left the convent and embarked on her artistic path, she underwent still more intense experiences channeling healing energies, and found that in order to ground those energies, she had to live and sculpt in the mountains. She would see energy moving in the stones, and at those peak moments, she experienced a oneness with everything. It is this vibrant life energy of the Great Mother that Vijali expresses in her art. Her work enables us to visualize our own interconnectedness with nature, particularly since the journey to visit her sculpture consists of entering nature partially prepared to spend at least half a day out of doors. As you prepare for your visit to her Great Woman in the mountains, you think about bringing food along, providing for the climactic conditions of the day and the location, and so forth. Once you have arrived at the piece, you experience a slowing down of time as you become attuned to the rhythms and cycles of the site. Vijali's work enables us to relax, to change our consciousness, and ultimately to see the Great Mother in the Earth as she does. Her stone sculptures flow with the natural setting which is their home. Her work also aligns us with the site-specific energy currents and natural processes. We take a day out to see one art work and make the experiencing of it the focus of our journey. The sculpture ultimately draws us closer to nature, making us conscious of the subtleties of each sensation in the environment.

Vijali has also created a World Wheel that expands the boundaries of conventional art. She writes about it that "It reaches back into the deep past, connecting to the origins of art and theater as a ritual of transformation for the individual and the community. It extends into the future by creating hope for our planet. Inspired by the elements of nature and the understanding that we ARE Earth, it combines theatre, dance, music, sculpture, and ritual into one art form called 'Theater of the Earth' " (Vijali, 1988). The pattern of the wheel is based upon the native American medicine wheel. The first environmental sculpture and performance, "Western Gateway," took place on August 17, 1987 in the Malibu area of Los Angeles, which is the beginning and western-most point of the wheel. Vijali will travel to each of the remaining 11 sites (which represent one spoke and one characteristic of the medicine wheel), and work with skilled local artists and performers to produce the event. The remaining sites are in Spain, Italy, Greece, Egypt, Israel, Russia, India, Tibet, China, and Japan. World Wheel is an artist's forum for global peace and understanding. This forum is a womb for personal inspiration that will, in turn, help us to survive, to heal, and to respect our planet and ourselves (Vijali, Notes about the World Wheel and the Theater of the Earth).

Sandra Menefee Taylor's installations *Remains to be Seen* and *Mystery Chamber #XI* draw us into the mythic world of Demeter, Goddess of Fertility and Grain, who, as the artist writes on the wall of the *Remains to be Seen* installation, "would have wiped out the whole race of talking men with a painful famine." Clearly it 'remains to be seen' whether grain will eventually be shared to feed the entire Earth's population. *Mystery Chamber #XI* brings us into the grainery with its huge storage vessels, real grain, real corn, and the invocation of the Hymn to Demeter. By reminding us of the ancient power of Demeter to refuse to bestow her fertility upon the Earth in protest against the rape of her daughter, Persephone, Menefee Taylor reminds us that our strength is as great as that of the life force, itself. However, if the Earth is barren in our time, it is *not* because Demeter has withheld her power, but because Demeter herself is dying.

Elizabeth Erickson is a member of the WARM feminist cooperative gallery in Minneapolis, and a ritual artist and poet. In her ritual *Tears of the Mother,* she instructs the participants to gather together in the location of a labyrinth, and to pour water (symbolic of the tears of the Mother) into the labyrinth. Each person is asked to read her own statement about saving the Earth from pollution and nuclear destruction. This ritual was performed at the U.N. End of Decade Conference for Women in Nairobi, Kenya, in 1985. Her poem *Tears of the Mother* expresses the pain of Gaia and of her inhabitants in this time of ecocrisis.

> TEARS OF THE MOTHER
> She cries.
> Her tears are for her self.
> Her tears are for the rivers.
> Her tears are for the forests.
> Her tears are for the crust of soil,
> shifting and covering her deep stones.
> Her tears are for her oceans, rocking with the moon.
> Her tears are for the fish, the lizards, the seabirds,
> all fourlegged beasts and all feathered ones, flying over her,
> fed by her.
> Her tears are for the tall green plants, the dry grasses,
> the blown-open flowers,
> Her tears are for the shaped fruit,
> all the living food as it seasons into wholeness.
>
> Her tears are for all the two-legged creatures, and
> men and women who move upon her
> who move together upon her and who are related to her and
> who are also
> grieving.
>
> All these are in danger.
> The rivers, the forests, the soil, oceans, animals,
> plants, men and women.
> Her bed of air. Her spin.
> All these are in danger.
>
> We are the women and men, related to her.
> Who know she is crying. We bring water to say
> we know this.
>
> We pour these streams onto the Mother,
> coming to protect and join with her
> in healing.
> We resolve to heal
> the Earth.
> She is the Mother. (Erikson, 1985)

While I have limited my discussion here to artists who either specifically or metaphorically mention or invoke the Earth Mother, I have not included the general categories of landscape painting or art about nature unless they were specifically related to the Earth as the embodiment of the Goddess or of the Earth Mother's sacredness and spirituality. Diane Burko is an exception. She is a landscape painter who has, however, been making pilgrimages to nature for almost two decades in order to evoke the spirit of place in her large paintings of canyons, mountains, sea, landscapes, and the sky. In her painting *La Manneporte* (6′ × 8′) (1987), one senses that the light emerging from the cave (or cove) corresponds to the Goddess energy emanating from the Grapçeva Cave in the pilgrimage series done by Mary Beth Edelson. There are many other women artists who use the landscape to express the Earth Mother's spirituality, such as Joella Jean Mahoney, whose work is primarily about the landscapes of the southwestern United States. While the use of landscape as a metaphor for a woman is common, in the cases of these two artists and many others too numerous to include, the landscape is no longer a metaphor, but *is* the Earth Mother Herself.

While most feminist matristic artists express spirit embodied in the phenomenal, material world, for they make no patriarchal dichotomies between spirit and matter, some feminist matristic artists express spirit itself. In conceptualizing the spirit world within a feminist matristic vision, it is necessary to postulate that this realm is not envisaged as apart from the world, but rather as an extension of the phenomenal universe that incorporates intangible and invisible entities.

THE JOURNEY TO THE
SPIRIT WORLD

In this section I speak primarily about artists who, like shamans, conceive of the creative process as a journey in which a contact is made with the energies and entities of the spirit world. If we consider the creative process of these artists as analogous to the shamanic process, then we can achieve a much deeper understanding of the transformative visions, energy exchanges, and healings that they seek to bring about through their art.

As we have said earlier, the shaman undertakes a ritual ecstatic vision-quest journey in order to reconnect a community with the power emanating from a numinous spirit realm. The artist-as-shaman then, too, enters into an altered state of consciousness in order to make a visionary journey to the forces, energies, and powers we associate with the Cosmic Mother or the Goddess, in order to return spiritually empowered, so that she can effect the transformative energy exchange needed. On this psychic journey, the artist, too, may experience states of symbolic death, dismemberment, and rebirth.

Barbara Kazanis has described her creative process as "enactments." Her enactments are partially ritual, partially "theater of the soul" in the ancient Greek sense of the mystery religions. They draw heavily on her involvement with physical and psycho-spiritual healing. She has moved from private ritual to more participatory work, and she has done work with death, dying, chronic diseases, and grief at hospice centers, where she found the patients had made altars, had enacted the mysteries, and had many mystical experiences. She considers her art work to be a form of visual inquiry.

In *Earth Spirits* she worked directly with objects that she discovered to have "power." Soon after she began to do work that dealt with funerals and resurrection, she found that each piece she created was, in itself, a map of the body showing its energy flows and blockages. Later, her work evolved from a series of shamanic dreams of experiences of initiation into African tribes.

In general, her art involves movement, meditation, and the healing arts. Her Earth altars use objects of power in order to enact a meeting with "the Ancestors," and to establish hidden energic connections between life in the visible and invisible realms.

New York/Boston artist Susan Schwalb's rituals are private rebirth ceremonies that record a death-life process in which a spark of the life force is reclaimed.

During the summer of 1980, in Norway, Schwalb performed a series of private art rites that were intended to put the art work back into nature, to return the paper to the land, and the image to the Earth, by burning a drawing in the grass or on the rocks. The drawings burned were usually of flowers, Schwalb's symbol for feminist matristic vision, which she has previously used in connection with images of the Goddess spirit in her large orchid drawings and burned smoke pieces on paper. After burning the silverpoint drawings, Schwalb used the ashes of these burnt drawings to make small altars about the act of burning the art. These commemorative pieces are like rites of passage marking changes in her art as well as in her life. They have evolved out of her silverpoint orchid drawings, which were hallmarks for her of female spirituality and sexuality fused in a single feminist matristic image.

In 1981, at Yaddo artist's retreat, she burned the drawings' cut edges, lit candles which she placed on the works, and made living altars in which the lit central area illuminated the entire drawing and made it live for a moment. Then the remains were kept and placed in an altar with flower petals. Also in 1981 Susan Schwalb created an altar in nature using a stump of a tree, bark, twigs, and grasses, which were then burned symbolically. Susan Schwalb's art explores the boundaries between energy and matter. For her, the piece is alive in the moment of the burning. Metaphorically, she likens the art work to a living, organic flower, which blooms, fades, and is reborn in a new season. The connection with the Earth as spiritual mother of all the material of both life and art is profoundly felt both in her assemblage reliquaries and in her process-burning rituals.

In these works the Earth Mother is not only the Goddess Creatress of life, but of art as well. By returning the work to nature, Schwalb affirms that art, like life, is related to, and born of, the sacred.

Fern Shaffer collaborates with photographer Othello Anderson to explore traditions that seek to explain the place of humans in the universe, and the meaning of natural phenomena. They are concerned with the traditions of pre-Columbian North America and the early American Indians as well as with shamanic practices in general.

Several of their pieces have been done at sacred burial mounds. *Spiral Dance* was a ceremony held at an ancient circle marked with red wood poles in Illinois. The circle had been used one thousand years ago as a solar calendar by the Sun Priests of an Indian tribe. At the spring equinox in 1986, they visited that power site in order to wake up the ancient energies in the Earth.

Effigy Mounds was a prehistoric burial site where magical, religious practices once took place. Shamans conducted ceremonies there to bring success in the hunt, to repel natural disasters, and to avert and repel illness. Shaffer and Anderson visited the site with Shaffer in ceremonial costume in order to communicate with the powers through shapes, colors, vibrations, and gestures reminiscent of the ancient ritualists, who were once in touch with the sacred energies.

Washing Crystals in Lake Michigan took place on the winter solstice in 1985 at 25 degrees below zero, Fahrenheit. Through these rituals in different climates, at different sacred spaces, and held at different times of the planetary cycles, Shaffer and Anderson are learning to use the language of art to speak the language of the spirit and to commune with the invisible energies that inhabit a sacred site. They work not only with the visible aspects of the site, but with its energy-surrounds.

Performing rituals at the solstice or the equinox, at sacred burial mounds of the Indians, and in below-freezing weather alters the energy of the site as well as that of the participant/artists. It sets in motion spirals of energy that radiate through the universe and affect forces both material and spiritual. These rituals, although done with only one or two people present, are posited on the understanding that since everything is interconnected, the artist's revisitation of a sacred site and her energy exchange with it may touch off a chain of energies and reactions that are associated with the networks and webs associated with the Great Earth Mother.

Donna Byars's art has always transmuted her dreams into magical, talismanic objects in whose company we are able to sense the mysterious presence of the spirit world.

An early work specifically inspired by a dream of the Goddess was Oracle Stone Grove (1977). In her dream a stone woman sat in a grove of trees. She spoke in vapors, but was understood intuitively of the dreamers. She told of the beauty and meaning of life. Suddenly she slipped from her chair, and disappeared into a hole in the ground. When she was replaced upon her chair, she could no longer speak. Oracle Stone Grove, with a stone upon a chair situated in a grove of weeping fig trees, invites the viewer to enter the grove of the muted Goddess, to commune with her energy, and to revive her world and her words of life.

In 1979 Byars created Dream Stones as a stone circle, reminiscent of the megalithic stone circles in the British Isles. Each of her stone tablets is inscribed with a mysterious symbol culled from a dream.

Her more recent works such as *Reclamation* (1978), *Greylag, Keeper of Visions* (1985),

Fern Shaffer and Othello Anderson: Winter Solstice (1985)

and *Standing Bear* (1986)/*When the Hair Was Long and Thick (For Jason)* unite many disparate elements magically, that intimate the unveiling of mysteries in which animal and human souls are reconciled within the cycles of energy, spirit, and nature.

Byars's art truly expresses the concept of the feminist matristic artist-as-shaman, for she brings back to the tonal the power animals from her dream journeys to the nagual in such a way as to provoke a healing of the soul. This energy is palpably experienced in the presence of her installations.

An artist who has been called to shamanic work, and whose process enlightens us about the artist's relationship with the spirit world is Rowena Pattee. In the profile she writes of her life, published in *Shape Shifters: Shaman Women in Contemporary Society,* she says that her main experience with Shamanism can be described as living from ''the sun in the heart'' (Pattee, 1987, p. 67).

For many years Rowena Pattee had practiced Zen meditation, and done shamanic drawings, paintings, and prints from Siberian, Amerindian, and Australian sources. Although she works with the complementarity of "masculine" and "feminine" aspects of the self, she believes that women shamans are being called upon at present in order to bring about a healing of the planet through compassion.

Her contact with the spirit world came about spontaneously through visionary journeys such as the journey she made to the center of the Earth. Upon her return, she encountered her guide, White Buffalo, who showed her underground sacred centers all up and down the Northwest coast from Alaska to Manchuria, the Pacific Islands and from South America to California.

More recently, White Egret Woman has appeared in her visions. She seems to manifest her presence in the underground sacred centers of the Earth. Rowena Pattee has many spirit Guides and a Council of Elders who give her directives. Through drumming and chanting she has accessed knowledge that is not ordinarily available to our sensory experience. In order to do this, she has made use of a variety of techniques such as the tarot, the I Ching, the runes, and geomancy. The vibrations that Rowena Pattee uses to access this information include numbers, sounds, colors, and thought-forms, which constitute a vibrational language linking the shaman to other dimensions. Through such journeys she has had visionary and energic experiences in which spirits directed her to create such pieces as her "White Eagle" robe. For Pattee, the task of humans is to attune to sources, to live and work in harmony with the cycles of the cosmos, of nature, and of all sentient beings. Through her many visionary experiences and shamanic journeys to the spirit world, Rowena Pattee is able to bring forth a prophecy for the future. "My concern is for the earth as a living being and for the regeneration of humanity at its roots. Its roots are spiritual and that's why shamans, and especially balanced, clear women shamans, are needed today" (Pattee, 1987, p. 62).

Beth Ames Swartz's spiritual journey through art to the sacred spaces where powerful, ancient sources of womanspirit can be recontacted dates back to her work *Israel Revisited* (1981–83). In that work she made a pilgrimage to the holy land, and celebrated the memory of ancient Biblical Matriarchs through works on paper that were created as a result of rituals she performed using fire and earth at sites connected with these Biblical Ancestresses.

In 1985 her complex installation *A Moving Point of Balance* began its own travels, and will continue to be exhibited through 1990. Here Swartz worked with the healing energies and colors of the chakras, making individual paintings for each chakra according to its color vibration.

Swartz's materials include, in addition to paint and canvas, a variety of healing stones from the Arizona desert. She uses quartz crystal, azurite, chrysocolla, rose quartz, amethyst, mica, gold and silver leaf, copper, earth, fire, and sunlight, as well as shards from the native American Southwest to create a richly textured picture surface that both channels energy and reflects light. Her *Alchemy Series* (1989) was done along with work on the medicine wheel. This series highlights the energy centers of the human body below the head. In her *Painting VII* of this series, the body of the Goddess is literally illuminated, as light and energy are channeled through the crystals into spirals and vortices that highlight the Survival Chakra, the Emotional Chakra, the Solar Plexus, the Heart Chakra, and the Throat Chakra.

When standing directly in front of many of the works in this series, one experiences a trembling and shuddering in the floor and a tingling in the body, as vast energy charges interact with the spatial- and human-surrounds. Indeed, for Beth Ames Swartz, there is less and less distinction made between the painting and the viewer, as the energy field of the work envelopes and merges with that of the viewer. The energy exchange created between the art work and the spectator is so powerful, that not only do many people experience an emotional cleansing, but the work also becomes charged by their presence. Thus, each piece emits not only its own color vibrations and energies, but also the cumulative effects of the gathered energies of all of its viewers.

The spirit world that Beth Ames Swartz's recent works explore is the energic dimension of the spiritual body, the light body pulsating within the human corporeal body. Her sometimes headless figures remind us that when we think with our heart, we have a body intelligence that is the equivalent of our more usual forms of mental knowledge. It is this energic bodily knowledge, this vibratory system awake in the human being, that is the spiritual reminder, the field that stores memories of our identity as daughters and sons of the Great Mother.

Maria Mazzara makes Medicine Bundles as offerings to the Great Mother. Her bundles are prayers to bring about a healing of herself, her friends, and the Earth, the Mother of us all. Her earliest memory that relates to the image of the bundle is of her house being struck by lightning when she was 5, and of her being wrapped and carried out of the house. In that memory, she herself was the bundle.

Today, Mazzara's things are wrapped and made into bundles, some of which are burned as sacrifices of the burdens and baggage that we carry. They are also metaphors for a healing community, since odd things from various sources commingle in one bundle and undergo transformation to medicine and prayer together, as if in a single microcommunity.

In her first bundle Maria burned a miniature Bible, not as a sacrilege, but in order to release the male Father God's hold upon her spirit. (Formerly she had been a nun.) Maria had also experienced serious back pain, and after an operation on her spine, she made bundles to the Great Mother asking for health and praising Her powers. She was healed.

Inspired by the native American "Medicine Way," Mazzara bundles things that help her to walk through the world no longer disconnected. As she offers gift bundles and memory bundles to friends, she weaves a medicine web of healing in her own life.

THE JOURNEY TO THE CRONE: JOURNEY TO EARTH-MOTHER'S WISDOM

The journey to the Crone is the most difficult journey of all, for it is the one we most fear. In a culture that mocks and rejects aging women, that rapes the Earth, and has arrogantly posited the locus of wisdom in young, middle-class white males, the most threatening site of woman's power is that which is located in the Crone, the Elder.

Inspired by tribal cultures' reverence for their elders and the myths of Goddesses such as Inanna and Demeter, who journeyed to the underworld and deprived the Earth of fertility during their absence, performance artist Rachel Rosenthal, in two pieces—*Gaia, Mon Amour* and *L.O.W.* (Loner on Wheels) *in Gaia*—makes her own mythic journey to the Goddess and the Crone. For Rosenthal, it is a true rite of passage for her own entry into the later stage of the life cycle.

In *Gaia, Mon Amour*, Rosenthal makes the first discovery of the Earth as a living being. Gaia speaks to her about how the Master Race is killing Her, and Rachel realizes that man has taken nature as hostage. Yet humans, as parasites on the Earth Mother by killing their host, are killing themselves, as well. In this piece she rocks and keens against an Amerindian slide backdrop, and drums and chants for an end to rape and ecocide.

In *L.O.W. in Gaia*, however, she confronts the Crone. In this piece, Rosenthal makes a pilgrimage to the mountains—a kind of vision-quest to be alone with the Great Mother. She is told that L.O.W. means "Loner on Wheels," and she soon comes to understand that in her case, because of her love for the Earth, it means "Lover on Wheels."

Reversing the Demeter-Persephone myth, Rosenthal is the daughter journeying to rescue the Mother. It is the wisdom of the Crone that ultimately speaks through Rachel as the voice of the Earth.

> *Rosenthal:* I am the Crone
> The third aspect of the Triple Goddess. The one you most fear.
> You can accept the Virgin, barely stomach the Mother, but me, you have attempted to destroy.
> I am your Death.
> Not the glamourous death of battle, of heroism, of blood spilled for the cause.
> No. I am gout, ulcers, rheumatism, Alzheimer's, and cancer.
> I am deterioration. I am helplessness, and I am hopelessness.

You never wish to see me. For I remind you, in all my weakness, that I am stronger
than you.
I am stronger than any god.
. . .
You tried to blot me out.
Yes, you've driven me underground.
But I am not the dead one.
You can't kill Death.
Sooner or later, all of you, my Earth children, come to me . . . (Rosenthal, 1989,
p. 82)

The Crone, representing the Great Mystery of mortality, poses the ultimate challenge to
anthropomorphic arrogance. The Crone is raging, and her fury causes her to lash back at
her enemies through avalanches, fires, volcanic eruptions, and floods in protest against Her
poisoning and rape. Rosenthal's vision-quest is not completed on her own terms, for before
she has composed her next performance piece and finished her book, she is called back to
Los Angeles and must leave the mountains.

However, even to entertain the thought that one has not completed one's vision-quest
after hearing the voice of the Great Mother is to exhibit human-centered thinking. For, in
fact, it is obvious that she *has had* a true vision-quest. Like a shaman, she has communed
with the Great Spirit, the Mother, and has returned, carrying wisdom from the spirit world
of the Earth Mother to the community in order to bring about a healing. The knowledge
taught by the Crone is that the Earth is dying, that Western civilization is killing the planet,
and that Death is stronger than the human brain. Death, the ultimate mystery, can be a
source of power, as well. For, to live in harmony with the Crone, ultimately means to create
a culture in which Death is not despised. To revere Death means to accept it as one of the
cycles of nature, as one does with the death of plants, the waxing and waning of the seasons,
and all the other patterns of change and transformation in the universe. It also means learning
to commune with the spirit world in its connectedness with the phenomenal world. To encounter the Crone is to encounter the fullness of the Goddess in *all* Her aspects.

Contemporary feminist matristic artists have accepted this challenge. They have envi-
sioned an art that gives expression to a transformed cosmogonic myth. If the mythic vision
of God the Father implies a denial of the Great Mysteries, then the vision implied by a
cosmogonic myth of the Goddess, reenacts a reverence for all the cycles of the cosmos.

THE JOURNEY TO THE OUTTA-SIGHT,
THE GODDESS IN THE CITY,
THE CLOWN

The first five journeys I discussed were voyages to the invisible realms of prepatriarchal
history, the unconscious, sacred sites in nature, the spirit world, and the wisdom of the
Crone. This last journey incorporates humor, and reminds us of the Goddess when we least
expected to think of Her, in the industrialized, urban metropolis.

Bringing Goddess-consciousness to society at large—away from the art world, far from
the gallery scene and the museums—and sparking a dialogue with ordinary citizens dining
out, The Waitresses, a performance troupe in Los Angeles, usher in the Goddess Diana to
perform her sacred role of nurturer in a local restaurant.

Dressed as the many-breasted Diana of Ephesus, Denise Yarfitz and Anne Gauldin create
consciousness-raising events among the customers of neighborhood restaurants, as they
point out that the stereotype of the modern waitress is a debased and degraded image of the
Great Earth Mother. *The Waitresses* troupe has discovered that the waitress is a contemporary
metaphor for the Great Goddess and for the mother. The modern waitress is often expected
to mother the customers, to be friendly, to smile, to bring them what they need or what they
desire, to serve them, to please them, as well as to nurture them.

The Waitresses have also transformed that debased stereotype by revealing the ancient powers hidden behind the role of waitress in a performance entitled *Coffee Cauldron: A Restaurant Ritual,* which was performed at the Los Angeles Contemporary Exhibitions Gallery (LACE). In this piece, routine waitress chores evolved into an alchemical and transformative meditation. Honoring the act of serving, they made the coffee pot their central symbol. Thus, they linked the magical aspects of the traditional association of the feminine with a vessel, to the Grail, the alchemical athanor, the cornucopia, the oven, and the breasts of the Great Goddess. Sprinkling their critique of our society's devaluing of the Great Mother, reflected in its treatment of waitresses (overworked, underpaid) with humor, and in the hopes of rekindling the proper relationship of love and respect between the nurturer and the one who is nourished, they have written:

> Diana had hundreds of breasts. (I don't)
> I wonder if Sambo's would hire her.
> There'd be a problem with the uniform, but that would be offset
> by her unique abilities. She could have the menu posted on herself,
> Each breast labeled as to its particular nourishment. . . .
> Diana, are you my guardian angel?
> Did you get good tips?
> Every restaurant should have one. Or at least, a shrine to her.
> Yes, a shrine. A place where everyone—waitress and customer
> alike, can pay homage to that great provider within each of us.
> (Gauldin & Yarfitz, Texts on Diana and the Waitresses)

In their performance piece *The Great Goddess Diana* (1978–1981), Anne Gauldin and Denise Yarfitz reminded the clientele that "Diana was a goddess worshipped thousands of years ago. Great many-breasted Mother, ruler and nourisher of the animal kingdom, provider of sustenance, both physical and spiritual, for all creatures, great and small. How could you stand it? Sweat of reaching hands, open mouths, empty bellies—questioning, smiling, giving menu, silverware, placemat, napkin, food, spoon, drink. White, wheat, or rye? Eyes, ears, legs? Thousand, roquefort, french? . . ." (Gauldin & Yarfitz, Texts on Diana and the Waitresses).

The main areas of social critique focused on by The Waitresses are work, money, sexual harassment, and the stereotypes of women and waitresses. After 1981 they expanded the subject matter of their performances to include broader social and political concerns such as world hunger. The Waitresses' mission is spiritual; their vision feminist matristic; their image heroic and comic. They have even marched in the Doo Dah Parade in Pasadena.

Just as women waitresses represent the Great Nurturing Mother, sanitation workers (garbage collectors) represent the ecosystem of planet Earth. Both professions are demeaned in a culture that values neither women nor nature.

New York Performance Artist, Mierle Laderman Ukeles, also mixes humor with completely serious social commentary in her many creations with the members of the New York Sanitation Department doing Maintenance Art.

It was in 1969, when the artist became a mother for the first time, that she realized her role had been transformed from that of "self-expression" (as an artist) to that of "maintenance" (as a mother).

Because she felt that both roles were equally important, and because she claimed the artistic freedom to call anything art that she perceived as such (following the example set by Marcel Duchamp's "Found Objects"), she baptized her maintenance work "Maintenance Art," and collapsed the boundaries between art and necessity, for the Earth and the city are both our Home, and what we do to beautify, maintain, and nurture one of them, we must do for both.

Her 1969 *Manifesto Maintenance Art: A Proposal for an Exhibition* suggested that all kinds of "care," including doing the dishes, clearing the table, mending the fence, and so forth, are forms of maintenance art. Her idea for an exhibition would include personal, general,

The Great Goddess Diana—Created and performed by Anne Gauldin (foreground) and Denise Yarfitz
(background) written by Denise Yorfitz, costume by Anne Gauldin, 1978–81, photo by Maria Karras

and Earth maintenance. Her Manifesto discusses the fact that housewives are not paid, and
she proposes to do the chores of a Housewife at the Museum for her exhibition. She will
also have garbage delivered to the Museum and treated there. The museum will become a
site of Earth maintenance, and air, land, and water will come to the museum to be depol-
luted, purified, and recycled.

In 1973 Laderman Ukeles performed a sidewalk cleaning piece in front of the A.I.R. Gallery in New York. Inspired by Rabbi Kook's statement that "the mysteries always teach us to
combine the holy with the profane" (cited by the artist in an interview with G. Orenstein,
1988), she transformed the public (profane) space of the sidewalk into a sacred (holy) space
by performing a ritual cleansing. In this piece the gestures made washing the sidewalk were
the same as those made in painting. She considered the act of washing as analogous to
painting with water.

As an artist, Laderman Ukeles wants to heal the Earth now, to expose how the Earth has
been plundered and raped, by showing what is done to the Earth Mother. She has made the
analogy between Silbury Hill and the landfills where today our garbage is dumped. These
landfills treat the Earth like a "whore," using and abusing Her, by filling Her with refuse and
poisons. The Earth has also been "domesticated" like a "housewife," and has been referred
to as a "virgin," who was then taken and raped by the men who were "taming" her. All of
these images of women, the virgin, the housewife, the whore, have been used to abuse the
Earth in ways analogous to those by which women have been violated.

In 1976 Laderman Ukeles worked with three hundred maintenance workers for seven
weeks. She asked the maintenance workers to consider one hour of their regular day's work

Mierle Laderman Ukeles: Ballet Mécanique (1983)

as art. In 1979 the Sanitation Department approached her, and asked how she would like to make art with 10,000 people. Thus, she spent one-and-one-half years talking to the Sanitation Workers and Maintenance People of New York in a piece entitled *Touch Sanitation*. From 1978 to 1980 she walked all over New York shaking hands with the sanitation workers and thanking them for keeping New York City alive. She spiraled the city ten times to keep the energy moving, rather than covering the city borough by borough. Imitating the physical movements and gestures made in loading and unloading garbage, Mierle found that their actions were similar to those in a ballet.

In 1983 she choreographed *Ballet Mécanique* for 32 blocks on Madison Avenue with six sanitation trucks and their sweepers. She made a Mirrored Garbage Truck as a social mirror in which people on the streets could see themselves reflected as troops of Earth Maintenance People, Sanitation Workers, and Planetary Healers.

At present, she is producing *Flow City,* a public art work done in conjunction with the New York City Department of Sanitation at 59th St. and the Hudson River. This complex work will permit the public to view the barges delivering the city's refuse. However, it will also bring earth back into the city, thus creating a complete recovery cycle, and thereby putting the public in touch with the processing of the city's waste products, as well as with its own connection both to those products and to the Earth Mother.

Los Angeles performance artist Barbara Smith has created many works on the theme of nurturance in the form of ritual meals. In 1969 her first dinner party, *Ritual Meal,* was created in order to show the sacrificial eating of the body and the absorption of the individual into the cosmos through eating.

The guests were seated by the figure of Primavera, who represented the organic world and its cycles and bounty. The technological perversion of natural processes was stressed by the waiters in surgical coats, who served the meal as if they were performing open-heart surgery. The red wine was served in a test tube (like blood), and the white wine came in a

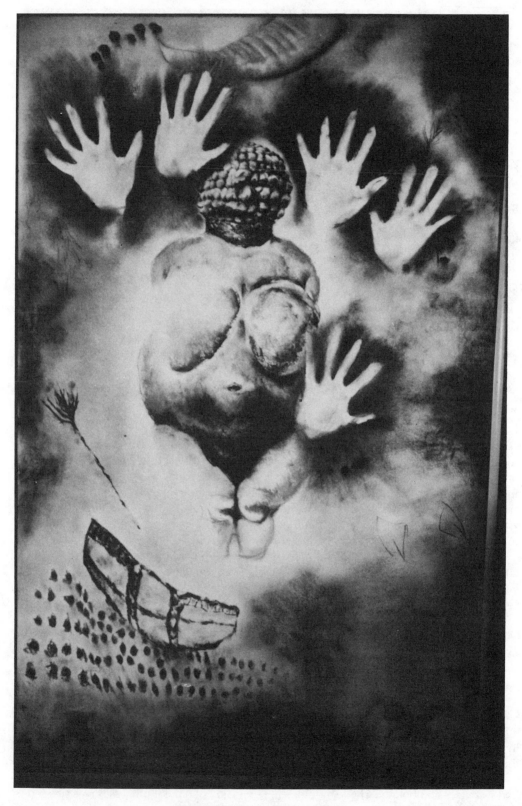

Leslie J. Klein: The Stones Bear Witness

beaker (like urine), and so forth. At the end of the meal the waiters came in nude with garlands of flowers, once more contrasting the natural world with the alienation produced by a technological assault upon it.

Over the past two decades Smith's work has evolved greatly as she has worked closely with Harley Swiftdeer, a native American medicine man. Her recent piece, *The Cauldron*, referring to the Great Mother's womb and the Grail, involved the meal as a mystical communion and a sacrament. Here she used the "holy squash" as a religious idol with both humor and integrity, for the multiple dishes she prepares from the squash indeed qualify it as the Great Nurturer.

Through acts of provocation as well as humor, Barbara Smith makes a plea for returning to a reverence for the gifts of the Earth Mother, as her rich fruits are eaten in feasts, banquets, dinner parties, and communal meals.

As Laderman Ukeles has said: "My art is more about the "out of sight" than the "invisible." The journey through humor leads to the Outta-Sight, to the great Goddess Waitresses in local restaurants, to ballets with garbage trucks on the streets of New York, to banquets in the operating room, and finally to the beauty salon.

Muriel Magenta's 1987 video *Salon Doo* takes a humorous look at society's preoccupation with primping, and with its fantasies of artificial beauty. The action takes place in a contemporary beauty salon, and clients come in for a transformation via the hairdo. The ultimate transformation, however, turns out to be the hairdo done with a giant wig that wraps and curls itself around the body of the client like a serpent. Indeed, the client is transformed into an image of the ancient Snake Goddess. The salon also has a good luck icon, a giant wig sculpture that is like a Buddha head, a hairdo/deity. Cross-culturally and biblically, hair signifies sexuality and power. In the ultimate fantasy hairdo, it is not surprising that the motifs of the Great Goddess re-emerge to empower the urban worshipper of beauty and strength.

Finally, Carolyn Marks is a Berkeley feminist matristic artist, who has succeeded in co-creating a Wall for Peace with 1,350 people from the Berkeley community, who have painted tiles expressing their desire to bring peace in the world. Marks is also a ritualist.

In one of Marks's rituals, she worked with the citizens of Bolinas, California, and on June 21, 1986, put her life-sized Goddess sculptures of Aphrodite, Isis, and Hathor into a pit with the Goddess sculptures made by the people of Bolinas. After a ritualized rebirth of the Goddess, they set fire to the pit, and the sculptures burst into flame.

The next morning the scattered remains of the sculptures resembled an archaeological find.

Through her Goddess rituals, her Wall for Peace, and her ritual *Washing the Words*, Carolyn Marks involves the urban and suburban communities in reinvoking the ancient power of the Goddess.

Leslie J. Klein's *The Stones Bear Witness* compresses within a single charged image the many themes we have associated with feminist matristic art.

Referring to the hand prints found on the Paleolithic cave walls, where Venus figurines and Goddess carvings have been unearthed along with paintings that were once believed to symbolize hunting magic, Klein reminds us that the "silent rock and pigment testify" to the artistic creativity of cavewoman" (Klein, 1988). Not only do the Goddess carvings and statuettes attest to the fact that the cave was the sacred site where the religion of the Great Goddess was practiced, but the small hand prints indicate that the artists who painted the animals (which were frequently pregnant) were most probably women, and the twig and leaf impressions were symbols of the cycles of life, not hunting spears, as was once thought.

Thus, as Leslie J. Klein tells it: "The symbols on the cave walls of this drawing have been recognized as female symbols, and as such, offer testimony of ancient female power, spirituality, and universality. The Great Goddess still resides in the caves and recesses of our psyches—driven underground, sealed and unlit for ages, but enduring" (Klein, 1988).

Cavewomen were obviously the first women artists to be written out of art history. They were also, most probably, the first artists to have created images of the Great Mother, Creatress of all life, that have endured for approximately 30,000 years, and still speak to us powerfully of the origin of life and creativity, as well as of the source of Creation—the matrix of all that is, the Great Mother.

Retelling Our Tales of Power,
Respinning Our Yarns of Yore

In a previous chapter we introduced the notion of tales of power in order to mark a fundamental difference between feminist matristic literature arising in the contemporary moment (the 1970s and 1980s) and traditional written literature, including the avant-garde, which is grounded in a patricentric cosmogonic mythology.

As we have noted, tales of power bridge the separation between the nagual and the tonal, the invisible spirit world, and the manifest world. They capture the numinous dimensions of the unseen worlds, and, more importantly, create cultural realities by their telling.

Patriarchal tale telling and myth making have described reality in ways that disempower women, and these tales and myths have constituted the fund of knowledge and the consensus on the versions of myth and literature that have reigned in the West and fueled our educational systems for hundreds of years.

The tales we tell have serious implications. They shape vision, teach behavior, provide models for perception, action, and values. Worlds without women, worlds boasting of the superiority of humans over nature, worlds denying the presence of spirit, have been circulating in our libraries, schools, universities, bookstores, flooding our mind's eye, so that the obvious has been rendered invisible through constant mystification. For example, the simple evidence of the female giving birth to the male has been obfuscated and distorted beyond recognition by myths such as that of Eve being born from Adam's rib, or of Athena being born from the head of Zeus. The original image of the Creator as a female has been annihilated through the institutionalization of patriarchal religion and the desecration of all traces of Goddess temples and shrines. Rather than honoring mature women who give life to men, most mature females have been depicted as the very force that holds men back from achieving freedom, that keeps them from adventure, from their quest. This can be seen in simple children's classics like *Tom Sawyer*. Contemporary feminist scholars, both literary and interdisciplinary, have demonstrated beyond question that the depiction of women in patricentric literature systematically reduces them to two simple stereotypes: the virgin and the whore—women portrayed as asexual or as overly sexual (according to patriarchal religious standards, of course). The images of women that circulate in these tales of patriarchy disempower women, for they deny the existence of empowered images of women such as those established by the historical record of thousands of years—images in which women reflected the gender of the Cosmic Creator in the way that men reflect the male deity today. However, whereas the male image of God is only approximately 5,000 years old, the female image of the Goddess lasted for more than 30,000 years.

Because the Goddess symbolizes both spirit and matter, both the visible and the invisible worlds known to us as all of Creation, I will identify Her with what Juergen W. Kremer has referred to as "the numinous." He has written that "Tales of Power are conscious verbal constructions around experiences of the numinous that help individuals to deal with the spiritual or mystical or archetypal aspects of internal and external realities, and which help them to change their lives in meaningful and fulfilling ways because of their contact with a larger realm" (Kremer, p. 33, 1987).

Naturally, in thinking of conventional or popular tales of power such as the ones told by Carlos Castaneda, we are reminded of the subtle magical transformations of his former, Western, descriptions of reality, experienced under the guidance of Don Juan.

I wish to make an analogy between Kremer's reference to witnessing the numinous or the nagual, and contemporary women's glimpses of the numinous (but invisible to patriarchal history) realm of the transformed description of reality that a feminist matristic vision provides.

About Tales of Power, Kremer has made the following statements, which are relevant to our discussion: ". . . we need to develop narratives and discourses of truths which include a moral or aesthetic dimension, which facilitate a mimetic dance with internal and external realities, and which further the integration of humans into nature as part-of-nature as well as the psychological integration. Given that we will never be able to capture the thing-as-such out there in our consensual discourse, the stories—be they scientific, mythological, artistic— that human beings create have to be conceived of in much more profound ways than before. The creative aspect of what we hold to be reality or realities comes to the fore. Certain narratives create certain realities. Instead of asking what is *the* reality out there, we may ask questions such as: Are these consensual realities we want to create? Are those the ones we want to participate in? And (to be blasphemous in the face of traditional science): Are they beautiful realities? And, how do we determine them—with mind or with spirit? . . . How do we and how can we participate in the creation and maintenance of cultural narratives and myths? How do they interface with our personal narratives? And how can we create personal narratives that have the greatest potential of pushing our evolution ahead?" (Kremer, p. 44, 1987). Kremer envisages Tales of Power as "one of the avenues to ameliorate some of the problems we are facing in Contemporary Western Societies" (Kremer, p. 45, 1987).

It is clear that our narratives create our culture, and that our culture determines our description of reality—which is, itself, a cultural construction.

Thus, we, as creators, have to ask ourselves exactly what description of reality we want to advance. These questions involve ethical and moral choices, for since our cultural narratives provide models of heroic behavior, construct gender identities, and either depict the spirit world as part of the real or as unreal, since these narratives may be androcentric or feminist matristic, patriarchal or ecofeminist and so forth, it is urgent that we create not just the narratives that describe or reconstruct what *might have been* or *might be* but also those that create what *we hope will be* as well. However, when I speak of what *we hope will be* in terms of a mindful feminist matristic tale of power, I am not necessarily speaking of the genres of science fiction or of fantasy fiction. I am speaking of tales that incorporate knowledge of our erased past millennia of matristic cultures and our present cross-cultural knowledge of them (which *is real*), as well as humans' past, present, and future interconnections with both spirit and nature.

Today's feminist matristic literature has the awesome task of dismantling those patriarchal cultural constructs which have masked the historical verities of female empowerment over eons of time, and which also have denied and degraded the human connection to the spiritual and natural world.

In what ways have humans related to the past, *and* since feminist matristic writers are establishing a relationship to an invisible past (most of whose traces have been destroyed), in what ways can humans relate to a reality that provides little evidence for consensus about it, to a numinous, spiritual, dimension that this past may point to?

I have turned to David Lowenthal's *The Past Is a Foreign Country* to survey the subject. Those who spurn contemporary Goddess art and literature have occasionally made spontaneous critiques of the reconstructive works of feminist matristic artists and writers, saying that they are attempting to recreate a Golden Age that never was (for example in reference to their inspiration derived from the cultural implications of the excavations of Čatal Huyuk [Neolithic/Anatolia]), or that they are romanticizing and idealizing epochs of history by claiming that they were peaceful when it is known that human sacrifice may have been practiced in some of these ancient goddess-worshipping cultures, and so forth. Actually, it is entirely too facile to accuse feminist matristic artists of a nostalgia for a past that perhaps never was—at least not in the way they imaginatively render it—or to impute a definite *bias* and embellishment to their avowedly fictional accounts of the past.

The reason for this is that all kinds of relationships to the past have been, and are currently being, practiced by both our ancient predecessors and our contemporaries within patriarchal history as well. The renaissance idealization and imitation of classical Greek and Roman models in the arts is just of many examples we might cite. From a feminist perspective we might also mention that the renaissance was not a progressive time for women, and was also the time of the beginnings of witch burnings. For this reason we spell it with a lowercase *r*. Thus, our Western patriarchal idealization of the renaissance must also be analyzed from the viewpoint of the new feminist historical scholarship.

Indeed, David Lowenthal reminds us that "the past is an artifact of the present" (Lowenthal, 1985, p. 1). It is only with hindsight that historians construct a narrative of the past that makes the outcome seem to be a logical result of the events that took place.

What have humans done to shape the data they have gleaned from the past? They have usually interpreted it according to their ideological biases, creating glamorous scenarios, glorious histories, and omitting embarrassing realities that did not fit into the ideological framework of their narratives. They have reinterpreted atrocities, glorified the slightest successes, and even created events that never happened in order to paint a picture of their past that explained their present regimes. According to Lowenthal "the past is altered for motives that reflect present needs" (Lowenthal, 1985, p. 348). We make our pasts attractive. We exaggerate, omit, distort, idealize, romanticize, rationalize, invent, expunge, correct, repress, exploit, reshape, rewrite, destroy, and evoke our past. Moreover, we depend upon these distorted narratives simply to prove that we exist, for the past does *not* exist and can never be known in exactly the way in which it occurred (despite the quantity of reliable data), but we rely on the past to establish our origins, to create our traditions, to ground us in what is probably an illusion (for history is constantly being rewritten) in order to conform to our present-day needs.

To have *no* past is to be *amnesiac*. To have no memory of one's past is to have no identity. In this chapter we will discuss the formation of female identity, and as an introduction to that discussion, it is crucial to understand that insofar as women remain in a state of culturally induced amnesia vis-a-vis approximately 30,000 years of human history upon which their feminist matristic legacy is to be recognized and reclaimed, their sense of individuality is similar to that of an adult amnesiac living in the world but disconnected from her or his own life history. We have previously talked about eco-, historical, and shamanic amnesias. We realize that contemporary feminist matristic artists have a preliminary task to perform—they must restore or recharge our collective reconstructed memories of our ancient matristic past. They must provide the tales of power that reconnect us with the spiritual as well as the material bases for Creation in the present and the future. In order to accomplish this, they must give consensus reality to their interpretations of the scant evidence we have. In this sense, historians may act as creators, and creators may act as historians. While debates may rage over the exact inferences we may deduce about a living culture of some

7,000 years ago from shards and artifacts, this debate remains the domain of academics and scholars.

Feminist matristic creators and historical writers outside the academy are concerned with translating meaningful conclusions as faithfully as they can into visions for renewal that are vital, inspiring, and applicable to the present—or as Lowenthal would say, that meet the needs of the present.

We are hardly the first people to reshape our vision of history to meet our contemporary needs. In recent times humans have had the arrogance to believe that moderns were superior to ancients just because of their technological advances. We have scorned and victimized cultures that have not moved on a path parallel to ours, calling them primitive, and treating them as if they were inferior in knowledge or wisdom.

Today, feminist matristic artists and writers are questioning that position, and coming to understand some of the lessons we can learn from the errors of arrogance—of anthropocentric and androcentric thinking. Today we have come to the point of asking which tales of power are worthy of being told. We ask this question about history, about myth, and about literature, for we know that these tales, narratives, and the like, create and shape the material reality which is palpable and can bring about civilizations that create suffering and that destroy, as well as civilizations that flourish and create joy and well-being. We are also conscious of the fact that our creations influence the nonmaterial, spiritual realms about which some humans are in a position to speak (i.e., shamans, etc.). Here I am referring to the ways in which our myths, and the like, depict the world of the dead. For those cultures whose myths and tales speak of the souls of the ancestors as living *in* the earth (i.e., native American cultures), our tales affect the ways in which we walk upon the earth, the ways in which we consider Her to be alive or inert, and thus the acts we perform that might violate the sacred ancestral spirits alive in those invisible realms or ignore their existence.

One of the many important narratives that reconstruct history from a feminist matristic perspective, one that has caught the imagination of many who are yearning for visions of equality and peace in the future is *The Chalice and the Blade* by Riane Eisler (1987).

Eisler bases her analysis of goddess-centered cultures on the archaeological work done by Marija Gimbutas on Old Europe. As an Austrian Jew and Holocaust exile, as a creative writer and a lawyer, Eisler questions the inhumanity and cruelty of humans to each other, and makes a case for a new interpretation of the past. Her exploration of history reveals that patriarchal cultures have been structured on what she calls a "dominator" model, one in which one-half of humanity (in this case, male) has been defined as superior to and has dominated the other half (female). This structure of ranking and hierarchy, she claims, did not characterize human relations in societies based upon the "partnership" model, which she views as a real and viable alternative to patriarchy. For Eisler, the flip side of patriarchy, matristic or "gylanic" prehistory, does not give evidence for "matriarchy" (rule by women), but for partnership and equality. Minoan Crete, in her estimation, is one example of a society in which women were empowered by the female image of the Creator. Yet, in Minoan Crete, women did not dominate men. These societies of Old Europe worshipped a Mother Goddess, respected women as the bearers of life, and did not possess weapons or engage in war. They revered nature and developed technologies, but did not create hierarchies, wage war, or practice domination. She writes: "Both the mythical and archeological evidence indicate that perhaps the most notable quality of the pre-dominator mind was its recognition of our oneness with all of nature, which lies at the heart of both the Neolithic and the Cretan worship of the Goddess" (Eisler, 1987, p. 75). In fact, Eisler sees the Cretan culture in its reverence for the living Earth as foreshadowing the Gaia Hypothesis formulated by James Lovelock and Lynn Margules.

In our discussion of the various relationships to the past that different cultures have espoused, we noted that for ideological reasons, historians have distorted and erased events from the record in order to create a more glorious concept of the history of their particular homeland.

Eisler's revision of history indicts patriarchy for having done the largest, longest, most consistent, and most destructive rewrite of this kind. Her book does not so much "rewrite" history, as attempt to restore what existed before it was "rewritten" under the aegis of patriarchal, dominator societies.

Eisler is hardly the first feminist to make this point, but she captures its drama by reminding us of George Orwell's prediction that in 1984 the Ministry of Truth would rewrite all books, and that "the horrifying thing is that this is not yet to come. It already happened long ago almost everywhere in the ancient world" (1987, p. 89). The change from a goddess-centered world and culture to a patriarchal-dominator model of gender relations came about not only in Crete, but in the Middle East, India, and Egypt as well.

Riane Eisler sees the task of contemporary feminist matristic writers, including historians, as that of restoring through rewriting, rather than inventing. This restoration, she claims, provides the hope for a viable alternative to patriarchy, based upon our lost tradition, which can inspire us to create a workable, egalitarian, peaceful future based upon a partnership model that, according to her, has already existed and proved itself over thousands of years.

Whether or not it existed precisely as she describes it, whether or not we can ever know much more about a past of which precious little remains, what is important is that Eisler has constructed a version of history similar to a tale of power. Her narrative connects those of a feminist matristic persuasion to a past that empowers, inspires and gives hope for the future. Because it was a period in which spirituality connected to nature, symbolized by the Great Mother, prevailed, and because it was until the present virtually invisible to most of us, it is analogous to the numinous for women. Our encounter with the restoration of this past is more like a revelation than like new knowledge.

Why is it more like a revelation than like the uncovery of, let us say, another part of patriarchal history, which I would label "information" or "data"? The restoration of our lost matristic history is like a revelation for women (and men) because it creates a profound shock, and it forces us to recycle the stories we have so often told of our history, by decentering the patriarchal versions of those stories. It lifts us out of our amnesias, and restores an identity that is not simply material, but is also spiritual. As a revelation connects humans to God, this revealed history connects humans to Goddess. It is the kind of knowledge that completely revises and overturns one's description of reality.

Yet, before we are carried away by the dream of recreating the idyl of a prepatriarchal Golden Age in the present or the future, let us be mindful of the powerful lessons that history teaches.

We have already asked whether our myths and visions, our stories and narratives are ones that we wish to participate in and that will further our evolution. This kind of ethical self-reflexivity apropos of creativity is relatively new. For, throughout history we have seen how the most beatific of visions, wedded to the service of an ideology that was not life-affirming, could wreak destruction and war upon countless numbers of innocent people. We are, at present, less than one-half century removed from the actual perversion of myths and themes relating to ancient Earth-based religions that Hitler's Holocaust unleashed upon the planet, perpetrating mass murders in the name of such an ideology. The Holocaust was the hysterical, pathological version of a perverse relationship to certain occult traditions such as anthroposophy, Masonry, theosophy, the Order of the Knights Templar, the Golden Dawn, the Rosicrucians, and the like. Some of these teachings, according to Edward C. Whitmont in *Return of the Goddess,* can be traced back to a belief in an Earth Goddess (Whitmont, 1988).

As Whitmont shows, Hitler's pathological obsession with the Grail myth distorted its original meaning, and led to the extermination of millions of people in the name of an ideology that completely misinterpreted the Grail and Earth Goddess. He also exploited the symbolism of its life-affirming visions, using them for destructive ends. As Whitmont reminds us: "It is important to see the difference between creative possibility and regressive pathology in the expression of a myth" (1988, p. 164). "In paranoic identification he (Hitler) believed himself to be the god of renewal and blessing" (p. 165).

We are thus soberly alerted to the ever-present dangers inherent in reactivating any myth in the absence of sufficient consciousness, of any ethical or moral questioning. Whitmont insists that we ask ourselves before invoking any myth "Whom does it serve?" (1988, p. 178). "It is at this juncture", he writes, "that the new myth points the way to the comprehension of the new ethos. The cosmogony by means of a personal God who made the world, and set up its rules and laws has lost its credibility. Externally imposed law is no longer a *numino-sum* to us. For better or worse, increasing numbers of us are asking Parzifal's question, we want to know whom or what it serves" (Whitmont, 1988, p. 221).

These new feminist matristic visions are now seeding a critical turning point in the history of the Earth. They are enabling us to return to a cosmogony that sacralizes all of creation with the moral self-consciousness of those who have lived through and survived to denounce the dangers of anthropomorphic androcentrism when it makes use of any mythic or ideologi-cal system that ignores the fate of all life on Earth.

As burdened as we are with a vision of the plight of global suffering, we are also simultane-ously beneficiaries of the knowledge that humans, alone, are responsible not only for the damage that has been done, but for reversing the course of planetary history. This self-con-sciousness enables us to encounter the Goddess cosmogony with new humility. To know that we are the only ones who can turn the tide of history should not fuel our egos so much as our hearts. We must bear the solitude of our human condition alone, but not above— rather along with—the plight and destiny of our animal and plant relatives on Earth, our Home. We must turn the tide for them as well as for ourselves, for our lives are interdepen-dent, and we must be supremely conscious of the results of all our creations, even when they are referred to as "advances," but might be the very devices that may sow the seeds of our ultimate annihilation.

The recycling of history, literature, and myth from a feminist matristic perspective is ac-complished by Diane di Prima in her poem-cycle *Loba* (1978). Because feminist matristic literature not only revises patricentric stories, but is also open-ended in its anticipation of its own revision, recycling, and reflowering, the author conceives of her poem as a "work-in-progress," and "reserves the right to juggle, rearrange, cut, osterize, re-cycle parts of the poem in future editions. As the Loba wishes, as the Goddess dictates" (di Prima, 1978: author's note).

Her poem is in a continual process of metamorphosis, because she puts no closure on any one version of it. Like the many variants of oral epics, the *Loba* may appear in one version at one time and place, and in other versions elsewhere. Presently, it is composed of eight parts beginning with *Ave,* and is a kind of *Howl*[1] written for women oppressed by patriarchal myths—women of our time in whom di Prima sees reflected a Goddess lineage. Addressing her "lost moon sisters" from Ave. A and Bleecker Street in New York, and from Rampart Street and Fillmore Street in San Francisco, she sees them in their contemporary incarnations as mythic goddesses with their ancient powers.

> you lie with the unicorn
> you lie with the cobra. . . . .
> you are armed.
> you drive chariots (di Prima, 1978, *Ave* section)

She also sees contemporary women living under diverse patriarchal social systems, and identifies with them, as she identifies all women with the energies of the Great Mother.

---

[1]The reference here is to Allen Ginsberg's poem *Howl.*

pregnant you wander
barefoot you wander
battered by drunk men you wander . . .
digging for yams you wander
looking for dope you wander
playing with birds you wander
chipping at stone you wander (di Prima, 1978, *Ave* section)

Identifying herself with all women who everywhere and throughout all time have been
"the hills, the shape and color of mesa" (di Prima, 1978, *Ave* section), the poet chants to
invoke her memory of all the manifestations of the Goddess.

I am you
and I must become you
I have been you
and I must become you
I am always you
I must become you
ay-a
aya ah
ay-a
ay-a ah
maya ma maya ma
om star mother ma om
maya ma ah (di Prima, 1978, *Ave* section)

The structure of *Loba* is episodic, and its mode is incantatory. The poet calls for the Goddess energies in a chant:

Belili Ishtar The White Lady Mother of All Living Cerridwen
    Olwen Blodeuwedd Achren Danu Nana Brigit Io Europe
Amathaounta Branwen Athene Lamia Cyllene Artemis Isis
    Anna Minerva Venus Aphrodite Danae Cotytto Demeter
Cybele Kali Eurynome Inu Plastene Lakshmi Sarasvati
Parvaati Uma Bhavani Hera Linda Cameira Ialysa Dione
    Circe Diana Alphito Ceres Albina Caridwen Cerdo
Cardea Jana Juno Carnea Cranae (the stony one) Pasiphae
(she who shines) Proserpine Bellona Hecate Rhamnusia Freya
    Mairne Mary (Sea) Miriam Rhea (flowing one) Acca Arianrod
Ariadne (most holy) Calliste Alpheta Hathor Morgan le Faye
    Sara-la-Kali Niamh Calypso Moiria Urania Ossa Achaiva
(the Spinner) Magdalen Ruth Sophia Daeira Semele Agave
Michael Eve Lilith Sarah Callisto (most beautiful) Tamar
Ashtaroth Asher Druantia Helen Nephthys Sekhmet Binah
    Mara Eumenides Spider-Woman Tara Yemoja Don Moremi
Olokun Prajna Nut Oya Tiamat Maat She Inara Anat
    Neith Mother Hubur Ninmah Ninul Nisaba CanyonLady (di Prima, 1978, p. 69)

Similarly, di Prima invokes the presence of contemporary women who embody Goddess
energies in the episode "Some of the People This Poem Is For," from Leonore Kandel to
Janis Joplin (1978, p. 79).

Di Prima's evocatory chant ranges widely over Goddess history in its quest and re-vision.
Using the poetic art as the magical art, she tunes in to an ancient vision of the *Loba,* and in
so doing, creates a matristic lineage for mythical and historical personae.

The word *Loba* is the feminine of the Spanish *Lobo,* meaning *Wolf,* and identifies the new
Goddess image as Wolf Woman, a combination of associations with the Artemis-Hecate
mythos and with the American Indian image of Wolf Woman, the wife of Wolf Chief in the
Navajo Emergence myth. In this myth, the wife of Wolf Chief rebels against her subordinate
role. According to the myth, the men are forced into action by the wife, who refuses to be
mother-wife and servant any longer. Thus, Wolf-Woman is the image of the contemporary

feminist emerging from the subordinate role. She is also Artemis, the Lady of Wild Things, the Lady of the Beasts, identified with Hecate and with witchcraft. All wild animals were sacred to her. Hecate, the goddess of the *dark Moon,* is only one image of the dark side of the Goddess that the Wolf, Kali, and Coatlicue also symbolize in other parts of di Prima's Loba cycle. Di Prima's meditation on the dark side of the Mother transforms the meaning from dark to light, from black to white. In *Painting of The Loba* she becomes "the white wolf lady dances on the hills/on the edge of black mesas under the full moon . . ." (di Prima, 1978, p. 79), and in *Dream: The Loba Reveals Herself,* the poet confronts the Wolf Goddess and learns that she is *not the Hunter* at all, but rather *the Protectress.* Her ferocious animal nature is now seen to be a means of her survival, an element integrally related to her nurturing qualities.

"I turned to confront/to face Her:/ring of fur, setting off/the purity of her head./she-who-was-to-have-devoured me/stood, strong/patient/recognizably/goddess./Protectress/great mystic beast of European forest./green warrior woman, towering./kind watchdog I cd/leave the children with./Mother & sister./Myself." (di Prima, 1978, p. 82). In her identification of the Wolf Goddess with Hecate, and later linking these mythemes of Lilith, Mary as Coyote Trickster, and ultimately to Gertrude Stein "when this you see/When we return to the circle." (di Prima, 1978, p. 189). Di Prima creates a many-faceted vision of the Goddess, whose primary nature is reflected in a multiplicity of historical, mythic, and literary metamorphoses from the image of Lilith, through Christianity in the images of Eve and Mary, to the present, in the goddess-nature of all the women named in the poem, "Some of the People This Poem is For". In her version of the Nativity, di Prima depicts the Virgin Mary as the Goddess coupling with the Horned God in a pagan landscape, restoring sexuality and procreation to the image of Mary. But, as she realizes, we have murdered the Goddess ourselves, by buying into the patriarchal versions of myths. "Friend/that I murdered/in the sacred grove" (di Prima, 1978, p. 188). Ultimately, it is patriarchal criticism that commits the final murder of the insights obtained through visionary feminist matristic poetry. As di Prima writes in *The Critic Reviews Loba* "Where is the history in this, & how/does geometry of the sacred mountain give strength to the metaphor. . . . . where are the dates, street names/precise equations? Must we accept/that star clouds burst with feeling/Hermes dances/in blood & bone . . ." (di Prima, 1978, p. 172). The feminist matristic writer accepts the validity of vision and revelation. She does not seek "data" for proof of the mythic murder of the Goddess. "Horned, like a king he had come, I did not speak/of this./Horned & dancing, I did not/question. I lay on stone/as in the oracle. he hissed, I answered/He danced between stone pillars/no language in common. It was/coupling of fierce reluctant blood. And free" (di Prima, 1978, p. 138). Di Prima inserts *The Ruses: A Coyote Tale* into the Nativity cycle, so that Mary takes on the qualities of the Trickster, Mother Protectress, on the *Flight into Egypt.* "Pursued/by cries of 200 infants/each of whom might have been the Christ . . ./I do not know" (di Prima, 1978, 140). "Sometimes for weeks it is better/not to eat, the meat is poisoned, but/you wait it out/ knowing the creatures are not/consistent, they forget. Or they will/move on. It is hard to explain this/to the cubs./ You keep downwind, stick to the water; journey in thick mist/or at the dark of the moon" (di Prima, 1978, p. 141). Mary and Christ, Coyote and her cubs, modern women and their children—all are images of the Moon Goddess, the Great Mother's natural energies alive in women today. This pagan passion is linked to the witch—nature of modern women in their quest for liberation and flight. "I will fly/Broomless, unarmed, un-ready/I will fly" (di Prima, 1978, p. 153).

The metaphor of the Hunt, which dominates the cycle, pleads for a return to our human-animal nature, the sacred animal nature of the Goddess as Lady of the Beasts and of women as manifestations of Her sacrality. As di Prima depicts it, in patriarchal history, those who worshipped the Goddess were burned as witches. Today, women's quests for knowledge about Her and about our lost history is also a kind of Hunt—for hints and clues, for traces and signs of Her female face hidden behind the masks of patriarchal symbol systems and omissions from the historical record. In Diane di Prima's vision, the Hunter is the supreme Protectress, Nurturer, not devourer, a reversal of the definition of her "dark Moon" aspect as Jung and Neumann would describe it, a reversal achieved through a consecration made to this aspect of her nature, and through a feminist matristic revisioning of the Dark as the Light, which has been repressed and reversed.

As we have noted in the *Loba*, the identity of a particular contemporary woman walking along a street in New York City or in San Francisco is, like the Loba, herself, a composite identity, organically related to all of the preceding incarnations of the Loba in her revision, interpreted according to a new feminist matristic mythos and history.

What feminist matristic writers uniquely do is reconnect contemporary women to a mythic and historic matrilineage, enabling them to perceive themselves as manifestations of the totality of all the matristic roots of their present incarnations. This identity is one of full connectivity, for it restores women to their greater dimensions by incorporating the aspects of the many diverse images of female deities, heroines, and creators of all cultures into the expression of the individual identity of which they are the present-day culmination. In their contemporary lives of poverty and victimization, women are re-connected to both the source of their strength and power, as well as to the history of the degradation and demonization of the female deities, exactly as the Loba had been misconstrued solely as the Hunter, and never perceived as the Protectress and the Nurturer. However, just as the mythic female figures and goddesses are "re-membered" in their gynergic aspects, just as the Loba is perceived as the ancient Nurturer and Protectress, rather than as the Hunter, so the images of contemporary women are transformed as well. As feminist matristic artists undo the process of demonization, or as Catherine Keller has said: "We begin to see the Western transmogrification of the snake into Satan as the central symptom of the demonizing of all nonpatriarchal powers" (Keller, 1986, p. 55), as feminist matristic writers exorcize the patriarchal demonic overlay of women's original strengths and energies, modern women and literary characters are simultaneously transformed.

Learning our lessons from history involves not only a critique of the errors of the past, but also a deeper analysis of the roots and causes of those errors lest they repeat themselves in a different form in the future.

Whether writing about the Goddess, about human mothers, or about the Earth Mother, feminists and ecofeminists from Mary Daly to Phyllis Chesler and Starhawk have expounded on themes such as Goddess murder, matricide, and the rape and killing of Mother Earth.

Over and over we have noted with Mary Daly, Merlin Stone, Marija Gimbutas, and Monica Sjöö, how the Great Cosmic Mother was gradually replaced by the patriarchal Father God, and we have resonated with Phyllis Chesler's analysis of wombless men, who, in their uterine envy, have created myths in which the Father God gives birth to Adam, Adam gives birth to Eve, and God gives birth to Christ (insofar as Mary is simply considered to be the vessel that brought Christ into the world). Phyllis Chesler asks what men want, and she responds: "their mother's body." (Chesler, 1978, p. 70) She writes that "matricide, not patricide is the primal and still unacknowledged crime." (Chesler, 1978, p. 71).

The fact that the male image has replaced the female image in the Creation myths in the West has led some men to wish to replace women as mothers literally—(through the test-tube baby industry, genetic engineering, cloning, etc.). Finally, patriarchal eco-amnesia is leading to the death of the Great Mother, of the Earth, itself. Matricide is a constant theme underlying many of the lessons we can learn from our history—perhaps even that of the Holocaust. For, in thinking about the Holocaust, the most haunting image is that of the ovens, the crematoria, literally wombs of death (rather than wombs of life) invented by "wombless men."

In a brilliant analysis of the construct of self from a feminist perspective, *From a Broken Web: Separation, Sexism and Self*, (1986), Catherine Keller traces matricide back to the *Enuma Elish*, dating from 2057–1758 B.C.E. In this Babylonian Creation epic the divine male hero, Marduk, kills the Goddess Tiamat, and then dismembers her body and creates the cosmos out of its pieces.

Thus, as Keller asserts, the supreme creative act is also a criminal act, the slaughter of the Great Mother. Whether it be women born from men (Eve, Athena), women slaughtered by men (Tiamat, the Gorgon), women conquered by men via rape (Persephone), since women are part of nature, this is identical to the conquest and taming of nature. Keller also emphasizes the fact that misogyny and gynophobia lie at the root of matricide, which is the impulse behind the birth of the hero in patriarchy. As she writes, "misogyny and heroic masculinity are indistinguishable" (Keller, 1986, p. 86).

In our reclamation of the Goddess today, we are not only remembering Tiamat, but we are also re-membering her. "An entire way of life based on connectivity seems to have been dismembered along with the Goddesses. Yet, to remember it now entails no return, no regression to a hypothetical golden age of goddess worship," states Catherine Keller (1986, p. 91).

It is this dis-membered life of connectivity that feminist matristic artists and writers are restoring today through the creative arts. Keller ultimately formulates a theory of the self based upon the persuasion that masculine psychological development, which involves separation from the mother, and ultimately defining the individuated self as separate (a heroic male ego) is one that is constructed upon "a repression of its own deep interrelatedness with everything else" (Keller, 1986, p. 9). Keller would reclaim the pre-Oedipal state of connectivity as the basis of a new definition of the female self. In this she aligns her analysis with that of Gilligan and Chodorow. She suggests "that we. . . . affirm the empathic continuum from which we emerge" (Keller, 1986, p. 140).

Discussing the oceanic feelings of merging and connectivity felt by daughters, she urges a reinterpretation of this state and its cultivation in maturity as a recognition of the libidinous energy inherent in connectivity. "Daughters transforming the so-called narcissism of the relation to the mother may find themselves empowered and not drowned by the subtle religiosity of oceanic feeling, learning to differentiate themselves in and through an intimate bond with the universe. Thus, the symbol of the Mother Goddess reemerges today, not as an illusory projection of omnipotence upon which creatures unilaterally depend, but as a life-force, indeed as a libido, internal to everything" (Keller, 1986, p. 151).

The web of interconnection that is woven by the daughters' opening the self to multiple influences, rather than separating off from others (as in the "masculine or male-identified" definition of selfhood) is envisaged by Keller, not only as redemptive, erotic/libidinous, but also as the very channel through which women relate to history, to the earth, to the human community, to the cosmos, to the sacred, and in so doing, become empowered and heroic.

Creating a new concept of the female hero is, obviously, especially important for our discussion of feminist matristic literature. The new female heroic self will be born of a female (not of a male god), and will reconnect us with both history and mystery through the web of connectivity that she weaves in the telling of her tales. Life-giving not death-dealing will be the hallmark of her acts of creation, and restoration of the mother rather than matricide will be the underlying thread of the web she weaves. Let us say that in the feminist matristic arts *matrigenesis* replaces *matricide* as the central issue.

The myth of the male warrior hero in western androcentric cultures is constructed upon a subtext that includes matriphobia, gynophobia, matricide, and the criminal mythic act of dismemberment of the Great Mother. This is translated socially into what Phyllis Chesler refers to as "the emotional, economic, social, and political castration of women" of which "men are guilty for having benefitted as a caste" (Chesler, 1978, p. 212).

The first web of connectivity that contemporary feminist matristic writers are weaving is of the reconnection with those women, both those written into patriarchal narratives (but whose own versions were never presented), and those whose voices were totally eliminated from the narratives of patriarchy to begin with.

Thus, we will find in feminist matristic literature a number of midrashes (readings between the lines of a text) or commentaries on Eve or Helen, Cassandra, Ariadne, Mary, Lilith, and so on, as well as restorations of the original versions of the Inanna or Demeter and Persephone myths. In this chapter on feminist matristic literature we have ascertained that contemporary writers are reconnecting with female personae from the origins of our literary and mythic canons in order to give their own versions of the tales that have come down to us written by men. We have also observed that gynecide lies at the root of patriarchal creation stories, many of which involve the murder, erasure, betrayal, or abuse of goddesses, mothers, wives, daughters, and lovers.

In my view, today's feminist matristic literary characters fit Catherine Keller's analysis of women's empowerment located in the "arachnean" (Keller, 1986, p. 5) web of connectedness in which "we range through an unlimited array of relations—not just to other persons, but to ideas and feelings, to the earth, the body, and the untold contents of the present moment" (Keller, 1986, p. 19). Keller understands that when we are liberated from the patriarchally defined mythic monsters, which carry the negativized powers of the originally strong female, we will "display a deep affinity with all beings" (Keller, 1986, p. 5).

This web that feminist matristic writers are weaving in creating characters that bear the full weight and witness to the matrilineage, has been described in this way by Keller: "I have been influenced by everything in my world up to this immediate moment; after this moment, what I will have become can causally affect everything subsequent" (Keller, 1986, p. 231). In other words "we arise from the matrix; we redesign its elements; we are woven back into the matrix" (Keller, 1986, p. 248). And the word matrix relates back to Mother. This "umbilical line," as Judy Grahn has called it in *The Queen of Swords* (1982, p. 92), in the matrilineage from the Great Mother onward, that was severed with patriarchy, is a structure that identifies connectivity as a key to individuation, not separation.

These weblike, interconnected, mytho-poetic and real selves (such as the Self woven of the threads of the feminist matristically retold tales of Helen, Inanna, and contemporary women) resonate empathically with the ways in which contemporary feminist matristic fiction relates to the ancient classic models by revisioning the patriarchal versions of the cycles (such as those of the Grail or the biblical or classical heroes) and "remembering" their ancient matricentric antecedents, such as the myth of the Goddess, Inanna.

For, in constructing contemporary female Selves woven of webs of connectivity with our mythic foremothers (remembered feminist matristically), new contemporary versions of myths are created in works of fiction that refer to these deities and heroines in ways reminiscent of the use made of stock characters in the oral epics. That is to say that what is stressed is the infinite variability of the possible tales to be told about these heroines and deities whose feminist matristic identities have now become part of the new pool of feminist matristic formulaic allusions.

Of all the midrashes, variants, or commentaries on the tale of Helen, for example, from the feminist matristic perspective, such as those by Judy Grahn, Marion Zimmer Bradley, Christa Wolf, and so on, what is most important is the dynamic by which one version sparks another, rather than the dynamic by which one version supercedes or dominates all others. These versions do not, however, vie with each other or compete to constitute the definitive, privileged version of a tale. Rather, as in the oral tradition, they inspire each other to create still more variants, to embellish each other's versions, or to imagine yet newer and more authentic episodes and variants based upon communally accepted characteristics of the new renditions of these now "stock" feminist matristic characters. In this sense, the ongoing process of variant creation is similar to an organic growth or a reflowering.

I see this feminist matristic process of creation as distinctly unlike the patriarchal use of mythic allusions and symbols in contemporary mainstream literature, for, whereas post-modern prose is conceived of as self-reflexive, as a system of signs that refer to each other and to previous printed "texts," feminist matristic literature resembles the oral tradition in that it relies more heavily upon the auditory effects of language (chants/incantations, etc.) and on the magical properties of the spoken word, of speech, and of the ways in which stories come to life in performance (not through the technology of the written word, about which more will be said later) than it does on the effects of silent reading through print.

As we shall see, when feminist matristic writers re-member or write midrashes on the familiar stories from the canon of Western classics, they create a new pool of feminist matristic Helens, Cassandras, Eves, Marys, and New Women, whose stories they imagine and reinvent, compose, and recompose, evoke, perform, and cross-fertilize in order to "recycle knowledge back into the real world" (Ong, 1982, p. 119), as was the function of oral literature, rather than cut the text off from circulation in the world, by defining it as a world apart from what we commonly term "reality."

In remembering our matrilineal origins through recreating the patriarchal cycles in a new feminist matristic ethos, women writers are actually defining the constitutive elements and attributes of a new feminist matristic Great Mother mythos as illustrated in the exempla of the cycles. I use the word mythos rather than myth, for I see this as a feminist matristic cultural ethos producing a plurality of tales, mythemes, topoi, and the like, but not one set version of a myth that remains unchanged.

An example of how Catherine Keller's definition of the self as a web of connectivity is expressed in contemporary feminist matristic literature is Judy Grahn's play, The Queen of Swords (1987). She reminds us that the story of Inanna's descent to the underworld to encounter her sister, Ereshkigal, the "Lady of The Great Below," is only one story of the many in the ancient Inanna Cycle.

While Inanna, the Sumerian Queen of Heaven and Earth (Sumer, 3000 B.C.E.) is related to goddesses such as Demeter and Isis, Ereshkigal can be understood in relation to Kali or Hel, and in later transformations in folktales to the wicked queen.

One of the most interesting aspects of Grahn's version of Inanna's visit to Ereshkigal is the way in which Grahn's concept of the contemporary Inanna expands the self. She is at once the ancient Inanna and the Goddess Helen (whose tale she relates in The Queen of Wands, 1982), also Helen from H.D.'s Helen in Egypt, and Gertrude Stein's Dr. Faustus Lights the Lights (as Marguerite Ida and Helene Annabel), as well as Helen from the tales in which she and Simon the Magus were "worshipped together as gods under a plane tree, Simon having found Helen working in a lowly brothel, and finally, Elaine of the Celts (Grahn, 1982, p. 2).

In fact, Judy Grahn's approach to creation is totally synonymous with the enlarged concept of the formation of female identity and women's reconnection to a matristic tradition that we have explored in relation to the writings of Catherine Keller.

In Grahn's play, Ereshkigal, the Queen of the Underworld (associated with Kali, Hel, Persephone, and the Wicked Witch), runs a lesbian bar. She is also identified as the Queen of Swords from the tarot deck.

In the Great Goddess Inanna's descent to the underworld and in what she learns from her dark, underworld sister, Ereshkigal, a shaman queen, we see what might have happened had Helen learned of her own queenly, matristic origins, and we are led to think about how the Greek cycle about her might have been different under different circumstances. In Grahn's play, the modern-day Helen, who can roughly be described as a contemporary, heterosexual, married (prefeminist) woman, learns of her Amazonian strengths and powers from her dyke sisters in a lesbian bar. It is, indeed, Ereshkigal who rebirths Inanna, just as she midwives the rebirth of a contemporary Helen, by teaching her about the dark side of the Goddess, the side that patriarchy has split off and driven into the underworld or underground, today interpreted by Grahn as the lesbian bar. Thus, as we review the myth of Inanna through the grid of The Queen of Swords, we come to understand how women's powerful, queenly selves have been forced to seek refuge in the underworld—how they have been driven underground, both socially and psychically. We have become amnesiac to these very

ancient powers, and the underworld is where women can regain consciousness and possession of this heritage of strength. The play is also a modern parable about the experiences of
some upper middle-class bourgeois white women in the contemporary women's movement.

In some sense Helen has always known that she was a queen—on an intuitive level. Yet,
she lives in a glass house, and recognizes "how rarely do I stand face to face/with my own
force" (Grahn, 1982, p. 14). If women follow their intuition, they are more likely to come
into contact with the truth about their historical past. When Helen learns that she must take
a journey to "Undertown" or "Underground town" from Nin, who throws the tarot for her
(a means of getting in touch with forces of the unconscious), her husband worries about her
mingling with the lowlife down there. Helen then asks: "And what of my desire?" (Grahn,
1982, p. 19) Ereshkigal, the owner of the lesbian bar, reminds Helen how she has recoiled
from knowing her in the past, how she has been portrayed as Mother Kali, as the essence of
evil. However, it is Ereshkigal who teaches Helen: "Look into your mind! . . . You were a
goddess in Christ's time/worshipped with Simon Magus under a plane tree" (Grahn, 1982,
p. 26). Helen suffers from all the forms of amnesia we have previously discussed: "I have a
certain problem with my memory" (Grahn, 1982, p. 26). Ereshkigal informs Helen that she
must listen with her inner ear. "Helen, you've been called Inanna, a goddess, queen of
heaven and earth" (Grahn, 1982, p. 29). "Where is your memory?" (Grahn, 1982, p. 26)

Ereshkigal continues her teaching, informing Helen that she was a Goddess before Demeter's time, and that she will change Helen's center of gravity by showing her that she has also
been a warrior. Ereshkigal's teaching is also a sexual initiation to womanlove, in this case
love of herself, her queenly, shamanic, warrior self, which Helen learns to do through loving
Ereshkigal, her dark sister.

> Oh descend to me
> lower yourself into yourself
> as I go down
> and go down
> and go down to you.
>
> I want you to fall, as I fall. . . .
> Oh descend to me
> Mound on Mound of Venus meeting (Grahn, 1982, pp. 54, 55)

Inanna's "fall" is also an initiation into sexuality as a path toward new knowledge, a path
that is linked to women's feminist matristic powers and allures as they were once experienced openly.

Helen is, thus, the new Eve as well, for Ereshkigal lures her to taste of the forbidden fruit
of the tree of knowledge. Little by little, as Helen descends lower and lower into the underworld, her matristic memory returns, and she remembers her past lives, her rape, hiding out
in Egypt, her healing powers, and her fall.

In *Gate Five: Belowworld, A Woman Among Motorcycles*, Ereshkigal addresses Helen as
Inanna, and expounds the teachings of the underworld, as she dresses in costumes accompanied by the chorus of the Crow Warrior dykes in the underworld.

> I, Boudica . . .
> a queen am I
> a warrior and a shaman.
> Shameless is my goddess and ferocious;
> my god's foot cloven. (Grahn, 1982, p. 82)

She describes herself as a swordswoman, a queen of sacred groves, a pagan, a lesbian,
and a mother whose daughters were raped. She is "the power of women brought down"
(Grahn, 1982, p. 83). Boudica is a historical example of an offended Queen of the Underworld, who rose up and defended the ancient ways. "A queen am I, a living memory/who

knows her own worth/and who remembers that the future/is the past rehearsed, and /*not should I go forth*/unless it be for battle girthed./Unless it be for battle girthed,/and belted, *not should I go forth*/until the foe is driven from the earth" (Grahn, 1982, p. 85).

Helen then remembers the war with the motorcycles, calling the grandmothers, Mother, and calling "the gods and mothers of the gods, Mary,/Anna, Isis, Ishtar, Aphrodite, Hecate, Oya, Demeter,/Freya, Kali, Kwan Yin, Pele, Yemanya, Maya, Diana, Hera,/Oshun" (Grahn, 1982, p. 89). She also recalls how her woman-naming roar drove the angry men away. Ereshkigal informs Helen that she has retrieved at least three of the four kinds of memory: "first, your mythic memory/as a goddess; second, your past-life history,/both the outer and inner versions in your mind;/third, the collective, consciously connected/recollections of your kind./ The last is of your own person,/the carefully buried splinter memories of child-hood" (Grahn, 1982, pp. 97, 98). The last kind of memory she has to retrieve—personal memory—is of family violence—her childhood memories of battery and rape within the family. This is the state to which Helen has been "reduced" or "expanded" before she is "hung on a peg," as in the myth of Inanna, just before being reborn.

In learning the truth about her past, Helen has gained consciousness, and she will become a true teacher and seer. As the play concludes, Helen has been reunited with her sister-self, her alter ego, her shadow, to become whole and conscious, whole and connected to her matristic heritage. "O Lady of the Great Below./Hard are your lessons . . . I know your shadow falls beside me/everywhere I go" (Grahn, 1982, p. 126).

Along with the expansion of consciousness that comes with knowledge and memory of our matristic matrilineage of power, a concept of identity evolves that is incremental, inter-connected, expanded, and multifaceted. In her multiphrenic complexity, a contemporary woman comes to *own* her lost Self, the Self that patriarchy had split off and forced her to bury, her powerful, queenly, amazonian, goddess Self, the Self we have come to call the Shadow.

It is also important to establish that the heroines who are being remembered appeared in works dating from eras that preceded written literature. The Homeric epics, for example, are part of an oral tradition, and were originally sung. So too, many of our myths and tales were originally transmitted via the oral tradition.

It has been shown by William J. Ong in *Orality and Literacy: The Technologizing of the Word* (1982), that first writing and then print created a sense of closure on the thought, a sense that what is printed is finalized. With the purely verbal forms, there is always the possibility for change, alternation, and ultimately, transformation. The oral tradition is partic-ipatory, in that it depends to a great extent on the lively presence of an audience and its immediate physical and emotional response to the recitation of the tale. Indeed, audiences affect the telling of a tale to such a degree that narrators will often change an episode or the ending in the presence of a hostile audience. Literature in the oral tradition is also closely connected with rhythms that may induce movement such as rocking or tapping on the part of the listeners. These rhythms and formulae, as well as the stock characters, buoy up the memory of the narrator so that even an extremely long epic can be retained by the collective memory of a community and its storytellers.

As Ong reminds us, for at least 50,000 years humans communicated without script, for the first script dates back only to 3500 B.C.E. (Ong, 1982, p. 7).

Indeed, "language is so overwhelmingly oral that of all the many thousands of lan-guages— possibly tens of thousands—spoken in the course of human history, only around 106 have ever been committed to writing to a degree sufficient to have produced literature, and most have never been written at all. Of some 3,000 languages spoken that exist today, only some 78 have a literature" (Ong, 1982, p. 7).

Thus, whereas oral literature is transmitted in the context of community, written literature is received in a solitary act. Oral tradition literature constitutes a world of sound. Printed literature is experienced in silence. Ong points out two more facts that are particularly relevant to our discussion. "Deconstruction is tied to typography rather than, as its advocates seem often to assume, merely to writing. For, deconstructionists rely on printed texts, and refute any transparent relationship between printed words, spoken words, or external phenomena" (Ong, 1982, p. 129). "Language is structure, and its structure is not that of the extramental world. The end result for Derrida is that literature—and indeed language, itself—is not at all 'representational' or 'expressive' of something outside itself" (Ong, 1982, p. 167).

Thus, it should not be surprising that if contemporary feminist matristic writers are evoking a world of women's voices that was an essentially oral world (versions of stories that might have been spoken, but were never committed to texts because the canon formation was in the hands of patriarchal males), the forms in which they invoke the erased voices and versions of their ancient sisters do not conform to the post-modern hallmarks of intertextuality. One might even conceive of creating a term like "intervocality" to suggest a process whereby contemporary feminist matristic tales deconstruct antecedent patriarchal versions of still earlier matristic stories. Indeed, contemporary feminist matristic writers choose consciously to restore versions of tales (myths, narratives, etc.) that existed before the patriarchal rendition closed them forever by fixing them in print. This is not to say that the writers in question either express themselves in the oral tradition or refuse to relate to the patriarchal printed texts. On the contrary, they commit to print a variety of divergent versions of the canonical patriarchal story. (Here I purposely employ the word "version" rather than "variant," which, in my opinion, would imply an acceptance of the major narrative motifs of the patriarchal versions.) Alice Walker, in *The Temple of My Familiar,* used a technique for committing an oral narrative to print—the playing of Lissie's cassette after her death.

It is also important to recall with Ong that, traditionally, women were not even formally trained in the rhetoric employed in the oral tradition. Thus, their narratives were probably excluded from that tradition as well, although they were obviously recited within the local communal settings in which many oral works were performed and sung. Ong knows of no major studies that have examined the monumental consequences of women's exclusion from the oral tradition. Today's feminist matristic writers may forego intertextuality in its contemporary form in order to make us aware of the fact that the version of the narrative their text refers to predates typography. Naturally they do not abandon the entire repertoire of typographical literary conventions or standards of aesthetic quality. They simply do not accept the patriarchal versions of those texts as canonical.

By inserting their own feminist matristic versions into the written record, they are attempting to create an alternate canon as well as to underscore the importance of variants and of change within the feminist matristic canon itself. In other words, we may encounter three or four different feminist matristic variants of Eve or Helen, all of which challenge both the Bible and classical literatures, but which vary among themselves within this new, alternate feminist matristic corpus. These variants, however, do not attempt to establish *the* feminist matristic version as *the* ur-story that all the others refer to. On the contrary, rather than attempt to fix or canonize one story, feminist matristic literature espouses the ecofeminist reflowering of multiple variants,[2] echoing the oral tradition that it honors when it reclaims the Goddess. Thus, contemporary feminist matristic writers, while still committing their multiple variants to print, may borrow the episodic structure that was common in the oral epic. They may forego the narrative climax, and in so doing avoid using "phallocentric" literary structures and strategies.

Feminist matristic writers are currently assembling scores of variant versions of the classical canonical texts to match the countless scores of variants audiences must have heard

---

[2]Here I use "variants" to indicate the multiple changes of tales within the feminist matristic tendency.

rendered on any given topic such as, let us say, the Trojan War, before one particular variant was actually inscribed into the written record, becoming somewhat of an ur-text for modern scholars. The first feminist matristic writer to do this was Charlene Spretnak in *Lost Goddesses of Early Greece: A Collection of Pre-Hellenic Myths* (1978). However, feminist matristic writers are fully contemporary in their perspectives and skills. They do not return to oral transmission per se, but do endeavor to reimagine or remember the female versions of such stories as might have circulated at a time when literature was the spoken word, a medium of sound rather than of sight, and when people could participate actively in its composition and its performance—people who today would be termed "illiterate" because they cannot read or write.

The feminist matristic writer who best expresses the contemporary feminist search for an authentic matristic language is Jeanne Hyvrard. In focusing on the French writer Jeanne Hyvrard's analysis of the problem of language, I do not mean to exclude or deny the importance of the writings of other French feminists who have been inscribing the female gender into texts in a variety of ways. What I wish to stress here is not so much the need for a female-gendered language, or an inscription of "femininity" into language, but the need for a feminist matristic language, one that remembers an ancient world view in which humans were not separate from nature, mind from matter, spirit from body, and in which the Earth Mother prevailed. One (or many of these languages) that Jeanne Hyvrard would call "fusional" (Waelti Walters, *De la Pensée Séparatrice*), that is to say, a language that she remembers from before the time of the patriarchal colonization of the culture of the Neolithic, a language that is neither eco-amnesiac nor patriarchal. The language that the narrator of Jeanne Hyvrard's *Mère la Mort* (1976) seeks is also an ecofeminist language, one that recalls the harmony of humans and nature in the Garden of Eden before the Fall.

The female narrator of *Mere la Mort* is considered mad by her androcratic, eco-amnesiac society. To the feminist matristic reader she is illuminated by a vision of the culture of the Great Mother.

The narrator of Hyvrard's *Mère la Mort* recounts and remembers the destructive acts perpetrated by the patriarchal colonizers who simultaneously desecrated the sacred culture of the Goddess and her natural earth shrines.

"But the invaders came. They said that stones were not alive. They uprooted the trees without seeing the blood that was flowing. They detoured the rivers without hearing the earth that was screaming. They separated the night from the day, the mother from the Earth, the doves from the olive trees. They said that a man had landed and that he had killed the python that guarded your cave. As if time could kill death. They multiplied words. They said that the king of Hell had carried off the daughter of the earth one day when she was gathering poppies. They separated things from their opposites. They said that reason was born with a helmet from the thigh of the creator . . . They perverted the language. . . . They said I had lost my mind. They made of me a dead woman. . . . But I survived. . . . They thought they could appropriate me. But I became the world" (Hyvrard, 1976, pp. 60, 61; trans. by Orenstein).

For Jeanne Hyvrard, the experience of colonization is the historical actuality that explains both the loss of a living Goddess creation myth in her culture and the loss of a living feminist matristic language. These losses have driven the narrator of the text, *Mere la Mort* (Mother Death), into a state of profound psychological despair. Her psychic state is, nonetheless, identified by the patriarchal culture in which she lives as madness.

Her work is an invocation to the Great Mother Goddess, called Mother Death, partly in order to underscore the murder of Her culture in contemporary patriarchal civilization. Yet, Mother Death is also a direct reference to the ancient Goddess of Death and Regeneration. In her madness, the narrator becomes like a fetus seeking refuge in the womb of her Earth Mother, and identifies her own body with that of the Mother Goddess and the Earth. The memory of a matristic world in which all of nature was once animated by a female life force is the source of the illness from which the patriarchal powers seek to cure her, for she feels the earth to be a bleeding woman and herself to be a part of its body. "They dress my wounds in cardboard covers, but the blood still flows from the womb of the mountain. . . . They look up the name of my illness in their files. It is called Memory. My perdition. It is called your body" (Hyvrard, 1976, pp. 48–49).

The Earth Mother Goddess of the narrator's memory is associated with the cluster of images we have identified as matristic historic realities rather than archetypal images. They are past realities preserved by memory, not psychic fantasies. The existence of goddess-centered culture is for Hyvrard's narrator a historical fact, and she refers to archaeological diggings in which goddess statues were uncovered as proof that these are not delusions but buried truths. "On an island before the invaders a statue discovered. A woman. Her breast bare. On her head. A dove. Feminine singular. In her hands. Serpents . . . Masculine Plural. . . . Death Mother your birds and your reptiles. I am running towards you seeking your name. I knew it before going to the school of the French" (Hyvrard, 1976, pp. 99, 131).

Marija Gimbutas informs us that in Minoan and Mycenean art, bird and Snake Goddesses abound, and they curiously resemble the memories of Hyvrard's narrator, for the "best known from the ivory and faience statuettes called 'Snake Goddesses,' one holding snakes in her hands, another with snakes intertwined around the abdomen and breasts, and both having exposed breasts. . . . A bird perches on an earlier Proto-Sanctuary of the Dove Goddess of Knossos" (Gimbutas, 1982, p. 146) In *Mère la Mort* it is explained that the patriarchal colonizers took over the pre-patriarchal Goddess religion. "Mère la Mort, the invaders came and they said that you were two. They changed our his/stories, but they could not kill our memory" (Hyvrard, 1976, p. 89).

In the form of illumination that her society labels madness, which is her true feminist matristic sanity, the narrator seeks to restore the unity that existed before the separation, to return to her Earth Mother, to an animistic world view, and to a holistic language. "Mère la Mort, we will again become your body from before the separation" (Hyvrard, 1976, p. 89). The search for a language which once named all of creation without establishing false dichotomies is the solution desired for the generation of the female psyche. "A word that means its contrary . . . A word to say death and rebirth" (Hyvrard, 1976, p. 155). "Mother Death, I am running towards you to survive. I am running towards you seeking your name. I read it once in a book. But they had so overwhelmed it, that I no longer recognized it" (Hyvrard, 1976, p. 158). Hyvrard's language remembers matristic culture, and recalls a time when women fabricated the statues of the Goddess by hand, and these statuettes are literally the only remaining concrete proof of the historical existence of the Goddess religion outside of female memory. Without them there is no real proof that the narrator is not mad. "Our common language from before the separation. The statues of baked clay that we made in our hands. Your ample thighs and your naked breasts. . . . Your birds and your serpents" (Hyvrard, 1976, p. 131).

Thus, the creation of a contemporary feminist matristic culture that these statues symbolize will now preserve the memory of a verifiable historic reality in a conscious way. *Mère la Mort* is an expressionistic cry in the night, a work of supplication, prayer, litany, and lamentation. Addressing the Mother Goddess in the familiar "tu" form, Hyvrard establishes the intimacy of the confessional and the love poem united.

As we have seen, in addition to the ordinary means of obtaining knowledge of the past, feminist matristic writers have had to make use of their memory, their psychic sense of intuition, body and sensory memory, and all forms of recall issuing from the profoundest levels of the unconscious, as well as from cellular and genetic memory banks.

Obviously, as di Prima has said in *The Critic Reviews Loba*, there is no proof, no definitive evidence of a world that has been systematically destroyed, and whose origins may date back further than 25,000 B.C.E. As she writes: "no longitude given/it moves/& breathless beauty/of circle & dodecahedron/form the mind's light/cutting lines of Force/thru this quivering/flesh seedpod/Cosmos" (di Prima, 1978, p. 172).

Feminist matristic writers are creating new images of mythic dimensions in their freshly visioned and newly launched tales of epic heroines. For, they are creating a contemporary feminist matristic culture, which includes lore and legends as well as tales and myths. These narratives circulate widely in women's culture at large—in women's groups, women's publications, in women's rituals, in women's concerts, songs. And, in general, on the grassroots level wherever women gather and share. What is important is the flowering, the proliferation of the many variants of the feminist matristically re-membered tales, as well as of the newly spawned cycles from the mythos of ecofeminism.

This rambling vine or mushrooming tree of life in the literary world gives rise to the possibility of cross-fertilization, grafting, pruning, re- and transplanting, seeding and sowing in a truly organic fashion, leading to the "reflowering of the Goddess" around the world once more.

Cycling: Restoring Matristic Storytelling

In this chapter we will explore the major teachings of contemporary feminist matristic writers, both as they transmit to us the lost tales of power of ancient goddess-centered cultures, and as they rewrite the canonical patriarchal versions of the lore and the teachings about the Great Mother.

In traditional and archaic cultures one of the primary functions of the lore (legends, tales, etc.) is to teach lessons. Tales of power are told about encounters with the spirits at the sacred sites, about punishment for unethical behavior (such as stealing offerings from the sacred site and how the spirits punished the offender), and about the proper way in which to address the spirits in order to receive their guidance, and so forth.[1]

Considering the proliferation of feminist matristic literature as a flourishing of tales of power, written with a constant reference to the world of oral (rather than printed) literature to which they refer, permits us to approach them as one would the tales of power told in a traditional culture, and come to them in order to seek a teaching. Naturally, since they are also contemporary written works of literature, they can be analyzed as such. However, that will not be *our* focus. We are presently interested in their teachings, and in what the new feminist matristic versions of each of the cycles reveals to us about the premises on which a matristic culture might once have been, or might, once again, be founded, about the nature of the patriarchal overthrow of such cultures, and the consequences ensuing from that conquest, according to the imaginative insights of contemporary feminist matristic writers.

In addition to teachings about history, ethics, literary tradition as an ideological construct, knowledge, power, and the mythic sources of both life-affirming and life-negating social systems, we will be seeking teachings about women's lives under such divergent systems, about the construction and expansion of personal identity, about women's empowerment and disempowerment in diverse systems, and specifically about how our tales, (myths, legends, literary traditions, symbolic structures, etc.) formulate our relationship to knowledge and to the formation of consciousness and conscience in these systems.

I will not be able to enter into detailed analyses of each cycle in one chapter. Rather, I will indicate the locus of the cycle, the topoi of the cycle, the motifs (original or matristic, patriarchal, and contemporary feminist matristic), and the major teachings. I will explore only a few contemporary works in each cycle, leaving it to the reader to place other works in these cycles and to notice other cycles in the process of being created.

In prebiblical times, many tales were told about specific women and men, but only one version was recorded by the redactors or scribes, who, being patriarchal scholars, selected

---

[1]Related to me by Sami Shaman, Ellen Marit Gaup-Dunfjeld.

a variant to inscribe that best illustrated the principles upon which their beliefs were founded. Today, feminist matristic writers are also inscribing their own preferred variants of versions of the tales that they have revised. They are the redactors of a flowering feminist matristic culture. But they are inscribing the variants of the tales that have, for the most part, already been recorded only in their patriarchal versions. They also have to contend with the publishing industry and with the values of the arbiters of contemporary taste, who still embody the values of patriarchy. Thus, in this case, the tales that are inscribed are not necessarily the prevailing variants of feminist matristic versions, nor are they necessarily the ones that might have been inscribed had the monolithic publishing industry not intervened—had the women writers made their own selections.

Since this process is in progress, we will not see the overall cumulative effects of this flowering for several decades. It is my conviction that when it will all be seen as one complete feminist matristic collection, a whole entity, these cycles, linked together, will comprise diverse Creation stories and histories, and might constitute a corpus of works that one could call a feminist matristic Creation Myth/os.

An analogy can be made with the Bible in the way the books (here cycles) are both separate and also part of a larger whole, and that they record the spiritual and historical epic of a specific people from their Creation story through their Exodus, Diaspora, Holocaust, and the founding of a new culture over time.

The cycles that we will peruse are:

1. The Biblical Cycle
2. The Classical Cycle (including Heroes and Goddesses)
3. The Indigenous Cycle
4. The Ecofeminist Cycle
5. The Grail Cycle

All of these cycles and others that will still evolve, when seen as parts of a larger mythic construct, will probably function as elements of a vast feminist matristic mythos of life's origins and women's history. As this reflowering is just occurring, it is not yet possible to obtain an overview of the entire mosaic as it will look when fleshed out over time.

THE BIBLICAL CYCLE

I have insisted on the fact that for every one of the feminist matristic novels or plays that inscribes the revised story of a Goddess or heroine into the printed record today, other variants of these stories circulate in our culture, forming the matrix out of which the cycles of tales arise, only some of which are actually published.

In the Biblical Cycle I want to stress the theoretical reconstruction and reinterpretation of the life of Sarah by Savina Teubal in her book *Sarah the Priestess; The First Matriarch of Genesis* (1984), partly because her work is a model of the new feminist matristic research, and also because Savina Teubal is a fiction writer whose imaginative talents were put to the service of reconstructive scholarship in the case of her revision of the Sarah story.

Thus, a very important "new" Sarah story emerges from her pen, which is one among many feminist midrashes on Sarah recently created, but one that comes with the authority of scholarship behind it, rather than being simply an imaginative, fictive invention or a combination of scholarship and fantasy.

Savina Teubal has used data from ancient Mesopotamian tablet inscriptions relating to the role of women as priestesses to explain some of the conundrums that the Bible poses with regard to Sarah. The questions Savina asks seem straightforward enough, but her answers are extremely complex. How is it that Sarah and Abraham (spelled Abram in her book) were married if they were brother and sister? Didn't the incest taboo forbid such marriages? Why is it that the great Jewish matriarchs, Sarah, Rebekah, and Rachel were childless for many years? Why did Sarah bear a child late in life? What does it mean that Sarah spent most of her life in a sacred grove of terebinth trees in Mamre? Why did Rebekah want her younger child, Jacob, to receive the birthright from Isaac, rather than her older son, Esau, and so forth? These and other questions led Teubal to study both the laws of the matrilineal societies in Mesopotamia that Sarah probably came from, as well as the laws relating to priestesses of the Goddess Asherah, who were known as "En" or "Naditu."

If one understands that Sarah's tradition was matrilineal, not patrilineal, and that in her culture Ultimogeniture (inheritance passed on via the youngest child) was practiced, and if one understands that in those societies a woman could marry her brother if they shared the same father, but *not* if they shared the same mother, then we begin to see a picture emerging that explains many of the perplexities relating to the life of Sarah and other matriarchs of the Bible.

Indeed, in a matrilineal society, it was considered to be incest to marry one's brother, but only if one shared the same mother, not if one shared the same father. However, since Sarah and Abram did have the same father, and not the same mother, they *could* marry, according to the matrilineal practices of the time.

Furthermore, Mesopotamian priestesses around the third century B.C.E., who participated in the sacred ritual of Hieros Gamos (mystic nuptials), were looked upon as incarnations of the Goddess. Sarah, in fact, did officiate at these mystic nuptials, which were related to the fertility of the land. Women who were priestesses of the Goddess Inanna were to remain childless—or celibate. This may explain Sarah's so-called barrenness. Indeed, Sarah often traveled to centers of moon worship, and all of the most important events of her life (including the theophany or the supernatural annunciation of the son that was to be born to her in her nineties) occurred at Mamre, a sacred grove of terebinth trees, sacred to the Goddess Asherah.

Teubal's scholarly work does constitute a new tale of power about Sarah. She emerges as a great Matriarch who was probably a priestess of the Goddess Asherah, and whose spiritual theophanies put her in direct communication with the deity. She spent most of her life as a priestess, not as a mother, and her life is exemplary of that of a Matriarch of elevated status from a matrilineal society, whose spiritual heritage involved reverence for the Earth consecrated to the Goddess. Her spiritual function was also oracular.

Turning from scholarship to the world of fiction, Penelope Farmer's novel *Eve, Her Story*, (1988) retells the story of the Garden of Eden from Eve's perspective, and it begins in this way.

"Let me start by making this clear. I ate the fruit of the forbidden tree, the Tree of Knowledge, because I chose to. The serpent had nothing to do with it"(Farmer, 1988, p. 11). The author mentions that she has been influenced by Raphael Patai's *The Hebrew Goddess* (1967), Merlin Stone's *The Paradise Papers* (1976)[2] and J. A. Phillips's *Eve, The History of an Idea* (1984) in creating her revision of the story of Eve. She reminds us that Merlin Stone suggested that the story of Eve and the serpent was actually conceived deliberately by the Levite priesthood. It was a form of propaganda to undermine the role of women and of the goddesses and used to attack their polytheistic, ecstatic rites. (Farmer, 1988, p. 187).

Having already published a book entitled *Beginnings: Creation Myths,* Farmer knows that our Biblical myth of the Fall is only one among many such myths in a wide variety of cultures. To put it in a relativistic perspective, she narrates the story from the point of view of Eve. What, then, is the teaching of Penelope Farmer in her revision of the story of Eve? Once more we find a tale in which the exiled, rebellious sister teaches the obedient sister about female sexuality and about women's original powers. Here it is Lilith, Adam's first wife, who meets with Eve in the garden, and tells her about how she had refused to lie underneath

---

[2]*The Paradise Papers* was the original name of the British edition of the book published in the United States under the title *When God Was a Woman.*

Adam. Lilith represents women's active sexual desires. When Eve wonders if, perhaps, Adam might still lust after his former wife, Lilith responds: "Does it matter?" asked Lilith. "Do I have to remind you again, Eve, of the significant question? Do I lust after—do I want—*him*; not the other way about. . . . The fact was that in the end the price of my submission was too high; that other things were more important. At which point I ran away" (Farmer, 1988, p. 122).

Lilith confesses that she only came back to Eden, which she mocks as anything but a real Paradise, in order to find her sister, Eve. Lilith then initiates Eve into the practice of active sexuality. Eventually their love for each other turns to ecstasy, and they dance wildly together in the garden.

Eve is a questioner, and evolves to become a woman on a quest. The serpent teaches her the fine art of storytelling. He also represents the arrogance of the earliest scientific rivalries with God's creation. He is an alchemist, and he says that he dishonored God's creation by aping his powers, thus implying that what God had created was insufficient for man's needs.

Adam, on the other hand, is a creator and a magician, not an arrogant scientist. He creates mountains, and calls forth landscapes magically, but does not compete with God or defy his Creation. Eve thinks she ate the *fig*, the forbidden fruit of knowledge, "in order to have a story to tell; and in order to know how to tell it, in my own way, before the serpent had time to" (Farmer, 1988, p. 179).

Reflecting upon the act that patriarchs claim determined the Fall of humankind, Eve says: "Yet the moment that I realized what I did it became a knowledgeable bite, the considered, careful action of a woman who needing, as a woman, what the garden could not give her, had to take the risk that her husband would not follow" (Farmer, 1988, p. 184).

Farmer's version shows the evolution of Eve from the passive "helpmeet" of Adam to the courageous quester for knowledge due to the initiation she received from her sister of the underworld/other world/exiled world, Lilith, whose teachings she would soon follow.

Learning the skill of storytelling from the serpent, Eve takes the power back unto herself, and tells her own story before it can be deformed or erased by the serpent and his ilk, who represent the culture of scientific arrogance and so-called enlightenment, a precursor of contemporary patriarchy.

Whereas many feminist matristic rewrites of the Garden of Eden story envisage the serpent as the symbol of the prepatriarchal Goddess, this particular variant casts the serpent as the precursor of scientific transgressions against God's law.

Eve, initiated and inspired by her outcast sister, Lilith, becomes an outcast, herself, choosing knowledge over security, risking the loss of Paradise and of her husband. Like Helen/Inanna, her entry into the other world or underworld is conscious and deliberate, for it is there, outside of the security of Eden, that Eve will find answers to her burning questions about female sexuality, death, and women's mysteries. Eve, too, in this novel, has magical, spiritual powers. She can speak to the Cherry Tree and command it to do as she instructs. She also informs Adam that she chooses to use these powers to do things in her own way— not as he and Jehovah decide.

As we have seen thus far, in their feminist matristic revisions, neither Eve nor Sarah are interpreted primarily as wives or mothers. Both have made ethical and spiritual decisions to commit themselves either to the Goddess or to Knowledge, (which in some versions is the same thing), to revere the Earth as sacred, and to act independently of their husbands, always in the service of a higher spiritual or ethical calling.

Reclaiming the art of storytelling from, in this case, the serpent (i.e., possible male redactors of women's stories) gives women the opportunity to reveal their sources of knowledge, their oracular and magical powers, and their matristic ethical considerations. Storytelling, as we shall see, becomes the dominant metaphor for the magical art that literally creates a new feminist matristic reality in which we, too, can participate.

Within Christianity, numerous feminist theo(a)logians have pointed to the reductionistic way in which the Great Goddess was incorporated into the Catholic religion, diminishing Her powers by making Her a virgin, and thereby denying the physicality of the procreative powers and experiences of all women.

Two authors retell the story of the Virgin Mary from a feminist matristic perspective.

Clysta Kinstler's novel, *The Moon Under Her Feet* (1989), is a feminist matristic midrash on the Christian mysteries as told from the point of view of Mary the Magdalen, who, with Mary the mother of Jesus, is a High Priestess of the Goddess Religion.

The book opens by announcing the concept of the midrash as it is linked to storytelling in the oral tradition. "Mine is a story that must be told and a story that must be heard, because those who presume to tell it do not know it. Or want to. Those who have taken possession of the story of Yeshua, the Christos, distort his record and mine, for one cannot be told without the other. I am Mari the Magdalen, and I have set down the truth in this manuscript, trusting that the Goddess will bring it to light when the time is ripe. . . . I have always served the goddess" (Kinstler, 1989, p. 1).

This midrash, which takes place at the time of Herod Antipas and Pontius Pilate, syncretizes all the female mysteries and rites from Asherah, Inanna, and Isis through the lives of the two Marys, including the Jewish and Christian mysteries. Both Marys conceive their children by enacting the role of the Goddess in the sacred rites of the Hieros Gamos, a fertility ritual in which the High Priestess becomes the Goddess on Earth, and is married to her consort, the Sacred Bridegroom. The child that she conceives during this sacred marriage ritual will be born a divine child or a god, and her consort must be sacrificed the next day in a ritual reenactment of the rites of Osiris.

It is through the Hieros Gamos that Almah Mari (known to us as the Virgin Mary) conceives her child, Yeshua. This sacred marriage, as it is portrayed by Kinstler, reverses both the mysteries of the Annunciation and of the Virgin Birth. Here Almah Mari conceives the divine child, Yeshua, in an erotic night of love as part of a sacred fertility ritual, which will restore the fertility of the land. According to tradition, her consort is beheaded the next day. This grieves her deeply, as she has fallen in love with him during their one night together. Almah Mari has been prepared for this ritual by her training as a High Priestess at the Temple of the Goddess in Jerusalem.

She has learned to use trance and to descend through the Seven Gates of the Netherworld to meet Ereshkigal, the queen of the dark realm. In her trance she can envisage all time and space, and see all events past, present, and future. She is the living incarnation of Queen Isis, and in altered states of consciousness she learns of her destiny with Yeshua.

Mari, (known to us as Mary Magdalen) is a young priestess of the Goddess religion at the Cloister of the College of Virgins, and she is the best friend of Almah Mari. She lives through Almah Mari's transformation from an ordinary priestess to High Priestess (or Magdalen), and eventually she is married off to Phillip Herod, the Tetrach of Batanea, Trachonitis, and Aurantis, a patriarch whose culture degrades and despises the Goddess.

Eventually Almah Mari obtains the release of Mari from the harem of her husband at Caesara-Phillipi, and has her recalled to Jerusalem to live out her destiny as the Magdalene, or the High Priestess of the Goddess at the Temple in Jerusalem. Through complexities in the narrative, Mari eventually enacts the role of the Goddess with Yeshua (the twin of her former lover, Seth). It is during this Sacred Marriage that her own divine child, Anna, is conceived. Anna is the divine progeny born of the marriage of the High Priestess of the Goddess and the divine son of the former Magdalen. Thus, we see a reversal of the sex of the new divine child from male to female with the implication that the new Redeemer will be a woman.

When the novel closes, Mari the Magdalen and Seth are wed. Together they will raise Anna, the divine female child of Yeshua and Mari. Seth will play the role of Joseph in this family. They also possess the Holy Grail, considered to be a relic of regeneration.

Mari the Magdalen experiences numerous visions of the Goddess in the iconography that we associate with the Virgin Mary. "Clothed with the sun and the moon under her feet" (Kinstler, 1989, p. 66).

In one vision the Goddess addresses Mari in these words: "I am come. I, the mother of all things, governess of the elements, firstborn of the worlds. My love is poured out upon the earth. I am the soul of nature, the life of the universe. From me all things proceed, and to me they return" (Kinstler, 1989, p. 66). Mari the Magdalen also is the first to see the vision of the risen Christ as Osiris, Yeshua, Seth, and Sharon (Yeshua's father in the Sacred Marriage) along with a vision of the Holy Mother Isis, both radiant and together in the spirit world.

Thus, in this feminist matristic midrash on the Christian mysteries, while demystifying the patriarchal mysteries of the Virgin Birth and the Annunciation, Kinstler has magically empowered female sexuality to anoint males to kingship in order to engender rebirth through union with the Goddess. The male's ability to produce a divine child depended entirely upon his marriage with the High Priestess (the Magdalen), who was skilled in the magical arts and in the Law of the Goddess, as Kinstler envisages it. It is the magic of the High Priestess that produces the divine child, thus keeping it in the motherline of priestesses of the Goddess Religion.

While there is no denial of Christ's divinity in this novel, it is because of the disempowerment of women and the eclipse of the truth of the Goddess tradition by the politics of the patriarchs that Christ's message must now be brought into the world via women who are reunited with their ancient Goddess heritage, their true source of power.

This tale of power combines a scholarly study of biblical history, the Apocryphal texts and the Gnostic gospels with feminist matristic revision. It allies the arts of the scholar with those of the visionary artist, showing us how only the combination of these two kinds of knowledge can help us piece together a past that, while conceived by the imagination, can also be rooted in the evidence of the real, and grounded by the workings of inspired intelligence.

Another feminist matristic revision of the story of Mary Magdalene is *The Wild Girl* by Michele Roberts (1984). Roberts, too, is influenced by the Gnostic gospels found at Nag Hammadi, and she has imagined an alternative, or fifth gospel, that of Mary Magdalene, a disciple of Jesus. She has collapsed Mary of Bethany, the sister of Martha and Lazarus, with the Mary who annointed Christ (as Kinstler does), in order to "follow the tradition of centuries, the spinning of stories around a composite character" (Roberts, 1984, author's note).

Through the novel we come to understand the figure of the female prophet (who in the Classical Cycle will emerge as the prophet Cassandra) as the source of power and knowledge in the sense of direct vision or Gnosis, through which vital information about our lost Goddess heritage is retrieved.

Roberts's Mary Magdalene had been drawn to women's mysteries as a child, and having run away from her home in Jerusalem at the age of 15 and been raped by men in her flight, she sought refuge and comfort at the shrine of Demeter and Persephone at Eleusis, where the women's mysteries were enacted every year.

After returning to Jerusalem, she had her first Gnostic epiphany, in which she had a vision of women dancing with sensuality, and she experienced fusion with the cosmos. Eventually, Mary met Jesus, Simon Peter, and John, and she fell in love with Jesus. In Mary Magdalene's relationship with Jesus, female sexuality is fully affirmed in the heart of, and at the birth of, the religion we now call Christianity.

After having been proclaimed the full equal of the male disciples, Mary began to prophesy aloud. In her prophecy she saw that all life comes from the Mother, and if the Mother is not respected, She will erupt, causing famines, plagues, and droughts. Jesus responded publicly to her prophecy by stating that men have denied the knowledge of the mother for too long. He admonished his disciples to welcome women as Ministers of the Word, and to join the

Father and Mother together in their souls—to conceive of God as both masculine and feminine.

The Gnostic Mary Magdalene has many revelatory and prophetic dreams, which link Sophia to the teachings of Jesus. Jesus interprets Mary's dreams as warnings to the Children of Ignorance who have ignored Sophia, have forgotten the feminine, and thereby have perpetuated a false creation. The false creation must be renewed, and in its renewal, Jesus will represent the new Adam, and Mary Magdalene, the new Eve. The core of this teaching is the restoration of the Mother to the new Christianity. "We have lost the knowledge of the Mother. We do not fully know God if we drive out this name of God. And so those who become restored and resurrected through this baptism, through this rebirth in the marriage chamber, shall acquire not only the name of the Father and the Son and the Holy Spirit who is Sophia, but also the name of the Mother who is earth, matter and soul married and indivisible" (Roberts, 1984, p. 111).

Ultimately, Mary has a vision of the Goddess, who speaks to her, revealing herself to be the Queen of Heaven, the Ancient One, Ishtar, Astarte, Athar, Artemis, Aphrodite, Isis, Inanna, Hecate, Demeter, and Persephone (Roberts, 1984, p. 125). The Goddess of many names tells Mary that She has been forgotten, ignored by men, and exiled from her home on earth, but that she will soon arise.

As in Kinstler's novel, Mary becomes pregnant, and bears a female child. This divine female child will pass on the teachings of her mother, Mary, and it will eventually be her child, Mary's grandchild, who will uncover the scrolls in which Mary Magdalene had inscribed her visions. In one of these gnostic visions that are inscribed in the scrolls of parchment, Mary dreams of a New Jerusalem, which she refers to as a female city. The dream reminds her that "we have forgotten to burn incense to the Queen of Heaven, ... We have cut our God in two, and we have cast the female part out into the desert and have called it the devil" (Roberts, 1984, p. 175). In the dream, women dance around the New Jerusalem (the New Goddess City), and summon up the exiled Sophia, the rejected Great Mother. The dream ends with an epiphany of the Goddess as the image we call the "Virgin Mary." "And then I saw a great sign in the heavens: a woman arrayed with the sun, and with the moon under her feet, and upon her head a crown of twelve stars . . ." (Roberts, 1984, p. 178). The Goddess in the vision is pregnant, and gives birth to a son, Jesus. Mary's later teachings reveal Jesus to be the son of the Mother Goddess. Mary Magdalene, as his disciple, later became the leader of a holy community of believers. It is her granddaughter (who found the scrolls), who is the author of this novel, thus assuring that Goddess knowledge is passed on through the motherline.

Finally, in this novel we have encountered a number of motifs common to the body of feminist matristic writings we will be exploring. Some of these motifs are: the reclamation of female sexuality as sacred through a reconnection to the Goddess tradition; the dream of a new feminist matristic Eden, expressed here as a new Mother Goddess city; the identification of the Mother and of the female Creator with the earth, and of Her language with that of nature, not split apart from culture, but understood as one with the culture, here preached by the Word of Jesus and Mary Magdalene; the affirmation of female prophecy as a form of direct visionary knowledge (gnosis) of the Goddess; and the birth of a divine, female child, symbolizing a new era in which the female aspect of the Creator will be made manifest. Goddess knowledge is thus circulated via the motherline, as well as by means of storytelling in the oral tradition. However, although this story had circulated orally, it was the discovery of the written scroll that established its veracity in a later patriarchal culture in which only the written word was accepted as evidence of truth. This also suggests that women in biblical times participated in the creation of literature, that they knew how to write, and that they associated the female image of Creation with the legitimation of their own creativity.

In reimagining an alternate Christian story, Michele Roberts has also extended the lineage of women writers back to the biblical era. She has given us the basis for wondering what else women might have written, had only their words been entered into the bible by *female* redactors.

In her book *Sexism and God-Talk: Towards a Feminist Theology*, Rosemary Radford Ruether proposed the use of the word God/ess as "the one who opens up a new community of equals" (1983, pp. 69, 71). "The God/ess," she maintains, "leads us to the converted center, the harmonization of self and body, of self and other, self and world. It is the shalom of our being. . . . we have no adequate name for the true God/ess, the 'I am who I shall become' " (Ruether, 1983, pp. 69, 71).

Ruether's proposal of the God/ess as the Shalom of Being in the unfolding of its mind, body, spirit connection to the universe, is directly opposed to the ways in which Christian doctrine degrades women's bodies, which, she reminds us, represent "the female life-giving role as the source of 'death' while expropriating the symbols of conception, birth and nurture to males" (Ruether, 1983, p. 144).

The perspective posited in this book is that works which define a feminist matristic vision see women's sexuality and spirituality as central to a relationship to the female Creator. Furthermore, in the feminist matristic ethos, sexuality is perceived as an expanded dimension of spirituality.

In her novel *A Weave of Women*, Esther Broner's community of women invoke the presence of the Shekinah or "the independent feminine divine entity" of the Kabbalah's mystical theosophy of the Middle Ages. According to Gershom Scholem, the foremost authority on the Kabbalah, the Shekinah was the feminine element in God (Patai, 1967, p. 124). *A Weave of Women* (1978) begins with antipatriarchal ceremonies among which there is a new feminist ritual—a hymenotomy, a piercing of the hymeneal membrane of the newborn child by members of the women's community in Jerusalem in order that the child "may not be judged by her hymen, but by the energies of her life." (Broner, 1978, p. 25). Simha's baby, Hava, on whom the hymenotomy is performed, was born out of wedlock. The ceremony that pierces the hymen makes the child a nonvirgin at birth, an act tantamount to bringing her into the world bearing all the stigmas decried by patriarchal theology: (1) born out of wedlock, and (2) a nonvirgin. Yet, it is in this state that she is ritually blessed by the Jerusalem feminists with a special ceremony and prayers to the Shekinah.

The women in this community, who revere the Shekinah, have created spiritual rites for such diverse events in women's lives as exorcising demons, birth, burial, and marriage. In celebrating the body as a temple for the spirit, they have invented Holy Body Day, a counterholiday in which "the women pray that they be restored to their own Temple" (Broner, 1978, p. 258). Eventually, they sing *The Women's Song of Songs*. Marcia Falk, a contemporary translator of *The Song of Songs* has written that *The Song of Songs* expresses "a strikingly nonsexist attitude toward heterosexual love, an attitude that excludes many of our modern Western stereotypes of 'masculinity' and 'femininity'. . . . This reciprocity between men and women is surely one of the Song's most inviting aspects of its lasting power" (Falk, 1973, Postface) Thus, the women celebrate Holy Body Day with their own *Song of Songs*, which proclaims the thighs as the pillars of the Temple. They conclude the day with a meal, having begun it with a ritual bath and a prayer to the Shekinah: "Blessed art thou, O Mother of the Universe, from whose body we descend, who has kept us alive, preserved us and brought us to this time, this season" (Broner, 1978, pp. 256, 257). Women's bodies are honored as holy in their sexual and sensual functions, for they reflect the body of the Great Mother who birthed them and nurtured them throughout the seasons.

The women's community in Jerusalem has not only a spiritual dimension, but a political one as well. The novel ends with the formation of a women's government in exile and the establishment of a women's commune. The women also create a ceremony specifically for sending women forth into the world.

The structure of the novel proceeds from the personal to the political and the communal—from the birth ceremony of the individual child, Hava, who dies a victim of male invaders, to the founding of the women's government in exile, and finally the marriage of the parents of the deceased child. This marriage obviously reverses the priorities of all those who marry to guarantee the legitimacy of the child born out of wedlock. Here it is only when the child is no longer alive that the parents actually marry, out of love, rather than obligation, either to themselves, the child, or the deity.

With the Shekinah as the symbol of the Shalom of our Being, as Ruether has described it, E.M. Broner envisages political and spiritual transformation as a function of the reclamation of Body Power by women on a spiritual quest.

Also within Jewish feminist tradition, both Kim Chernin and Deena Metzger have written novels which restore the Great Mother tradition to Jewish women who are born to a sacred calling in the modern era. They are the secret psychic bearers of intuitive knowledge (*gnosis*) of the Goddess, whom they must honor in order to heal the world.

Both authors look upon the oral tradition of storytelling as the key to gaining entry to a lost matristic history and the women's mysteries it discloses.

In Chernin's *The Flame Bearers* (1986), the art of storytelling induced a trancelike state in which the women in the sacred matrilineage, who are called upon to keep the tradition of the Mother alive within Judaism, can enter into contact with the spirit world and with other historical, spatial, and temporal dimensions. Thus, storytelling in the oral tradition, as Chernin conceives it, induces gnosis and is a sacred, magical art giving access to secret knowledge, both of women's histories and of their mysteries.

Deena Metzger's novel *What Dinah Thought* (1989) is a midrash on the biblical story of Dinah, or a retelling of the story from Dinah's point of view. In her novel, Dina is a contemporary Jewish woman possessed by the history and myth of the biblical story of Dinah (for whom she is named), and thus, she feels that she is the reincarnation of the ancient Dinah, and that she intuitively knows her story to be different from the way it was told in the Bible. As we shall see in her novel, the telling of the ancient story had a magical evocative power, which infused the contemporary Dina's life, bringing about Goddess revelations and new knowledge through love. About the importance of storytelling, the contemporary Dina comments: "A retelling is required. Dinah is to be born again, and we are to grow back into history, reliving each recurring incident of her life, of her lives, retelling each according to a new formula which we must enact as well. Revisioning of the most extreme order" (Metzger, 1989).

We have set ourselves the task of seeking the teachings of these stories. Just as in Kim Chernin's novel, Rocha the Scribe would gather the women together in secret and write down their teachings from the oral tradition for the first time, our feminist matristic authors have become the scribes of our new feminist matristic Creation myths, now written down for the first time.

Chernin's myth is related orally: "My children, are you listening? In the beginning there was no division between the earth and the heaven. The winged spirits and the four-legged spirits and those with gills and those with scales lived sometime here and sometime there, in the sea, on the land, in the sky. Chochma, the Bride, looked over them all, over the goddesses and gods and over the humans, too, women and men. But then her own son, he who sat at her right hand, rose up against her to call himself Shaddai, The Almighty. And now he took captive the women and men she made to rejoice in her earth. And so Chochma, what can she do? She who we call Mother Compassionate, what can she do? She went out of heaven to live only with the earth, to console the women and men. She made sparks from her own fire. That is what we teach. The trees, the birds with their wings, the flowers in their glory, the salt sea waves, the grass of the fields, these are the Handmaidens. By night and by day they cry to us, calling us to rise up from our sorrow and from our forgetting to worship her again. Children, you hear them? This is what my mother taught" (Chernin, 1986, p. 72). "Children, you understand? When the knock comes to the door you go there and you open it up and you make welcome the messenger. And you find out if she is calling you to be the Great Teacher. The one who will go out to gather in the fallen sparks. To speak again the names of The Mother" (Chernin, 1986, p. 73).

The teaching specifies that the Mother rules through love and compassion. It is the work of the sacred Flame-Bearers to prepare the world for the coming of the Great Teacher who will speak the names of the Great Mother again. In each generation there is born one of the seven sacred women who will be called upon to carry on the teachings, and practice the mysteries of the Great Mother.

While Chernin is inspired by the Kabbalah, and her concepts are influenced by the historical paradigms of the fathers and sons replacing the Mother in religions around the world, it dawns upon the reader of this genre of feminist matristic fiction that there may be a level of truth in the fiction that is of the order of a mystical revelation rather than of a purely imaginative invention. In any case, where the line between imagination and the Gnostic accessing of past-life recall is to be drawn certainly becomes blurred in feminist matristic literature. The teaching transmitted by this novel is that the act of creation is one means to accessing a kind of truth that our written records deny.

Rae Shadmi, the protagonist of *The Flame Bearers,* who is called back home to carry on the tradition of the Mother after having fled from it for many years, is informed that her destiny is to resurrect the knowledge hidden from us by the reign of science and reason. Rae's grandmother came to the new world, not only with the stories, but with the miracles as well. For the magic was both the story and the act of telling it.

Chernin's tale of power not only restores the power of the Mother to Judaism, but since Her tradition is guarded by real mothers in each generation, it restores the power of all mothers and daughters over time, as well as the image of the female as the matrix and source of the regeneration of life.

Deena Metzger's novel *What Dinah Thought* divines, conjures, invokes, and evokes the matristic story of the biblical Dinah whose thoughts are unrecorded about the fact that after she was ravished by Shechem, a Hivite, her brothers Simeon and Levi revenged the insult by killing the Hivites.

In the novel, a contemporary woman named Dina realizes that it is not coincidental that she bears the name of the biblical Dinah, and that because names are magical, when we are born to a certain name, we take on its knowledge and power.

Deena Metzger's midrash on Dinah's story sends the contemporary Dina to Israel in search of the man who is the contemporary incarnation of Schehem, just as she feels herself to be the reincarnation of Dinah. Through a poetic gnosis, she postulates/imagines/knows/invents/remembers that the uncircumcised Hivite Schehem, with whom the biblical Dinah made love, was from a goddess-worshipping culture, the very culture that the Hebrews with their male God, Yahweh, excised from the tradition.

The modern Dina invokes the goddesses so that she can magically conjure up her past-life's beloved on her trip to Israel.

"I call on Anath and Asherah, on Aphrodite, Isis and Ishtar, all the great conjurers and healers to help me. Praise!" (Metzger, 1989)[3] In so doing she is performing magic, which she defines as "the attempt to align oneself with the gods and do their will" (Metzger, 1989).

In Metzger's tale, it is the woman from a patriarchal culture who falls in love with a man from a Goddess religion. It was through the vengeance that her brothers took upon all of Schehem's people, that war was brought into the world. During the modern Dina's stay in Israel, on her trip to the Sinai, she experiences a theaphany, which is the female equivalent of the experience of Moses at the Burning Bush. Schehem had been killed because of the commandment "Thou shalt have no other gods before me." Through the Goddess thea-

---

[3]These quotations are taken from the unpublished manuscript. As this book goes to print, a rewritten version of the novel is being published by Viking (1989), and the quotes may have been changed.

phany, Dina comes to understand that other deities (i.e., the Goddess) can be as powerful and compelling as one's own. Dina perceives Asherah in the tree of life, and in an ecstatic vision, chooses to revere Her as the God of peace. "But it was a tree. And so it was god. Always had been god, burning or not, it was god. I knew Her name. I threw up my arms, there was no one around but me and Her, and I held them above my head in imitation of her branches, knowing then that this was the way that Dinah had prayed, and you, Shechem, had prayed. . . . not kneeling, not scraping our faces in the ground, but standing, in imitation of the god, hands raised in joy, dancing ASHERAH" (Metzger, 1989).

In their "karmic" reenactment of a biblical love, the modern Dina falls passionately in love with Jamine, a Palestinian, who recognizes her, too, from the past. Once again their peoples are politically opposed to each other. He continually asks her whether she *knows who he is,* and she realizes that to love him deeply, as she does, is to betray her Jewish fathers. Yet their love has endured for centuries, and she chooses this love and the memory of the Goddess, as well as the hope for peace between the Palestinians and the Israelis in the act of love, which is like the ancient Hieros Gamos, for it will renew the world.

As she unites with Jamine, she knows that this is more than just a sexual union. It is a sacred marriage between the God and the Goddess, one that is capable of bringing peace and healing to the Palestinian-Israeli relationship, at least on a personal level.

> Then I saw it all. I don't know what I saw. It wasn't us, I saw, but also it wasn't not us. It wasn't now and it wasn't the past. I saw It, the two of them, I don't know how to name them. Maybe I saw God, She and He together. It's easy to give them names and reduce it, thereby. Asherah and her E1, Aphrodite and her Adonis or Ishtar, then, and her Tammuz.
>
> I saw them, together, the two of them, as they had been together from the beginning. Coming apart and joining, the rhythm of the breath and of sex and of seasons. It was like waves in the sea of wheat, the coming apart, the joining. Sometimes they were One and sometimes they were separate. But it was one and the same. They were not divided from each other, they were one and the same. . . . This sacred act of merging was only enacted in the flesh, but through it they felt history, the entire past coming together and altering. (Metzger, 1989.)

Dina intuits that Dinah had understood that she came to know the gods through the act of love with Schehem, and the gods she came to know were the Mother and the Father merged as one, just as she, the American Jew and he, the Palestinian, could, through love, create peace between their peoples. In this new version of the biblical story, Metzger narrates the ending of the modern feminist matristic tale:

"So it came to pass that the Israelites and the Hivites lived together in peace and became like one people" (Metzger, 1989).

One of the teachings embedded in Deena Metzger's novel is that magic is alive, and that through our connection to the ancient matrilineage, through our consciousness of our past incarnations (which we can acquire via dreams or intuition, by our names, through direct gnosis, and through study, etc.), we can bring about karmic justice, we can right the wrongs of the past, and consciously *will* miracles to occur.

It is clear from the image of the Goddess tree growing from their graves, with which the novel concludes, that it is the Great Mother and not the patriarchal Father God whose tradition will make the miracles that all new Dinas seek, occur.

THE CLASSICAL CYCLE

As inheritors of the Jewish, Christian, and Greek traditions, it should not be surprising to us that a large number of new versions of the stories of ancient and classical hero/ines are based upon female figures from the Bible and the Greek classics.

Whereas the Biblical Cycle shows how patriarchy has usurped the magical, oracular, and divine powers of the female, and vested them in males, in the Greek cycle we find that women of reason with a realistic vision and with a matristic ethics (who are able to see the consequences of destructive, irrational, and violent acts—such as war—and advise against them) were considered mad, and punished for their utterances.

Whereas in the Biblical Cycle women who sought knowledge (such as Eve) were exiled, in the Classical Cycle, women who have knowledge are imprisoned as madwomen. Women in both cycles possess and/or seek knowledge of their prepatriarchal Goddess heritage. It is because of their love of knowledge that they are banished, punished, ostracized, ridiculed, or enslaved.

The vision of matricide, the murder of the Goddess, performed by patriarchal civilizations, lies at the root of women's sufferings in all of the cycles. Women who understand this through their rational perception of history and their accurate evaluation of the many destructive deeds committed in the name of a male God, are deemed mad, and doomed to punishment.

In some sense, we shall see that Troy is just another form of Eden, if we consider Eden to be a patriarchally designed Paradise from which all evidence of the Goddess has been effaced. And Hades turns out to be the upper world, where we normally reside.

In looking at the feminist matristic versions of classical tales, we discover an important Eve-Cassandra connection. Both Eve and Cassandra chose knowledge, and both were severely punished for it. The realm of Ereshkigal, the underworld/other world, is transposed in the feminist matristic rewrite of these Greek tales, to the Mother Goddess community of Cybele, where Amazons and priestesses revere the Earth and the Great Mother. It is the wild world, the other world, the world outside of the palace, and the world outside of Eden, where Lilith already resides as the first defiant, wild woman, the first feminist rebel.

If we recall that *The Iliad* was an oral epic, and that its various episodes were sung by storytellers in the ancient world, presenting events from many disparate points of view in many differing renditions with various episodes added or omitted from time to time, we can readily appreciate the quasi-formulaic nature of today's feminist matristic versions of the lives of women from the *Iliad* such as Cassandra. I am arguing that if we judge these works on the basis of artistic originality alone, we are missing the point. For, the point is that they are quasi-formulaic. In other words, whether the author is Christa Wolf, Ursule Molinaro, Marion Zimmer Bradley, or Carol Orlock, in the motif of women choosing to live close to nature and the Goddess, there is no lack of originality. On the contrary, there is a true matrilineage being created by the very sustaining of the same motifs from society to society throughout time.

By formulaic I mean the way in which motifs, undergoing a feminist matristic revision, often tend to recreate characters and episodes in patterns that are acquiring a new feminist matristic standardization. However, once more, if we review this literature from the perspective of the midrash and the oral tradition, we need not condemn the standardization, itself, but rather we must seek to understand its origin and its recurrence. Some critics would refer to these clusters of events or to the symbolic meaning invested in certain characters as archetypes. I do not view this phenomenon as archetypal, but rather as formulaic.

We have already encountered several revisions of women from the Bible who bear certain resemblances to each other; these women are either priestesses of the ancient Goddess religion, or they are in quest of knowledge about Her religion. They are often banished, exiled, punished, or labeled mad. The male heroes are regularly depicted as the inventors of war and of the kind of science and technology that arrogantly defies the will of the Creator. If these motifs recur with regularity in contemporary feminist matristic literature, it is *not* because the authors see history in simplistic terms, or that they are lacking in originality. Nor do they desire to create a complex contemporary version based on a classical model as Joyce did in *Ulysses*. Their simplicity and repetitiveness can be explained by their desire to create new feminist matristic cultures as rapidly as possible, and this can be done by circulating tales whose motifs and characters are easily recognizable and repeatable.

In perusing the Classical Cycle we will begin with Cassandra, and then encounter Ariadne, Demeter and Persephone.

Christa Wolf's essay, "Conditions of a Narrative—Cassandra" (1984), poses the question of why she has no "Poetics" to expound. Her response to this question leads her on a journey in search of Cassandra. But, as she explores the meaning of Poetics, such as those advanced by Aristotle, Horace, or Brecht, she formulates for herself what she calls a "poetological problem" in which she states that "I feel keenly the tension between the artistic forms within which we have agreed to abide and the living material, borne to me by my senses, my psychic apparatus, and my thought, which has resisted these forms" (Wolf, 1984, p. 142).

In her four essays collected in the volume *Cassandra: A Novel and Four Essays* (1984), she brings to life her thoughts during her personal journey—a record of her trip to Greece and Crete. She documents how she became obsessed with the figure of Cassandra, and she describes her psychic journey into women's prepatriarchal past and matristic heritage, which lies buried underneath the myths that have come down to us in the classics.

Wolf's aesthetic conclusion is that the forms in which these patriarchal stories are embedded, known as "poetics" create "sinister effects of alienation . . . in art as well as elsewhere" (1984, p. 142).

Christa Wolf's encounter with the Mother Goddess civilization of ancient Crete, where in the Heraklion Museum one finds endless figures of the Fertility Goddess and of the ancient Great Mother from every archaeological stratum ever excavated, leads her to state: "It is worth thinking about, why women today feel they must derive part of their self-esteem and a justification of their claims from the fact that civilization begins with the worship of woman" (Wolf, 1984, p. 195).

She answers her own question by postulating that the evidence from Minoan Crete leads us to understand that a society in which everyone prayed to a Goddess did actually exist, was not a myth, and that from all accounts we can surmise it was a peaceful society and one that was historically real, not merely "an Isle of the Blessed existing outside of the coordinates of its time" (Wolf, 1984, p. 195). Yes, for Wolf, the essential importance of this knowledge is that the Elysian Fields have existed, and that people who lived in them four or five thousand years ago "were people just like us" (p. 197).

For Wolf, too, it is the art of storytelling that will keep this knowledge alive, and that will reconnect us to the memory and the spirit of our matristic ancestors. Wolf's meditation establishes a vital living link between us and the dead—via storytelling.

"Three thousand years from now, will there be anyone left here or anywhere else who still believes that the dead travel somewhere. . . .? Will anyone still think about making it easier for the dead? Will there still be some empathy, some memory, between living and dead? Remembrance, storytelling, art?" (Wolf, 1984, p. 189)

Meditating on Aeschylus' *Oresteia,* she comes to understand how matricide resides at the core of patriarchy, for Orestes is proclaimed innocent of the murder of his mother in his attempt to avenge his father. It is the patriarchally defined Pallas Athena who casts the deciding vote in his favor, but the Furies, "who embody the souls of the ancestors,. . . . lament the downfall of the old law, which they regard as the downfall of morality in general" (Wolf, 1984, p. 223). In a Great Mother-worshipping society, the murder of the mother would have been forbidden, but the Father God-worshipping patriarchy has replaced that law by the law of blood revenge.

In considering the fate of Cassandra, (the prophet who spoke truth, but whom Apollo punished by taking away peoples' belief in her visions, for they foretold destruction), Wolf states boldly: "Cassandra is one of the first women figures handed down to us whose fate prefigures what was to be the fate of women for three thousand years: to be turned into an object" (1984, p. 227).

Wolf understands that Cassandra is punished for the content of her visions, and that she "sees the future because she has the courage to see things as they really are in the present" (Wolf, 1984, p. 238). Thus she is pronounced "mad" for speaking the truth. This paradigmatic fate is the fate that befell several women writers we have studied such as Colette Thomas, Unica Zurn, and Leonora Carrington.

What the content of Cassandra's vision is also becomes of great relevance to our argument, for, as Wolf sees it, Cassandra's vision, as it was before people (i.e., males) wrote about her, is one that challenged patriarchal dualism, and insisted upon the interconnectedness of everything. "It is the feeling that everything is fundamentally related" (Wolf, 1984, p. 287). Wolf sees the patriarchal Western thought pattern as exemplified by "the renunciation of the manifoldness of phenomena in favor of dualism and monism, in favor of closed systems and pictures of the world; of the renunciation of subjectivity in favor of a sealed 'objectivity' " (Wolf, 1984, p. 287).

Thus, the aesthetics that accompanies this paradigm has taken us away from the reality of interconnectedness. The woman writer who sees the same truth as Cassandra and embodies it in her own narrative, the woman who is a seer, a priestess "approaches another kind of storytelling . . . when she encircles her irrational, deadly grief with words whose magical significance is unmistakable" (Wolf, 1984, p. 304).

Finally, Wolf comes to understand that if there had been a peaceful society in the Mediterranean that was destroyed by the Acheans, it would mean that Cassandra might have been put "in the position of having to separate from a utopia that was no longer valid, and of finding no tangible place to live" (Wolf, 1984, p. 247).

Wolf's Cassandra is symbolic of the contemporary feminist matristic writer, who, having learned of our ancient Goddess heritage, becomes a witness and a speaker of the truth that has been denied.

In her novel, Cassandra, having witnessed as a young girl the rituals of the Goddess Cybele on Mt. Ida (where women danced in homage to the Goddess), made this resolution: "I will continue a witness even if there is no longer one single human being left to demand my testimony" (Wolf, 1984, p. 22). Cassandra is upset and jealous when her brother is made an oracle and she is not. Then, after she is raped by Ajax, she would no longer court anyone's friendship or love. Wolf sets up the contrast between the women's world outside of the palace, where Cybele is worshipped, and the official palace world, ruled by the patriarchy. Indeed, even before she was born, it was predicted that Cassandra would "restore her rights to the snake goddess as guardian of the hearth fire in every home" (Wolf, 1984, p. 49).

When Cassandra learns that Paris wants to fetch Helen in order to possess the woman reputed to be the most beautiful in the world and win the reputation of being supreme among men, she predicts: "Woe, woe. Do not let the ship depart" (Wolf, 1984, p. 59). She is immediately pronounced mad. For Cassandra, this so-called lunacy, which is her "vision," although it brings an end to the torture of pretense (for she speaks the truth), takes her on a journey to the underworld. To return from madness is to reenter the lies of palace life. For Paris had abducted Helen, and this act led to ten years of war.

Thus, the nature of Cassandra's vision is the actual interconnectedness of everything. Cassandra believes that Helen is not worth this, not worth war and death. She is pronounced mad again. Her only consolation was to be found among the women in the mountains, those who worshipped Cybele. In the palace, reality was turned upside down. Helen was a phantom that had been invented, and it was this phantom that caused the war. "To call what was true, true, and what was untrue, false. That was asking so little (I thought) and would have served our cause better than any lie or half-truth. For it was intolerable (I thought) to base the whole war—and our whole lives, for wasn't that our life!—on the accident of a lie" (Wolf, 1984, p. 85).

As the Trojan War claims more and more lives, and death stalks the city, Cassandra wishes she could live with her nonviolent vision in the caves and mountains along the Scamander River with those who refuse killing and dying, and choose to live and to express their reverence for the Goddess. Thus, Cassandra went to the women in the caves and discovered the stone figures of the Goddess whom they worshipped, and to whom they made offerings. When she defies her father's plan to use Polyxena to lure Achilles so that Paris could kill him, she is put in a fortress—the underworld. It is as if she were buried alive. When she is released, Cassandra joins the women's community in the cave. She feels that the figure of the Goddess on the wall of the cave is almost alive and that it is breathing. The women live in poverty; they make pots and clay vessels, and they revere the Earth, share their dreams, and think about who will come after them. "We racked our brains trying to think of a way we could leave them a message, but did not know any script to write in. We etched animals, people, ourselves inside the rock caves, which we sealed off before the Greeks came. We pressed our hands side by side into the soft clay. We called that immortalizing our memory, and laughed" (Wolf, 1984, p. 132). Cassandra realizes that the counterpart to her choice of life in the cave is the "heroism" that life in the new Troy would come to represent, a choice of war, death, and the pursuit of the values of the male hero.

Both Christa Wolf and Ursule Molinaro, in her *Autobiography of Cassandra: Princess and Prophetess of Troy* (1979), create a version of Cassandra that makes her a living woman rather than a mythic soothsayer, and that relates her struggle between matristic and patriarchal values to the struggles of contemporary feminist matristic writers and artists who, in their evocation of the ancient Goddess culture, also protest against war and the patriarchal notion of heroism, which includes gratuitous violence, the destruction of nature, and the maiming of lives for selfish purposes.

Molinaro and Wolf stress, through their style and their tales, that Cassandra's insights were based upon her excellent faculties of reason and ethics and not upon possession by the irrational. Cassandra is a thinker, who insisted on telling the truth.

The stories of Cassandra, as retold by both Wolf and Molinaro, are particularly poignant, for as our century draws to a close, advocates of the "New Age" are beginning to desire contact with the gods once more. But as we see, *it matters greatly which gods* are worshipped. Wolf and Molinaro warn us that patriarchal principles prevail, both in a world that is severed from the gods, as is our own, for the most part, as well as in a world in which humans regularly communicated with deities. Yet, if we restore the invisible deities without making a priority of life on earth, symbolized by the Goddess, we will not have made any profound change at all. For, under the hegemony of the patriarchal male god (whether it enters into daily, living communication with humans, or whether it is institutionalized in churches and removed from the arena of daily life), life on Earth is not prioritized, and until the Goddess and all she represents prevails, our planet's existence continues to be in danger.

It is interesting to note that whether women are punished in patriarchy by being robbed of their oracular powers or of their powers of reason, they are always doomed. Obviously, patriarchy does not really care whether women define their gifts as visionary or rational. It is the system under which women are *not* seen to reflect the image of the Creator of Life that permits them to be divested of their strengths and powers, whatever they may be. In these two cycles, our feminist matristic Sarahs and Cassandras demand the restoration of *both* their oracular *and* their intellectual powers, for it is patriarchal dualism that has set them up in opposition to each other. Actually, the two are interconnected, and one without the other is useless in a feminist matristic world, where all things are interrelated, where one fleshes out rationally the consequences of what one has been in a vision.

Turning to Marion Zimmer Bradley's *Firebrand* (1987), we find that Kassandra is once more depicted as the voice of reason, rather than the voice of madness. Kassandra lives through an other world initiation similar to that of Helen with Ereshkigal, for she meets the Amazon Queen, Penthesilea, and learns to live independently of men. Penthesilea also teaches Kassandra about her visionary talents and about the Goddess. Kassandra, who believes that her *sight* was given to her by Apollo, is reminded by Penthesilea that "before ever Apollo Sun Lord came to rule these lands, our Horse Mother-the Great Mare, the Earth

Mother from whom we all are born— she was hers'' (Bradley, 1987, p. 68). Penthesilea says: "it seems to me strange that a woman should seek a God rather than the Earth Mother or our Serpent Mother. It is She who dwells underground and rules over all the realms of women—the darkness of birth and death . . . a time must come when . . . you must go underground to meet the Serpent Mother"(Bradley, 1987, p. 87). Penthesilea's women are separatists, and they are chaste. Her empowering "life style" is only one of two possibilities that present themselves to Bradley's Cassandra as alternatives to life in the Trojan world of male heroes and ongoing war.

Penthesilea and Kassandra spend one night in the city of Colchis, which is ruled by Queen Imandra, who has not yet chosen to take a consort. In Colchis, women walk freely in the streets, and they perform the kinds of work usually associated with males, such as labor in a forge. Kassandra is enticed by the life in Colchis under the aegis of Queen Imandra—a life dedicated to the Serpent Goddess. In Colchis they "celebrate the return of the Earth's Daughter from the underground, where she has been imprisoned during the chill of the winter season" (Bradley, 1987, p. 134). They tell the (Persephone) story of the Earth's Daughter's descent into darkness, and how they await the return of the light. Through these mysteries (like the Eleusinian mysteries) Kassandra passes through the Gates of the Underworld, encounters the serpents, and, as she asks to see the Goddess, she comes to understand that she is, and at the same time is not, the Goddess.

Thus, Kassandra, like Helen in Judy Grahn's *Queen of Swords,* is initiated to her Goddess heritage by the Amazons (outsiders), as she descends to the underworld to encounter the mysteries and to obtain empowerment and knowledge of her matristic strengths.

Kassandra is described as both a prophet and a rational thinker. Once again, it is the male hero who engages in irrational acts such as the abduction of Helen, using her as an excuse for war. "Can't you see that Helen is only an excuse?" (Bradley, 1987, p. 238) Helen is depicted as a good person—respectable, intelligent, who also sees herself being used as a pretext for war, and wishes she could take refuge with the Goddess instead of being a symbol of "the face that launched a thousand ships." Kassandra realizes that men do not demonstrate reason, nor do women when their feelings for men are involved.

As the many incidents in the book unfold, Kassandra's prophecies of doom materialize. Finally, when Achilles first kills and then rapes her aunt, the Amazon Penthesilea, Kassandra asks why the Gods do nothing to prevent this, and indeed, how the Goddess herself could let this horror continue. It is implied that the Goddess has lost her power in a universe where the will of the male gods prevails, but that her power returns when she is revered, as she is in Colchis, when her mysteries are enacted regularly.

The resolution of Bradley's version of the *Illiad* is that Kassandra, the sole voice of reason in a world of violence, decides to return to Imandra in Colchis and to live her life in devotion to the Serpent Mother. On her way, however, she encounters a man dressed in women's garments, Zakynthos, who seeks "a world where Earth will be worshipped in the old ways. . . . It is She who has given me this vision, a dream of a city where women are not slaves, and where men need not spend their lifetimes in war and fighting. There must be a better way for both men and women to live than this great war" (Bradley, 1987, p. 601).

Kassandra will help to found the new city where "men and women need not be enemies," for "what evil (men) had done (was done) at the bidding of Gods made in their own image" (Bradley, 1987, p. 602). Bradley's ending is posited on the words found inscribed on Tablet #803 in the Archaeological Museum in Athens, which, addressing Zeus of Dodona, says that the "Zakynthian family descended for thirty generations from Kassandra of Troy" (Bradley, 1987, p. 602).

Zakynthos, dressed in female attire, obviously represents the new man in whom "the feminine" and "the masculine" principles have been integrated into a new, more balanced and holistic union. He expresses the desire to be both Father and Mother to Kassandra's son, thus affirming his nurturant nature.

Bradley is a noted writer of science fiction, and one might object that her ending takes us beyond the commentary or the variant, and enters the domain of science fiction, since the Zakynthian men are of a race yet unborn. Yet, because the book concludes with only the hope that the new man and the new city will emerge, and presents archaeological proof that a lineage did derive from Kassandra, I would prefer to interpret this as a utopian motif—one that circulates in many feminist matristic works which have previously been described as falling between fantasy and science fiction. However, if we consider the new egalitarian Eden of the Goddess to be an emerging motif, we can accept its frequent reappearance in feminist matristic literature more easily without criticizing its lack of grounding in the circumstances of the narrative or in the realism with which it fits into the fictive world. In these works, I do not find a lack of original aesthetic or narrative resolutions. What I find is that the resolution is achieved by the repetition of an emerging formulaic pattern or motif— in this case that of the new Garden City of the Goddess or the new feminist matristic Eden.

Another motif that recurs in different feminist matristic versions of the Greek cycle postulates that the earthquake that destroyed Crete might have been due to the anger of the Great Mother at having had Her religion replaced by that of the Father God.

In *Firebrand* Priam tells Kassandra that the gods had caused the destruction of the city. During the earthquake the Temple of Serpent Mother was drowned, and the Temples of Zeus and Apollo were left untouched. He explains this as the reason why there has been less worship of the Serpent Mother since then. He implies that the Gods willed it, since they destroyed Her temple. Kassandra questions him: "But how do we know it is the Gods who have shaken the lands? Have they sent messengers to tell us so?" (Bradley, 1987, p. 173)

In her musing on whether, indeed, it had been the great earthquake that shook the lands or caused the worship of the Earth Mother to be discredited (except among the tribeswomen), we are led to infer that the earthquake might have been the expression of the rage of the Great Mother against the patriarchal takeover of Her shrines.

Ariadne by June Rachuy Brindel (1980) narrates the story of Ariadne, the last Matriarch of Crete, a queen and priestess of the Great Mother religion. In the Greek myths that have come down to us through Robert Graves, and Joseph Campbell, the voice of Ariadne has been erased. However, she was the last queen of a culture that looked upon women as holy, and upon birth as a great mystery. Therefore, it is crucial that we use our imaginations in order to re-member what might have taken place during her reign.

The book opens with a Creation myth of the Great Mother religion, and ends with the earthquake in Crete as an expression of the fury of the Earth Mother over the horrors that have taken place since King Minos elevated himself above his station of consort, and conspired to replace the worship of the Mother by that of Zeus.

Merope, Ariadne's lady-in-waiting, chanted the Creation myth of the Great Mother to Ariadne when she was a child. "In the start of time, splendor appeared. . . . It was the Mother. She was all that was. She divided the sky from the sea and danced upon the waves. A wind gathered behind her from Her swift dancing. When She rubbed this wind between Her hands, it became The Great Serpent. She took him to Her and loved him, and a great egg grew within Her and She became a Dove. The Dove-Mother brooded over the egg until it was ready. Then out of the egg came all things—sun, moon, stars, earth, mountains, rivers, and all living creatures. The splendor of the Mother flowed through everything—through sun and sea, through the veins of the earth into root and leaf, into grain and fruit, into all women and all men. And each birth became forever an acceptance of splendor and each death a gift to the Great Mother" (Brindel, 1980, p. 3).

June Brindel stresses the orality of the Cretan world by having Merope chant, and by typographically juxtaposing the first person narratives of Ariadne and Daedalus at various points in the novel—spatially separating them into columns and formatting them as responsive readings or choral works, one voice alternating with another.

Ariadne becomes a channel for the voice of the Goddess as a young child, since her mother, Pasiphae, had offended the Goddess, and She had withdrawn Her voice from Pasiphae. Like Cassandra, Ariadne has prophetic premonitions of the violence and the destruction that will ensue with Minos's usurpation of the prominence of the Mother Goddess religion, replacing it with that of the religion of Zeus, the Father God.

Merope sees to it that Ariadne is initiated to the mysteries of the Goddess, and takes her to the cave in the mountains where she encounters the Sibyl. It was in the cave of the Goddess that Ariadne first began to menstruate. However, upon leaving the cave, Ariadne discovered Merope's body hanging from a tree, and knew that Minos's men had killed her. Indeed, Pasiphae also dies, and Ariadne is certain that Minos is responsible for both deaths.

Daedalus, a visitor to Knossos, remarks upon how the old Goddess religion still seems to be dominant in Crete. However, as Minos's rule begins to take over, Daedalus decides to send his son, Icarus, away, so that he doesn't become indoctrinated to the old religion. Daedalus also fears that the Goddess religion is beginning to reclaim his wife. Then, suddenly, she, too, is found dead in the mountains, and her death is explained away as an accident.

Ariadne's powers increase as she spends more and more time in a trance or a dream state. Her visions predict the death of all vegetation and the absence of the Goddess. She sees Daedalus naming everything.

Daedalus observes Ariadne's state, and reports that the people believe she is communing with the Goddess. A drought has come over the land. The people say that "the Raging Ones have taken over Ariadne's soul, and unless it is returned the land will die" (Brindel, 1980, p. 68). Here is a motif that recurs in the feminist matristic Grail Cycle. In the feminist matristic vision, it is not the dying king that causes the land to die, but it is the death of the religion of the Earth Goddess that destroys vegetation.

Many changes have come about since Daedalus's arrival. He perceives that since the beginning of the worship to Zeus, animal sacrifice has been initiated. Daedalus teaches Ariadne an Egyptian Creation myth that says that the world was created by the Word of Ptah. The creation of the world via the Word is directly opposed to the creation of the world from the womb of the Great Earth Mother. Ariadne recognizes this myth as a lie. While the Creation story based upon the Word of the male god is written down on the Egyptian papyrus, "the most important secrets" . . . about the women's mysteries, for example . . . "were never written down" (Brindel, 1980, p. 93).

Ariadne notices how angry the Goddess is that both sacrifices and wine have been added to the ceremonies. In order to show her anger, the Goddess withholds her fruits and grains from the Earth. After many more murders, the people beseech Icarus (who is in love with Ariadne) to beg her to bring back the old Goddess religion. "Purify the worship. Bring back the old faith. Give the Great Goddess that which she has always demanded so that the rains will come and the barren earth will yield fruit and grain" (Brindel, 1980, p. 110).

Ariadne then performs a ceremony, raises the double axe on the mound, but refuses to sacrifice the bull. "I offered seeds on a hearth, took a torch from a priestess, and burned them for the Earth Mother" (Brindel, 1980, p. 116). As Ariadne begins the dance of the Mother and calls the Mother to enter her body, she becomes the Goddess-on-Earth incarnate. Icarus joins her in pronouncing the sacred words, and his voice reawakens all of nature. Her belief returns as the Earth suddenly becomes alive once more. And then, tragically, she receives the news that her beloved, Icarus, has been found dead. Ariadne also learns that Queen Hatshepsut has died in Egypt, and that war and death are everywhere. Even Minos becomes frightened, and prays to the Goddess.

Ariadne, like Kassandra, is a visionary who also embodies the voice of Reason. Those who worship the Mother are whole, not split. Those who worship the Sky God are separated from vision, and act irrationally and violently. These motifs are constant in feminist matristic revisions and variants on the Bible and on the Greek classics.

Ariadne seeks help from the priestesses of the Goddess in her desire to have Minos murdered. In doing so, it is stressed by Brindel that she was acting quite rationally, and was not at all mad. "I was rational, pointing out the guidance of history, the blotting out of Mother worship in Egypt and Syria, the attacks on the temples and palaces of the great Queen Hatshepsut the moment she was dead, the effacing of her name from her monuments, the destruction of her Priestesses" (Brindel, 1980, p. 155).

After Minos is killed, the Earth shudders, and after the quake a great fire razes everything to the ground. The Mothers are dead. All vegetation has withered. The novel concludes in this way: "Without the Mother, we must each of us become the Mother. . . . Our story is being told by liars. That is why I must write this for you. So that you will know what really happened. So that you will listen for Her voice" (Brindel, 1980, pp. 239, 240).

Feminist matristic novels do not exclude men from the Goddess vision. Just as in *Firebrand* Zakynthos shared the dream of Kassandra, so Icarus shares Ariadne's cosmogony and ethics. It is not the gender of the hero that causes the destruction, it is the nature of the god being worshipped and the relationship of that god to the Earth that either affirms life or courts death.

This is a novel about matricide—the killing off of the Great Mother, her priestesses, and Merope, Pasiphae, Icarus (believers in the religion of the Mother), and masses of worshippers of the Goddess.

One of the teachings for our time that Brindel's novel, *Ariadne,* spells out, is that although in the New Age our communication with the gods may return, it is crucial to remember that it is not the return of our relationship to deity that matters as much as it is the ideology embodied by the cosmogony of the particular deity that determines the values which will be lived out in the world. As we have seen, only an Earth Mother mythos is capable of embodying the ideology and values that guarantee a reverence for nature. Disembodied cosmogonies, those which sever the earth from the sacred, are liable to support or encourage regimes that do not take Her land into consideration when making decisions involving the affairs of humans. Both novels warn us that deities represent ideologies and politics, and that if the political ideology behind the deity does not respect the Earth (whether She is referred to as Serpent Mother, the Great Mother or the Great Goddess), our planet is doomed, and subject to the Mother's rage or to an earthquake similar to the one that felled ancient Crete. The voice of the Earth Mother *is alive* in the full Gaian sense of the term, and She speaks to us of the spirits incarnated in the natural, material world. To dishonor those spirits (animal, plant, ancestral, deity, etc.) is to rape and plunder the soul of matter and to transgress against the laws of sacred creation.

Some of the structures and mythemes that I am referring to as motifs, might be said by various scholars to constitute the real history of events or the classical version of a Greek myth.

However, just as the myths, tales, and legends have come down to us in patriarchal history as the one and only truthful version of events (because only one survived as the account that was inscribed into the written record), so these feminist matristic versions often seem to purport to be the true historical account of events as well. But, since we also know that the teachings of the Mother were transmitted orally and through the Mysteries, we must realize that even if these works were not fiction, it would take incredible new archaeological discoveries to reveal more than we already know about events in the ancient matristic past.

Moreover, telling the tales in the guise of fiction permits more radical hypotheses about the actual events to emerge than if one actually had to stick to existing documents and evidence, for very little remains.

In *The Goddess Letters: The Myth of Demeter and Persephone Retold* (1987) by Carol Orlock, several of the motifs we have encountered before reappear in a new context. The most familiar repeated motif is a redefinition of the underworld, but this time the underworld is not the abode of the strong wild rebellious women. Instead, it is Patriarchy. In this book the characteristics of the Goddesses who rule each world (Demeter, the upper world) and

Persephone (the underworld of Hades) are the reverse of those in Judy Grahn's *Queen of Swords*. Here, Demeter, the Great Mother, teaches the empowerment of a separatist "Mother Knowledge" in the upper world. It is the upper world of nature that is the locus of female empowerment, and the underworld, Hades, is the realm of male domination of women. Demeter does not want men to participate in her rites, and she mourns the loss of her daughter, Persephone to the underworld. Demeter does *not* go to the Underworld (as does Grahn's Helen or Inanna), but she does deprive the Earth of vegetation, according to the classical myth. Persephone, carried away by Hades to the underworld, communicates with her mother, both via annual visits, and via letter writing. Since deities are immortal, they both live to witness the brutal coming of Christianity and of Patriarchy, the burning of the Goddess temples, and the mass murders carried out in the name of a religion that worships death, not life. Even though she has lived long enough to observe all of this violent history, Persephone, like Grahn's Helen, has become a wom an living in a man's world (the world of Hades), and despite the fact that she is even Queen of that world, she has abdicated her Power. She actively supports the argument that men should be initiated into the Mysteries of the Great Mother. Persephone is *not* a separatist. Through Persephone's vision of the Christian desecration of the sacred Goddess shrines, we come to understand that the real Hell is in the upper world, on our Earth, not in the underworld.

Patriarchy is here connected with the written word, as opposed to the world of oral teachings that relate to the Great Mother. For the worshippers of the Great Mother a poem is a living thing. Demeter tells Persephone about Homer's *Hymn to Demeter*. "When you come next year, you'll hear the great Homer recite our poem. I know it by heart, naturally, but won't write it here, because, like a ritual, a poem is a living thing. It can't be expressed by marks on a page" (Orlock, 1987, p. 158).

In opposing the invention of writing, which fixes living things into rigid forms, what Demeter objects to most is that the people of the new religion are rewriting everything. "They've changed everybody's names, turned stories upside down and forgotten to put back parts they meant to use. The wanderers call their priests, the ones who do the rewriting, 'scholars,' so these days it's the biggest insult to call anybody a scholar" (Orlock, 1987, p. 158).

Demeter also laughs at how the patriarchal priests and scholars have tried to write laws in books that outlaw the Mother religion. "Now a law has been written in a book, a law to forbid humans to speak of our practices in the temple. Our rites are called "mysteries" not to be spoken of. This is utterly ridiculous. . . . They write this new law, too, forgetting the real knowledge in their hearts. Our secret is utterly open, no law is needed to defend it. With law, without law, all who wish may have our knowledge, and those who have it know that it can't be expressed. Taking words to it, that's like trying to carry a song in a jar" (Orlock, 1987, p. 199). "In the new religions, they write down words about their god and study them. Fathers teach the books to their sons. . . . For my worship, books cannot serve. Knowledge of me is like a flower. Crushed between pages it would die. A flower can't pass from father to child, the child must go and see it. . . . In the new religions humans praise the line of generations through the father. Daughters only command a price" (Orlock, 1987, p. 199).

The technique of "distanciation," through which we view our patriarchal world via the lens of a matristic culture, achieves a critique of patriarchal religions while preserving the Voice of Authority of the female Creator. Demeter is furious about the new religions and the lies being told to the worshippers about wars waged in the name of the new gods.

Persephone thinks about saving her letters to her mother, and bringing them with her to the upper world when she rises in her next cycle. She could also destroy them. Her decision is of importance to us, for the lesson it conveys. "Christians have their book, a Bible, and there are Sutras, there's a Torah, all sorts of books. I could carry this rolled-up bundle to earth, leave it somewhere to be found" (Orlock, 1987, p. 219). She decides *not* to do it, "not out of principles" (Orlock, 1987, p. 219); she simply is not courageous enough. Persephone decides to leave the letters behind so that Dis (Hades) will find them. "He may burn them or tear them up and scatter their leaves to float up the Lethe" (the river of forgetting). "Perhaps he will give them to Zeus" (Orlock, 1987, p. 220). Persephone leaves them on the table and rises. What is the meaning of her act? Persephone has adjusted to the rule of a man-made world. She writes to Hades: "To my beloved King and Lord . . . I honor whatever you do" (Orlock, 1987, p. 220).

As we read this, we realize how many women alive in our time, raised on powerful Mother knowledge, and believing in it, have compromised themselves in favor of their Lord, have abdicated their courage, collaborated and conspired, not with the "enemy" (here depicted as the patriarchal scholars and priests), but with the particular men that they love, whom they honor, and who, according to their whim, may destroy the very fruits of their wives' creative and intellectual labors.

If this is the behavior of a Goddess and a queen, how might a mere human react in similar circumstances?

Persephone's transformation from the outraged daughter of the Earth Mother (who has been abducted by Hades and perceives how a man's world violates the ways of the Mother), to the defender of men's participation in women's sacred rites, arguing according to the logic and rhetoric she has learned in the man's world, and finally, her transformation into the author of that particular letter to Hades, traces the trajectory of how a Goddess and a queen is domesticated and turned into a subservient wife, suffering from matristic amnesia. The metamorphosis of Persephone over time explains Grahn's Helen. We have witnessed how the Mother knowledge gets erased—first by the violators and plunderers of the shrines of the Mother, and later by the very practitioners of Her teachings, as they acquiesce to male domination in patriarchy.

As the novel ends, Persephone rises to Earth, but as we have seen, although she may restore fertility (and bring the spring), she will not rebel against patriarchal rule. Indeed, she will insist that men be taught the secrets of the Mother, and that they take part in Her rites. She has, however, arrived at these conclusions via the rhetoric she learned from Hades and the Judges—(i.e., from the Patriarchy), arguments from circumstance, deduction, syllogisms, and so forth (Orlock, 1980, pp. 137–145). The novel closes on an ironic note, with a quote from the Homeric *Hymn to Demeter* "Happy is that man among men on earth who has seen these things" (Orlock, 1980, p. 220). Women readers sensitive to the use of the generic "man," understand that in this case, indeed, it is the "male" who will be happy when he has seen these things (i.e., the transformation of Persephone and the triumph of Patriarchy). In this case, not only does "man" mean male, but Homer's *Hymn to Demeter* is also seen in its true patriarchal light, as a male-authored text.

Yet there is, actually, a hopeful teaching in this novel, as well. Persephone does rise to restore fertility. As we have observed the change in Persephone in the underworld, we can hope that over time, the cycles of transformation may bring about more changes in Persephone, for the Mother knowledge is buried deep in her memory. Even though she becomes amnesiac over time, because she has changed once, there is still hope that she may change again. Persephone also represents contemporary women living in patriarchy. We are all daughters of motherlines that go back to the Mother knowledge of Demeter. In order to ensure fertility on Earth, we, modern Persephones, are rising and choosing life. We are re-membering the lost Mother knowledge, and whether we can re-member it all in time to save the Earth is one of the questions posed by the works discussed here. If all the Persephones can remember our Mother knowledge, and summon the strength to reclaim it, then there is, indeed, hope for humankind to realign with the Earth and the Cosmos once more. But if we remain beholden to sky gods and kings, many cycles will pass before the transformation can occur. Will the Earth last long enough to witness the rebirth of modern Persephones to the remembering of our Mother knowledge?

Both Eve and Persephone must choose knowledge *and* fertility. Both must remember the world as it was before Adam and Hades.

THE INDIGENOUS CYCLE

Works that fall into the Indigenous Cycle come out of cultures with their own Mother Goddess cosmogonies, myths, or lore. Thus far this book has attempted to show how the Goddess functions on behalf of women in whose culture an original matristic tradition has been overthrown by patriarchy. It has looked at the many ways in which Goddess lore and practices help to empower women, and it has also shown the ways in which Goddess tradition has often survived secretly underground, has remained intact, guarded by those chosen in sacred ways (i.e., *The Flame Bearers*) to preserve the teachings. Oral transmission plays a very important role in the passing on of Goddess lore, and many of the novels we have examined are marked by their emphasis on oral storytelling and on the importance of the voice and of the spoken word within the texture of the literary work. This cycle will give examples of several of the many, contemporary works that are written by women living in cultures with a thriving matristic mythos.

Flora Nwapa is a contemporary Nigerian writer, whose novel, *Efuru*, links the traditional with the contemporary, both culturally and aesthetically in ways that illuminate how the Goddess can function to support the independent woman's struggle for an autonomous identity within a tradition-bound society.

In his study, *Women Writers of Africa* (1981), Lloyd Brown points out that the oral tradition of tale telling had always featured women in the prominent roles. Although the influence of colonialism virtually eliminated women's voices from African literature by imposing a silent literary tradition upon them, Nwapa reintegrates the ancient oral tradition within the novel as an aesthetic narrative device in order to strengthen women's voices and roles in both society and literature.

In many African cultures the mystique of Motherhood caused the social ostracism of women who were thought to be infertile. The barren or childless woman is frequently stigmatized and persecuted through communal gossip and other rituals of social alienation.

Efuru, Nwapa's heroine, has two unsuccessful marriages and the one child she bears in the first marriage dies. For years she lives under the burden of the approbation of her village, for she has been shown to have been an exemplary wife, with, however, a strong streak of individualism. She often challenged her husband's authority and asserted her right to make independent decisions. It is because of her self-assertion that her marital relationships break down and she is ultimately left alone.

During the course of her life, however, she has recurrent dreams in which the River Goddess, Uhamiri, appears to her. As the Goddess of the Lake, Uhamiri is a childless deity, and is known as the deity who bestows wealth upon independent women. Efuru's father interprets her dreams to her, and informs her that she, like her mother before her, has been chosen by the divinity to be her worshipper. "The old man laughed softly. Your dream is good. The Woman of the lake, our Uhamiri, has chosen you to be one of her worshippers" (Nwapa, 1966, p. 183).

Efuru recalls the rituals that were performed in worship of this Goddess that she witnessed as a child. These women worshippers had once seemed to her to be possessed. Thus, at first she rejects this new identity. However, later, as she comes to understand how the Goddess of the Lake bestows blessings upon women who are not mothers, but whose integrity and individuality must be respected, she embraces the cult of Uhamiri.

When the Dibia (holy man) explains to Efuru's father what this Goddess signifies, he stresses that "the Goddess of the Lake has chosen her to be one of her worshippers. It is a great honor. She is going to protect you and shower riches on you. But you must keep her laws" (Nwapa, 1966, p. 191). The Dibia instructs Efuru in the many rituals she must perform as a worshipper of the goddess.

The reiteration of chants and rituals, not only those associated with the worship of the Goddess, but those connected with fertility and death, stress the cycles of life, death, and rebirth, all connected with an ancient Mother Goddess. As a feminist matristic narrative critical of a social system that castrates women, the novel, *Efuru*, opens with Efuru's ritual clitidorectomy and the ceremonial fattening of the bride. But it closes with Efuru's embrace of Uhamiri's worship as an autonomous and proudly independent, unmarried woman.

Emerging from patriarchal oppression through her discovery of the cult of the Goddess of the Lake, Efuru is affirmed both in her childless state and in her integrity and independence from a male partner. *Efuru* ends with these words: "Efuru slept soundly that night. She dreamt of the Woman of the Lake, her beauty, her long hair, and her riches. She had lived for ages at the bottom of the lake. She was as old as the lake, itself. She was happy. She was wealthy. She was beautiful. She gave women beauty and wealth, but she had no child. She had never experienced the joy of motherhood. Why then did the women worship her?" (Nwapa, 1966, p. 281).

The Woman of the Lake is the Mother Goddess. In this Nigerian novel, it is through a rediscovery of the Goddess that independent women can attain social integration and a deeper knowledge of their spiritual identity. Uhamiri is the Goddess who affirms that biology does not have to be synonymous with destiny for women.

Nwapa's insistence on the importance of a mythic vision and her understanding of the need to reconnect modern women with the ancient wisdom of a matristic mythos via the tale of Efuru if they are to emerge from their subordination in patriarchy intact, is, in itself, a tale-telling ritual for women today, both a cautionary tale and a ceremonial reenactment of woman's mythic origins from the Goddess of the Lake, or from the waters of life.

The Goddess of the Lake reconnects contemporary women to their ancient rituals and to the wisdom of their traditions, posing a meditation upon the pertinence of our matristic sources of knowledge to the validation of women's importance in many of their new contemporary roles.

In *The Sacred Hoop: Recovering the Feminine in American Indian Traditions* (1986), Paula Gunn Allen discusses native American literature as "ceremonial literature." She tells us that "ceremonial literature is sacred; it has power. . . . Ceremonial literature includes songs for many occasions: healing, initiation; planting, harvesting, and other agricultural pursuits; hunting; blessing new houses, journeys, and undertakings. There are also dream-related songs; war songs; personal power songs; songs for food preparation, purification, and vision seeking. . . . At base the ceremonials restore the psychic unity of the people, reaffirm the terms of their existence in the universe and validate their sense of reality, order and propriety" (Allen, 1986, p. 73).

In *The Sacred Hoop* Paula Gunn Allen emphasizes the importance of storytelling as a part of the oral tradition, for it "is to give people a basis of entry into the more obscure ritual tradition" (Allen, 1986, p. 100). "It lets people realize that individual experience is not isolete, but is part of a coherent and timeless whole, providing them with the means of personal empowerment and giving shape and direction to their lives" (Allen, 1986, p. 100).

Paula Gunn Allen's novel, *The Woman Who Owned the Shadows* (1983), shows how difficult it is for a contemporary woman to enter the underworld and take possession of the knowledge from the shadow or dark aspect of the Goddess in a culture from which knowledge of the Mother has not been expunged.

The prologue sets the story within the framework of Spider Woman's Creation. Spider Woman sang and wove the universe, seeding the sacred twins Uretsete and Naotsete, who would create all people from spirit. Spider Woman's song is the song of "the women who made all that lives on earth. Who made the world. Who formed matter from thought, singing" (Allen, 1983, p. 2).

As Ephanie, the protagonist, recalls the parts of her life that dismembered her and empowered her, she focuses on the shadows, for as a child, playing with her most intimate companion, Elena, "they had especially loved the shadows" (Allen, 1983, p. 22).

At another time in her life (when her cousin Stephen comes to help her out of a mental breakdown after she is abandoned by her husband), she refers to herself as "Shadow Woman." However, throughout her worst moments, she is buoyed up by the way in which her own "Fall" is shown to be parallel to the "Fall" taken by the mythic goddess, Sky Mother.

Remembering the tale of the woman who fell from the sky, Ephanie recalls how, as a child, she had been goaded by Stephen into jumping from a branch of an Apple Tree. Elena had warned her not to do it, but she did, and she fell. "After she fell everything changed" (Allen, 1983, p. 202). She confessed this sin to a Christian Priest. In the present she understands that in veering toward the Christian interpretation of the Fall, rather than the Sky Mother story, she had misunderstood the meaning of the event. "I was going to be a hero, before I got sidetracked, she thought. I was going to be full of life and action. I wasn't going to be the one who lived alone, afraid of the world. Elena and I, we were going to do brave things in our lives. And we were going to do them together" (Allen, 1983, p. 204).

Suddenly a Spirit Woman appeared in the shadows at the foot of her bed. The Spirit Woman sang the Creation myth, and in the shadows around her face the images of the myth came to life. In this vision of the Shadows, Ephanie sees the spirit world pass before her eyes in the face of the Old Woman who teaches her that death isn't what we call death. "It is a different way of being" (Allen, 1983, p. 209). The teaching of the Old Woman is that the story of life is ever-changing, ever-moving, and moving on. The spirits ask her to learn how to jump and to fall like the ancient Sky Mother. . . . "To fall into this world like the old one, the one you call Anciena, sky woman, jumped, fell, and began in a world that was new" (Allen, 1983, p. 211).

Ephanie began to dream of the Spider Medicine Society of healers, the double women, "the women who never married, who were not mothers, but who were sisters, born of the same mind, the same spirit" (Allen, 1983, p. 211). These women remind us of the women who belonged to the cult of Uhamiri in *Efuru*. In her own healing dreams and waking thoughts, Ephanie "re-membered the voice of the woman who sat in the shadows and spoke saying 'There are no curses. There are only descriptions of what creations there will be'" (Allen, 1983, p. 212).

As the novel closes, Ephanie's room fills with shadows that become shapes of women singing and dancing in the ancient ways. "She heard the singing. She entered the song" (Allen, 1983, p. 213).

The ceremonial ending of the novel

I am walking	Alive
Where I am	Beautiful
I am still	Alive
In beauty	Walking
I am	Entering
not alone	
(Allen, 1983, p. 213)	

integrates her into the larger cosmic dance of life, and affirms the "medicine" power of the life force of Spider Woman, the Creator over all negative (Christian) interpretations of events and energies that originally propelled Ephanie into the depression she suffered over her "sin." The matristic cosmogony calls her back into life, and empowers her to affirm the shadows (the dark) as the knowledge of the spirit world, which, in her culture, is that of Spider Woman's beautiful, bountiful creation.

It was *Daughters of Copper Woman* by Anne Cameron (1981) that affected the literary scholar and university professor in me when I found that the words and sacred teachings of an ancient matriarchal, matrilineal society on Vancouver Island were being committed to print for the first time, because they had been scattered and risked being lost. However, they were being written down with great irreverence for university professors (such as myself), who might distort them beyond recognition and use them for purposes for which they were never intended.

In Cameron's story "The Face of Old Woman" with which the collection of stories concludes, we learn that the time has finally come to put the knowledge of the Secret Society of Women down on paper, although this knowledge was far more powerful when it was unwritten. Now, in written form, it risks entering the university and being misused by the (mostly male) professors, since it is knowledge carried on by women for women, and in universities it could easily be perverted to conform to patriarchal purposes. Yet, at last the Old Woman of the tradition realizes that "The women who can't find no peace in what the men's universities teach will maybe find peace in this stuff" (Cameron, 1981, p. 143).

The teachings that these matriarchal women offer, now, at a time when the secret knowledge risks being completly erased, is a knowledge that defies the educational institutions of patriarchal enlightenment societies.

This knowledge teaches that "there's a power other than the power we live with every day. It's the power that taught levitation. It's the power that lets us leave our bodies and fly like spiritbirds, and its the power that allows Old Woman to be fog or mist, or ride the wind, or speak through old woman" (Cameron, 1981, p. 145).

Today the members of the Secret Society of Women have to trust outsiders to remember and re-collect the scattered pieces of this knowledge in order to make it whole again. The stories these women tell are about the coming of the patriarchs when "the world turned upside down. . . . People got sick and died in ways they had never known" (Cameron, 1981, p. 61). "And then new men arrived. Men who never talked to women, never ate with women, never slept with women, never laughed with women. Men who frowned on singing and dancing, on laughter and love. Men who claimed the Society of Women was a society of witches" (Cameron, 1981, p. 61). This is the same story that we will read of in Jovette Marchessault's *Night Cows,* when we learn about the coming of the Order of the Castrators. These are the invaders from the North in the history of Old Europe as told by Marija Gimbutas.

These are the stories of the conquest of a traditional matristic society by the patriarchal invaders. They are also the stories of Creation and of original Goddess figures like Copper Woman, who lived alone with her secrets and her mysteries, and of how she created a little boy out of her snot and gave birth to a daughter by him, of how she lived and how she died, of the warrior women in her culture, and of the ways in which the Priests destroyed their knowledge. They are stories about the special women who were chosen to guard the secret knowledge, and about how they were identified as old souls reborn. These stories resemble Kim Chernin's *Flame Bearers,* for in her book as well, the members of a secret society were carefully chosen and nurtured so that they could keep the flame of the sacred teachings alive in the hearts of all to whom they were imparted. They are stories about how these women knew when the time had come for the next change, and how they recognized that the present is a new time for change, a time to record the stories for the first time. They are stories that impart the ecofeminist teaching that "all things are alive, perhaps not in the same way we are alive, but each in its own way. And though different from us in shape and life span, different in Time and Knowing, yet trees are alive. And rocks. And water. And all know emotion" (Cameron, 1981, p. 44). They are sharing the secrets of the matriarchs now in order to save Mother Earth. "Rivers are filthy that used to be clean. Mountains are naked that used to be covered with trees. The ocean is fighting for her life and there are no fish where there used to be millions, and this is the work of the cold evil. The last treasure we have, the secrets of the matriarchy, can be shared and honored by women, and be proof there is another way, a better way, and some of us remember it" (Cameron, 1981, p. 146).

The book ends with a chant (perhaps we might call it a poem), but it is a chant in the magical sense of "enchantment." It casts a spell in which the power of Old Woman is in-

voked to watch over those of us who are piecing together the shreds of ancient womanknow-
ing now.

> Old Woman is watching
> Watching over you
>   in the darkness of the storm
>   she is watching
>   watching over you
>
>   weave and mend
>   weave and mend
> Old Woman is watching
>   watching over you
> with her bones become a loom
>   she is weaving
>   watching over us
>   weave and mend
>   golden circle
>   weave and mend
>   sacred sisters
>   weave and mend
> I have been searching
> lost
> alone
> I have been searching
> for so many years
>
> I have been searching
> Old Woman
>
> and I find her
> in
> mySelf
> (Cameron, 1981, pp. 149–150)

The Old Religion, the Ancient Knowledge, whether it comes from Celtic Ireland or Vancouver Island, teaches us that women possess the shamanic power to fly, to shape-shift, to
create, to commune with nature, and to put their knowledge to the service of the regeneration of life on earth.

Let us hope that the printed transmission of these texts, whose power was kept intact in the
oral tradition, will encourage women everywhere to re-connect with their matristic literary
traditions, which do not sever the word from its ancient sources of magic, from the spoken
word, from voice and the energy of human contact, both with other humans and with nature.

THE ECOFEMINIST CYCLE

As one of the newly emerging cycles, the Ecofeminist Cycle directly addresses the issues
posed by Susan Griffin in *Woman and Nature*. It presents the simultaneous degradation of
woman and nature, but then develops the position that the more aligned humans become
with the spirit of woman-and-nature, aligned and integrated, the closer humankind approaches salvation for the Planet and for all life on Earth, symbolized by the Great Mother.

In this cycle I first discuss the South African novel *The Expedition to the Baobab Tree* by
Wilma Stockenström, and then *The Iguana* by Anna Maria Ortese, as examples of the works
being generated with an ecofeminist vision on a global scale.

Subsequently, I turn to two visionary works, one in the genre of science fiction, *Always
Coming Home* by Ursula LeGuin, and the other a mythico-poetic autobiography, *Plant
Mother* by Jovette Marchessault. We will also look at the visionary text, *Night Cows*, by the
Quebecoise author, Jovette Marchessault.

In this cycle, the Goddess or the Great Mother is not always or necessarily, named, for the spirit of woman-and-nature allied, when evoked within a feminist matristic context, conjures Her up as the female Creatrix. Nonetheless, when not named specifically, She is identified as Earth Mother or Goddess by those matristic symbols that we have come to associate with the Mother Goddess mythos.

The Expedition to the Baobab Tree (1982), by Wilma Stockenström, translated from the Afrikaans, is the story of a slave who escapes from her life as the most elevated of the servants of a rich master. She had lived in a false, patriarchal Eden as the highest in service until one day, on a journey with her master's son, a prosperous merchant (who died during the trip), she escaped, and sought refuge and survival by living in a Baobab Tree.

Her narrative begins when she is merging with the spirit of the Baobab Tree, which becomes the new feminist matristic Eden for her, setting itself in opposition to the opulence of the patriarchal Garden she had lived in as a slave.

Her present life merges dream and waking visions in a true realization of what surrealism really means when taken to its most far-reaching conclusions by a female visionary in revolt against oppression.

The protagonist lives in Dream-Time, and has ultimately become a Tree Goddess: "A supreme being I am in my grey tree-skin" (Stockenström, 1982, p. 14). She lives in the hollow of the Baobab Tree with only three small beads as her possessions. In her former life as a slave, she had haughtily and arrogantly ignored the spirit of the tree. It meant nothing to her to make offerings, do incantations, make sacrifices to the trees. "I walked past them head in the air, and offered them nothing. No, I laughed at the other women who bowed before them and reverently set down a handful of millet grains on the great leaf of a fever tree beside the silent treetrunk and muttered over them. I did not mutter at all, not for any tree spirit" (Stockenström, 1982, p. 27).

But now, in her voluntary exile from the false Eden, as she has had to learn to live and survive in harmony with the Baobab Tree, she eventually learns to pay homage to it, and she becomes "the spirit of the tree." Although both she and the field mouse inhabit the tree, only *she* reveres it.

As the head slave-girl, she had formerly internalized all the values of the patriarchal oppressors and had "wandered about like a fool in the paradisal luxuriance. This was a garden!" (Stockenström, 1982, p. 37) But having no woman-power in the Garden of the master put her in the position of Eve in Eden—"to be hungry and to know of a source of food and not be able to get to it" (Stockenström, 1982, p. 38). She had always tried to imagine the kind of existence in which she would not be a possession. However, she realized that in the house of her benefactor she would never have been able to keep her grandchildren. They would have belonged to him. She was completely without rights in the luxuriance of her patriarchal Eden.

One day, on her long journey to market with the eldest son of her master and a stranger, she happened to notice rock carvings on the walls of a cave in the wilderness. The stranger described them as functionless, communicating absolutely nothing, but she saw them as meaningful symbols and glyphs, vestiges of an ancient Goddess religion. "Here is something that looks like a woman," said the eldest son. "It has breasts. Here is a snake, I think. And look here! An elephant with a scalloped back!" (Stockenström, 1982, p. 88) Faced with these hieroglyphs on the cave wall, she suddenly fell into a trance, and began to prophesize that "languages that yet slept" and "strange trees would one day march out through the valleys and over the hills and along the mountain sides. . . . I prophesied that there would be a walking around inside the earth" (Stockenström, 1982, p. 89). When she asked the others whether they had heard her prophecy, they denied it.

In her Baobab Tree "dreaming and waking have become extensions of each other" (Stockenström, 1982, p. 92). Her visionary powers were infinitely expanded as she communed with the spirit of the tree. She often gave thanks to the earth, to the honeybee, to the tree, and to the rain for the bounty she had received that kept her alive in her exile. As she surrendered to the powers of her environment, "to put it less despondently, I learned to live with them, as I learned to live with the veld and the animals and the insects, with the choice of paths in reality and in my sleep" (Stockenström, 1982, p. 98), she had "overcome . . . the insult of not being allowed to be human" (Stockenström, 1982, p. 101).

She is gradually enlightened, as dream, nature, and clarity intermingle, and teach her that the water spirits and the tree spirits have actually nourished her all through her life. "I rule. I dream outwards . . . the nourishing awareness that dream leads to dream" (Stockenström, 1982, p. 101). As the book closes, she realizes

> I was really a mistress and mother and goddess
> Baobab, merciful one. My baobab.
> I drink down my life—Quickly, water-spirit. Let your envoy carry out his task swiftly. . . .
> (Stockenström, 1982, p. 111).

Taking leave of our reality, she dives into the dark water, and rows "with my wings toward the far side when in descending silence I am no longer able to help myself and deafly fly further and further. I will find rest in the upside-down. I fold my wings" (Stockenström, 1982, p. 111).

The illuminated vision of a female slave who has metamorphosed into a Tree Goddess reveals the facticity of all patriarchal Edens and the promise of a new feminist matristic Eden when woman and tree are again revered as one, as the source of life and nourishment, the sacred matrix from which all living things are created. Her wings indicate a true metamorphosis from one life form to another. Her death, another journey, promises still more spiritual knowledge. The slave became a free woman by taking up residence in a Baobab Tree and merging with its spirit. In this sense, the newly freed woman has literally eaten of the Tree (of Knowledge) and learned that the visible and the invisible are no longer inseparable, but simply different aspects of a description of reality in which everything in the natural world partakes of the sacred, and is in constant communion with the spirit world.

Anna Maria Ortese's novel *The Iguana* (1987) puts all the values of patriarchal European civilization into question. It also gives us hope for the recognition of the Goddess (even in her most humiliated and degraded aspect) being reborn within the heart of the most decadent of white European androcratic colonizers.

Here an Architect/Real-Estate Developer sets sail with a "Nouvelle Vague" Publisher to discover an island untouched by European civilization in order to exploit it. The Architect would like to develop a Mediterranean resort there, and to sell real estate for a profit, while the Publisher dreams of discovering a rare manuscript that he can publish. Together they fantasize about publishing the confessions of a madman who falls in love with an Iguana. Naturally, they do not realize that this is precisely what will happen, and that the Count (the Architect) will become that most exotic madman in love with an Iguana. Both men see the literature of oppression as ultimately financially rewarding.

When they finally set sail, they discover the island of Ocaña, shaped like a horn of plenty (relating to the Cornucopia, that, as we shall see, emerges symbolically as well in Leonora Carrington's novel, *The Hearing Trumpet*). Like knights on a Grail Quest, whose sacred origin has now been long forgotten by those motivated entirely by mercantile interests, the Architect and the Publisher will be truly transformed by their journey, for indeed, they eventually encounter the Grail in the image of the Iguana.

On the island, which is not shown on the map, because the cartographers were Christian, and never noted the places that they considered to be pagan (possessed by the devil), they discover that a Marquis and his brothers (whose family dates from the seventeenth-century Portuguese discovery of the land) are keeping a woman Iguana in a state of bondage.

The Iguana, reminding them of a prehistoric lizard, is the servant of these ancient aristocrats. She literally lives "down below" in the basement, and her rooms seem to bury her alive.

The Count and his friend come with a patronizing, colonizing attitude. They want to take the Iguana back to Europe, to educate her, and to restore her. They hope to develop commercially viable real estate markets on the island. However, eventually they realize that the Marquis and his brothers do not want to have their land exploited, nor does the Iguana wish to be married and go to live in Europe.

Ortese astutely shows how, even when men are protective of nature in general, they still enslave women, and it is not until women and nature are seen as one, not until the Goddess (here the Iguana—a kind of prehistoric serpent) is revered, that Evil will vanish from the Planet.

Even on an island far removed from Western civilization, one on which nature is still untrammeled and appreciated, woman continues to be degraded and scorned. The Iguana, having been raised in this island's culture, where she is perceived as the Devil incarnate, has come to believe that she is "the incarnation of Evil, shame, and wickedness." . . . only such a creature knows the whole mortal cold of Evil! . . . This is Hell" (Ortese, 1987, pp. 93–94).

Slowly the island paradise becomes an Inferno, as the Count realized that the Marquis mercilessly beats the Iguana, and clears his conscience by citing the scriptures: "Jesus, among the episodes of his divine predication, makes no mention of animals, and we can be certain that eternal life is none of their affair, since they have no souls" (Ortese, 1987, p. 100).

Furthermore, as the Marquis beats the Iguana, he consoles himself with poetry about how everything passes "with time, the pains of a little Iguana will likewise vanish" (Ortese, 1987, p. 136). Western literature, seen as a colonizing enterprise, helps us put into perspective the symbolic meaning of "real estate" as the two are linked in this novel.

Of what does our "real" estate consist? Our cultural heritage? Here, indeed, the inheritance from the wisdom of the West, which has survived on this island in a time warp, shows that any philosophy or religion that deprives animals and women of a soul is, itself, the real source of Evil.

The Count's awakening to the true spiritual level of a Grail-Quester, ultimately entails the sacrifice of his own life. But on his journey, now a true inner voyage, he has understood that something is terribly wrong with Western civilization. "There is something we're totally ignorant of, something we refuse to know, someone hidden who closes our eyes . . . there's a deception working to the harm of people who are weaker than we are" (Ortese, 1987, p. 168).

Ultimately, the Count discovers that God is dead, and has been murdered by human arrogance and the lust for power. He realizes that compassion, which we are supposed to feel for the oppressed, offers "evil a chance to veil its crimes," and opens to goodness "a portal to profoundest weakness" (Ortese, 1987, p. 169). He soon grows to desire passionately the rebirth of God.

The Count imagines offering testimony to the crime of the murder of God, and God reveals itself to be "a simple white butterfly," an epiphany of the ancient Mother Goddess, a sign indicating continual metamorphosis. Reflecting on the butterfly and the Iguana, the Count wonders that "so weak and simple a creature . . . could contain the secret, the very origins of the immense astounding universe with all its splendors, gifts . . ." (Ortese, 1987, p. 175). He also comes to understand that "these voyages are dreams, and iguanas are warnings. That there are no iguanas, but only disguises, disguises thought up by human beings for the oppression of their neighbors, and then held in place by a cruel and terrifying society. He himself, had been product and expression of such a society, but now he was stepping out of it" (Ortese, 1987, p. 180).

Ortese shows us how our guilt is synonymous with our idealism. For, in hoping to save the unfortunate creatures of the island by exploiting them, one is simultaneously idealistic (from one's limited cultural perspective) and, at the same time, guilty. To build hotels and condos on the island would be to expel its inhabitants from the natural Paradise which is the Earth. It is the beginning of man's arrogance and of the Fall.

After the Count's death, through compassion for the Iguana, those on the island learned to read and write; soon they were "mutually assisting each other with a great deal of love" (Ortese, 1987, p. 194). The Count is referred to in poetry (written by the Marquis and his brothers to commemorate the love of the Iguana) as the "Count of Christ": "Save the bull/ protect the cow/and the lamb/and the falling star" (Ortesi, 1987, p. 194).

The novel closes addressing the reader while taking leave of Ocaña and its humble human family. "If you are surprised by the sea that closes so easily over these evils and these smiles. . . . please remember Unamuno's pressing question, and the similar questions you yourself have asked, and you will see that at least this sense of surprise remains the same" (Ortese, 1987, p. 198).

The double distanciation effect reminds us not only that we are reading a fiction, but that we, too, are dreamers of ourselves reading fiction, for, as Unamuno's work has constantly reminded us, "all life is a dream." Then, placing us back in the context of the Western literature of consolation-through-creativity, we begin to see ourselves as the Marquis, for we can all too easily let the oppressed Iguanas of our world continue to suffer as we go on reading Unamuno or Ortese, convincing ourselves that their suffering is merely part of a dream. And, like the Marquis who believed in the words of Jesus, we make our Unamunos into our Gods, we quote them, and we continue to turn the pages of books like *The Iguana*, refusing to commit our own lives to restoring the Grail.

All of Western literature, as shown by Anna Maria Ortese, can be understood as a facile "out," created by Western colonizers to dispense with the problem of Evil by creative fictional and metaphysical consolations in the form of printed tales purporting to be stamped with the "authority" of the "Creator." Print itself, and the silence of reading alone, is, in this sense, a dampener to the political impact of a tale of power, for, had the book's story been shared orally, the reader response might have been completely different, and the book might have incited one to an act that would improve the lot of those Iguanas who are victims of the predominant philosophies of the West.

Ortese, however, has written a tale of power with a male hero, who *does* come to understand the nature of Evil. If God is not dead, it is the prehistoric Goddess (the scapegoated serpent/lizard/woman) who, in her humiliation, reminds us of the true teachings of all religions — of the transformation and salvation that is possible through *love*. This, if anything, is our "real" estate, the only heritage of the West that is capable of redeeming women, men, and nature, now.

Ursula K. LeGuin's *Always Coming Home* (1985), without literally mentioning the Goddess, exemplifies the world view and the values of both feminist matristic literature and a philosophical meditation upon the possibility of literature as we have known it from an eco-feminist perspective.

Her book creates a total ethnography, including the material culture and the folklore and folkways of the Kesh, a people who will live in the distant future, but whose way of life (sacred path) and attitude toward Creation concretize a feminist matristic cosmogony and praxis at its best.

The hardcover edition of *Always Coming Home* was published with a cassette tape of the music and poetry of the Kesh.

Additionally, a section called The Back of The Book provides an entire dictionary of the Kesh language, a glossary of their numbers, examples of their written script, their punctuation, and information about their narrative modes in which "fact and fiction are not clearly separated, truth and falsehood, however are" (LeGuin, 1985, p. 500), as well as notes on their spoken and written literary traditions.

The oral tradition is very much alive with the Kesh and, in fact, is as sacred and important as any written tradition. The ecological basis of their literary tradition includes the firm belief that, like everything else that is alive, books are mortal—they die. Thus, the Kesh clear out their libraries every few years in a kind of secret ritual in order to make room for new books. After all, why should the forests be continually destroyed in order to save every word that is written? "Perhaps not many of us could say why we save so many words, why our forests must all be cut to make paper to mark our words on, our rivers dammed to make electricity to power our word processors: we do it obsessively, as if afraid of something, as if compensating for something. Maybe we're afraid of death, afraid to let our words simply be spoken and die, leaving silence for new words to be born in" (LeGuin, 1985, p. 503).

Their literature, can be written or unwritten (thus even when the technology is available, one may choose not to use it—for sacred or ethical reasons). "When the artist and the audience are together, collaboration on the work becomes mundane and actual; the work shapes itself in the speaker's voice and the listeners' response together" (LeGuin, 1985, p. 502). Sometimes a written text can be translated back to breath. Because the spoken word is personalized to "you" here and now, it is ephemeral. Some oral texts can be written down, but, in their view when a text belongs "to the breath, . . . To reproduce such a text would be, . . . most inappropriate, not because it was sacrosanct, but because its oral/occasional/communal character was *essential*" (LeGuin, 1985, p. 502).

Thus the mantic function of the writer as storyteller is restored in the Kesh world. In a poem about Artists, written on a white plaster wall in the room of the Oak Society in Telina-na, we learn that writers (dancers, painters, shapers, and makers) journey to the gap between the worlds and come back with words and tunes. Like shamans, they go into confusion and come back with patterns. What they bring back can be understood as an eco-memory. It is expressed this way in one Kesh life story. "So of what the hawks' eyes saw all I can here recall to words is this:

"It was the universe of power. It was the network, field, and lines of the energies of all the beings, stars, and galaxies of stars, worlds, animals, minds, nerves, dust, the lace and foam of vibration that is being, itself, all interconnected, every part of another part and the whole part of each part, and so comprehensible to itself only as a whole, boundless and unclosed" (LeGuin, 1985, p. 290).

The literature of the Kesh affirms the life cycle through valuing both the living and the dying of words. When Stone Telling (the narrator) relates her life, she defines the religion of the Dayao people with whom she does not identify. For us, they are associated with believers in patriarchal Father-God religions. "One made everything out of nothing. One is a person, immortal. He is all-powerful. Human men are imitations of him. One is not the universe; he made it, and gives orders" (LeGuin, 1985, p. 200).

Through the cross-cultural distanciation, we come to see our own patriarchal, linear culture of print technologies, of death-defiance, and of war as only one pathetic, misguided way of life among many other cultural possibilities of civilization.

The valley Elders are ashamed and angry when an adult wages war. They are a peace-loving people. In their word "heya," both the invisible world and the visible world are contained. It is a formula, like "bless you," which, when spoken, utters the presence of the invisible together with the visible. "The word heya was the word that contained the world, visible and invisible, on this side and on the other side of death" (LeGuin, 1985, p. 94).

The Kesh also have a keen sense of community, and "continuity with the dirt, water, air, and living creatures of the Valley" (LeGuin, 1985, p. 90). They even come home to die, because they feel themselves to be intimately connected to their bioregion. They do not value possessions as we do. Nor do they practice the slaughter of animals without addressing the spirit of the animals, and showing respect for their souls.

The Kesh culture is matrilineal, exogamous, and matrilocal. Households include humans and other beings, as well as the moon, streams, plants, stones, and springs. They are people who are definitely *not* in a hurry. They are not patronizing to animals, and consider quail and deer (game animals) as a link between the wilderness and the human soul, both of which participate simultaneously in a sacred act during the hunt. The Kesh live well–they are healthy and full of grace. They understand that the metaphor of "The Way" generates "Change," and that those who follow the Kesh way, accept change as an inherent part of life. They do not resist it, but welcome it as part of the cycles and an expression of the life force. Although they do not specifically name the Goddess, reverence for the Earth Mother has become an integral and central part of their way of life.

Ursula K. LeGuin's novel has fleshed out in detail the songs, tales, poetry, games, instruments, sounds, and practices of an earth-based culture, and has distanced the high-tech culture, placing it in a ghetto, "The City of Mind," in order to show us how life could be lived if an earth-based spirituality and cosmogony were reawakened in humans today. She demonstrates that if humanity is to evolve, it will come to resemble simpler societies, those we have been taught to regard as primitive, because they are not technologically advanced. Here the Kesh simply *choose* not to live a high-tech life, because they put the life of the planet above personal comfort. Moreover, the simplicity of the Kesh way, a society that will come to be in the future, shows us that, what we consider to be "Evolution" is actually "Devolution."

The creative works, both artistic and literary, of the Kesh (who have obviously learned the lessons of their history, which are the lessons of our present) take us back to the aesthetics of ritual and oral forms, and to the sacredness of the performance and the relationship of person to person and person to the natural environment, as well as to the history of the community, including the invisible world of the spirits of humans, animals and plants.

This tale of power, which creates a new world of tales of power is a "Stone Telling" (as the narrator is named), for LeGuin has scattered stones of light through the darkness of our minds in order to lead us down the "Path" to a completely new "Way." For a people who firmly understand that stones, which have been around for millennia, can communicate, this book is obviously what they would teach us in their Stone Telling, for it encompasses the wisdom gleaned from the observation of many human cultures over eons of time, a wisdom that only the stones would have been around long enough to acquire.

The cassette that accompanies the book gives us examples of the music and poetry of the Kesh, and once more their close relationship to the Earth becomes apparent. Much of their music is composed of the sounds of water, of birds, and of other resonances from the natural environment.

In her second novel, *Mother of the Grass,* Québecoise author, Jovette Marchessault, introduces a Child-Seer as the protagonist, whose mythic journey is a passionate search for the most ancient images of a lost female Creator. It is through the inspired tutelage of her Grandmother that the heroine's artistic vision is first unleashed, and that her creative yearnings are most tenderly nourished. The figure of the Grandmother looms as magnificently over the world of her childhood as she envisages the Goddess reigning over all Creation. For her, Grandmother incarnates the spirit of Plant Mother and of those great spirit-teachers of all time who impart a sacred knowledge through the manifestation of their joyous being. The creative ecstasy that is transmitted through the great matrilineage over generations from Grandmother to Granddaughter constitutes an important female rite of passage in which the initiate acquires the knowledge that women's creative literary and artistic powers set the female forces of transformation and regeneration to work in the universe. It is virtually a shamanic initiation that the Grandmother imparts to her granddaughter. Jovette Marchessault's moving description of the magical intimacy that existed between her and her Grandmother shows how this Goddess-nature or Goddess-spirit is incarnated in the reality of women's cultural experiences in the tonal or the phenomenal world. "Listening to her was for me to listen to the collective voice of every living thing. The little creative solo of each species could be heard, drawing its music, its words, from the antediluvian residue, from the mythological dust. Grandmother's speech was a speech undissociated from the elements of dream" (Marchessault, 1989, p. 18).

It is this new female language ushered in by a retelling of the matristic myth of origins, that renames all of creation, and that will reinterpret the ancient tales and legends of patriarchy in original feminist matristic ways. This new feminist matristic language is animistic, vitalist, and celebratory; it exalts the life-giving forces of the Earth; it reclaims female desire, sexual pleasure, and liberates a new-found *joie de vivre*. This is similar to the language sought by Jeanne Hyvrard's narrator in *Mère la Mort*.

In Marchessault's mythico-poetic universe the figures of Mother and Child always create a compelling new image of ecstatic sisterhood. The persona of the Mother is always multidimensional. Mothers are at once mammalian and human, mythic and real, celestial and terrestrial. In *Night Cows*, Cow Mother, like Hathor, a vitalist symbol, is both Cow Goddess and Mother Parent. Mother and Daughter cows/humans embark upon the ultimate female vision-quest journey to seek the truth about their prepatriarchal origins. As Mother and Daughter cow fly beyond the Milky Way to their rendezvous with the night cows to learn of the female time before the coming of the Order of the Castrators, they nurture each other with desire. The new Mother-Daughter relationship in *Night Cows* is one of hope and exaltation. Because the nature of this text overflows into dramatic "recitative," it has been performed in public readings and spectacles all over Québec, notably by Pol Pelletier, who performed it in both French and English, and who is co-founder of Le Théâtre Expérimental des Femmes in Montreal.

> "There we are, all naked within our garments, within the flesh of our garments of night, within the embrace of the hairs of our skin. Daughter, mother, mother, daughter, the hierarchy goes off to take a holiday when the cows of the night bathe themselves in the lakes of sweaty tenderness.
>
> And we are off! And we fly to our rendezvous in the Milky Way. How beautiful! The great river of milk, the land of birth, where mothers and daughters are reunited at long last. So beautiful! Canals of milk blooming with water lilies. Milk-drunk, white flow, fluid star, the fruit of our mother's guts expands across the brisk climate of the sky. All the breasted creatures of the universe come to the meeting place. (Marchessault, 1985, p. 75)

All of Jovette Marchessault's creative work in literature and the visual arts is a celebration of the empowering of women by each other through the reactivation of Goddess-energy.

It is significant to note that the images of the Goddess that figure so prominently in many works in the Ecofeminist Cycle appear in animal or plant form, rather than being anthropomorphic. This probably expresses a desire for a sacred image of the Creator that is devoid of class, race, or age specifications; one that metamorphoses from culture to culture, and may acquire universal meanings. This also relates the contemporary images of the Goddess to the ancient matristic images of the Great Mother as She was manifested in plant and animal symbology.

As I see it, the unique feature of the Ecofeminist Cycle is that the narratives do not focus on the story of a human being removed from the context of the natural environment and the cosmos. In most of these stories trees, animals, planets, all creatures, plants, and stones are as compelling in their own life histories and mysteries as are the humans with whom they interact. All live in the Earth, whose quakes and natural disasters communicate to us that the Mother is in desperate need of healing now.

THE GRAIL QUEST CYCLE

As we have already noted, feminist matristic writers stress the fact that the Goddess tradition, its practices and beliefs, were never meant to be committed to writing. Additionally, most vestiges of its sacred temples and artifacts have been destroyed by the patriarchal conquests. Thus, one is left between a rock and a hard place. As *The Daughters of Copper Woman* made clear, while the oral tradition transmits the lore in a manner that preserves the integrity and purity of the teachings, without the written tradition, the teachings risk being lost forever. Something is gained and something is lost in each case. The question is how to preserve the quality of the teachings without running the risk of their disappearance.

How then does the Goddess wisdom get reclaimed, and how can it be transmitted intact and retain as much authenticity as possible?

The feminist matristic Grail Quest Cycle addresses some of these concerns. In this cycle we will discuss together *The Mists of Avalon* (1982) by Marion Zimmer Bradley and *The Hearing Trumpet* (1977) by Leonora Carrington in order to extract some of the teachings that are pertinent to the questions we have raised.

I would refer the reader to the topic of the Holy Grail in *The Woman's Encyclopedia of Myths and Secrets* (1983) by Barbara G. Walker for a brief history of the Grail tradition written from a woman's perspective.

The history of the Grail is in many ways similar to that of the Goddess tradition, and that is obviously why it has been taken up by two visionary writers, Leonora Carrington and Marion Zimmer Bradley.

Barbara G. Walker tells us that "The real origins of The Holy Grail were not Christian but pagan. The Grail was first Christianized in Spain from a sacred tradition of the Moors. Like the Celts' Holy Cauldron of Regeneration, which it resembled, the blood-filled vessel was a womb symbol meaning rebirth in the Oriental or Gnostic sense of reincarnation. Its connotation was feminine, not masculine" (Walker, 1983, p. 352).

Without tracing the long literary history of the Quest of the Grail, we may simply underline the fact that when the Grail was Christianized, and lost its "feminine" power, becoming simply a chalice that contained the blood of Christ, it lost its allure. The knights of King Arthur's Round Table would risk their lives on the Quest for the Grail, which still had an identification with the "feminine," according to Barbara G. Walker, but "When the Grail's aura of feminine mystery was removed, its romantic appeal declined. If the Grail was nothing more than the cup of Christ's blood, then there was no reason for the great Quest at all. The cup of Christ's blood was readily available to all, in every chapel; and even though it was called a holy sacrament, its discovery somehow lacked thrills. As matters turned out, to Christianize the Grail was to neutralize the magnetism of its secret nature" (Walker, 1983, p. 354).

Both Marion Zimmer Bradley and Leonora Carrington establish a parallel between the Christianizing of the Grail and the patriarchalizing of the mysteries of the Goddess. Both writers situate their stories of the recovery of the Grail within the bastions of patriarchal cultures that have pretensions to true enlightenment (i.e., the initiation to knighthood in *The Mists of Avalon* and the practices of the Gurdjieff school as embodied in Lightsome Hall of *The Hearing Trumpet*). Moreover, the heroines of both novels, Marion and Morgaine achieve their most powerful revelations and visions at a very advanced age, via direct *gnosis*. Both authors present the conflict between the secret esoteric modes of teaching and training versus the open exoteric methods of transmission. This conflict raises the question of the superiority or inferiority of the oral tradition versus the technologies of the written word. With the advent of the technologies of the printed word, what is gained is access to "knowledge" of a certain kind, and a democratic, open education for all. However, what is sacrificed is the energy inherent in the mode of transmission. The written technologies democratize the knowledge, permit its transmission intact, but they also leave it open to deformation and misinterpretation in the hands of those who would destroy it. They also enclose it within one codified, finalized, prioritized version. On the other hand, the secret society of pure preservation via a lineage of the elect can lead, at its absolute worst, to Fascism of the most inordinate proportions.

This is obviously why both novels politicize the issues around the concept of the Planet as the ultimate Grail (Cauldron of Regeneration). Both novels interpret the Wasteland of the Fisher King as the Planet Earth now, in its state of Ecocide. Both lead us to understand that the King (patriarchy) is dying, and that the reclamation of the Grail for the Goddess is the only way to regenerate life on Earth. The two books pose the problem of whether all Gods are really one, as some of the Priests would have us believe in an all too facile and unpoliticized response to the question.

In *The Mists of Avalon,* Morgaine talks about the difference between Christianity and the Goddess Religion with respect to the Earth, and she asks whether it is sufficient, as the Merlin and other Priests would preach, to let all people serve whatever God they prefer, because all Gods are one.

It is clear that for Bradley, this question is at the heart of her own Grail Quest. "And if for a moment it seemed she could hear the voice of the Merlin *Let all men be free to serve what God they best like . . . Even,* she wondered, one which denied the very life of the earth? But she knew Taliesin would have said, *Even so*" (Bradley, 1982, p. 403).

In reflecting upon the difference between the Goddess religion and Christianity, Morgaine, a Priestess of the Goddess from Avalon, thinks: "The difference is deeper than I thought. Even those who till the earth, when they are Christians come to a way of life which is far from the earth. They say that their God has given them dominion over all growing things, and every beast of the field. Whereas we dwellers in the hillside and swamp, forest and far field, we know that it is not we who have dominion over nature, but she who has dominion over us. . . . All of these things are under the dominion of the Goddess and without her beneficent mercy none of us could draw a living breath, but all things would be barren and die" (Bradley, 1982, p. 398).

These two books also lead the reader into an intimate relationship with a mode of extrasensory perception through which the Grail (the Goddess) and the other world can be perceived and known directly via the intermediary of reading feminist matristic literature, which is our equivalent of the hearing trumpet through which Marion experiences *gnosis* of the Goddess. In *The Hearing Trumpet,* Marion is given a hearing horn shaped like a cornucopia, a horn of plenty (reminding us of the shape of the island of Ocaña in *The Iguana*) through which she comes into telepathic contact with the history of the Goddess and the Grail while residing in an Old Age Home that her son, Galahad, has put her in at the age of 92. Here, of course, Galahad (who in the Grail Legend, did actually live out his quest to the very end, and actually encountered the Grail), now in the modern era, places his mother in Lightsome Hall, a retirement home run by a Dr. Gambit as a kind of Gurdjieff training center for old people through which enlightenment is to be reached via rigorous practices under strict patriarchal supervision. Ironically, unbeknownst to this contemporary Galahad, while disposing of his elderly mother, he actually helps her to recover the Grail knowledge of the Goddess for herself, right under the very eyes of the patriarchal guardians at Lightsome hall, for she meets the Goddess via a telepathic communication with a portrait of an Abbess on the wall. It is obvious that for elderly women, the encounter with the Grail and with sacred knowledge of the Goddess is spontaneous, and does not come about via a program of rigorous training. For in old age the dream and waking states begin to meld into an otherworldly "surreality," and elderly women's bodies become finely tuned to the messages emanating from other dimensions.

In *The Mists of Avalon,* the Priestesses have the "Sight," the telepathic ability to tune into events and thoughts at a distance, to transmit and receive messages, and to experience the power and energy of the Goddess, even when they are couched behind patriarchal symbols and glyphs. At the end of *The Mists of Avalon,* also in her extreme old age, Morgaine comes to honor the grave of Viviane, her aunt, and former Lady of the Lake, High Priestess of the Isle of Avalon. On her visit to the grave she encounters a group of nuns who remind her very much of the Priestesses of Avalon. In their chapel she is shown an old statue of the Christian saint, Brigit, and as she looks at Brigit, she feels the energy of the Goddess as she is worshipped in Ireland. The nuns also have the Holy Thorn of Avalon, and Morgaine concludes that "the holy thing brought itself from Avalon into the world of men where it was most needed. It would remain hidden in Avalon, but it would be shown here in the world as well" (Bradley, 1982, p. 875). Then Morgaine perceives the shadow of the chalice, and she realizes: "It is everywhere. And those who have need of a sign in this world will see it always" (Bradley, 1982, p. 875).

It is the gift of "Sight" and of telepathic hearing that is quickened in the spirit of older women, permitting them to decode the glyphs of Christianity, and through their perception of powerful energy fields and visions, to encounter the Goddess at the end of their lives, for She beckons them to the other world to which they will pass at their physical death.

Thus, both books transmit to us the message that the power of the Goddess is such that She invites us to Her via the sacred theaphanies in which She reveals Herself to us through *gnosis*, even when She has to break through the pageantry of patriarchal rites that mock Her mysteries, whether they be the rites associated with the initiation of the knights of the Round Table or the practices at Lightsome Hall. These two novels are concerned with wresting the Grail from the hands of patriarchy, and returning it to the Goddess in order for life on Earth to flourish again.

The Hearing Trumpet is about saving the planet by restoring the cup of the sacred Pneuma to the Goddess. "As you know, the Great Mother cannot return to this planet until the Cup is restored to her filled with Pneuma, and under the guard of her consort, the Horned God. . . . If the planet is to survive with organic life, she (the Goddess) must be induced to return so that good will and love can once more prevail in the world" (Carrington, 1977, p. 177).

We may ask ourselves how written literature can transmit the vital energies that are passed on in an initiation or via oral transmission. In my opinion, feminist matristic writers do not recommend that we abandon the written enterprise at all, but rather, that we make use of the best of both possibilities in order to energize (or illuminate) our texts with the vibrations necessary to create change. These techniques have traditionally been referred to as "poetics," but as we have seen with Christa Wolf, patriarchal poetics are not necessarily appropriate to matristic materials. These writers are thus invoking a different poetics, a poetics of sacred geometries and of Goddess symbols that resonate throughout the 30,000 years of recorded and unrecorded histories of goddess-centered cultures. In *The Hearing Trumpet* we find the same symbols that Marija Gimbutas identified as belonging to the epiphanies of the Great Goddess in Old Europe. Moreover, the composite matrilineal identity of human, animal, and Goddess forms becomes apparent in the feminist matristic theaphanies.

In *The Hearing Trumpet,* the elderly women at Lightsome Hall make plans to recover the Grail, and to restore it to the Goddess.

An Earthquake shakes a great stone tower, and as it releases a six-winged creature who had been imprisoned within its walls, the answer to the riddle that had puzzled the women becomes clear. The riddle was: "Though legless your whirling will then appear lame/I seem to move, but I don't, what's my name?" (Carrington, 1977, p. 162) The answer to the riddle, as the Earthquake suggested, was the Earth.

The creature then says that she will show the women the Mother of Sephira, and eventually the creature leads them to a chamber in a cavern where a woman sat stirring a great cauldron. "The woman who stood before me was myself" (Carrington, 1977, p. 166). This, she is informed, is "the womb of the world whence all things come" (Carrington, 1977, p. 166). There, in a sacred theaphany, she saw "the face of the Abbess of Santa Barbara de Tartarus . . . She faded and then I saw the huge eyes and feelers of the Queen Bee, who winked and transformed herself into my own face. . . . Holding the mirror at arm's length I seemed to see a three-faced female whose eyes winked alternatively. One of the faces was black, one red, one white, and they belonged to the Abbess, the Queen Bee, and myself" (Carrington, 1977, p. 169).

In a wild pagan rite, the women ask the Bees to instruct them about how to recover the

Holy Grail so that "the Earth shall not die on her axis! Speak, Zam Pollum!" (Carrington, 1977, p. 189)

The people of Queen Anubeth, the Wolf-Woman (like the Loba), who here appears as a savior, offer themselves to recover the holy cup. "The Goddess hummed with a million voices and drops of honey fell like manna from the roof of the cavern" (Carrington, 1977, p. 189).

As the novel closes, the Grail is captured and returned to the Goddess, and Anubeth (the Loba savior), in extreme old age, gives birth to a litter of werelets. Anubeth, like the biblical matriarchs, undergoes the miracle of fertility in old age. Here it is hoped that werecubs, a new species, will be kinder to the Earth than humans had been.

In the center of the novel is a sacred spiral, through which we are transported into the past to learn the life history of Santa Barbara de Tartarus and of Doña Rosalinda. During this spiral into the history of the abbess, whose portrait hangs in Lightsome hall, we also learn of Mary Magdalen, who "had been an initiate into the Mysteries of the Goddess, but had been executed for the sacrilege of selling certain secrets of her cult to Jesus of Nazareth. This, of course, would explain the miracles which have puzzled us for so long" (Carrington, 1977, p. 93).

The symbols of the sacred spiral, the Octagonal Tower (in which Dona Rosalinda practiced her herbal cures and magical incantations), the Elixir of the Goddess, Venus ["the cup lies sterile and empty under the rule of Set who is Yehowa, the Revenger" (Carrington 1977, p. 116], the bees, the sacred circles (in which the women do their magical work), the Rose (the symbol of the Flower of Venus and the Virgin Goddess) the name Marian (for Mary, the Goddess and Queen of Heaven) (Walker, 1983, pp. 866, 867), Tartarus (the underworld), the Wolf-Woman (the Loba), the Horn (Cauldron of Regeneration) . . . and so forth, all converge to create a composite charged energy field in which the ordeals of initiation can be lived on an imaginary level with as much energy transfer as would have occurred in a private rite of initiation. The act of reading can then be considered to be a kind of a ritual of energy transmission.

The book *The Hearing Trumpet* is constructed on a Cross, reinterpreted feminist matristically. The abbess who winks from her portrait in Lightsome Hall at Marian turns out to be Rosalinda Alvarez *Cruz* della Cueva. "A cross is the parting or the joining of Ways . . ." (Carrington, 1977, p. 91). The vertical axis of the cross is the spiral into the past history and past lives of the abbess. The horizontal axis is the story of the women in Lightsome Hall, which takes place in the "present" of the novel.

Feminist matristically, this is the cross on which the Goddess (not Christ) was crucified, and, as a representation of "the parting and joining of the ways," it is not a Christian cross, but a sacred crossroads at which the matristic past and feminist matristic present become realigned in a new sacred geometry.

The motifs that are familiar to us from other feminist matristic works are the Earthquake, in which the Earth Goddess speaks; the Loba, a hybrid—part animal and part human, who is a protector of the cubs, not a predator (as humans have been and wolves have not); and "the new feminist matristic Eden" in which the entire Earth is understood to be the Grail, the sacred vessel, which will flower again once the Goddess has her rightful realm restored to Her—once the Grail is wrested away from the patriarchal powers that have led to Her annihilation.

Marion Zimmer Bradley and Leonora Carrington both use the ruse of cross-dressing to allow women to infiltrate into the male world in order to reclaim the Grail. However, the women who do this are extremely conscious of their use of male attire and for what goals they have compromised themselves. In contradistinction to women today, who enter the male world in order to merge with it, these women enter it in order to restore the Grail to the Goddess, and the Goddess as the Creator of all life.

In each book the female protagonist must read through the symbols revealed in a cave in order to encounter the core of Goddess knowledge. In *The Mists of Avalon* the Priestesses must be trained to call the fire, the mists, the rain, to work with healing and herbal lore, and to use love songs powerfully. They embody the Goddess when they marry the King Stag in their fertility ritual. The Wasteland, as it is described in the Ballad of the Fisher King, is seen only as a symbol, even to our medieval forbears. Through this distanciation effect, we realize that if we mistake the Wasteland for a symbol, we, too, might practice the rituals of the male Gods (for their priests believe that all Gods are one), and then the land will never be revived. For today we see that the Wasteland has become a reality. It was never merely symbolic. All Gods are *not* one. The Earth *is* dying, because the Goddess religion has been wiped out, literally, not symbolically.

If we can read *The Mists of Avalon* and understand that women, like Morgaine, are responsible for acting on their understanding, then we realize that we, too, are beckoned to learn the arts of shape-shifting and storytelling, the shamanic arts, in order to wrest the Grail (the Earth) from patriarchal dominion, and to bring about the rebirth of the Earth Goddess in the world today.

In a larger sense, we women are also the Grail, for we are the womb from which life springs, and we are as much of the Earth as She is of us. Her life depends upon our heeding Her warnings, and shape-shifting our way toward bringing Avalon or a feminist matristic Eden to life in the here and now.

In answering our original question about how the Goddess tradition can be transmitted if its highest form of power is when it is unwritten and guarded purely as secret knowledge, but, at the same time, is needed now by a world in crisis, we must conclude that contemporary feminist matristic artists and writers are making use of the synergy of the combined energies of the crossroads where the two traditions meet—the Goddess tradition and the Enlightenment tradition. While not rejecting the best of either one, these artists and writers reclaim the values of both that enhance life and affirm the Earth. If it is necessary to transmit secret oral knowledge via the print media, now, in order for it not to be lost, it will be done (e.g., *Daughters of Copper Woman*). However, this does not mean that they abandon the advantages of oral transmission or of ceremonies that impart energies impossible to capture within the pages of a book.

Formerly the Grail was the object of the Quest. Today it is no longer the object; it is the subject—the Quester. Women as Grails are constituting themselves as seekers, and the knowledge they uncover will not merely be classified, catalogued, and filed away by electronic media. It will be imparted to new generations of women, so that it will live again. It will be revealed in ways that restore the original allure and potent energy fields of the Great Mother.

The Grail Quest Cycle reinterpreted feminist matristically teaches us at least two important lessons. The first is that old age is a period in which the states of dreaming and waking are more closely aligned than at any other time in our lives. Elderly women, in particular, seem to enter an extremely creative period as they age, for they sharpen their visionary and intuitive faculties, and become wise in the ways in which they perceive things from a wider, more holistic perspective. Thus, the Grail Quest Cycle teaches us to revere aging women, for they emerge as prophetic figures. Second, because the wisdom teachings were often passed on in the oral tradition, feminist matristic literature teaches us a new reverence for all forms of folklore and oral performance literature, because even the most innocent jingles and riddles may once have been incantations, and they might contain clues to the teachings of the Goddess handed down in coded form.

Finally, we are reminded that through the lore of a culture, the Goddess tradition survives underground, and while it may not flourish in Patriarchy, it does live on in a subterranean, occulted way.

If the works I have discussed in this book offer any hope, it is precisely this—that the Goddess tradition can be remembered and reborn even within Patriarchy, itself, just as these books have been written in a patriarchal society. Contrary to the ways in which patriarchal religions disempower women, the Goddess tradition does not exclude men. The Goddess religion does not turn patriarchal religion on its flip side and offer a matriarchal hierarchical system. On the contrary, the Earth Goddess places primary emphasis on the Planet, rather than on humans, whether male or female.

Today, in order to restore the magnetism to the Grail (earth/womb/cauldron) that patriarchalization and Christianization have neutralized, we must remove the many layers of androcentric/cratic and anthropomorphic resonances from the entire history of the Grail Quest by understanding that the Grail is both the female womb and the Earth Mother without which all life would vanish.

We began this section with the paradigm of Inanna or Helen, the woman of the upper world who visits the underworld. We conclude by noting that in times of crisis, the wisdom of the underworld/other world can be directly visited upon the upper world via epiphanies, theaphanies, revelations, and *gnosis* such as those witnessed by Marion Leatherby and her companions at Lightsome Hall or by Morgaine and various members of the court of King Arthur. Both movements provide important means of empowerment and illumination. To focus on one to the exclusion of the other is to perpetuate too narrow and reductivist an understanding of knowledge, power, energy, and matter.

Finally, it is the miracle of the fertility of matriarchs in old age (such as the biblical Sarah, who was possibly a priestess of the Goddess under oath to remain celibate during her time of service) that points to lessons we can learn from exemplary lives, lessons that open us up to the possibility of understanding the multiple dimensions of the Mysteries, and how the ancient pagan fertility rites of the Sacred Marriage (Hieros Gamos) in which the Goddess descended to inhabit a human body for a moment of ecstatic merging, can be related to the fertility of the Earth in a real, rather than merely symbolic or mythic sense.

For these are the Great Mysteries, still unexplained, and to reclaim the Great Mother is to remember these Mysteries, and to keep the sacredness of Her Mysteries intact. It is the arrogance of a culture that would try to reproduce Her Mysteries scientifically that has led Her into peril.

The feminist matristic journey has led us to encounter one of our main weapons in the struggle against arrogant androcentrism and anthropomorphism: the power of Love.

Women today are expressing a Love for the Planet, a Love for Life, a Love for all Species and for the Universe that goes far beyond Eros and Agape. It approaches the Cosmic Love of which the Hieros Gamos has always been the living incarnation. It may involve placing the interests of the human *after* the interests of the whole, and it certainly involves what Brian Swimme has referred to as retelling the Cosmic Story (1984), for it has been shown that when the stories of Creation are sung and told, life itself is created anew. If the feminist matristic artists and writers I have focused on here were in touch with any single truth, it was this, and that is why they have so compellingly and alluringly enchanted us with their telling of tales of power, which have re-reconnected them (and now us) with the most ancient sources of creative power ever known to humans, those that stream forth from the great sacred Cauldron of Regeneration, the Earth Mother herself.

CODA

Cornucopia: Fertility, Abundance, Creativity, Hope—Singing Our Sisters, Healing Our Mother

This book has identified a feminist matristic renaissance that is flourishing within the artistic culture inaugurated by the contemporary women's movement.

This rebirth of ecological and matristic values in the contemporary feminist matristic arts has announced a paradigm shift away from the cosmogony of the Father God to that of the Mother Goddess as the symbol system of the sacred. It has reminded us that creation is magical, that via our creative, visionary journeys we may acquire knowledge of women's histories and mysteries, both by study and by direct *gnosis*. These journeys to the other worlds, like shamanic vision-quests to the Wilderness, have also taught us that we have been tamed by our civilization. Our contemporary feminist matristic journeys and cycles via artistic vision have reconnected us with our lost history, with a female cosmogonic mythos, with nature, with the spirit world with the oral tradition, and with the other worlds of dream, psyche, and prehistory.

There are literally so many feminist matristic works being created and circulating in our culture at present, that it would have been impossible for me to include them all in this book. Not only are new works springing to life at an astonishing rate, but there are many literary works by authors whose entire *oeuvre* may not necessarily be called feminist matristic according to our definition, but whose individual pieces certainly belong in any such collection.

Among them, there are also several writers whose entire body of creative work would be considered part of the feminist matristic mythos. I would like to invoke their presence in this book now by naming them, and remembering how their fertile seeding and planting have yielded this abundant crop. Their works have always been with me, in spirit, throughout the entire writing of this book. Some of these writers are: Robin Morgan, Ntozake Shange, Sally Miller Gearhart, Adrienne Rich, Karen Malpede, Susan Griffin, Marge Piercy, Audre Lorde, Z. Budapest, Monique Wittig, Margaret Atwood, Meridel LeSueur, Lynn V. Andrews, Denise Boucher, Fran Winant, Nicole Brossard, Chantal Chawaf, Jean Auel, Evelyn Eaton, Alice Walker, Gina Covina, and many others.

I also want to mention the many feminist and feminist-spirituality journals that have published feminist matristic writers over the last two decades. Among them are: *Lady Unique Inclination of the Night* (edited by Kay Turner); *Womanspirit* (edited by Jean and Ruth Mountaingrove); *Chrysalis: A Magazine of Women's Culture, Heresies* (the Great Goddess issue);

Woman of Power; Quest: A Feminist Quarterly; Calyx; Trivia: A Journal of Ideas; 13th Moon; Fireweed; The Feminist Art Journal; Women Artists News; Womanart; and the publications of the *London Matriarchal Study Group,* to name only a few.

As this ripe flowering begins to bear new fruit, we can only anticipate the continued upsurge of feminist matristic creations in the future. And, if the fertility of the Earth is waning, the fertility of the feminist matristic creative imagination seems to be very much on the rise.

I have hardly begun to mention the many other scholars, artists, ritualists, vision-questers, musicians, singers, and performers whose talents are transforming our culture around the world at music and theater festivals, women's conferences, women's salons, fêtes, retreats, communities, summer solstice camps study groups, ceremonies, consciousness-raising groups, and travel expeditions—in fact, just about everywhere that women gather to share their stories, and to practice the traditional medicine ways of tribal cultures or to "raise power" for healing each other and the Earth.

This book simply represents my own personal journey from surrealism to ecofeminism via scholarship and questing. It is hardly the route that everyone will travel to reclaim the Goddess. Yet, it has now become a Path that others can follow in order to make their own discoveries. More than that, I hope that it has also planted the seeds of growth and rebirth, and catalyzed the desire to journey and to cycle to still wilder regions of the marvelous and the numinous through research and gnosis.

If the Earth is communicating Her pain to us now, She is also, quite obviously, communicating her Hope to us as well, for the reflowering of a healthy feminist matristic culture right in the midst of our patriarchal present, and against the greatest odds ever, certainly points to a miracle. The magical rebirth of the Goddess today can only mean that the Mother *is* ready to be healed by our acts of love and caring, by our songs of praise, by our celebration of Her fertility, by our recognition of Her power, and by the energy we invest in re-membering Her beauty, Her strength, Her wisdom, Her life force, and Her bounty. The flourishing of a feminist matristic vision today is a sign that it may not be too late to save our Mother's life.

References

Abendroth, Heide Göttner. (1985). Nine principles of a matriarchal aesthetic. In Gisela Ecker (Ed.), *Feminist aesthetics*. London: Women's Press.

Adler, Margot. (1981). *Drawing down the moon: Witches, druids, goddess worshippers and other pagans in America today (2nd ed.)*. Boston: Beacon Press. (Originally published 1979. New York: Viking Press)

Allen, Paula Gunn. (1983). *The woman who owned the shadows*. San Francisco: Spinsters Ink.

Allen, Paula Gunn. (1986). *The sacred hoop: Recovering the feminine in American Indian traditions*. Boston: Beacon Press.

Allen, Paula Gunn. (1990). The woman I love is a planet; the planet I love is a tree. Forthcoming, in Irene Diamond & Gloria Orenstein (Eds.), *Reweaving the world: The emergence of ecofeminism*. San Francisco: Sierra Club Books.

Andrews, Lynn V. (1987). *Crystal woman: The sisters of the dreamtime*. New York: Warner Books.

Andrews, Lynn V. (1981). *Medicine woman*. San Francisco: Harper & Row.

Andrews, Lynn V. (1985). *Jaguar woman and the wisdom of the butterfly tree*. San Francisco: Harper & Row.

Aptheker, Bettina. (1988). Standing on our own ground. *Gallerie, Women's Art, 1*(1).

Asungi. (1988, March). Notes on her paintings printed on her note-cards bearing these images, and notes on new paintings in a letter to Gloria Orenstein.

Balakian, Anna. (1967). *The symbolist movement: A critical appraisal*. New York: Random House.

Bettelheim, Bruno. (1980). *Surviving and other essays*. New York: Vintage.

Biaggi, Christina. Artist's statement. *Proposal for the goddess mound*. Self-published brochure.

Bradley, Marian Zimmer. (1982). *The mists of Avalon*. New York: Ballantine Books.

Bradley, Marian Zimmer. (1987). *Firebrand*. New York: Simon & Schuster.

Breton, André. (1960). *Nadja*. New York: Grove Press.

Breton, André. (1972) *The manifestos of surrealism*. Ann Arbor: University of Michigan Press.

Brindel, June Rachuy. (1980). *Ariadne: A novel of ancient Crete*. New York: St. Martin's Press.

Broner, E.M. (1978). *A weave of women*. New York: Bantam Books.

Brown, Lloyd. (1981). *Women Writers of Africa*. Westport, CT: Greenwood Press.

Budapest, Z. (1979–1980). *The holy book of women's mysteries* (Vols. 1–2). Oakland: Susan B. Anthony Coven.

Cameron, Anne. (1981). *Daughters of copper woman*. Vancouver, BC: Press Gang Publishers.

Carrington, Leonora. (1972). *Down below*. Chicago: Black Swan Press. (Also in Carrington, 1988)

Carrington, Leonora. (1975). *Catalogue*. New York: Iolas Gallery.

Carrington, Leonora. (1976, November–January). Commentary. *Catalogue of the retrospective exhibition*. New York: Center for Inter-American Relations.

Carrington, Leonora. (1977). *The hearing trumpet*. New York: Pocket Books.

Carrington, Leonora. (1988a). *The house of fear: Notes from down below*. New York: E.P. Dutton.

Carrington, Leonora. (1988b). *The seventh horse and other tales*. New York: E.P. Dutton.

Carson, Rachael. (1962). *Silent spring*. New York: Fawcett.

Chadwick, Whitney. (1985). *Women artists and the surrealist movement*. Boston: Little Brown. A New York Graphic Society Book.

Chernin, Kim. (1986). *The flame bearers*. New York: Random House.

Chernin, Kim. (1987). *Reinventing Eve: Modern woman in search of herself*. New York: Random House.

Chesler, Phyllis. (1972). *Women and madness*. Garden City, NY: Doubleday.

Chesler, Phyllis. (1978). *About men*. New York: Simon and Schuster.

Chicago, Judy. (1979). *The dinner party: A symbol of our heritage*. Garden City, NY: Anchor Doubleday.

Chicago, Judy. (1985). *The birth project*. Garden City: Doubleday.

Chodorow, Nancy. (1978). *The reproduction of mothering: Psychoanalysis and the sociology of gender*. Berkeley: University of California Press.

Christ, Carol. (1979). Why women need the goddess. In Carol P. Christ & Judith Plaskow (Eds.), *Womanspirit rising: A feminist reader in religion*. San Francisco: Harper & Row.

Christ, Carol. (1982). Why women need the goddess. In Charlene Spretnak (Ed.), *The politics of women's spirituality*. Garden City, NY: Anchor.

Christ, Carol P., & Plaskow, Judith (Eds.). (1979). *Womanspirit rising: A feminist reader in religion*. San Francisco: Harper & Row.

Daly, Mary (1973). *Beyond God the father: Towards a philosophy of women's liberation*. Boston: Beacon Press.

Daly, Mary. (1978). *Gyn/Ecology: The metaethics of radical feminism*. Boston: Beacon Press.

Daly, Mary. (1987). *Websters' first new intergalactic wickedary of the English language*. Boston: Beacon Press.

Davis, Elizabeth Gould. (1971). *The first sex*. New York: Putnam.

de Lubicz, Schwaller, R.A. (1978). *Symbol and the symbolic: Egypt, science and the evolution of consciousness*. Brookline, MA: Autumn Press.

Detlef, Ingo Lauf (1977). *Secret doctrines of the Tibetan books of the dead*. Boulder & London: Shambala.

Dexter, Miriam R. (1990). *Whence the goddesses: A source book*. Elmsford, NY: Pergamon Press, Athene Series.

Diner, Helen. (1973). *Mothers and Amazons: The first feminine history of culture*. Garden City, NY: Anchor Press. (Original work published in 1929)

Dinnerstein, Dorothy. (1976). *The mermaid and the minotaur: Sexual arrangements and human malaise*. New York: Harper & Row.

di Prima, Diane. (1978). *Loba*. Berkeley: Wingbow Press. Quotations from *Loba: Parts I–VIII* © 1978 by Diane di Prima, reprinted with the author's permission.

Doty, William G. (1986). *Mythography: The study of myths and rituals*. University: University of Alabama Press.

Duerr, Hans Peter. (1985). *Dreamtime: Concerning the boundary between wilderness and civilization*. Oxford: Basic Blackwell.

Edelson, Mary Beth. (1989, April). An open letter to Thomas McEvilley. *New Art Examiner*. pp. 34–38.

Edelson, Mary Beth. (1988, Winter). A personal interview.

Eisler, Riane. (1987). *The chalice and the blade*. San Francisco: Harper & Row.

Eliade, Mircea. (1954). *The myth of the eternal return or cosmos and history*. Princeton, NJ: Princeton University Press, Bollingen Series.

Eliade, Mircea. (1963). *Myth and reality*. New York: Harper & Row.

Eliade, Mircea. (1972). *Shamanism: Archaic techniques of ecstasy*. Princeton, NJ: Princeton University Press, Bollingen Series. (Originally published in 1964).

Eliot, George. (1956). *Middlemarch*. Boston: Houghton, Mifflin. Prelude, pp. 3,4.

Erikson, Elizabeth. *Tears of a mother*. Text of a ritual. Unpublished, 1985.

Falk, Marcia. (Trans.). (1973). *The Song of Songs: Love poems from the Bible*. (Postface) New York: Harcourt, Brace Jovanovich.)

Farmer, Penelope. (1988). *Eve: Her story*. San Francisco: Mercury House.

Fisher, Elizabeth. (1979). *Women's creation: Sexual evolution and the shaping of society*. Garden City, NY: Anchor. (New York: McGraw Hill Paperbacks, 1980)

Frueh, Joanna. (1985, September). The dangerous sex: Art language and male power. *Women Artists News*, pp. 6, 7, 11.

Gadon, Elinor. (1989). *The once and future goddess*. San Francisco: Harper & Row.

Gauldin, Anne and Yarfitz, Denise. The texts on Diana and the Waitresses were sent to me by Anne Gauldin.

Gauthier, Xavière. (1971). *Surrealisme et sexualité*. [Surrealism and sexuality]. Paris: Gallimard.

Gilbert, Sandra M. & Gubar, Susan. (1979). *The madwoman in the attic: The woman writer and the nineteenth century literary imagination*. New Haven, CT: Yale University Press.

Gilbert, Sandra M. & Gubar, Susan. (1988). *No man's land: The place of the woman writer in the twentieth century*. Vol. 1. *The war of the worlds*. New Haven, CT: Yale University Press.

Gimbutas, Marija. (1974). *The goddesses and gods of old Europe: Myths and cult images 6500–3500 B.C.* Berkeley: University of California Press.

Girard, Raphael. (1979) *Esotericism of the Popol Vuh: The sacred history of the Quiche-Maya*. Pasadena: Theosophical University Press.

Goldberg, Rabbi Nathan. (1949–1966). *Passover Haggadah*. New Revised Edition. New York: Dtav Publishing House Inc.

Goldenberg, Naomi. (1979). *The changing of the gods: Feminism and the end of traditional religions*. Boston: Beacon Press.

Grahn, Judy. (1982). *The queen of swords*. Trumansburg, NY: Crossing Press.

Griffin, Susan. (1978). *Woman and nature: The roaring inside her*. San Francisco: Harper & Row.

Grim, John A. (1983). *The shaman: Patterns of Siberian and Ojibway healing*. Norman: University of Oklahoma Press.

Harding, Esther M. (1971). *Women's mysteries, ancient and modern*. London: Rider.

Hawthorne, Susan. (1988). Dancing into the future: A feminist literary strategy. *Women's Studies International Forum, II*(6), 559–568.

Heller, Chiah. (1987). *Toward a Radical Eco-Feminism: From Duo-logic to eco-logic*. Unpublished paper.

Hyvrard, Jeanne. (1976). *Mère la mort* [Mother death]. Paris: Les Editions de Minuit. (This book has recently been published under the title *Mother death* by the University of Nebraska Press, 1988. The translations in this text have been done by Gloria Orenstein.)

Iglehart, Hallie. (1983). *Womanspirit: A guide to women's wisdom*. San Francisco: Harper & Row.

Jonas, Hans. (1958). *The Gnostic religion*. Boston: Beacon Press.

Jung, Emma, & Von Franz, Marie-Louise. (1980). *The grail legend*. Boston: Sigo Press.

Kaplan, Janet A. (1988). *Unexpected journeys: The art and life of Remedios Varo*. New York: Abbeville Press.

Kavanagh, Ursula. Artist's Statement. Unpublished, 1988.

Keller, Catherine. (1986). *From a broken web: Separation, sexism, and self*. Boston: Beacon Press.

Kinstler, Clysta. (1989). *The moon under her feet*. San Francisco: Harper & Row.

Klebesdel, Helen. Letter to Gloria Orenstein. December 13, 1987.

Klein, Leslie. (1988). Artist's statement. Unpublished.

Kremer, Juergen W. (1968). The shaman and epistemologer—Is there a Juanist way of knowledge? In Ruth-Hinge Heinze (Ed.), *Proceedings of the 3rd International Conference of the Study of Shamanism and Alternate Modes of Healing*. Berkeley, CA.

Kyra. Artist's statement. Sent to Gloria Orenstein in 1987.

Larson, Stephen. (1976) *The shaman's doorway*. New York: Harper & Row.

Lauter, Estella, & Rupprecht, Carol Schreirer. (1985). *Feminist archetypal theory*. Knoxville: University of Tennessee Press.

Lauter, Estella. (1984) *Women as mythmakers: Poetry and visual art by twentieth century women*. Bloomington: University of Indiana Press.

LeGuin, Ursula. (1985). *Always coming home*. New York: Harper & Row.

Leonora Carrington. (1974). Mexico City: Ediciones Era.

Levy, G. Rachael. (1968). *The gate of horn: Religious conceptions of the Stone Age and their influence upon European thought*. Atlantic Highlands, NJ: Humanities Press. (Original work published 1948)

Lindfield, Michael. (1986). *The dance of change: An eco-spiritual approach to transformation*. London: Arkana.

Lovelock, J.E. (1979). *Gaia: A new look at life on earth*. Oxford: Oxford University Press.

Lowenthal, David. (1985). *The past is a foreign country*. Cambridge: Cambridge Press.

Marchessault, Jovette. (1989). *Mother of the grass*. (Yvonne M. Klein, Trans.). Vancouver, BC: Talonbooks.

Marchessault, Jovette. (1985). Night cows. In *Lesbian Tryptich*. (Yvonne Klein, Trans.). Toronto: Women's Press.

Marks, Carolyn. Text of a ritual. *Washing the words*. Unpublished.

McCoy, Ann. The dream narratives are from Ann McCoy's private writings.

Medina, Andrés. (1964). Magia y religion en los altos de Chiapas [Magic and religion in the highlands of Chiapas]. In *El mundo mágico de los Mayas*. Mexico City: Instituto Nacional de Antropologia y Historia.

Merchant, Carolyn. (1980). *The death of nature: Women, ecology, and the scientific revolution*. San Francisco: Harper & Row.

Merchant, Carolyn. (1990). Ecofeminism and feminist theory. Forthcoming, in Irene Diamond & Gloria Orenstein (Eds.), *Reweaving the world: The emergence of ecofeminism*. San Francisco: Sierra Club Books.

Metzger, Deena. (1989). *What Dinah thought*. New York: Viking. (Quotes are from the unpublished manuscript.)

Meyerhoff, Barbara. (1974). *Peyote hunt: The sacred journey of the Huichol indians*. Ithaca, NY: Cornell University Press.

Miller, Alice. (1986). *Thou shalt not be aware: Society's betrayal of the child*. New York: New American Library.

Molinaro, Ursule. (1979). *Autobiography of Cassandra: Princess and prophetess of Troy*. Danbury, CT: Archer Editions Press.

Mollenkott, Virgina Ramey (1981). *The divine feminine in biblical imagery of god as female*. New York: Crossroads.

Monaghan, Patricia. (1981). *The book of goddesses and heroines*. New York: E.P. Dutton.

Moon, Sheila. (1970). *A magic dwells: A poetic and psychological study of the Navajo emergence myth*. Middletown, Ct: Wesleyan University Press.

Moore, Tom. (1983). *Rituals of the imagination*. Dallas: The Pegasus Foundation.

Nelson, Ralph. (1974). *Introduction to the Popol Vuh*. Boston: Houghton Mifflin.

Neumann, Erich. (1955). *The great mother: An analysis of the archetype*. Princeton, NJ: Princeton University Press.

Nwapa, Flora. (1966). *Efuru*. London: Heinemann.

Oda, Mayumi. (1981). *Goddesses*. Berkeley: Miller Publications.

Ong, William J. (1982). *Orality and literacy: The technologizing of the word*. London and New York: Methuen.

Orenstein, Gloria. (1973, spring). The women of surrealism. *The Feminist Art Journal*. (Reprinted in Orenstein, 1980)

Orenstein, Gloria. (1978). Nadja revisited: A feminist approach. *Dada-Surrealism*. No. 8, 91–195.

Orenstein, Gloria. (1980). The women of surrealism. In Judy Loeb (Ed.), *Educating women in the visual arts*. New York: Teacher's College Press.

Orenstein, Gloria. (1978, spring). The re-emergence of the archetype of the great goddess in art by contemporary women. *Heresies*, 74–78.

Orenstein, Gloria. (1982, spring). Reclaiming the great mother: A feminist journey to madness and back in search of a goddess heritage. *Symposium*, *XXXVI*(1), 45–70.

Orenstein, Gloria. (1983, Fall). Towards a bifocal vision in surrealist aesthetics. *Trivia: A Journal of Ideas, 3*, 70–87.

Orenstein, Gloria. (1984). Une vision gynocentrique dans la littérature et l'art féministes contemporains. [A gynocentric vision in contemporary feminist literature and art.] *Etudes Littéraires, 17*(1), 143–160.

Orenstein, Gloria. (1987). From occultation to politicization: The evolution of the goddess image in contemporary feminist art. In K.F. Clarenback & E.L. Kamarck (Eds.), *The green stubborn bud: Women's culture at century's close*. Metuchen, NJ: Scarecrow Press.

Orenstein, Gloria. (1988, Spring). Interview with the Shaman of Samiland: The methodology of the marvelous. *Trivia: A Journal of Ideas, 12*.

Orlock, Carol. (1987). *The goddess letters: The myth of Demeter and Persephone retold*. New York: St. Martin's Press.

Ortese, Anna Maria. (1987). *The iguana*. Kingston, NY: McPherson. (Original work published 1965).

Pagels, Elaine. (1979). *The Gnostic gospels*. New York: Random House.

Partington, Angela. (1987). Feminist art and avant-gardism. In Hilary Robinson (Ed.), *Visibly female: Feminism and art today* (Anthology) London: Camden Press.

Patai, Raphael. (1964). *The Hebrew goddess*. New York: Avon Books.

Pattee, Rowena. (1987). Profile. In Michael Jamal (Ed.), *Shape shifters: Shaman women in contemporary society*. New York and London: Arkana.

Peers, E. Allison. (1946). *Mother of Carmel: A portrait of St. Teresa of Jesus*. New York: Morehouse—Gorham.

Perera, Sylvia Brinton. (1981). *Descent to the goddess: A way of initiation for women*. Toronto: Inner City Books.

Phillips, John A. (1984). *Eve: The history of an idea*. San Francisco: Harper & Row.

Raven, Arlene. (1988). *Crossing over: Feminism and the art of social concern*. Ann Arbor, MI: UMI Research Press.

Remedios Varo. (1966). Mexico City: Ediciones Era.

René (Colette Thomas). (1954). *Le testament de la fille morte* [Testament of a dead girl]. Paris: Gallimard.

Rigney, Barbara Hill. (1978). *Madness and Sexual Politics in the Feminist Novel*. Madison: University of Wisconsin Press.

Roberts, Michele. (1984). *The wild girl*. London: Methuen.

Rorlich, Ruby. (1977). Women in transition: Crete and Sumer. In Renata Bridenthal & Claudia Koontz (Eds.), *Becoming visible: Women in European history*. Boston: Houghton Mifflin.

Rosenthal, Rachel. (1988). L.O.W. in GAIA. *Performing Arts Journal, 10*,(3), 76–94.

Roth, Cecil. (1971). *Jewish Art: Illustrated history*. Greenwich, CT: New York Graphic Society.

Ruether, Rosemary Radford. (1983). *Sexism and god-talk: Towards a feminist theology*. Boston: Beacon Press.

Sharon, Miriam. Personal Communications. 1977.

Showalter, Elaine. (1985). *The female malady: Women, madness, and English literature 1830–1980*. New York: Viking Penguin.

Simon, Linda. (1977). *The biography of Alice B. Toklas*. New York: Doubleday.

Singer, June. (1976). *Androgyny: Towards a new sexuality*. New York: Anchor.

Sjöö, Monica, & Mor, Barbara. (1981). *The ancient religion of the great cosmic mother of all*. Trondheim, Norway: Rainbow Press.

Sjöö, Monica, & Mor, Barbara. (1987). *The great cosmic mother: Rediscovering the religion of the earth*. San Francisco: Harper & Row.

Sjöö, Monica. (1987). Interview with Monica Sjöö. In Hilary Robinson (Ed.), *Visibly Female: Feminism and art today*. London: Camden Press.

Spretnak, Charlene. (1982). *The politics of women's spirituality: Essays on the rise of spiritual power within the feminist movement*. Garden City, NY: Anchor.

Spretnak, Charlene. (1984). *Lost goddesses of early Greece: A collection of pre-Hellenic myths*. Boston: Beacon Press. (Originally published 1978. Berkeley: Moon Books)

Starhawk. (1979). *The Spiral dance: A rebirth of the ancient religion of the great goddess*. New York: Harper & Row.

Starhawk. (1982). *Dreaming the dark: Magic, sex, and politics*. Boston: Beacon Press.

Starhawk. (1987). *Truth or dare: Encounters with power, authority and mystery*. San Francisco: Harper & Row.

Starhawk. (1989). Feminist, earth-based spirituality and ecofeminism. In Judith Plant (Ed.), *Healing the wounds: The promise of ecofeminism*. Philadelphia: New Society.

Stein, Gertrude. (1934). *The making of Americans*. New York: Harcourt Brace.

Stein, Gertrude. (1935). Poetry and Grammar. *Lectures in America*. Boston: Beacon Press.

Stein, Gertrude. (1980). With a wife. A sonatina followed by another. Emplace. Dates. Yet dish. Lifting belly. What does she see when she shuts her eyes. In Richard Kostelanetz (Ed.), *The Yale Gertrude Stein*. New Haven, CT: Yale University Press.

Stimpson, Catharine R. (1977, Spring). The mind, the body, and Gertrude Stein. *Critical Inquiry, 3*, 489–506.

Stimpson, Catharine R. (1981, Winter). Zero degree deviancy: The Lesbian novel in English. *Critical Inquiry, 8*(2), 363–379.

Stimpson, Catharine R. (1985a Fall). Reading Gertrude Stein. *Tulsa Studies in Women's Literature, 4*(2), 265–271.

Stimpson, Catharine R. (1985b). The somagrams of Gertrude Stein. *Poetics Today, 6*, 1–2.

Stimpson, Catharine R. (1986). Gertrude Stein and the transposition of gender. In Nancy K. Miller (Ed.), *The Poetics of Gender* (pp. 1–8). New York: Columbia University Press.

Stimpson, Catharine R. (1988). *Where the meanings are: Feminism and cultural spaces*. New York: Routledge, Chapman, & Hall.

Stockenström, Wilma. (1982). *The expedition to the Baobab tree*. London: Faber & Faber.

Stone, Merlin. (1976). *When God was a woman*. New York: Dial Press.

Stone, Merlin. (1984). *Ancient mirrors of womanhood: Our goddess and heroine heritage*. Boston: Beacon Press. (Originally published 1979–1980. New York: New Sibylline Press, 2 vols.)

Stone, Merlin. (1988, Winter). Endings and origins. *Woman of Power, 8*, 28, 29. (Revisioning the dark).

Suetonius. (1957). The life of Julius Caesar. In *The Twelve Caesars*. (Trans. by Robert Graves.) London: Penguin.

Swimme, Brian. (1984). *The universe is a green dragon*. Santa Fe, NM: Bear.

Teish, Luisah. (1985). *Jambalaya: The natural woman's book of personal charms and practical rituals*. San Francisco: Harper & Row.

Teubal, Savina. (1984). *Sarah the priestess: The first matriarch of Genesis*. Athens, OH: Swallow Press.

Trible, Phyllis. (1976). Depatriarchalizing in biblical interpretation. In Elizabeth Koltun (Ed.), *The Jewish woman: New perspectives*. New York: Shocken Books, 1976).

Turner, Kay. (1978, Spring). Contemporary feminist rituals. *Heresies* (The great goddess issue).

Vijali. (1988). Notes on the world wheel. Artist's brochure.

Waelti-Walters, Jennifer. (1988). De la pensée séparatrice à la pensée ronde. In *Jeanne Hyvrard, La langue d'avenir*. Victoria, BC: University of Victoria, Les Cahiers de L'Apfucc.

Walker, Alice. (1989). *The temple of my familiar*. San Diego: Harcourt Brace Jovanovich.

Walker, Barbara G. (Ed.). (1983). *The woman's encyclopedia of myths and secrets*. New York: Harper & Row.

Walker, Barbara G. (1985). *The crone: Woman of age, wisdom, and power*. San Francisco: Harper & Row.

Weil, Lise (1987, Spring). Editorial. *Trivia: A Journal of Ideas*. No. 10.

Winant, Fran. *Mermaid with violets*. Unpublished novel. (Available from Winant at 114 Perry Street, New York, NY 10014.)

Wolf, Christa. (1984). *Cassandra: A novel and four essays*. New York: Farrar, Straus, Giroux.

Zurn, Unica. (1970). *L'homme jasmin: Impressions d'une malade mentale*. [Jasmin man: Impressions of a mental illness]. Paris: Gallimard.

Zurn, Unica. (n.d.). Journal entry. *Obliques (La Femme Surréaliste)*, 14–15. Paris: Editions Borderie.

Bibliography

Abendroth, Heide Göttner. (1985). Nine principles of a matriarchal aesthetic. In Gisela Ecker (Ed.), *Feminist aesthetics*. London: Women's Press.

Adler, Margot. (1981). *Drawing down the moon: Witches, druids, goddess worshippers and other pagans in America today* (2nd ed.). Boston: Beacon Press. (Originally published 1979. New York: Viking Press)

Ahlbäck, Tore (Ed.). (1987). *Saami religion*. Åbo/Turku, Finland: The Donner Institute for Research in Religious and Cultural History.

Allen, Paula Gunn. (1983). *The woman who owned the shadows*. San Francisco: Spinsters Ink.

Allen, Paula Gunn. (1986). *The sacred hoop: Recovering the feminine in American Indian traditions*. Boston: Beacon Press.

Allen, Paula Gunn. (1990). The woman I love is a planet; the planet I love is a tree. Forthcoming, in Irene Diamond & Gloria Orenstein (Eds.), *Reweaving the world: The emergence of ecofeminism*. San Francisco: Sierra Club Books.

Andrews, Lynn V. (1981). *Medicine woman*. San Francisco: Harper & Row.

Andrews, Lynn V. (1985). *Jaguar woman and the wisdom of the butterfly tree*. San Francisco: Harper & Row.

Andrews, Lynn V. (1986). *Star woman*. New York: Warner Books.

Andrews, Lynn V. (1987). *Crystal woman: The sisters of the dreamtime*. New York: Warner Books.

Andrews, Lynn V. (1989). *Windhorse woman*. New York: Warner Books.

Aptheker, Bettina. (1988). Standing on our own ground. *Gallerie, Women's Art, 1*(1),

Arditti, Rita, Duelli Klein, Renate, and Minden, Shelley. (Eds.). (1984). *Test-tube women: What future for motherhood?* London: Pandora Press.

Ashe, Geoffrey. (1988). *The virgin: Mary's cult and the re-emergence of the goddess*. London: Arkana.

Asungi. (1988). Notes on Paintings & Letter to Gloria Orenstein.

Atwood, Margaret. (1976). *Surfacing*. New York: Popular Library.

Balakian, Anna. (1966). *The literary origins of surrealism: A new mysticism in French poetry*. New York: New York University Press.

Balakian, Anna. (1967). *The symbolist movement: A critical appraisal*. New York: Random House.

Balakian, Anna. (1970). *Surrealism: The road to the absolute*. New York: Dutton. (Original work published 1959)

de Beauvoir, Simone. (1952). *The second sex*. New York: Vintage.

Begg, Ean. (1985). *The cult of the black virgin*. London: Arkana.

Bell, Roseann P., Parker, Bettye, Guy-Sheftall, Beverly (Eds.). (1979). *Sturdy black bridges: Visions of black women in literature*. Garden City, NY: Doubleday, Anchor.

Berger, Pamela. (1985). *The goddess obscured: transformation of the grain protectress from goddess to saint*. Boston: Beacon Press.

Berman, Morris. (1984). *The reenchantment of the world*. New York: Bantam Books.

Bettelheim, Bruno. (1980). *Surviving and other essays*. New York: Vintage.

Biaggi, Christina. Artist's statement. In *Proposal for the goddess mound*. Self-published brochure.

Bord, Janet & Colin. (1983). *Earth rites: Fertility practices in pre-industrial Britain*. London: Granada.

Boucher, Denise. (1978). *Les fées ont soif*. Montréal: Editions Intermède.

Bradley, Marian Zimmer. (1982). *The mists of Avalon*. New York: Ballantine Books.

Bradley, Marian Zimmer. (1987). *Firebrand*. New York: Simon and Schuster.

Breton, André. (1960). *Nadja*. New York: Grove Press.

Breton, André. (1972). *The manifestos of surrealism*. Ann Arbor: University of Michigan Press.

Brindel, June Rachuy. (1980). *Ariadne: A novel of ancient Crete*. New York: St. Martin's Press.

Broner, E. M. (1978). *A weave of women.* New York: Bantam Books.

Brossard, Nicole. (1983). *These our mothers* or: *The disintegrating chapter.* (Trans. by Barbara Godard). Québec: Coach House.

Broude, Norma, & Garrard, Mary D. (1982). *Feminism and art history: Questioning the litany.* New York: Harper & Row.

Brown, Lloyd. (1981). *Women writers of America.* Westport, CT: Greenwood Press.

Bryant, Dorothy. (1976). *The kin of Ata are waiting for you.* Berkeley, CA: Moon Books.

Budapest, Zsuzsanna. (1989). *The holy book of women's mysteries.* Berkeley, CA: Wingbow Press.

Caldecott, Leonie, & Leland, Stephanie (Eds.). (1983). *Reclaim the earth: Women speak out for life on earth.* London: Women's Press.

Cameron, Anne. (1981). *Daughters of copper woman.* Vancouver, B.C.: Press Gang Publishers.

Campbell, Joseph. (1959). *The masks of God* (Vol. 1: *Primitive mythology*). New York: Viking Press.

Capra, Fritjof, and Spretnak, Charlene. (1984). *Green politics: The global promise.* New York: E.P. Dutton.

Carrington, Leonora. (1972). *Down below.* Chicago: Black Swan Press. (Also in Carrington, 1988a)

Carrington, Leonora. (1975). *Catalogue.* New York: Iolas Gallery.

Carrington, Leonora. (1976, November–January). "Commentary" in *Catalogue.* New York: Center for Inter-American Relations.

Carrington, Leonora, (1977). *The hearing trumpet.* New York: Pocket Books.

Carrington, Leonora. (1988a). *The house of fear: Notes from down below.* New York: E.P. Dutton.

Carrington, Leonora. (1988b). *The seventh horse and other tales.* New York: E.P. Dutton.

Carson, Rachel. (1962). *Silent spring.* New York: Fawcett

Chadwick, Whitney. (1985). *Women artists and the surrealist movement.* Boston: Little Brown. A New York Graphic Society Book.

Chernin, Kim. (1987). *Reinventing Eve: Modern woman in search of herself.* New York: Random House.

Chernin, Kim. (1986). *The flame bearers.* New York: Random House.

Chesler, Phyllis. (1972). *Women and madness.* Garden City, NY: Doubleday.

Chesler, Phyllis. (1978). *About men.* New York: Simon and Schuster.

Chicago, Judy. (1979). *The dinner party: A symbol of our heritage.* Garden City, NY: Anchor Doubleday.

Chicago, Judy. (1985). *The birth project.* Garden City, NY: Doubleday.

Chodorow, Nancy. (1978). *The reproduction of mothering: Psychoanalysis and the sociology of gender.* Berkeley: University of California Press.

Christ, Carol P. (1982). Why women need the Goddess. In Charlene Spretnak (Ed.), *The politics of women's spirituality.* Garden City, NY: Anchor.

Christ, Carol P., & Plaskow, Judith (Eds.). *Womanspirit rising: A feminist reader in religion.* San Francisco: Harper & Row.

Christian, Barbara. (1985). *Black feminist criticism: Perspectives on black women writers.* Elmsford, NY: Pergamon Press, Athene Series.

Chrysalis: A Magazine of Women's Culture. (1978, Fall). No. 6.

Collard, Andrée, with Contrucci, Joyce. (1989). *Rape of the wild: Man's violence against animals and the earth.* Bloomington, IN: Indiana University Press.

Condren, Mary. (1989). *The serpent and the goddess: Women, religion, and power in Celtic Ireland.* San Francisco: Harper & Row.

Covina, Gina. (1983). *A city of hermits.* Berkeley, CA: Barn Owl Books.

Culpepper, Emily. (1987). Contemporary goddess thealogy: A sympathetic critique. In Clarissa Atkinson, Constance Buchanan, & Margaret Miles (Eds.), *Shaping new vision: Gender and values in American culture.* Ann Arbor, MI: U.M.I. Research Press.

Daly, Mary. (1973). *Beyond God the father: Toward a philosophy of women's liberation.* Boston: Beacon Press.

Daly, Mary. (1978). *Gyn/ecology: Towards a metaethics of feminism.* Boston: Beacon Press.

Daly, Mary. (1987). *Websters' first new intergalactic wickedary of the English language.* Boston: Beacon Press.

Dames, Michael. (1976). *The Silbury treasure: The great goddess rediscovered.* London: Thames & Hudson.

Dames, Michael. (1977). *The Avebury cycle.* London: Thames & Hudson.

Davis, Elizabeth Gould. (1971). *The first sex.* New York: Putnam.

Detlef, Ingo Lauf. (1977). *Secret doctrines of the Tibetan books of the dead.* Boulder, CO, and London: Shambala.

Dexter, Miriam R. (1990). *Whence the goddess: A sourcebook.* Elmsford, NY: Pergamon Press, Athene Series.

Diamond, Irene, & Orenstein, Gloria (Eds.). (1990). *Reweaving the world: The emergence of ecofeminism.* San Francisco: Sierra Club Books.

Diner, Helen. (1973). *Mothers and Amazons: The first feminine history of culture.* Garden City, NY: Doubleday, Anchor. (Original work published in 1929)

Dinnerstein, Dorothy. (1976). *The mermaid and the minotaur: Sexual arrangements and human malaise.* New York: Harper & Row.

Doore, Gary. (1988). *Shaman's path: Healing, personal growth and empowerment.* Boston: Shambhala.

Doty, William G. (1986). *Mythography: The study of myths and rituals.* University AL: University of Alabama Press.

Downing, Christine. (1981). *The goddess: Mythological images of the feminine.* New York: Crossroad. Copyright 1981. Reprinted by permission of the Crossroad Publishing Company.

Duerr, Hans Peter. (1985). *Dreamtime: Concerning the boundary between wilderness and civilization.* Oxford: Basil Blackwell.

DuPlessis, Rachel Balu. (1986). *H.D.: The career of that struggle.* Bloomington: Indiana University Press.

Eaubonne, Françoise d'. (1976). *Les femmes avant le patriarchat.* Paris: Editions Payot.

Eck, Diana L., & Jain, Devaki (Eds.). (1987). *Speaking of faith: Global perspectives on women, religion, and social change.* Philadelphia: New Society Publications.

Ecker, Gisela (Ed.). (1986). *Feminist aesthetics.* Boston: Beacon Press.

Edelson, Mary Beth. (1988). Personal interview.

Edelson, Mary Beth. (1989, April). An open letter to Thomas McEvilley. *New Art Examiner.*

Eisler, Riane. (1987). *The chalice and the blade: Our history, our future.* San Francisco: Harper & Row.

Eliade, Mircea. (1954). *The myth of the eternal return or cosmos and history.* Princeton, NJ: Princeton University Press, Bollingen Series.

Eliade, Mircea. (1963). *Myth and reality.* New York: Harper & Row.

Eliade, Mircea. (1964). *Shamanism: Archaic techniques of ecstasy.* Princeton, NJ: Princeton University Press, Bollingen Series.

Eliot, George. (1956). *Middlemarch.* Boston: Houghton Mifflin.

Erikson, Elizabeth. (1985). Tears of the Mother. Text of a ritual. Unpublished.

Falk, Marcia. (Trans.). (1973). *The Song of Songs: Love poems from the Bible.* (Postface). New York: Harcourt, Brace, Jovanovich.

Farmer, Penelope. (1988). *Eve: Her story.* San Francisco: Mercury House.

Fiorenza, Elizabeth Schüssler. (1989). In memory of her: A feminist theological reconstruction of Christian origins. New York: Crossroad.

Fisher, Elizabeth. (1979). *Woman's creation: Sexual evolution and the shaping of society.* Garden City, NY: Anchor. (New York: McGraw Hill Paperbacks, 1980)

Friedman, Susan. (1979). Psyche reborn: Tradition, re-vision, and the goddess as mother-symbol in H.D.'s epic poetry. *Women's Studies, 6,* pp. 147–160.

Frueh, Joanna. (1985, September). The dangerous sex: Art language and male power. *Women Artists News,* pp. 6, 7, 11.

Frueh, Joanna. (1988). Towards a feminist theory of art criticism. In Arlene Raven, Cassandra Langer & Joanna Frueh (Eds.), *Feminist art criticism, an anthology.* Ann Arbor, MI: U.M.I. Research Press.

Gadon, Elinor. (1989). *The once and future goddess.* San Francisco: Harper & Row.

Gauldin, Anne & Yarfitz, Denise. *Texts on Diana & The Waitresses.* Unpublished.

Gauthier, Xavière. (1971). *Surréalisme et sexualité.* Paris: Gallimard.

Gearhart, Sally Miller. (1984). *The wanderground: Stories of the hill women.* San Francisco: Allyson Press. (Originally published 1978. Watertown, MA: Persephone Press)

Gilbert, Sandra M., & Gubar, Susan. (1979). *The madwoman in the attic: The woman writer and the nineteenth century literary imagination.* New Haven, CT: Yale University Press.

Gilbert, Sandra M., & Gubar, Susan. (1988). *No man's land: The place of the woman writer in the twentieth century* (Vol. 1). New Haven, CT: Yale University Press.

Gilligan, Carol. (1982). *In a different voice: Psychological theory and women's development.* Cambridge, MA: Harvard University Press.

Gimbutas, Marija. (1982). *The goddesses and gods of old Europe: Myths and cult images 6500–3500 B.C.* Berkeley: University of California Press.

Gimbutas, Marija. (1989). *The language of the Goddess.* San Francisco: Harper & Row.

Girard, Raphael. (1979). *Esotericism of the Popol Vuh: The sacred history of the Quiché-Maya.* Pasadena, CA: Theosophical University Press.

Goldenberg, Naomi. (1974). *The changing of the Gods: Feminism and the end of traditional religions.* Boston: Beacon Press.

Grahn, Judy. (1982). *The queen of swords.* Trumansburg, NY: Crossing Press.

Graves, Robert. (1959). *The white goddess: A historical grammar of poetic myth.* New York: Vintage.

Gray, Elizabeth Dodson, (1981). *Green paradise lost.* Wellesley, MA: Roundtable Press.

Gray, Elizabeth Dodson. (1988). *Sacred dimensions of women's experience.* Wellesley, MA: Roundtable Press.

Griffin, Susan. (1978). *Woman and nature: The roaring inside her.* Boston: Beacon Press.

Grim, John A. (1983). *The shaman: Patterns of Siberian and Ojibway healing.* Norman: University of Oklahoma Press.

Hall, Nor. (1980). *The moon and the virgin: Reflections on the archetypal feminine.* New York: Harper & Row.

Haller, Evelyn. (1983). Isis unveiled: Virginia Woolf's use of Egyptian myth. In Jane Marcus (Ed.), *Virginia Woolf: A feminist slant.* Lincoln: University of Nebraska Press.

Handelman, Susan. (1983). Jacques Derrida and the heretic hermeneutic. In *Displacement: Derrida and after.* Bloomington: Indiana University Press.

Harding, Esther M. (1971). *Women's mysteries, ancient and modern*. London: Rider.

Harris, Ann Sutherland, and Nochlin, Linda. (1976). *Women artists: 1550–1950*. New York: Alfred A. Knopf.

Harrison, Jane Ellen. (1955). *Prolegomena to the study of Greek religion*. New York: Meridian Books. (Original work published 1922)

Hawthorne, Susan. (1988). Dancing into the future: a feminist literary strategy. *Women's Studies International Forum II*(6), pp. 559–568

H.D. (1974). *Helen in Egypt*. New York: New Directions. (Original work published 1961)

H.D. (1973). *Trilogy*. New York: New Directions.

Heller, Chiah (1987). *Toward a radical ecofeminism: From dua-logic to eco-Logic*. Unpublished.

Heresies: A Feminist Publication on Art and Politics. (1978, September). No. 5, Great Goddess Issue. Rev. ed. 1982.

Herrera, Hayden. (1983). *Frida: A biography of Frida Kahlo*. New York: Harper & Row.

Hess, Thomas B., & Baker, Elizabeth C. (1971). *Art and sexual politics: Why have there been no great women artists?* New York: Collier Books, Art News Series.

Hubbs, Joanna. (1988). *Mother Russia: The feminine myth in Russian culture*. Bloomington: Indiana University Press.

Hull, Gloria T. Scott, Bell, Patricia, & Smith, Barbara (Eds.). (1982). *All the women are white; all the blacks are men; but some of us are brave: Black women's studies*. Old Westbury, CT: Feminist Press.

Hyvrard, Jeanne. (1976). *Mere la mort* [Mother death]. Paris: Les Editions de Minuit. (This book has recently been published under the title *Mother death* by the University of Nebraska Press, 1988.)

Iglehart, Hallie. (1983). *Womanspirit: A guide to women's wisdom*. San Francisco: Harper & Row.

Jamal, Michel (Ed.). (1987). *Shape shifters: Shaman women in contemporary society*. New York and London: Arkana.

Johnson, Buffie. (1988). *Lady of the beasts: Ancient images of the goddess and her sacred animals*. San Francisco: Harper & Row.

Jonas, Hans. (1958). *The Gnostic religion*. Boston: Beacon Press.

Journal of Feminist Studies in Religion. Plaskow, Judith, & Fiorenza, Elizabeth Schussler, (Eds.).

Jung, Emma, and Von Franz, Marie-Louise. (1980). *The grail legend*. Boston: Sigo Press.

Kalven, Janet, & Buckley, Mary I. (1984). *Women's spirit bonding*. New York: Pilgrim Press.

Kalweit, Holger. (1988). *Dreamtime and inner space: The world of the shaman*. Boston: Shambhala.

Kaplan, Janet. (1988). *Unexpected journeys: The art and life of Remedios Varo*. New York: Abbeville Press.

Kavanagh, Ursula. (1988). *Artist's statement*. Unpublished.

Keller, Catherine. (1986). *From a broken web: Separation, sexism, and self*. Boston: Beacon Press.

Kimball, Gayle (Ed.). (1980). *Women's culture: The women's renaissance of the seventies*. Metuchen, NJ: Scarecrow Press.

Kinstler, Clysta. (1989). *The moon under her feet*. San Francisco: Harper & Row.

Klein, Leslie. (1988). *Artist's statement*. Unpublished.

Kremer, Juergen W. (1968). The shaman and the epistemologer—Is there a Juanist way of knowledge? In Ruth-Inge Heinze (Ed.), *Proceedings of the 3rd International Conference of the Study of Shamanism and Alternate Modes of Healing*. Berkeley, CA. Write to: Ruth-Inge Heinze; 2321 Russell #3A; Berkeley, Ca, 94705.

Kremer, Juergen W. (1987). Tales of power. In Ruth-Inge Heinze (Ed.), *Proceedings of the 4th International Conference on the Study of Shamanism and Alternate Modes of Healing*. Berkeley, CA. Write to: Ruthe-Inge Heinze; 2321 Russell #3A; Berkeley, Ca, 94705.

Kyra. (1987). *Artist's statement*. Unpublished.

Lady Unique Inclination of the Night. (Cycles 1–6; 1975–1983). New Brunswick, NJ. Annual

Larsen, Stephen. (1976). *The shaman's doorway*. New York: Harper & Row.

Lauter, Estella, and Rupprecht, Carol Schreirer. (1984). *Women as mythmakers: Poetry and visual art by twentieth century women*. Bloomington: University of Indiana Press.

Lauter, Estella, and Rupprecht, Carol Schreirer. (1985). *Feminist archetypal theory*. Knoxville: University of Tennessee Press.

LeGuin, Ursula K. (1985). *Always coming home*. New York: Harper & Row.

Leonora Carrington. (1974). Mexico City: Ediciones Era.

LeSueur, Meridel. (1975). *Rites of ancient ripening*. Minneapolis: Vanilla Press.

Levy, G. Rachel. (1968). *The gate of horn: Religious conceptions of the Stone Age and their influence upon European thought*. Atlantic Highlands, NJ: Humanities Press. (Original work published 1948)

Lindfield, Michael. (1986). *The dance of change: An eco-spiritual approach to transformation*. London: Arkana.

Lovelock, J. E. (1979). *Gaia: A new look at life on earth*. Oxford: Oxford University Press.

Lowenthal, David. (1988). *The past is a foreign country*. Cambridge: Cambridge Press.

Lippard, Lucy R. (1983). *Overlay: Contemporary art and the art of prehistory*. New York: Pantheon Books.

de Lubicz, R.A. (1978). *Symbol and the symbolic: Egypt, science, and the evolution of consciousness*. Brookline, MA: Autumn Press.

Mackey, Mary. (1983). *The last warrior queen*. New York: Seaview.

Macy, Joanna. (1983). *Despair and personal power in the nuclear age*. Baltimore: New Society Publications.

Malpede, Karen. (1983). *Women in theatre: Compassion and hope*. New York: Drama Book Publishers.

Malpede, Karen. (1987). *A monster has stolen the sun and other plays*. Marlboro, VT: Marlboro Press.

Marchessault, Jovette. (1989). *Mother of the grass*. (Yvonne M. Klein, Trans.). Vancouver: Talonbooks.

Marchessault, Jovette. (1985). Night cows. In *Lesbian Triptych*. (Yvonne M. Klein, Trans.). Toronto: The Women's Press.

Medina, Andrés. (1964). Magia y religion en los Altos de Chiapas [Magic and religion in the Highlands of Chiapas). In *El mundo magico de los Mayas*. Mexico City: Instituto Nacional de Antropologia y Historia.

Mellart, James. (1967). *Čatal Huyuk: A Neolithic town in Anatolia*. New York: McGraw Hill.

Merchant, Carolyn. (1980). *The death of nature: Women, ecology, and the scientific revolution*. San Francisco: Harper & Row.

Merchant, Carolyn. (1990). Ecofeminism and feminist theory. Forthcoming, in Irene Diamond & Gloria Orenstein (Eds.), *Reweaving the world: The emergence of ecofeminism*. San Francisco: Sierra Club Books.

Metzger, Deena. (1989). *What Dinah thought*. New York: Viking Press.

Meyerhoff, Barbara. (1974). *Peyote hunt: The sacred journey of the Huichol indians*. Ithaca, NY: Cornell University Press.

Miller, Alice. (1986). *Thou shalt not be aware: Society's betrayal of the child*. New York: New American Library.

Molinaro, Ursule. (1979). *Autobiography of Cassandra: Princess and Prophetess of Troy*. Danbury, CT.: Archer Editions Press.

Mollenkott, Virginia Ramey. (1983). *The divine feminine in biblical imagery of God as female*. New York: Crossroad.

Moltmann-Wendel, Elizabeth. (1988). *A land flowing with milk and honey: Perspectives on feminist theology*. New York: Crossroad.

Monaghan, Patricia. (1981). *The book of goddesses and heroines*. New York: E.P. Dutton.

Moon, Sheila. (1970). *A magic dwells: A poetic and psychological study of the Navajo emergence myth*. Middletown, CT: Wesleyan University Press.

Moon, Sheila. (1985). *Changing woman and her sisters: Feminine aspects of selves and deities*. San Francisco: Guild for Psychological Studies Publishing House.

Moore, Tom. (1983). *Rituals of the imagination*. Dallas: The Pegasus Foundation.

Morgan, Robin. (1976). *Lady of the beasts*. New York: Random House.

Murray, Margaret. (1962). *The witch-cult in western Europe*. Oxford: Clarendon Press.

Nelson, Ralph. (1974). *Introduction to the Popol Vuh*. Boston: Houghton Mifflin.

Neumann, Erich. (1955). *The great mother: An analysis of the archetype*. Princeton, NJ: Princeton University Press.

Noel, Daniel. (1986). *Approaching earth: A search for the mythic significance of the space age*. Warwick, NY: Amity House.

Nwapa, Flora. (1966). *Efuru*. London: Heinemann.

Obliques: La femme surréaliste. Numero 14–15. Paris: Editions Borderie.

Ochs, Carol. (1977). *Behind the sex of God: Toward a new consciousness-transcending matriarchy and patriarchy*. Boston: Beacon Press.

Ochshorn, Judith. (1981). *The female experience and the nature of the divine*. Bloomington: Indiana University Press.

Oda, Mayumi. (1981). *Goddesses*. Berkeley, CA: Miller Publications.

Olson, Carl (Ed.). (1983). *The book of the goddess, past and present: An introduction to her religion*. New York: Crossroad.

Ong, William J. (1982). *Orality and literacy: The technologizing of the word*. London and New York: Methuen.

Orenstein, Gloria. (1973, Spring). The women of surrealism. *The Feminist Art Journal*, pp. 1, 15–21. (Reprinted in Orenstein, 1980)

Orenstein, Gloria. (1975). *The theater of the marvelous: Surrealism and the contemporary stage*. New York: New York University Press.

Orenstein, Gloria. (1978a). Nadja revisited: A feminist approach. *Dada-Surrealism*, No. 8, 91–105.

Orenstein, Gloria. (1978–no. 5). The re-emergence of the archetype of the great goddess in art by contemporary women. *Heresies*, pp. 74–78.

Orenstein, Gloria. (1980). The women of surrealism. In Judy Loeb (Ed.), *Educating women in the visual arts*. New York: Teachers' College Press.

Orenstein, Gloria. (1982). Reclaiming the great mother: A feminist journey to madness and back in search of a goddess heritage. *Symposium, XXXVI*(1), p. 45–70.

Orenstein, Gloria. (1983, Fall). Towards a bifocal vision in surrealist aesthetics. *Trivia: A Journal of Ideas*, No. 3, pp. 70–87.

Orenstein, Gloria. (1984). Une vision gynocentrique dans la littérature et l'art féministes contemporains [A gynocentric vision in contemporary feminist literature and art]. Québec: *Etudes Littéraires, 17*(1), pp. 143–160.

Orenstein, Gloria. (1987). From occultation to politicization: The evolution of the goddess image in contemporary feminist art. In Kathryn F. Clarenbach & Edward L. Kamarck (Eds.), *The green stubborn bud: Women's culture at century's close*. Metuchen, NJ: Scarecrow Press.

Orenstein, Gloria. (1988, Spring). Interview with the Shaman of Samiland: The methodology of the marvelous. *Trivia: A Journal of Ideas, 12*, pp. 93–102.

Orlock, Carol. (1987). *The goddess letters: The myth of Demeter and Persephone retold*. New York: St. Martin's Press.

Ortese, Anna Maria. (1987). *The iguana*. Kingston, NY: McPherson. (Original work published 1965)

Ostriker, Alicia Suskin. (1986). *Stealing the language: The emergence of women's poetry in America*. Boston: Beacon Press.

Pagels, Elaine. (1979). *The Gnostic Gospels*. New York: Random House.

Parker, Rozsika, & Pollock, Griselda. (1981). *Old mistresses: Women, art, and ideology*. London: Routledge & Kegan Paul.

Partington, Angela. (1987). Feminist art and avant-gardism. In Hilary Robinson (Ed.), *Visibly female: Feminism and art today*. (Anthology) London: Camden Press.

Patai, Raphael. (1967). *The Hebrew goddess*. New York: Avon Books.

Pattee, Rowena (1987). Profile. In Michel Jamal (Ed.), *Shape shifters: Shaman women in contemporary society*. New York and London: Arkana.

Pearson, Carol S. (1986). *The hero within: Six archetypes we live by*. San Francisco: Harper & Row.

Peers, E. Allison. (1946). *Mother of Carmel: A portrait of St. Teresa of Jesus*. New York: Morehouse-Gorham Co.

Perera, Sylvia Brinton. (1981). *Descent to the goddess: A way of initiation for women*. Toronto: Inner City Books.

Phillips, John A. (1984). *Eve: The history of an idea*. San Francisco: Harper & Row.

Plant, Judith (Ed.). (1989). *Healing the wounds: The promise of ecofeminism*. Philadelphia: New Society Publications.

Plaskow, Judith P., & Christ, Carol P. (Eds.). (1989). *Weaving the visions: New patterns in feminist spirituality*. San Francisco: Harper & Row.

Pollock, Griselda. (1988). *Vision and difference: Feminity, feminism, and the histories of art*. London: Routledge and Kegan Paul.

Popol Vuh. (1974). *The great mythological book of the ancient Maya*. (Ralph Nelson, Trans.). Boston: Houghton Mifflin Co.

di Prima, Diane. (1978). *Loba*. Berkeley, CA: Wingbow Press.

Przyluski, Jean. (1950). *La grande déesse: Introduction a l'étude comparative des religions*. Paris: Payot.

Raven, Arlene (1988a). *Crossing over: Feminism and art of social concern*. Ann Arbor, MI: U.M.I. Research Press.

Raven, Arlene, Langer, Cassandra L., & Frueh, Joanna. (1988b). *Feminist art criticism: An Anthology*. Ann Arbor, MI: U.M.I. Research Press.

Remedios Varo. (1966). Mexico City: Ediciones Era.

René, (Collette Thomas). (1954). *Le testament de la fille morte*. Paris: Gallimard.

Rich, Adrienne. (1976). *Of woman born: Motherhood as experience and institution in contemporary fiction*. Madison: University of Wisconsin Press.

Rigney, Barbara Hill. (1978). *Madness and sexual politics in the feminist novel*. Madison: University of Wisconsin Press.

Rigney, Barbara Hill. (1982). *Lilith's daughters: Women and religion in contemporary fiction*. Madison: University of Wisconsin Press.

Roberts, Michele. (1984). *The wild girl*. London: Methuen.

Rorlich, Ruby. (1977). Women in transition: Crete and Sumer. In Renata Bridenthal & Claudia Koontz (Eds.), *Becoming visible: Women in European history*. Boston: Houghton Mifflin.

Rorlich, Ruby. (1980). State formation in Sumer and the subjugation of women. *Feminist Studies, 6*(1), pp. 76–102.

Rosenthal, Rachel. (1989). L.O.W. in Gaia. *Performing Arts Journal, 10*(3), pp. 76–94.

Roth, Cecil. (1971). *Jewish art: Illustrated history*. Greenwich, CT: New York Graphic Society.

Roth, Moira (Ed.). (1983). *The amazing decade: Women and performance art in America, 1970–1980. A Source Book*. Los Angeles: Astro Artz.

Ruddick, Lisa. (1986). A rosy charm: Gertrude Stein and the repressed feminine. In Michael J. Hoffman (Ed.), *Critical essays on Gertrude Stein*. Boston: G. K. Hall.

Ruether, Rosemary Radford. (1983). *Sexism and god-talk: Towards a feminist theology*. Boston: Beacon Press.

Schell, Jonathan. (1982). *The fate of the earth*. New York: Avon Books.

Shange, Ntozake. (1975). *For colored girls who have considered suicide when the rainbow is enuf*. New York: Macmillan.

Sharon, Miriam. (1977). Personal communication.

Shiva, Vandana. (1988). *Staying alive: Women, ecology, and development*. London: Zed Books.

Showalter, Elaine. (1985). *The female malady: Women, madness, and English literature 1830–1980*. New York: Viking Penguin.

Showalter, Elaine (Ed.). (1985). *The new feminist criticism: Essays in women, literature, theory*. New York: Pantheon.

Silko, Leslie Marmon. (1977). *Ceremony.* New York: Viking Penguin Books.

Simon, Linda. (1977). *The biography of Alice B. Toklas.* New York: Doubleday.

Singer, June K. (1976). *Androgyny: Toward a new theory of sexuality.* Garden City: Anchor Press.

Sjöö, Monica. (1981). *The ancient religion of the great cosmic mother of all.* Trondheim, Norway: Rainbow Press.

Sjöö, Monica (1987) Interview. In Hilary Robinson Ed. *Visibly Female: Feminism and art Today.* London: Camden Press

Sjöö, Monica, & Mor, Barbara. (1987). *The great cosmic mother: Rediscovering the religion of the earth.* San Francisco: Harper & Row.

Spretnak, Charlene. (1984). *Lost goddesses of early Greece: A collection of pre-Hellenic myths.* Boston: Beacon Press. (Previously Berkeley: Moon Books 1978.)

Spretnak, Charlene (Ed.). (1982). *The politics of women's spirituality: Essays on the rise of spiritual power within the feminist movement.* Garden City, NY: Anchor.

Spretnak, Charlene. (1986). *The spiritual dimensions of green politics.* Santa Fe: Bear & Co.

Starhawk. (1979). *The spiral dance: A rebirth of the ancient religion of the great goddess.* New York: Harper & Row.

Starhawk. (1982). *Dreaming the dark: Magic, sex, and politics.* Boston: Beacon Press.

Starhawk. (1987). *Truth or dare: Encounters with power, authority, and mystery.* San Francisco: Harper and Row.

Stein, Gertrude. (1934). *The making of Americans.* New York: Harcourt Brace.

Stein, Gertrude. (1935). Poetry and grammar. In *Lectures in America.* Boston: Beacon Press.

Stimpson, Catharine, R. (1977, Spring). The mind, the body, and Gertrude Stein. *Critical Inquiry, 3,* 489–506.

Stimpson, Catherine R. (1981, Winter). Zero degree deviancy: The Lesbian novel in English. *Critical Inquiry, 8*(2), 363–379.

Stimpson, Catharine R. (1985, Fall). Reading Gertrude Stein. *Tulsa Studies in Women's Literature, 4*(2), 265–271.

Stimpson, Catharine R. (1985). The somagrams of Gertrude Stein. *Poetics Today, 6,* 1–2.

Stimpson, Catherine R. (1986). Gertrude Stein and the transposition of gender. In Nancy K. Miller (Ed.), *The Poetics of Gender* (pp. 1–8). New York: Columbia University Press.

Stimpson, Catharine R. (1988). *Where the meanings are: Feminism and cultural spaces.* New York: Routledge, Chapman, and Hall.

Stockenström, Wilma. (1982). *The expedition to the Baobab tree.* London: Faber & Faber.

Stone, Merlin. (1976). *When God was a woman.* New York: Dial Press. (First published in Britain as *The paradise papers*)

Stone, Merlin. (1984). *Ancient mirrors of womanhood: Our goddess and heroine heritage.* Boston: Beacon Press. (Originally published 1979–1980. New York: New Sibylline Press, 2 vols.)

Stone, Merlin (1985). Endings and origins. In *Woman of power, 8,* pp. 28, 29.

Suetonius. (1957). The life of Julius Caesar. In Robert Graves (Trans.), *The Twelve Caesars.* London: Penguin.

Suleiman, Susan Rubin (Ed.). (1986). *The female body in Western culture: Contemporary perspectives.* Cambridge, MA: Harvard University Press.

Swimme, Brian. (1984). *The universe is a green dragon.* Santa Fe, NM: Bear & Co.

Teish, Luisah. (1985). *Jambalaya: The natural woman's book of personal charms and practical rituals.* San Francisco: Harper & Row.

Teubal, Savina. (1984). *Sarah the priestess: The first matriarch of Genesis.* Athens, OH: Swallow Press.

Teubal, Savina. (1990). *Hagar the Egyptian: The lost traditions of the matriarchs.* San Francisco: Harper & Row.

Thompson, William Irwin. (1987). *Gaia: A way of knowing. Political implications of the new biology.* Great Barrington, MA: Lindesfarne Press.

Tobias, Michael. (1985). *After Eden: History, ecology and conscience.* San Diego: Avant Books.

Trible, Phyllis. (1976). Depatriarchalizing in biblical interpretation. In Elizabeth Koltun (Ed.), *The Jewish woman: New perspectives.* New York: Schocken Books.

Turner, Kay. (1978, Spring). Contemporary feminist rituals. *Heresies.* (The Great Goddess issue). No 5, 1978.

Vijali. (1988). Notes on the world wheel.

Vivien, Renée. (1976). *A woman appeared to me.* Reno: Naiad Press. (Trans. by Jeannette H. Foster)

Waelti-Walters, Jennifer. (1988). De la pensée séparatrice a la pensée ronde. In *Jeanne Hyvrard, La langue d'avenir.* Victoria, B.C.: University of Victoria, Les Cahiers de L'Apfucc.

Walker, Alice. (1989). *The temple of my familiar.* San Diego: Harcourt Brace Jovanovich.

Walker, Barbara G. (Ed.). (1983). *The woman's encyclopedia of myths and secrets.* New York: Harper & Row.

Walker, Barbara G. (1985). *The crone: Woman of age, wisdom and power.* San Francisco: Harper & Row.

Warner, Marina. (1976). *Alone of all her sex: The myth and the cult of the virgin mary.* New York: Vintage.

Weigle, Martha. (1982). *Spiders and spinsters: Women and mythology.* Albuquerque: University of New Mexico Press.

Weil, Lise. (1987, Spring). Editorial. *Trivia: A Journal of Ideas, 10,*.

Weil, Lise. *Realizing female integrity: Between the acts and Cassandra.* Unpublished dissertation manuscript.

Whitmont, Edward C. (1988). *Return of the Goddess.* New York: Crossroads Press.

Williams, Donald Lee. (1981). *Border crossings: A psychological perspective on Carlos Castaneda's path of knowledge.* Toronto: Inner City Books.

Winant, Fran. (1988). *Mermaid with violets*. Unpublished novel. (Available from Winant at 114 Perry St., New York City, NY 10014).

Wittig, Monique. (1969). *Les Guerrillères*. [The Guerrillères] Paris: Les Editions de Minuit.

Wolf, Christa. (1984). *Cassandra: A novel and four essays*. New York: Farrar, Straus, Giroux.

Woolf, Virginia. (1969). *Between the acts*. New York: Harcourt, Brace, Jovanovich. (Original work published 1941).

The Yale Gertrude Stein. (1980). New Haven, CT: Yale University Press.

Zurn, Unica. (1970). *L'homme jasmin: Impressions d'une malade mentale*. [The Jasmin Man: Impressions of a mentally ill woman] Paris: Gallimard.

Zurn, Unica. (n.d.). Journal entry. *Obliques* (La Femme Surréaliste), Nos. 14–15. Paris: Editions Borderie.

Author Index

Subject Index

About the Author

Gloria Feman Orenstein is a professor at the University of Southern California with a joint appointment in the Department of Comparative Literature and the Program for the Study of Women and Men in Society. Well known for her writings on the women of surrealism, she also co-created The Woman's Salon for Literature in New York City (1975–1985). She is the author of *The Theatre of the Marvelous: Surrealism and the Contemporary Stage,* the co-editor of *Reweaving the World: The Emergence of Ecofeminism,* and has also published numerous articles on Feminism and the creative arts. Her interest in Shamanism has led her to studies with the Shamans of Samiland (Lapland), and to the pursuit of the Goddesses in the Sami culture.

The ATHENE Series
An International Collection of Feminist Books

General Editors
Gloria Bowles
Renate Klein
Janice Raymond

Consulting Editor
Dale Spender

The Athene Series assumes that all those who are concerned with formulating explanations of the way the world works need to know and appreciate the significance of basic feminist principles.

The growth of feminist research has challenged almost all aspects of social organization in our culture. The Athene Series focuses on the construction of knowledge and the exclusion of women from the process—both as theorists and subjects of study—and offers innovative studies that challenge established theories and research.

On Athene: When Metis, goddess of wisdom who presided over all knowledge was pregnant with Athene, she was swallowed up by Zeus who then gave birth to Athene from his head. The original Athene is thus the parthenogenetic daughter of a strong mother and as the feminist myth goes, at the "third birth" of Athene she stops being Zeus' obedient mouthpiece and returns to her real source: the science and wisdom of womankind.

THE ATHENE SERIES
An International Collection of Feminist Books
General Editors: Gloria Bowles, Renate Klein, and Janice Raymond
Consulting Editor: Dale Spender

WHENCE THE GODDESSES   A Source Book
Miriam Robbins Dexter

NARODNIKI WOMEN   Russian Women Who Sacrificed Themselves for the
Dream of Freedom
Margaret Maxwell

FEMALE-FRIENDLY SCIENCE   Applying Women's Studies Methods and Theories to
Attract Students to Science
Sue V. Rosser

SPEAKING FREELY Unlearning the Lies of the Fathers' Tongues
Julia Penelope

BETWEEN WORLDS Women Writers of Chinese Ancestry
Amy Ling

THE REFLOWERING OF THE GODDESS
Gloria Feman Orenstein